Invitation to Critical Thinking

Invitation to Critical Thinking

Vincent E. Barry
Bakersfield College

Holt, Rinehart and Winston
New York   Chicago   San Francisco   Philadelphia
Montreal   Toronto   London   Sydney
Tokyo   Mexico City   Rio de Janeiro   Madrid

Library of Congress Cataloging in Publication Data

Barry, Vincent E.
  Invitation to critical thinking.

  Includes index.
  1. Logic.   I. Title.
BC177.B35   1984   160   83−18680

ISBN 0-03-059383-2

Copyright © 1984 by CBS College Publishing
Address correspondence to:
  383 Madison Avenue
  New York, N.Y. 10017

4 5 6 7   090   9 8 7 6 5 4 3 2

CBS COLLEGE PUBLISHING
  Holt, Rinehart and Winston
  The Dryden Press
  Saunders College Publishing

To Richard Fischer, Laird Coates, and David Morgen, who proved that youth is not always wasted on the young

Preface

One of the most exciting new developments in informal logic is the emergence of courses designed to help students assess real-life arguments. In attempting to develop students' analytical and evaluative tools, these courses go far beyond the teaching of informal fallacies. Variously named—Critical Thinking, Reasoning, Argument, Logic—they all share the goal of trying to equip students with the skills they need to assess ordinary, everyday arguments logically and to use these assessments in preparing intelligent pieces of logical criticism. Inasmuch as *Invitation to Critical Thinking* shares this goal, it is written with such courses in mind.

Approach

How can this goal best be achieved? Drawing on my own teaching experience and the commendable research done in the field, I decided early on in the preparation of this book that it would (1) help students to assess multiparagraph arguments, which they often find troublesome; (2) teach them how to cope intelligently with the mass media, for much of the material that forms the basis of real-life arguments derives from advertising, prime-time television, and news; and (3) show them how to apply the principles of correct thinking to their own argumentative essays, for success in college, not to mention intellectual development in general, largely depends on an ability to compose coherent, logical, and cogent essays.

The book's intended emphasis on longer arguments called for the inclusion of the following items:

1. A procedure for the elimination of extraneous material from arguments
2. A method for casting arguments; that is, for discerning and portraying their structures
3. Strategies for filling in missing premises
4. Instruction on language and meaning
5. Guidelines for the construction of criticism and evaluation

Organization

Invitation to Critical Thinking organizes the preceding items into four parts: "Awareness," "Analysis," "Evaluation," and "Generation." Part One ("Awareness") consists of Chapters 1—3, which are intended as a kind of consciousness-raising. Before students learn how to cope with arguments, they are made aware of some common blocks to effective thinking, the centrality of language in thinking, and the impact of the mass media (i.e., advertising, television, and news) on thinking.

Part Two ("Analysis") consists of Chapters 4—6, which systematically introduce students to argument and develop specific skills for identifying arguments, casting them, and filling in their missing premises. Although the analysis and evaluation of arguments cannot be neatly separated, I have tried to develop students' analytical skills before having them criticize and assess arguments. There are two reasons for this. First, to cover analysis and evaluation simultaneously, I think, so blurs the instruction that students fail to understand either thoroughly. Second, I have found that well-honed analytical skills greatly facilitate the evaluative process; and conversely, underdeveloped analytical skills impede, even preclude, incisive evaluation.

Part Three ("Evaluation") consists of Chapters 7—10. These chapters teach students what the criticism of arguments involves; introduces the various devices (i.e., informal fallacies) that arguers use to intensify or downplay their messages; sets up a seven-step procedure for argument evaluation; and shows students how to apply this procedure to argumentative essays.

Part Four ("Generation") consists of Chapter 11, which can be viewed as the capstone of the book. It teaches students how to apply what they've learned to the writing of their own argumentative essays.

Topics

The organization of the book hints at some of the topics covered. The following list pinpoints special or unique topics that are included:

- What critical thinking is and is not (Chapter 1)
- Some common obstacles to critical thinking, including cultural conditioning and hasty moral judgments (Chapter 1)
- The functions of language (Chapter 2)
- Language devices used to slant communication, including bias words and assumption-loaded labels (Chapter 2)
- Persuasive advertising techniques (Chapter 3)
- Television's reality warp (Chapter 3)
- Prime-time television as a transmitter of ideology (Chapter 3)
- How judgments of newsworthiness are shaped by journalists' judgments of reality and values; their news sources; and the dictates of time, space, and money (Chapter 3)
- Unexpressed premises and premise support as essential aspects of the anatomy of arguments (Chapter 4)
- A casting method that makes use of tree diagrams (Chapter 5)
- Directions for casting rhetorical devices (e.g., background information and repetitions of the same assertion) (Chapter 5)
- Methodology for filling in missing premises (Chapter 6)
- An informal approach to validity (Chapter 7)
- Assessment of the truth of premises using the notion of justification (Chapter 7)
- The justification of various types of assertions: logical, semantic, systemic, empirical, and evaluative (Chapter 7)
- In-depth consideration of value assertions (Chapter 7)
- Thirty-two common informal fallacies, grouped according to whether they are used to intensify by association (e.g., testimonials and statistics, polls, and surveys) or downplay by (a) omission (e.g., half-truths and false analogy); (b) diversion (e.g., ad hominem and straw man tactics); or (c) confusion (e.g., equivocation and inconsistency) (Chapter 8)
- A seven-step format for evaluating arguments that requires students to give an overall evaluation (Chapter 9)
- The anatomy of the argumentative essay, including consideration of thesis, organization, main points, and development patterns (Chapter 10)
- The outline as an alternative casting method for argumentative essays (Chapter 10)
- The need for audience inventory and determination of persona in writing one's own argumentative essays (Chapter 11)
- Arguable theses (Chapter 11)
- Writing theses (Chapter 11)
- Anticipating objections to one's own arguments (Chapter 11)
- The use of observation, personal experience, informed opinion, and organized research in supporting one's theses (Chapter 11)
- Organizational patterns for developing argumentative essays: inductive, pro-and-con, cause-and-effect, and analysis-of-alternatives (Chapter 11)
- The use of an outline to test the logical relationships between one's thesis and main points and between support material and main points (Chapter 11)

I have tried to write a readable text devoid of jargon. In many instances, this called for substitute terminology and a level of coverage that, while clear and accurate, did not obfuscate with needless detail. Consistent with this intention is the inclusion of many timely, lucid, and stimulating examples.

Learning Aids

The book is studded with pedagogic devices. Each part begins with an overview of the material to be covered in its chapters, and each chapter opens with the highlights of the chapter in the sequence of coverage. "Quick Check" exercises with comments are embedded in almost every chapter for immediate reinforcement, and "Applications" for further study and analysis end each chapter. Also included are chapter summaries, diagrams, charts, and tables that distill coverage for easy comprehension.

Beyond this, the book contains guidelines, strategies, and directions to ensure mastery of basic critical thinking skills that include

- A three-step strategy for identifying arguments (Chapter 4)
- A three-step method for casting arguments (Chapter 5)
- Guidelines for casting the rhetorical features of arguments (Chapter 5)
- Strategies for identifying incomplete arguments (Chapter 6)
- Guidelines for filling in missing premises (Chapter 6)
- A format for argument analysis and evaluation (Chapter 9)
- A sample outline as an alternative casting method for argumentative essays (Chapter 10)
- A procedure for writing thesis statements for argumentative essays (Chapter 11)
- Methods for selecting subjects for argumentative essays (Chapter 11)
- A method for testing the logic of one's own argumentative essays (Chapter 11)
- A sample outline for testing the logic of one's own essays (Chapter 11)
- Ways to develop an argumentative essay (Chapter 11)
- Strategies for ending an argumentative essay (Chapter 11)

Acknowledgments

The collective thought and energies of many individuals have gone into the writing of this book. I want to thank Holt philosophy editor David Boynton for his generative ideas and timely encouragement and senior project editor H. L. Kirk for shepherding the book through editing and production. Especially constructive were the reviews of Professors Philip A. Pecorino, Queensborough Community College; Peter A. Angeles, Santa Barbara City College; Phyllis L. Woloshin, Oakton Community College; and Anita Silvers, San Francisco State University. Any errors or faults are, of course, my sole responsibility.

V. E. B.

Contents

PART TWO   Analysis

PART THREE   Evaluation

8   Detecting Bias: Intensify/Downplay   203

9 Applying a Format   245

10 The Extended Argument   260

PART FOUR   Generation

11 Writing the Argumentative Essay   293

Invitation to Critical Thinking

PART ONE

Awareness

Blocks to Critical Thinking

Not too long ago a student popped into my office clutching a magazine. "Got a minute?" Bob asked me. When I said I did, he opened the magazine he was carrying, shoved it under my nose, and asked "Have you read this?"

The article he was referring to was headlined SMILE, YOU'RE ON CANDID CAMERA—AND THE EVENING NEWS! I hadn't read it.

"I don't know what to make of it," Bob said, obviously exercised over what he'd read.

I took a few minutes to read the article, which was written in the aftermath of Abscam. You may recall that Abscam was the name given to the FBI's sting operation that used hidden television cameras and recording devices to trap congressmen preparing to take bribes from agents posing as Arabs. The author of the article was convinced that the technology of television, as evidenced by Abscam, could provide a crude alternative to the procedures of justice established over hundreds of years. Not only were sophisticated surveillance devices proliferating, but, more important, in 1981 the U.S. Supreme Court had ruled that videotapes introduced as evidence during trials constituted public information. As a result the Abscam tapes, as well as any others introduced as evidence in a trial, could be released to network television. The author claimed that this ruling effectively permitted television networks to commission muckraking tapes for themselves and then show them on the evening news, thereby smearing people's reputations and convicting them in the court of public opinion.

I admitted to Bob that the subject was important and the author's treatment of it provocative. He agreed, expressing profound concern about the article's implications. "Frankly," he said, "it scares me to death. I mean, how much privacy do any of us have? Why, we're liable to find ourselves starring in the news some night, in a somewhat less than flattering role." He went on to express outrage that the Supreme Court had provided a legal basis for a seemingly dangerous and unwarranted violation of individual privacy. Bob continued talking like this for some minutes, punctuating his indignation with such expressions of confusion as "I just can't believe this" and "I just don't know what to make of this."

I expect that Bob is like many of us: We read or hear something and simply don't know what to make of it. Put another way, we are often unable to react critically to the information or claims we encounter. As a result we react emotionally—with fear, anger, outrage, even despair. The other side of the coin is that, unable to formulate intelligent viewpoints of our own, we rely on the same kinds of emotional, even irrelevant, appeals to back up what we assert.

The unfortunate part of this whole episode is that Bob didn't need any technical background to respond intelligently to what he'd read. All he needed were some basic critical thinking skills. Had he had them, he probably would have spotted the distortion in the article. After all, by the author's own account, the Supreme Court decision applied to video surveillance *introduced as evidence during trials.* There really isn't anything too shocking about this. It's simply an extension of the principle that any testimony introduced as evidence during trials typically is public information. Certainly the court's ruling did not even imply, let alone authorize, a television network's conducting with impunity surveillance expeditions for broadcast on the evening news. Missing this point, Bob was sucked into the author's panic-mongering.

Perhaps like Bob you don't know what to make of much of what you read and hear. Or perhaps you don't know how to go about formulating rational positions on personal and social issues. If so, you can benefit immensely from developing some basic critical thinking skills.

This book should help you do just that. It is meant to assist you in developing a rational basis for your beliefs by providing procedures for analyzing, testing, and evaluating your opinions and those of others.

The book is divided into four main parts: "Awareness," "Analysis," "Evaluation," and "Generation." Part One ("Awareness") is devoted to consciousness-raising. It aims to make you aware of (1) the nature of critical thinking and blocks to exercising it, (2) the centrality of language in thinking and in expressing what is thought, and (3) the impact of the information environment on how we see and think about the world and ourselves.

Part Two ("Analysis") introduces you to some basic skills you need for understanding communication designed to convince you of something. Specifically it shows you how to identify arguments, portray their structures, and fill in their missing assumptions.

Part Three ("Evaluation") teaches you how to respond intelligently to arguments by systematically criticizing and testing them. It includes a seven-step procedure for argument evaluation and gives special attention to argumentative essays.

Finally, Part Four ("Generation") helps you apply what you've learned in the preceding parts to your own arguments. It shows you how to use your critical thinking skills in writing argumentative essays, such as those you are typically asked to compose in college.

This opening chapter attempts to make you aware of what critical thinking is and why most of us don't, can't, or won't think critically. Its underlying assumption is that the first step toward becoming an effective thinker is to develop habits of mind that allow a calm, rational examination of statements and issues.

Critical Thinking—What It Is and What It Is Not

Before proceeding, indicate which of the following five statements are true and which are false.

1. Critical thinking is the same as disagreement.
2. Critical thinking aims to embarrass or humilate, allowing you to dominate somebody else.
3. Critical thinking entails nitpicking.
4. Critical thinking requires no imagination or creativity.
5. Critical thinking can be applied only to the beliefs and positions of others.

If you think any of these statements is true, you are misinformed about critical thinking. But don't feel bad. There's widespread ignorance among the well- and not-so-well-educated about the nature and function of critical thinking. And the number of people who don't, can't, or won't think critically is even greater.

Just what is critical thinking? We can begin to answer this question by considering the five preceding statements.

1. Critical thinking is *not* the same as disagreement. There is a considerable difference between disagreement and critical thinking. A disagreement is a clash of views. When you assert an opinion and I deny it or state an opposing opinion, we are disagreeing but not thinking critically. For example:

You: Handguns should be outlawed.
  I: There should be no gun-control legislation.
You: There's far too much violence on television. Why, just the other night . . .
  I: Compared with movies, there isn't much violence on television.
You: Premarital sex increases the chances of a successful marriage. Why, look at my wife and me. . . .
  I: I don't see how having sex before marriage could improve the marriage's chances of succeeding.

Obviously disputes like this are commonplace. When the parties to the dispute feel strongly about their positions, they are likely to reassert them, as if stating them again and again, perhaps in other words, will establish their soundness. While such disagreements call for critical thinking if the parties to them are to reach agreement or enlightenment, they are not themselves examples of critical thinking.

Critical thinking involves determining and assessing the reasons for an opposing view. It aims to find out whether a position is worth holding, thereby serving as a basis for further discussion and inquiry that, ideally, will lead the disputants to a better understanding of an issue. You believe handguns should be outlawed; I don't. If we're thinking critically, we'll closely inspect the reasons for and against each position. We don't merely keep reasserting our positions. I look at the reasons for your position; you look at the reasons for mine. Just as important, each of us is willing to have our positions subjected to this kind of scrutiny.

2. Critical thinking *does not* aim to embarrass or humiliate, and it *does not* allow you to dominate somebody else. Thinking critically *does* give one a kind of power. After all, if you can determine and assess the reasons for a belief, if you can make a discussion more enlightening, you stand a good chance of getting to the nub of an issue, of solving problems, of gaining greater control over your life, of attaining truth. In short critical thinking does help you gain knowledge, and knowledge, as commonly observed, is a kind of power.

But notice that the power critical thinking gives you is the power that comes from knowing, from attaining truth and justified belief. It is not the tyranny of imposing one's will on another, of inflicting humiliation, or even of trying to persuade another of your viewpoint. The goal of critical thinking is the justification of belief. A belief is justified when better reasons count for it than against it. Critical thinking helps you take measure of your beliefs. When they are justified, you know you have a solid basis for believing what you do, that you can defend your beliefs if necessary, and that you have legitimate grounds for action. But I can never justify my beliefs by dominating or humiliating you, or even by persuading you to believe as I do. Those who think they can are tyrants, not critical thinkers.

3. Critical thinking *does not* entail nitpicking. A nitpicker is one who is unduly preoccupied with minutiae. The critical thinker, by contrast, is concerned with substance, not trivia. Yes, thinking critically requires analysis, which in turn calls for attention to detail. But the details the critical thinker attends to are both relevant to a position and significant to its support. They are not side or trivial issues.

For example, suppose you claim "Many children enjoy watching Saturday-morning television. So they aren't being exploited." Upon hearing this assertion, I reply "Just what do you mean by 'enjoy watching'?" We then spend the next several minutes exercising ourselves over the meaning of "enjoy watching."

Language clarification certainly is an important part of thinking critically.

If we don't have the same understanding of the meaning of words, we lack a common basis for thinking critically about a subject. But that doesn't mean that every term always needs to be defined before we can proceed to think critically. The use of some terms simply is not problematic. Such is the case here with "enjoy watching." What I understand by "enjoy watching" surely is close enough to what you understand by it for us to get on with the issue. Even more important, your position doesn't hinge upon the meaning of "enjoy watching." So when I ask you what you mean by "enjoy watching," I am nitpicking. Worse, I'm probably steering us down the path of some semantic dead end while illumination of the real issue lies in another direction.

Incidentally, nitpickers like to introduce irrelevancies. For example, suppose I said to you "But I know a kid who doesn't enjoy watching Saturday-morning television" or "Saturday-morning television is full of commercials" or "Saturday-morning television is replacing outdoor recreation." Maybe so, but these observations are irrelevant to the issue at hand: whether or not kids who enjoy watching Saturday-morning television are being exploited. So far I have offered nothing that shows I am thinking critically about what you asserted. What I have offered is a mix of hairsplitting and irrelevancy.

In contrast suppose I said to you "But is it necessarily true that when kids are enjoying themselves they are not being exploited?" Now I'd be getting at the heart of your position, of what you're assuming. It is this assumption that allows you to claim that because many kids enjoy watching Saturday-morning television they are not being exploited. I have zeroed in on something both relevant and significant to your position, something you and I must toss around if we're interested in thinking critically about this important matter. If at this point you accuse me of nitpicking, then you simply don't know the difference between thinking critically and nitpicking. And if you say that I'm dragging in side issues, you simply can't distinguish between the relevant and the irrelevant, the significant and the trivial.

Of course focusing on what is both relevant and significant to a position isn't always an easy matter. In fact, in complex discourse it can be a formidable challenge. Most of us need training to distinguish the relevant from the irrelevant, the significant from the trivial. In part the study of critical thinking is designed to provide this training.

4. Critical thinking *does* require information and creativity. Some view critical thinking as a dry-as-dust exercise in analysis. Although it's true that critical thinking requires painstaking analysis, it also can call for creative thinking, for it sometimes requires the formulation of examples to discredit a position. Here's a very simple example. Suppose a couple spends $62 in twenty minutes while shopping at a supermarket. Upon leaving the store, the husband mumbles "Sixty-two bucks in twenty minutes! Why, this inflation is out of control!"

His wife demurs. "Not necessarily," she says. "Just yesterday I was in there for over an hour and spent only twelve dollars. And the Warbucks next door just spent over thirty thousand dollars in ten minutes."

"Yes, but that was on a Mercedes."

"That's my point," says the wife. "Inflation isn't measured by how fast we spend our money but by how much our money can buy compared with some previous time."

This woman is thinking critically; she is examining what her husband asserted. But notice how she does it. Through an imaginative use of examples, she makes the point that inflation isn't measured by how fast we spend our money, as her husband implied, but by what our money can buy relative to some past time. When critical thinking calls for such imaginative use of examples, it is creative.

Critical thinkers are also being creative when they formulate possible solutions to a problem or explanations for a phenomenon. Think of a detective, and you'll see what I mean. Yes, good detectives must test and evaluate solutions or explanations; that is, they must think critically. But they must first be able to devise possible solutions or explanations, what in science are called "hypotheses." Failing that they can't solve the crime. Coming up with hypotheses requires a fertile imagination, a creative mind.

The relation between critical and creative thinking is perhaps best seen in the laboratory. Consider, for example, how medical researcher Ignaz Semmelweis *discovered* and *demonstrated* the importance of physician hygiene in patient care.

Between 1844 and 1846, the death rate from a mysterious disease termed "childbed fever" in the First Maternity Division of the Vienna General Hospital averaged an alarming 10 percent. Curiously the rate in the Second Division, where midwives rather than doctors attended the mothers, was only about 2 percent. How could the difference be explained? More important, did the explanation account for the disease itself?

Despite heroic efforts for two years to account for the higher rate of childbed fever in the doctor-supervised division, Semmelweis remained thwarted. Then one day a colleague accidentally cut himself on the finger with a student's scalpel while performing an autopsy. Although the cut seemed harmless enough, the man died shortly thereafter, exhibiting symptoms identical to those of childbed fever. A thought struck Semmelweis. Perhaps doctors and medical students, who spent their mornings doing autopsies before making their division rounds, were unwittingly transmitting to the women something they picked up from the cadavers.

By drawing on a vast repertoire of knowledge and experience but also on imagination and intuition, Semmelweis had devised a possible solution to the mystery of childbed fever. Now he had to criticize his explanation; that is, subject it to tests. If Semmelweis was right, then the disease could be checked by requiring the doctors and students to clean their hands before examining patients.

Semmelweis insisted that they do just that. Doctors and students were forbidden to examine patients without first washing their hands in a solution of chlorinated lime. *Voilà!* In 1848 the death rate in the First Division fell to less than 2 percent.

The point is that, although the critical and creative aspects of thinking can be distinguished, they cannot be easily separated. The effective critical thinker inevitably is creative. Sometimes, as in the example involving the husband and wife, creativity yields imaginative examples that point up the weakness of a position. Other times, as with Semmelweis, it yields solutions to a problem or explanations for a phenomenon that then must be tested and evaluated; that is, criticized. Still other times it yields imaginative leaps from assertions to their implications, thereby raising a discussion to a more illuminating level. In such cases a solution, explanation, or proposal has already been made. Upon hearing it the listener makes an imaginative inferential jump that typically is a test of verification. Consider, for example, this exchange:

> *SUE:* People who attempt suicide are looking for sympathy.
> *SAM:* You mean suicide attempts can be explained as appeals for sympathy?
> *SUE:* Exactly.
> *SAM:* If that's the case, then *we could at least expect suicide attempts to be rare in a society that's indifferent or hostile to its individual members.*

You'll probably agree that Sam's inference (which is italicized) shows considerable resourcefulness. For one thing, Sue never quite said what Sam inferred. In fact she may not have even considered the implication of her position. Furthermore, since no society like the one Sam envisions now exists, Sam probably has never lived in such a society. He may not even be aware of any. Nevertheless he's able to *imagine* one. And his hypothetical society is most germane, for if the suicide rate in such a society were low, then Sue's position would be supported. Thus, in thinking critically about what Sue said, Sam has devised an imaginative test for it.

5. Critical thinking can be applied *not only* to the beliefs and positions of others *but also to our own*. Although it's true that you can apply critical thinking scalpel-like to dissect the claims you encounter, its application is by no means confined to the views of others. How many times have you pondered a personal problem? Perhaps you once agonized about whether to go to college, or what to major in, or whether to marry. Furthermore, as an intelligent, responsible citizen you probably want to clarify your positions on important social issues: capital punishment, abortion, gun control, violence on television, nuclear arms control, and the like. The resolution of personal problems and the formulation of viewpoints on social issues call for critical thinking. Indeed, individuals who cannot think critically are like rudderless boats, destined to flounder through life at the mercy of every eddy and crosscurrent that touches them.

The preceding observations suggest that *critical thinking is a process that emphasizes a rational basis for beliefs and provides procedures for analyzing, testing, and evaluating them.* Critical thinking helps you understand and deal with the positions of others and to clarify your own. It aims to give you a basis for justifying beliefs and for directing further investigation and inquiry.

With these preliminary remarks behind us, let's now turn to another issue: the rarity of critical thinking. Although critical thinking may not be as rare as a dog without fleas, it is uncommon enough for us to wonder why. Why don't most people think critically? Why do people find thinking critically so difficult? Why is it that people can so often be taken in by hucksters and confidence artists when just a little critical thinking would protect them from exploitation? Answering these questions calls for a look at some blocks to critical thinking.

Blocks to Critical Thinking

Blocks to critical thinking impede us from arriving at a reasonable basis for belief. They are obstacles that we must not only be aware of but work zealously to avoid following blindly. Otherwise they will thwart our efforts to become more effective thinkers. There are far too many such blocks to give a complete list. Instead we'll focus on the primary ones, which include cultural conditioning, reliance on authority, hasty moral judgment, black-and-white thinking, labels, resistance to change, and frame of reference. Although these categories overlap, they are sufficiently different from one another to warrant separate coverage.

Cultural Conditioning

Cultural conditioning refers to the process by which society's attitudes and values are passed on to its members. Although the precise nature of cultural conditioning, including how it operates and what lasting effects it has, is uncertain, cultures unquestionably condition their members. In other words, you and I are to a large degree the products of the particular place and time in which we were raised. We have been significantly shaped by the customary beliefs, social forms, and material traits of that setting. The assumptions derived from this conditioning are so embedded in our view of things that we probably aren't even aware of much of it.

For example, most Americans "believe in" individuality. Individuality is a value toward which they have a favorable attitude. Likewise, many of us still believe in "the American dream": Through sheer hard work, we can become just about anything we want to become. And many Americans remain firmly committed to the idea of "progress" as measured by such things as an increasing gross national product, a higher standard of living, and a growing population.[1] The list of cultural assumptions that we've inherited could be extended to include the following:

Communism and socialism are evil.
There exists a single God who is all good and all powerful, and who intervenes in
       the lives of His creation.
The two-party format is the best way to structure our political system.
Capitalism is the best economic system ever devised.
We should never intentionally put to death the old and infirm.
Anybody can grow up to be President of the U.S.

---

[1]See Ray Kytle, *Clear Thinking for Composition*, 4th ed. (New York: Random House, 1982).

People should marry for love, not money.
Money is the root of all evil.
Money can't buy happiness.
Rich people aren't happy.
People should be physically punished for crimes.
Women are passive and men aggressive.
It's okay, even normal, for males to be sexually promiscuous, but not females.
The male should be the breadwinner.
Women make better nurses than men do.
Children should be seen, not heard.

The list goes on and on. In each case it is not so much observed specifics that lead us to an assumption but accepted beliefs regarding a particular aspect of culture: social behavior, sexual roles, politics, religion, economics, and so on.

What's the connection between cultural assumptions and critical thinking? Very simply, blindly accepting such assumptions leads to selective perception—to seeing only what we want to see. But critical thinking requires objectivity, a dispassionate and impartial examination of the evidence that confirms or disconfirms a position. When I think critically, I must try to put aside my preconceptions and biases about an issue; I must attempt to keep an open mind. While none of us can ever be completely objective, we can be impartial enough to allow our views to conform to the evidence instead of making the evidence conform to our views. *There may be good reasons for holding any cultural assumption.* But when we leave the assumption unexamined and allow it to bias our thinking, we violate a prerequisite of critical thinking: objectivity.

To see how cultural conditioning can block critical thinking, consider this simple statement: "Democracy is the best form of government because it allows people to participate in their governance." Probably not many Americans would question this statement because it's based on our cultural assumption that allowing people to participate in their governance is good and desirable. "But," you may be thinking, "isn't it? Doesn't everyone know that?" No. Communists don't believe that such a system of government is good and desirable. Neither do Fascists. Nor did Plato or Aristotle, to name just two of Western civilization's preeminent thinkers. If you're serious about critical thinking, then you must at some point examine such an assumption. What's to be said for it, what against it? Only then can you start thinking critically about the statement made above.

Reliance on Authority

Authority is an expert outside ourselves. The expert can be a single individual (a parent, a teacher, a celebrity, a clergy member, the President), a group of individuals (doctors, educators, a peer group, a national consensus), or even an institution (a religion, a government agency, an educational establishment). Whatever its form, authority is a common source of belief and knowledge.

Just think about everything you claim to know that is based on authority.

Facts and opinions about world history, the state of your health, the direction of the economy, the events of the day, the existence of God and an afterlife—the list seems endless, the topics unbounded. In fact, without relying on authority, we would know very little of what we ordinarily take for granted.

But there's a danger: We can so rely on authority that we stop thinking for ourselves. Puzzled about something, we might invoke some authority to decide the answer for us. When dealing with a controversial issue, we might find out what the majority thinks and, looking no further, adopt the same position. Following authority blindly is a block to critical thinking as well as an evasion of autonomy.

To get some idea of how influential authority can be, consider a series of experiments conducted by psychologist Stanley Milgram in the 1970s. You may know that Milgram's experiment consisted of asking subjects to administer strong electrical shocks to people whom the subjects couldn't see. The subjects supposedly could control the shock's intensity by means of a shock generator with thirty clearly marked voltages, ranging from 15 to 450 volts and labeled from "Slight Shock (15)" to "XXX—Danger! Severe Shock (450)."

Before you think that psychologist Milgram was sadistic, I should point out that the entire experiment was a setup: No one was actually administering or receiving shocks. The subjects were led to believe that the "victims" were being shocked as part of an experiment to determine the effects of punishment on memory. The "victims," who were in fact confederates of the experimenters, were strapped in their seats with electrodes attached to their wrists "to avoid blistering and burning." They were told to make no noise until a "300-volt shock" was administered, at which point they were to make noise loud enough for the subjects to hear (for example, pounding on the walls as if in pain). The subjects were reassured that the shocks, though extremely painful, would cause no permanent tissue injury.

When asked, a number of psychologists said that no more than 10 percent would heed the request to administer a 450-volt shock. In fact well over half did—twenty-six out of forty. Even after hearing the "victims'" pounding, 87.5 percent of the subjects (thirty-five out of forty) applied more voltage. The conclusion seems unmistakable: A significant number of people, when asked by legitimate authority, will hurt others.

Authority not only influences the behavior of people, it also affects their judgment, perhaps even more so. For example, consider these three lines:

A ————
B ——————
C ——

Which of the three matches this one?:

————

Undoubtedly B. Do you think you could ever be persuaded to choose A or C? Maybe not, but experiments indicate that some individuals can be persuaded to alter their judgments, even when their judgments are obviously correct. These experiments involved several hundred individuals, who were asked to match lines just as you just did. In each group, however, one and only one subject was naive; that is, unaware of the nature of the experiment. The others were confederates of the experimenter, who had instructed them to make incorrect judgments in about two-thirds of the cases and to pressure the dissenting naive subject to alter his or her correct judgment.

The results: When subjects were not exposed to pressure, they inevitably judged correctly. But when the confederates pressured them, the naive subjects generally changed their responses to conform with the unanimous majority judgments. When one confederate always gave the correct answers, naive subjects maintained their positions three-fourths of the time. But when the honest confederate switched to the majority view in later trials, the errors made by naive subjects rose to about the same level as that of subjects who stood alone against a unanimous majority.[2]

Make no mistake about it: Authority cows us. We are impressed, influenced, and intimidated by authority, so much so that, under the right conditions, we might even shuck our own values, beliefs, and judgments.

Certainly none of this is intended to imply that authority is never a legitimate source of opinion and belief. When (1) the authority asserting a given view is indeed an expert in the field, (2) authorities are generally agreed on that view, and (3) I can, at least in theory, find out for myself whether the view is valid, then I have solid grounds for relying on authority. But even then I must realize that the authority gets its force from the weight of evidence on which the view it asserts is based.

Authority plays such an influential role in our thinking that I will say more about it later in our study. Here it's enough to note that a slavish reliance on authority is foreign to critical thinking. When we make up our minds and base our actions not on the weight of evidence but on the say-so of someone influential, then we are mere lackeys, not critical thinkers.

Hasty Moral Judgment

A moral judgment is an evaluation of someone or something as good or bad, right or wrong. We make moral judgments all the time, and these are largely influenced by cultural conditioning. We term the child abuser an "evil person," and child abuse "wrong," "heinous," or "reprehensible." We denounce naked aggression and welcome efforts to rebuff it. We deplore the liar and admire the truth teller. We take positions on issues such as abortion, capital punishment, and pornography that reflect approval or disapproval. "Abortion should [or

[2]See S. E. Asch, "Effects of Group Pressure Upon the Modification and Distortion of Judgment," in M. H. Guetskow (ed.), *Groups, Leadership and Men* (Pittsburgh: Carnegie Press, 1951); S. E. Asch, "Opinions and Social Pressure," *Scientific American* (Sept. 1955):31−35; S. E. Asch, "Studies of Individual and Conformity: A Minority of One Against a Unanimous Majority," *Psychological Monographs* 70 (1956):9

should not] be legalized"; "Capital punishment is [or is not] the most effective way of deterring certain serious crimes"; "Pornography should [or should not] be carefully controlled." Value judgments all.

Often we make such judgments hastily. For example, we judge people on the basis of their looks, background, or associations. We base such judgments not on careful consideration of factual evidence but on emotion, prejudice, preconception, intolerance, or self-righteousness. Because hasty moral judgments are essentially nonrational—that is, unreasoned—they blunt the goals of critical thinking: insight and understanding.

Unquestionably hasty moral judgments are deeply ingrained blocks to thinking critically, for the values upon which they are based typically are imparted very early in our lives, well before we can seriously examine them and the belief systems they spawn. Thus, before we're mature enough to think intelligently about things like religion, race, sex, and politics, we have been exposed to the values of parents, teachers, clergy members, and others who participate in our moral development. As a result we tend to acknowledge what supports our acquired moral value systems and to ignore or dismiss what doesn't. We wall ourselves off from disclosure contrary to our preconceptions, thereby purchasing security at the price of insight and understanding.

This doesn't at all mean that you shouldn't have strong moral beliefs. But there's a big difference between moral convictions that precede deliberation and those that follow it. The former are hasty, the latter well considered. Presumably you want your moral beliefs to be as carefully thought out as any other kind—economic, political, educational, social. As we saw earlier, a primary goal of critical thinking is the formulation of justified belief. Since hasty moral judgments are not such beliefs, they thwart critical thinking.

Black-and-White Thinking

Black-and-white thinking refers to the tendency to place things in either/ or categories, ignoring the complexity of an issue. Here are some expressions of black-and-white thinking:

You're either for me or against me.
A person is either 100 percent American or he/she isn't.
Most people are either honest or crooked.
There is only one right way to do anything.
America—love it or leave it.
Guns don't kill people, people do.
There are two kinds of girls; those that do it and those that don't.

Several factors account for black-and-white thinking. One is the human desire for certainty. If we see things in mutually exclusive categories, we stand a far better chance of attaining a certainty than if we consider the complexities of an issue. Black-and-white thinking also results from the pervasive tendency to confuse negatives and opposites. When two things are genuine negatives, they exclude any middle ground. For example, "cold" and "not cold," "red" and "not red," and "conservative" and "nonconservative" are negatives: They exclude any gradations between their extremes. If the room is cold, it cannot be not cold; if the cloth is red, it cannot be not red; if the politician is conservative on an issue, he or she cannot be nonconservative on the same issue.

But negatives are not opposites, which allow for a number of gradations. "Cold" and "hot," "black" and "white," and "conservative" and "liberal" are opposites. There is plenty of middle ground between each term and its opposite. With negatives one of the two extremes must be true and the other false; but with opposites both extremes may be false. Thus the room may be neither hot nor cold, but pleasantly warm. The cloth may be neither black nor white, but green. The politician may be neither conservative nor liberal, but moderate.

Failing to perceive the difference between negatives and opposites, people apply a false logic to such concepts as democracy and justice, such states of mind as love and hate, or to human institutions, issues, and behavior.[3] They may falsely believe that if they feel anger or hate toward someone, they cannot at the same time love that person. Or they may believe that if individuals are to be held accountable for their actions, then such actions cannot at the same time be regarded as the outcome of social or environmental forces. Or they may hold that if welfare is abused by some recipients, it can't at the same time be unabused by other recipients. Such wrongheadedness can produce equally illogical proposals. For example: Regarding welfare fraud, *either* weed out all cheaters or abolish the system. In order to ensure world peace, *either* arm to the teeth or disarm. To deal with the problem of abortion, *either* disallow it or allow it on demand.

Still another explanation for the prevalence of black-and-white thinking can be found in the nature of our language. English is replete with polar opposites: "right/wrong," "good/bad," "happy/sad," "conservative/liberal," "love/hate," "smart/dumb," "sane/insane," "drunk/sober," "true/false." Some semanticists believe that the availability of such opposites encourages black-and-white thinking; it inclines us to view the world as clear-cut when in fact subtle variations abound. Whatever the explanations for black-and-white thinking, one thing is clear: It can be a block to critical thinking.

Labels

Labels are essential for communication. They make it possible for us to communicate a complex situation a piece at a time. The use of labels helps us react specifically to some part of the environment and to deal with new and unfamiliar environments by picking out familiar features. For example, there are about three billion entities in the world today corresponding to our label "the human race." We can't possibly deal individually with so many human beings. We can't even individuate the dozens we encounter daily. Instead we must group them, drawing the many into a single unit by means of a label.

[3]Kytle, *Clear Thinking*, p. 58.

But as useful as labels are, they can be blocks to thinking. First, by lumping things into categories, labels ignore individual differences. For example, to call Gloria Steinem a "feminist" is to ignore other aspects of her identity, for Steinem is also a "voter," "licensed driver," "taxpayer," "consumer," "author," and so on. Labeling her a "feminist" encourages us to see her exclusively in terms of that label. The result can be a distortion.

Linguist Irvin Lee gives a graphic example of how the very act of labeling causes us to overlook all other features of an entity, many of which might offer a more accurate representation than the label we choose.

> I knew a man who had lost the use of both eyes. He was called a "blind man." He could also be called an expert typist, a conscientious worker, a good student, a careful listener, a man who wanted a job. But he couldn't get a job in the department store order room where employees sat and typed orders which came over the telephone. The personnel man was impatient to get the interview over. "But you're a blind man," he kept saying, and one could almost feel his silent assumption that somehow the incapacity in one aspect made the man incapable in every other. So blinded by the label was the interviewer that he could not be persuaded to look beyond it.[4]

Besides causing us to overlook individual differences, labels encourage polarization. That is, they encourage us to view things as grouped in opposing factions, for example: "democracy/totalitarianism," "democrat/republican," "pro–capital punishment/anti–capital punishment," "capitalist/social-ist," "people who love America/people who do not," "people who pull their own weight/people who do not," and so on. Hence labels are one of the great blocks to finding alternative ways of thinking about the world. The fixed patterns of thought are not altered by incoming information but instead alter it. How many articles have you read that glibly use such labels as "profitability," "productivi-ty," "justice," "equality," "human rights," "individualism," "free enterprise," and similar abstractions? There's nothing necessarily wrong with such labels. But they can be used too conveniently to justify our views. Rather than allowing us to think critically, they inhibit analysis by obscuring, eliciting knee-jerk reac-tions, and forcing one to take sides.

Take, for example, the term "patriotism." "Patriotism" is so shrouded by notions of heroics and duty and virtue, by "my country right or wrong," that we must regard it as either honorable or dangerous.[5] Of course national spirit, in terms of individual culture or economic growth, is important, but because the term "patriotism" polarizes, it's of little use in discussing the important subject of national spirit. In fact it can block the intelligent, searching examination that the subject requires.

How can we escape labels? Challenge them, try to do without them, even establish new labels. In challenging labels ask yourself why you are using them. What do the labels really mean? Are they essential to your communication? Or are they clichés you are using because they are convenient? Watch out for the

---

[4]Gordon Allport, *The Nature of Prejudice* (Reading, Mass.: Addison-Wesley, 1954).
[5]Edward de Bono, *Lateral Thinking* (New York: Harper & Row, 1970), p. 217.

labels used by others. Ask youself why you must accept them. In challenging a label, you are not rejecting it. You are simply refusing to accept it blindly. Your purpose is to generate a new view of something, a view that the label may be blocking. In trying to avoid labels you are trying to discover what lies buried beneath them. You may find that there is much or little there. The key is realizing that in removing the block that labels create, you are allowing the free flow of information you need for effective thinking.

Resistance to Change

A big block to thinking effectively is the tendency to cling to preconceived notions, to set ways of viewing and doing things. As a simple example, consider chain smokers. How do some chain smokers contend with the blizzard of statistics that connect smoking to disease? They simply avoid such evidence, consider themselves exceptions to the rule, or so rationalize their habit that, in the end, they have more reasons for smoking than not.

Similarly, not many people regularly read political journals that present views contrary to the ones they hold. Probably even fewer have ever seriously investigated religious views incompatible with their own. And precious few ever consider alternatives to their views of what's right and wrong, good and bad. Indeed, many of us react to beliefs, values, and attitudes that challenge our own with self-righteous contempt.

The fact is that most of us not only avoid views contrary to our own, we systematically expel them from our experience. We resist change. Why?

We resist change partly because we perceive it as a threat to who and what we are and partly because we believe in the superiority of our own culture, in the view that "mine is better—my ideas, my values, my race, my country, my religion."

The history of science is rife with examples of this kind of resistance to change. For example, Galileo's astronomical treatise, the *Dialogue on the Two Chief Systems of the World* (1632), was a thoughtful and devastating attack on the traditional geocentric view of the universe proposed by the ancient Greek Ptolemy (second century A.D.) and accepted by most scholars and scientists of Galileo's time. Galileo's treatise was therefore an attack not only on the views of these authorities but also on their self-concepts. Predictably enough, they reacted violently. Pope Urban was persuaded that Simplicio, the butt of the whole dialogue, was intended to represent himself. His vanity bitterly wounded, the Pope ordered Galileo to appear before the Inquisition. Although never formally imprisoned, Galileo was threatened with torture and forced to renounce what he had written. In 1633 he was banished to his country estate. His *Dialogue*, together with the works of Kepler and Copernicus, were placed on the Index of forbidden books, from which they were not withdrawn until 1835.

In general we block out new information that threatens the existing beliefs[6] with which we are secure. For example, all of us like to think of our

---

[6] John Herman Randall, Jr., *The Making of the Modern Mind* (Boston: Houghton Mifflin, 1940), p. 235.

presidents as honorable and virtuous men whose actions are always motivated by the highest regard for the national welfare. As a result many of us dismiss the emergence of contrary information about a president as the brainchild of a crank or a sensationalist bent on personal gain. Perhaps it is. But we often form this opinion before even considering the evidence because it threatens our "taken-for-granteds."

How can you deal with such resistance to change? A good way is to become aware of two danger signals. Whenever you find yourself or others responding in one of these two ways, you or they are probably letting resistance to change block rational inspection of the situation.[7]

One danger signal is what psychologists term "reaction formation," which refers to an immediate, strong, and emotional reaction *against* something. A dramatic example of reaction formation is "white flight," a term used to describe the mass exodus of whites from a neighborhood when a black moves in. Often white flight is preceded by an equally emotional and irrational response prior to the sale of the house to the black. Thus, upon learning that a party is about to sell a house to a black, neighbors have been known to exert intense pressure on the seller to stop the sale. The pressure takes various forms, ranging from "moral suasion" to threats of reprisal. Unable to stop the sale and convinced that property values will plummet, or repelled by the notion of having a black neighbor, white homeowners abandon the neighborhood en masse. Racism aside, the irrationality of the behavior lies in the fact that, ironically, the white homeowners themselves reduce the market value of their property by advertising it as undesirable, which they effectively do by bailing out.

A similar problem is now occurring in the area of mental health. New laws have made it increasingly difficult to institutionalize persons or to keep them institutionalized indefinitely. In addition the latest professional thinking holds that an institutional environment is not always the best way to treat the emotionally disturbed. In many cases a treatment program that allows the patient to function in as nearly normal a social environment as possible seems far more therapeutic. The upshot of these new developments is the establishment of residential homes for carefully screened patients. One of the major obstacles to establishing such centers is that neighborhood residents initially react with a mixture of fear, anger, and hostility. In a word, they feel threatened, so much so that they sometimes refuse even to discuss the matter or will threaten court action to prevent the establishment of these homes. And yet where these centers have been established, for the most part they have meshed beautifully with the neighborhoods around them.

Of course, reaction formation need not be confined to phenomena like these. Strong emotional reactions also can be directed against some abstraction. For example, anything that even remotely smacks of socialism likely will elicit passionate disapproval from most Americans. This explains in part why proposals for such things as day-care centers, guaranteed minimum income, national health insurance, rent control, and a raft of other social welfare pro-

[7]Ray Kytle, *Clear Thinking for Composition*, 3d ed. (New York: Random House, 1977), pp. 62–63.

grams and proposals meet with immediate, vitriolic opposition. Perhaps such programs shouldn't be acted upon. But if not it is because they are ineffective and inadequate solutions to social problems, which can only be determined by examining them and the alternatives. The problem with an immediate, emotional reaction against something is that is precludes the analysis and evaluation of the issues.

A second danger signal is "primary certitude," which refers to an immediate, strong, emotional feeling *about* something. Individuals who engage in primary certitude are convinced that they have a corner on the truth and hence are unwilling to entertain any contradictory facts. You may have encountered people whose reactions, in effect, reflect this attitude: "Don't confuse me with facts, my mind is already made up" or "I don't care what you say, the fact of the matter is that. . ." Such reactions are dead giveaways of primary certitude.

You can find evidence of primary certitude in peoples' responses to almost any controversial issue. Take, for example, the rising incidence of violent crimes. Countermeasures typically recommended include installing tougher judges, giving stiffer penalties, and restoring the death penalty. While these recommendations are understandable, no causal relation has ever been established between the severity of physical punishment and the crime rate.[8] Similarly, a common proposal for dealing with the decline in U.S. productivity and competitiveness is to establish import quotas and tariffs. Yet experts tell us that the problem is not that simple. At the root of declining productivity and competitiveness are obsolete equipment and plants, failure to anticipate and meet consumer needs, a less pronounced work ethic among younger workers, increasing labor costs, and inflation. As with reaction formation, primary certitude cuts off the thorough and intelligent examination of an issue. It blocks effective thinking.

Frame of Reference

All of us have a tendency to see ourselves and the world according to our own frame of reference; that is, according to the organized body of accumulated knowledge and experience we rely on to interpret new experiences and guide our behavior. This frame of reference limits our perception. Perception refers to the process by which we give meaning to sensory stimuli. Although we speak of "seeing" an airplane or "hearing" music, we really are seeing light waves and hearing sound waves. The process by which we give meaning to light and sound waves is perception. We see light waves, but perceive airplanes, houses, trees, and other people; we hear sound waves, but we perceive a symphony, a baby crying, a dog barking, and a tree creaking.

Perception—giving meaning to sensory stimuli—occurs only in terms of the information in our frame of reference. For example, some African natives with no knowledge of airplanes perceive the jet plane as a big bird. In fact some natives refer to jets as *ndege mkubwa*, Swahili for "big bird." Those who are

[8]Kytle, *Clear Thinking*, pp. 64–65.

unfamiliar with jets can't possibly perceive them as such. Instead they perceive them in terms of the information stored in their frame of reference. Similarly the first automobiles were called "horseless carriages," and those many uniden-tified objects reportedly observed in the sky and variously described as saucer- or disc-shaped are termed "flying saucers."

Several important implications for critical thinking follow from the limita-tions to perception created by our frame of reference. First, in limiting percep-tion, the frame of reference limits our ability to recognize problems. For instance, persons unaware of its danger signals can't recognize the presence of a cancer in their bodies. Second, the frame of reference limits the acquisition of new knowledge, for knowledge is as necessary to acquiring knowledge as money is to making money. For instance, a student who knows nothing about geometry most certainly will flounder in a trigonometry course, and those of us with little or no knowledge of aerodynamics and thermodynamics can't begin to understand the scientific aspects of launching, sustaining, and recovering space craft. Third, false information in the frame of reference can be worse than no information at all. Individuals who are convinced that sucking on nectarine pits will cure cancer deprive themselves of potentially therapeutic medical treatment. Employers and labor unions who are certain that fatter paychecks are the only way to motivate workers overlook what may be more effective motivational devices, such as restructuring work and improving job atmo-sphere.

Lacking a rich and accurate frame of reference, we cannot think critically. If you want to think effectively, then, start stocking your mind with information. Of course this poses a problem, for the amount of information currently avail-able is awesome. None of us can hope to acquire more than a fraction of it. Nevertheless there are steps you can take to increase the information in your frame of reference.

The selection of information for your frame of reference largely depends on the kind of person you are and will become. More specifically, you might categorize the information you need in terms of career aspirations, social roles, and human potential.

If you wish to succeed in your career, you will surely need to acquire the necessary technical knowledge and to keep abreast of current developments in your field. But you will be more than a professional; you will also be a person who functions in numerous social roles—the role of spouse, parent, consumer, citizen, and so on. To be effective in these roles, you will need just as much information—in some cases more—as you need to succeed in a career. In general this calls for wide reading and study of the social, political, biological, and physical sciences. Beyond this you presumably wish to become everything you are capable of becoming: You wish to realize as much of your potential as possible. If besides success as a professional and a player of various social roles you desire fulfillment as a human being, you must at least expose yourself to what is termed the humanities, those branches of learning having primarily a cultural character, for example, philosophy, art, music, and literature.

But there is something further you must know—something more basic than what you need to succeed in a career or social role or as a human being.

You need the knowledge of how to act freely as a human being. Specifically you must first be able to learn for yourself. Lacking this knowledge you remain a slave to the ideas of others and the machines programmed by them. You must know how to think for yourself. If you don't you can never go beyond what others have learned or thought and again you remain enslaved to the ideas of others. In a word, you must know how to learn and think for yourself. Frankly, I can think of no better way to make this discovery than with a study of critical thinking. Indeed it's safe to say that lacking critical thinking skills, you will never know how to learn and think for yourself.

Summary

This chapter attempted to dispel some common misconceptions about critical thinking and to make you aware of some blocks to thinking critically.

1. Critical thinking is not the same as disagreement.
2. Critical thinking does not aim to embarrass or humiliate.
3. Critical thinking does not entail nitpicking.
4. Critical thinking does require imagination and creativity.
5. Critical thinking can be applied to our own beliefs, as well as to others'.

In a nutshell, critical thinking emphasizes the need for a rational basis for belief and provides procedures for analyzing, testing, and evaluating beliefs.

Many people don't, can't, or won't think critically. The main reason for this inadequacy is that people fall victim to certain blocks, clichéd patterns of viewing things. Some common blocks are cultural conditioning, reliance on authority, hasty moral judgment, black-and-white thinking, reliance on labels, and resistance to change.

Critical thinking is necessary if we are to make sense of what we hear and read, gain insight into the information and claims that bombard us, make discussions more illuminating, and develop and evaluate our own positions on issues.

Applications

1 Many subjects typically evoke hasty moral judgments that are culturally conditioned. For example "honesty" generally elicits the judgments "good" or "desirable" whereas "dishonesty" elicits the judgment "bad" or "undesirable." State the moral judgment that the following subjects typically elicit.

cheating on one's spouse	racially mixed marriages
equal opportunity	caring for the elderly
drug abuse	equal pay for equal work
pornography	free enterprise
violence	individuality
cheating on taxes	welfare

2 Many Americans probably would consider the following statements truisms. State your reasons for accepting or questioning them.

a A person who tries hard enough will eventually succeed.

b Rich people aren't happy.

c A college education is necessary to succeed in life.

d Honesty is the best policy.

e People who can't find a job simply aren't trying.

f Every cloud has a silver lining.

g The best defense is a good defense.

h The business of America is business itself.

i The best government is the one that governs least.

j Might makes right.

3 Specify whether an individual, a group, or an institution is the authority appealed to in the following passages.

a **JOE:** You know, I think I'm going to start banking at First Federal.

JILL: Why's that?

JOE: Well, I saw Fred Astaire do a commercial for them the other day. I figure a guy as successful as Fred must know something about saving money.

b **FRANK:** You know, I think all political parties should be entitled to TV time, not just the major ones.

WINNIE: I don't agree. The major parties represent the significant viewpoints. The other parties don't.

FRANK: Why do you say that?

WINNIE: Well, by far the vast majority of Americans belong to the Republican or Democratic parties. So what those parties have to say obviously is important.

c **JOYCE:** No more Tang for me. I'd prefer something more nutritious.

GEORGE: More nutritious? Don't you realize that NASA chose Tang for its astronauts?

JOYCE: No kidding! Hmm, maybe I won't switch after all.

d **BILL:** There's no question that humans are inherently aggressive.

JUNE: I disagree.

BILL: If you do, you'll have to buck some real heavyweights, like Darwin, Lorenz, and Ardrey. As for me I think their endorsement of the agressionist view offers conclusive evidence for it.

d **STAN:** There's no question that the Golden Rule is a sound moral principle.

STU: Why do you say that?

STAN: Because it's basic to every religion and society. You can go back thousands of years and find some version of the Golden Rule operating in society.

4 Which of the following statements would you take on authority? Why? Why not?

   a Hell exists (meaning the preternatural abode of evil and not, as philosopher Jean Paul Sartre once suggested, other people).

   b Sugar contributes to tooth decay.

   c The earth was once visited by astronaut gods.

   d $E = MC^2$

   e The Declaration of Independence was adopted on July 4, 1776.

   f Mercy killing is immoral.

   g The Mona Lisa is an outstanding painting.

   h Democracy is the best form of government.

   i The Vietnam War was necessary.

   j Laetrile is not an effective way to treat cancer.

5 State one political, one scientific, one medical, and one religious belief that you take on authority.

6 It's no secret that in our culture women traditionally have been expected to please men and to depend on them, while men play an active role. But the part that labels play in both reflecting and reinforcing this cultural assumption sometimes goes overlooked. For example, women are much more identified with something to eat (e.g., "sugar"), compared with pets (e.g., "chick"), and associated with plants (e.g., "clinging vine") than men are. How many food, pet, and plant labels for women can you list? How do such labels condition women to assume certain social roles?

7 Some labels communicate both a fact and a judgment of that fact. This makes discussions involving religious, racial, and political groups especially complex. For example, to many Americans the word "Communist" means simultaneously "one who believes in communism" (fact) and "one whose ideals and purposes are godless and repellent" (judgment). As a result sometimes it's necessary to speak and write in roundabout terms if you wish to avoid arousing traditional prejudices that hinder clear thinking. (The term "patriotism" was used in this chapter as an illustration.) Identify three such words and give a substitute for each that is less loaded.

8 Sometimes people assume that the label attached to a person or thing is a sufficient reason for drawing conclusions about the entities to which such labels are attached. Advertisers expect the typical consumer to make such an inference. For example, the manufacturers of Superflite Golf Balls presumably want golfers to infer from the label alone that using these balls will lengthen their drives. Similarly owners of "discount" stores presumably want shoppers to believe that everything in their stores has been discounted.[9] Give three examples of labels that presumably are intended as sufficient reasons for drawing conclusions about the objects to which the labels are attached.

9 Which of the following propositions would you strongly support or oppose? Try to account for your reaction in terms of the blocks discussed: cultural

---

[9]T. Edward Damer, *Attacking Faulty Reasoning* (Belmont, Calif.: Wadsworth, 1982), pp. 59–60.

conditioning, reliance on authority, hasty moral judgment, black-and-white thinking, reliance on labels, and frame of reference.

a Polygamy and polyandry should be legalized.

b "America the Beautiful," or some other song, should replace "The Star Spangled Banner" as our national anthem.

c The U.S. Constitution should be amended to permit persons under thirty-five years old to be President.

d College students should be allowed to determine curricula and take whatever courses they want for credit toward graduation.

e High school students should be allowed to smoke on campus.

f Sex education should be introduced in junior high schools and continue right on through high school.

g Parents should make birth control devices available to their adolescent offspring.

h The draft should apply equally to females as to males.

i There should be tax penalties for people having more than two children.

j A person convicted of drunk driving should receive a mandatory jail sentence.

k A pregnant woman, in consultation with her physician, should be allowed to have an abortion on demand.

l Prayer should be mandatory in all public schools.

m Television networks (CBS, NBC, ABC) should be allowed to televise pornographic programs after 11:00 P.M.

n Homosexuals should not be permitted to teach in elementary schools.

o All religious institutions should be required to pay taxes.

10 All the blocks to critical thinking that we discussed have one thing in common: They encourage a stereotyped way of looking at or describing something. As a critical thinker, you must challenge assumptions. In so doing you challenge the necessity of boundaries and the validity of individual concepts. The following three problems are designed to give you practice in challenging assumptions. If you cannot solve them, it's because you are starting from an incorrect assumption, from a stereotyped way of looking at things.

a You're a gardener. Your employer asks you to plant four olive trees so that each one is exactly the same distance from each of the others. How would you arrange the trees?

b Link up the following arrangement of nine dots using only four straight lines that must be made without your raising the pencil from the paper.

    • • •

    • • •

    • • •

c A man works in a tall office building. Each morning he enters the elevator on the ground floor, presses the button to the ninth floor, exits, and then walks up to the fourteenth floor. At night he enters the elevator on the fourteenth floor and gets out on the ground floor. Account for his behavior.

Language—The Limit of Our World

What we think, even how we think, cannot be separated from language. Our thoughts and beliefs about such things as education, politics, economics, religion, ethics, art—indeed, ourselves and our world—cannot be distinguished from the language we use to formulate them.

The relation between language and thought has two fundamental aspects. One is that language reflects what individuals or groups think about things. Language reveals how they order their experiences, what assumptions they make, and what perspectives they take. When Archie Bunker uttered such priceless malapropisms as " 'Sorry' ain't gonna clench my thirst," "You gotta grab the bull by the corns and heave ho," and "On the sperm of the moment, it's like making a sow's purse outta silk," he did more than make us laugh. He revealed himself to be pretentious and vain, ignorant and arrogant, and, in the unvarnished terms of his creator, Norman Lear— "a horse's ass."

Just as language can give insights into individuals, it can also tell us about groups. Have you ever wondered, for example, why we have only one word for "snow" and one for "camel"? "So what?" you may be thinking. "How many words for snow or camel do you need?" Lots, if you're an Eskimo or an Arab. In fact, in Eskimo separate words are used to distinguish many different kinds of snow, including soft, hard-packed, slushy, and wind-driven. And Arabic has more than 5000 names for camels, terms that pinpoint differences of age, sex, and bodily structure. In our world, making fine distinctions regarding snow and camels is trivial; for Eskimos and Arabs these distinctions are vital.

The second aspect of the relation between language and thought is that language influences thinking. We don't always—sometimes we won't or can't—distinguish between words and things. A slogan that rhymes, is alliterative (i.e., has a number of words that begin with the same sound), or has strong rhythm can move us to action. Seduced by "Fifty-four Forty or Fight," our ancestors nearly went to war in 1844. Some historians attribute much of the misery of the modern world in part to the fascination that Grant's "Unconditional Surrender" held for four generations of Americans.[1] In the 1952 and 1956 presidential elections, Republicans made hay with the catchy slogan "I Like Ike." In 1960 the Democrats wooed us with the pleasing and easily remembered "All the Way with JFK," while the Republicans offered the colorless and vague "Nixon's the One!" And who can forget the earthy, populist appeal of "Grits and Fritz" (Carter—Mondale)?

If you seriously examine your prejudices, you will probably find that many of them are, at base, verbal. A word becomes emotion-soaked, evoking a certain emotional response (take, for example, "patriotism," "free enterprise," "communism," and "atheism"). Then whenever the word is repeated, it evokes the same response, regardless of the situation it is describing, which goes unexamined. There's no attempt to be rational, to see what's actually occurring. The word triggers the response.

Presumably you want to think more effectively. If so, you must become aware not only of the blocks to critical thinking but also of the centrality of language in both reflecting and influencing what you think. Since a large part of thinking critically hinges upon your ability to detect bias in communication, the lion's share of this chapter will deal with that one topic. But there are other language concerns you should be familiar with: the nature of language, its functions and meaning, and word definition. These, too, are covered in the present chapter.

Language as a Convention

Today we find it hard to believe that people once thought that a natural connection existed between words and what words stood for, that for example the word "tulip" and the flower it referred to or "dog" and its referent were naturally connected. Not that anybody ever thought that a word was a thing, that the word "tulip" was the actual flower or "dog" the actual creature. But primitive peoples did believe that in nature there was a connection between words and their referents, just as surely as there was a connection between dark nimbus clouds and rain. Given this supposed natural connection, a word could never rightly be used to stand for anything other than what it stood for any more than dark nimbus clouds could mean anything else than rain.

But no such natural connection exists between words and their referents. Words are conventional as opposed to natural. Terming words "conventional"

[1]Bergen Evans, *The Word-A-Day Vocabulary Builder* (New York: Random House, 1963).

means that they are a human invention that has been adopted by the users of a language. Words are noises that human beings have assigned meaning to. Speakers of English use "cat" to refer to feline creatures, while speakers of French use "chat" and speakers of German use "katze." Some other word could do just as well for these peoples. Indeed, any word that you now know might have been used to stand for anything. Which word is the "right" word for a thing? Since words are conventional, there is no such thing as a right or wrong word for a thing. True, the noise assigned a thing may be hard to pronounce, ambiguous (sounding too much like the noises assigned other things), or difficult to spell; you could object to it on these grounds. But it would be foolish to object that the noise used to stand for a thing was the "wrong" noise.

Much the same can be said of syntax, which refers to the way words are put together to communicate thoughts and ideas. In English we put adjectives before nouns, as in "white house." In Spanish the adjective typically follows nouns: "casa blanca." Just as words are conventional, so are the ways we put words together. A young man who tells his girlfriend "I want to see you in the worst way" utters a syntactically ambiguous sentence, given the syntax governing the use of English. His girlfriend might object to his statement for this reason, but not because the word order he chose doesn't correspond to some "true" way to put words together.

The referents that words have, then, as well as their order in sentences, are not discovered, but assigned. Astronomers didn't discover and learn the names of the planets; they gave the planets their names. Any other names could have done just as well. So it is with all words. Inasmuch as another word for the objects chair or house or building could have been used, words are arbitrary. But although language is arbitrary, this does not mean that our choice of words and word order can be arbitrary. If you and I wish to communicate to other speakers of English, we must accept the conventions of the English language. The conventions themselves are arbitrary (that is, they could be other than what people have chosen to make them), but once established they dictate the words we use and how we put them together.

Think of the rules governing organized American football and you'll see what I mean. One rule states that the dimensions of the playing field between the end zones should be 100 yards; another prescribes exactly eleven participants per team. These rules are arbitrary; they could be other than what they are. In fact, Canadian football is played on a 110-yard field with twelve participants on a side. But—and this is the point—if you choose to play American football, then you must play by its conventions. If you play Canadian football, you must observe its conventions.

Of course, the conventions of games can change by common consent. Thus not long ago the so-called two-point conversion rule replaced the one-point convention in scholastic football. Accordingly, those who play high school or college football must now follow this convention.

By the same token, in playing the language game, you must abide by the conventions of the particular language in which you choose to communicate, in our case English. And you can rightly expect others to do the same. In departing from our language's conventions, we risk unnecessary confusion, which is the archenemy of clear and effective thinking.

The Rule of Common Usage

In *Through the Looking Glass*, Alice and Humpty Dumpty have the following conversation:

> ". . . there are 364 days when you might get un-birthday presents—"
> "Certainly," said Alice.
> "And only *one* for birthday presents, you know. There's glory for you!"
> "I don't know what you mean by 'glory,'" Alice said.
> Humpty Dumpty smiled contemptuously. "Of course you don't—till I tell you. I meant, 'there's a nice knock-down argument for you!'"
> "But 'glory' doesn't mean 'a nice knock-down argument,'" Alice objected.
> "When I use a word," Humpty Dumpty said, in a rather scornful tone, "it means just what I choose it to mean—neither more nor less."[2]

Just imagine the confusion that would reign if, like Humpty Dumpty, each of us used words to mean exactly what we wanted them to mean, "neither more nor less." To avoid such chaos and inconvenience, *follow common usage*. When you do use a word in a way contrary to common usage, tell your audience what meaning you intend. If you don't, they are justified in assuming that you are using the word in its conventional sense. The same applies when you're receiving information. If a writer or speaker doesn't inform you of a departure from common usage, you are right in taking for granted that the person is following common usage.

Some words are so indefinite in their present meaning that their continued use can be confusing and unprofitable. "Right," "democracy," "liberal," "conservative," "radical," "loyalty," "patriotism," "justice," "culture," and "sophisticated" are just a few of these many words. Recall our discussion of labels in the preceding chapter. As currently used these words are labels obscuring a nest of confusions. To avoid these confusions, writers sometimes drop these words entirely. Or they preserve the word but try to clarify it by using it in some special or precise sense that they stipulate to the audience. I'll say more of this technique shortly. Here it's enough to urge you to become sensitive to words with fuzzy meanings. Look for departures from common usage in what you read and hear and demand stipulation when the terms are hopelessly ambiguous. By the same token, take care to make clear the meaning of such words when you use them.

A Guide to Meaning, not Truth

It's important to realize that common usage is a guide to determining what we will use our words to mean. But neither common usage nor stipulated

---

[2]Lewis Carroll, *Through the Looking Glass*, in *The Complete Works of Lewis Carroll* (New York: Random House, 1936), p. 214.

departures from it necessarily determine whether the statements in which we use our words are true or false. For example, the statement "Dogs bark" is true, when (not *because*) each word in the sentence is used in its conventional sense. In a later chapter we will explore the concept of truth, for it plays a crucial role in critical thinking, specifically in argument analysis. Suffice it to note for the present that the statement "Dogs bark" is true because it reports an actual state of affairs that can be proved by observing the behavior of certain creatures, dogs. By the same token "Snakes bark" is false when each word in the sentence is used in its conventional sense. Although the words are used in accordance with their common usage, taken together they do not express an actual state of affairs.

Now suppose that a person who utters "Snakes bark" says, Humpty-Dumptylike, "Oh, by 'snake' I mean those domesticated carnivores you often see wagging their tail and chewing on a bone." Even so, this stipulated meaning of "snake" does not determine whether the statement "Snakes bark" is true any more than the common usage of "dog" determines the truth of the statement "Dogs bark." In both cases the truth depends not on the meaning of words but on confirmation of the behavior of the creature under discussion through observation of the world. A dog by any other name either barks or does not bark. If you say that a particular creature—whatever you call it—barks, and I say that the same creature—whatever I call it—does not bark, we are engaged in a factual dispute. A factual dispute is one that can be resolved only by a further investigation of the facts, not of the meaning of words.

Factual and Verbal Disputes

Some people like to think that in most cases disputes arise simply because of disagreement about the meaning of words, what they commonly term "a matter of semantics." In fact, most of the disputes that concern us are factual. Two people may disagree about how many planets there are in the solar system, or whether capital punishment is a deterrent, or whether the majority of people in the United States favor gun control, or whether jogging can prevent heart disease. There is no way to settle these issues except by investigating the facts of the case. No matter how clear the use of the words, such disputes defy resolution without appropriate data.

To be sure, some disputes are strictly verbal; that is, they can be settled by clarifying the meanings of the words involved. An example is the old dispute "If a tree falls in the forest and nobody is there to hear it, is there a sound?" Clarifying the meaning of "sound" will settle the dispute. Accordingly, if you're talking about sound waves, then certainly there are sounds whether or not anyone is there to hear the tree fall. But if you mean sound sensations—the experience of sound—then the falling tree makes no sound, for no one is there to experience the sound sensations. In this instance, then, clarification of a term is sufficient to resolve the dispute.

Moreover, sometimes the truth of what we say is simply a matter of definition. For example, the claim that vice is bad is true by definition because vice is defined as an immoral habit or practice; that is, as something bad.

Similarly, the claim that virtue is good is true by definition because virtue is defined as moral excellence; that is, as something good.

Certainly it's a good practice to ensure clarity in language usage and demand it of others. And surely some disputes can be settled and truth determined by language clarification. But in the vast majority of cases, following common usage is a guide to meaning, not to truth.

Quick Check on Disputes

Are the following factual disputes or verbal disputes?

1 JOHN: The Gilsons served a delightful little lunch.
   JOAN: The Gilsons served a magnificent banquet.
2 Brad has an old car. One day he replaces one of its defective parts. The next day he replaces another. Before the year is out, Brad has replaced every part in the entire car. Is Brad's car the same car he had before he began the replacements?
3 A bad peace is even worse than war. (Tacitus)
   The most disadvantageous peace is better than the most just war. (Erasmus)
4 Phil told his brother Fred "When I die I'll leave you all my money." A week later he thought better of his promise and decided to leave his money to his estranged wife instead. So Phil wrote in his will "I leave all my money to my next of kin" (his wife). Unknown to Phil his wife had died in a car accident. The day after he made out his will Phil himself died, and his money went to his next of kin—his brother Fred. Did Phil keep his promise to Fred or didn't he?
5 Our country: in her intercourse with foreign nations may she always be right; but our country, right or wrong! (Stephen Decatur)

   Our country, right or wrong. When right, to be kept right; when wrong, to be put right. (Carl Schurz)

Comments

1. Factual: John believes that the Gilsons served a small meal, whereas Joan believes it was big. It is possible, however, that their words don't express a factual dispute about the exact size of the meal but a difference in the amounts of food John and Joan are used to seeing served at a meal.
2. Verbal: If "same car" is taken to mean one that contains all, most, or the most important parts that it contained at some point, then Brad doesn't have the "same car." But if "same car" is taken to mean the project Brad's been working on all this time or perhaps the vehicle designated by a registation certificate, or some other constant, then it is the "same car."
3. Factual: It wouldn't do any good to define "bad peace" or "disadvantageous peace" here, for the parties are disagreed about whether it is to be preferred to war. What is now needed is an airing of the reasons for each position so that a comparative evaluation can be made.

4. Verbal: Phil did not keep his promise inasmuch as he didn't *intend* his money to go to Fred. In this sense he broke his promise when he made out his will. But if Phil's intention is not considered, he did keep his promise in that the assurance he gave Fred was, in fact, carried out.
5. Factual: In effect Schurz disagrees with Decatur's position that we should support our country even when it is wrong.

Functions of Language

So subtle and complicated an instrument is language that we often overlook its many uses. As a result we can get caught in the snares laid by language in the way of the thinker: We can fail to understand, or can even misinterpret, communication. A basic part of thinking effectively, then, is grasping how language functions.

We can impose some order on the rich variety of language usage by dividing it into four broad categories. Although this fourfold division is a simplification, it does pinpoint the main kinds of language usage essential to critical thinking.

1. Informative.   A main use of language is to communicate information. This is typically accomplished by formulating and then affirming (or denying) statements. *Language used to affirm or deny statements is said to perform an informative function.*

The following statements are typical examples of the informative use of language:

Washington is the nation's capital.
Laetrile is not an effective treatment for cancer.
U.S. presidential elections are held quadrennially.
Business administration is currently the most popular college major.
One out of ten Americans has herpes.
The Democrats have never controlled the U.S. House of Representatives.

Notice that the last statement is false. "Information" as used here is taken to include *misinformation*; that is, false statements as well as true. Furthermore, statements whose truth is in doubt, such as "Extraterrestrial life exists" and "The next President will be a Republican," are said to convey information.

2. Expressive.   Besides conveying information about the world, language also serves to express feelings. *Whenever language is used to vent or arouse feelings, it is said to perform an expressive function.*

Poetry furnishes the best examples of the expressive function of language:

So fair, so sweet, withal so sensitive,
Would that the Little Flowers were to live,
Conscious of half the pleasures which they give....
—*William Wordsworth*

The poet did not compose these lines to report any information but to express certain emotions he felt and to evoke a similar response in the reader.

But expressive language need not be confined to poetry. We express sorrow by saying "What a pity" or "That's too bad" and enthusiasm by shouting "Wow!" or "Right on!" And we express feelings of affection, passion, and love by murmuring "Darling" or "Honey" or like terms of endearment. None of these uses is intended to communicate information but rather feelings. Accordingly, expressive language is neither true nor false.

3. Directive.   *Language serves a directive function when it is used to cause or prevent overt action.* The clearest examples of directive discourse are commands and requests. When a teacher tells a class "Study for tomorrow's test," he doesn't intend to communicate information or express emotion but to cause a specific action: studying. When the same teacher asks the audiovisual technician to set up a projector in his classroom, he is again using language directively; that is, to produce action. If the teacher first asks the technician if she has a projector available, he is also using language directively, for questions typically are requests for answers. Like expressive language, directive language is neither true nor false.

4. Performative.   Language can also be used in the performance of an action, for expressing certain words in a specific context can bring something about. For example, suppose that during a marriage ceremony, the bride says "I do." Or, in bumping into you, I say "I apologize." Or, in christening a ship, a person says "I name this ship the *Nautilus*" and breaks a bottle of champagne across its hull. Or, after a heated discussion about the relative merits of baseball teams, a friend says to you "I bet you five bucks that the Dodgers make it to the World Series." Although all these utterances have the form of informative utterances, they certainly are not reporting the performance of some action that undoubtedly is done—the action of promising, apologizing, christening, betting. Rather, in saying what they do, the speakers are actually peforming the action. When the bride says "I do," she is not describing or reporting the marriage ceremony, she is actually carrying it out; when I say "I apologize," I am not describing or reporting the apology, I am actually performing it. Utterances of this kind, which include verdicts and promises, are called "performative utterances." *Language serves the performative function, then, when it is used in certain contexts to make something so.*

Multiple Functions

You don't have to be a linguist to realize that a given communication need not employ just a single language use. Indeed, most ordinary communication likely will exhibit multiple uses of language.

Consider, for example, this poem:

My heart leaps up when I behold
  A rainbow in the sky;
So was it when my life began;
So is it now I am a man;
So be it when I should grow old,
  Or let me die!

The Child is father of the Man;
And I could wish my days to be
Bound each to each by natural piety.
          —*Wordsworth*

Although this poem, like most, is primarily expressive discourse, it can be said to be informative in the sense that the poet is stating that the adult can learn from the child and directive in the sense that the poet is urging us to get in touch with the feelings and intuitions of childhood. On the other hand, a classroom lecture, essentially informative, may express something of the professor's own enthusiasm, thus serving the expressive function. By implication, it may also serve some directive function, perhaps bidding the class to verify independently the lecturer's conclusions.

The fact is that most ordinary language usage has mixed functions. This is an important point to remember when thinking critically about some discourse, for buried amid the rhetorical flourishes may lie the contentions that are the object of our critical inspection. I will say considerably more about this in later chapters when I discuss argument analysis and portrayal.

Quick Check on the Functions of Language

What language functions are exhibited by each of the following passages?

1 Baseball umpire: "You're out!"
2 A flat tax rate is outrageous because it favors the rich and penalizes the poor. This is why you must urge your legislators to vote against it.
3 Although we tend to look on our presidents as great men, some of them were indecisive, petty, unintelligent, and unscrupulous.
4 I wouldn't vote Democratic if I were you. Don't you realize the Democrats are the "war party"?
5 Thomas "Tip" O'Neill, the cantankerous Speaker of the House, is a crafty legislator whose political roots can be traced to the leftist-leaning philosophy of Franklin Delano Roosevelt.
6 "A civil war is like the heat of a fever; but a foreign war is like the heat of exercise, and serveth to keep the body in health." (Francis Bacon, *Essays*)
7 "War is the greatest plague that can afflict humanity; it destroys religion, it destroys states, it destroys families. Any scourge is preferable to it." (Martin Luther, *Table-Talk*)
8 "We must all hang together or assuredly we shall all hang separately." (Benjamin Franklin, to the other signers of the Declaration of Independence)

Comments

1. Performative
2. Informative: flat tax rates favor the rich and penalize the poor
   Directive: urge legislators to oppose a flat tax rate
   Expressive: to evoke feelings of outrage against the flat tax rate
3. Informative

4. Informative: the Democrats are synonymous with war
   Directive: don't vote Democratic
   Expressive: to evoke fear of the Democrats
5. Informative: O'Neill is the Speaker of the House whose philosophical roots can be
   traced to Roosevelt
   Expressive: to evoke feelings of distrust for O'Neill
6. Informative: civil wars weaken a nation; foreign wars strengthen it
   Directive: avoid civil wars; don't avoid foreign wars
   Expressive: to evoke antipathy toward civil wars and approval of foreign wars
7. Informative: war is destructive
   Directive: avoid war
   Expressive: to evoke antipathy toward war
8. Informative: unless we stand together, we will all lose our lives
   Directive: let's stand fast together
   Expressive: to evoke strong feelings of solidarity

Word Meaning: Denotation and Connotation

Critical thinking is concerned largely with informative statements. These statements are both the product and the object of critical inspection. They of course
both consist of words in certain arrangements. Unless we know the meanings of
these words, we cannot think critically about the statements that contain them,
nor can we respond intelligently to the statements. While there is much to be
said about meaning, I will confine my remarks to the meaning of general terms
that can apply to numerous particular items around us, for example, "bridge,"
"building," "school," "politician," "book," and the like.

In considering general terms, it's helpful to distinguish between two
senses of word meaning: the denotative and connotative. *The denotative, or
extensional, meaning of a word is the group of objects indicated by that word.* For
example, the denotation of "bridge" is that group of objects that we commonly
identify as bridges; the denotation of "building" is that group of objects to which
the term "building" commonly applies. In the denotative sense of meaning,
then, a word serves to designate or refer to role: It points to a group of objects.

It is not by chance, however, that the terms "bridge" and "building" refer to
the objects they refer to, for these objects share some common features or
properties. Bridges and buildings have characteristics that make them bridges
or buildings and not, say, tunnels or silos. The common characteristics of the
objects designated by a term make up the term's connotation or intensional
meaning. The connotation of a word, then, is the collection of properties shared
by all and by only those objects in a term's extension.

*The connotation of a word can be either conventional or subjective. A term's
conventional connotation is that set of properties we ordinarily accept as being
shared by the objects in a term's extension.* For example, we have agreed to take
the properties of being a closed plane curve, all points of which are equidistant
from a point within called the center, as the criteria for deciding whether a
figure is to be called a "circle." This agreement establishes a convention; thus we
speak of the *conventional* connotation or intension of a term. Because a term's

conventional connotation is public and can be discovered with the help of a dictionary, it is a most important aspect of word definition and of communication.

Quite often a word has special meaning for an individual or group of individuals because it evokes an emotional response. *The subjective connotation of a word refers to its emotional impact.* For example, the conventional connotation of "manipulate" is to handle, manage, or use with skill. One who displays such deftness is literally a "manipulator" or "manipulative." Nevertheless, in my relations with others I wouldn't want to be called either, and neither would you. The reason is that "manipulate" carries negative connotations in the context of human relations.

Again, the word "tabloid" designates a newspaper about half the size of a standard-size newspaper page. But most tabloid newspapers tend toward sensationalism. As a result "tabloid" carries a negative or pejorative meaning. To call a newspaper a tabloid is to put it down. Similarly the explicit meaning of "prima donna" is the principal female singer in an opera company. But no woman or man would want to be called a "prima donna" because the term carries the connotation of a vain, temperamental person.

Of course, subjective connotations need not be only derogatory. Many are complimentary: They carry a positive emotional charge. Words with such connotations include "statesperson" (as opposed to the negative "politician"), "moderate" (as opposed to the negative "wishy-washy"), and "professor" (as opposed to the negative "pedagogue"). Still other words carry no emotional impact at all: "house," "tree," "lamp," "car," "job," and so on.

Nothing is more essential to thinking effectively about what you read, hear, and write than sensitivity to subjective connotation. Only with such sensitivity can you understand both what someone means, which may be obvious, and what that person wants to suggest, which may be far more important than the superficial meaning. This doesn't mean that in thinking about a passage you must consider every single word for implications and subsurface meanings. Many words—articles, conjunctions, prepositions, and some adverbs—carry no emotional impact because they don't represent ideas but are used as connectives or relational devices. Other words, such as scientific or technical terms, are usually free of any subjective connotations; they don't evoke any vivid pictures or emotional responses. For example, "eschatology" is colorless compared with the words designating its chief concerns: "death," "judgment," "heaven," and "hell." But the fact remains that most words that stand for ideas do have a positive or negative emotional charge, and you must be sensitive to these connotations if you are to think effectively about the passages in which they are contained.

Recognizing Bias in Language Use

A bias is a predisposed point of view. Writers and speakers can communicate bias in many ways. One obvious way is simply to state an opinion: "The New

Federalism won't work"; "Capital punishment doesn't deter crime"; "A woman should not have a legal right to abortion." Another way is through the careful selection of material. If I want to prove that capital punishment doesn't deter crime, I might select only those data that support my position, suppressing those that don't.

But beyond these obvious ways of communicating bias, writers and speakers can use an array of language devices to slant material more subtly. I will mention just a handful: bias words, assumption-loaded words, suggestion of inference, extreme quantifiers and intensifiers, and euphemism. To be sure, these devices are a valuable part of language. But often they give information, not about the issue under discussion, but about the writer. They express the writer's attitudes and feelings and in fact are chosen by the writer to convey, if possible, these attitudes and feelings to the reader. Such devices are dangerous to critical thinking, for they can lead the writer or reader to confuse the exposure of an attitude with reasons for holding that attitude. This is why it's important for you as a critical thinker to become sensitive to these language devices, to recognize them for what they are: subtle attempts to shape your opinion through loaded language.

Bias Words

As we just saw, words can have connotations that are derogatory, commendable, or neutral. While we must always remember that a word owes much of its meaning to its context, we can still surmise what kind of bias certain words have acquired. Consider, for example, the words "liberty" and "license," as in the phrase "liberty, not license." There is no difference in what these words refer to: Each suggests the absence of restrictions on doing something. But when writers use "license" instead of "liberty," they are implying disapproval and presumably want their audience to disapprove as well. More important, the writer may be using the word "license" as a substitute for reasoning. Thus, when I term the publication and sale of pornographic material "license," I am saying that I don't like it. And I am loading my utterance in order to sway you to my opinion, not by reason but by bias.

Again, the word "fad" can refer to any belief or position that a person disapproves of. It also implies that the person adhering to the belief or position (the "faddist") attaches too much importance to it and that few others regard it with such enthusiasm. Thus, when I call jogging, jazzercise, and video games "fads," I am telling you more about my attitude toward these things than about the things themselves. Why does this matter? In the hands of a facile writer, bias words can be used to subtly lead an audience to the writer's position, not through reasoning but through an appeal to their emotions or prejudices.

Consider this passage taken from an essay on burnout, a widespread psychological syndrome in which individuals beset by exhaustion, physical illness, acute anger, depression, and self-doubt end careers and possibly their lives:

> One of the biggest difficulties with the concept of burnout is that it has become faddish and indiscriminate, an item of psychobabble, the psychic equivalent, in its ubiquitousness, of jogging. Burnout has no formal psychiatric status. Many psychoanalysts regard the malady as simply that old familiar ache, depression. Even so, plenty of professionals take burnout seriously. Psychological journals are heavy with analyses of burnout. [Lance Morrow, "The Burnout of Almost Everyone," *Time*, September 21, 1981]

The use of the word "faddish" indicates that the author believes that too much importance has been attached to burnout. His attitude is heightened by other word choices: "indiscriminate" (which connotes "confused" or "jumbled"), "psychobabble" (psychological gibberish), and "heavy" (indulging to an unusual or great degree).

The choice of words affects the tone of a passage, which in turn influences an audience's perceptions and thinking. When a journalist wishes to report the presence of 50,000 illegal aliens living in Los Angeles, she might write: "Fifty thousand illegal aliens are living in deserted buildings in Los Angeles" or "Fifty thousand illegal aliens are holed up in the warrens along the back alleys of lower Los Angeles." While both statements report the same fact, the second gives you a different impression from the first. Because "holed up" and "warrens" suggest verminlike creatures and "back alleys" reinforces this image, you might infer that these illegal aliens are unclean, perhaps a threat or a source of violence and upheaval. The words people choose to report facts can influence how you interpret those facts.

Since we have already discussed expressive language when examining connotation, we needn't belabor the point here. But do remember the following points about emotionally charged language:

1. Words with strong connotations bring into play a wide range of associations. "Dole" refers to a portion of money, food, and so forth, especially as given at regular intervals in charity. But it carries a derogatory connotation, as in "on the dole."

2. Some strongly charged words produce an almost automatic response. If we refer to abortion as "murder," the word "murder" will cause an almost reflexive reaction of horror, disgust, and violent disapproval, directed not only at the act of abortion but at those who engage in it. On the other hand, if we refer to abortion as "the termination of a pregnancy," the action of abortion will sound more respectable and official.

3. Emotive language provides clues to the preferences and commitments of the speaker or writer. An editorial writer who speaks in terms of the President's "lackeys," "stooges," "court," and "sycophants" is not likely a supporter of the administration. Changes in vocabulary are often a sign of changes in attitude. Today it's no longer appropriate to refer to alcoholism as a "weakness" or "character flaw" but as a "disease"; homosexuality is no longer a "perversion" or "sickness" but a "life-style"; youngsters who are unruly at school are not "antisocial" or "disciplinary problems" but "maladjusted."

These changes in vocabulary not only reflect a change in attitude, they also encourage us to perceive and think in terms of the new label.

Quick Check on Word Bias

Complete the following word tone table.

Complimentary	Derogatory	Neutral
leader of the people	demagogue	party or group leader
right-to-work advocate		
		government employee
		salesperson
		elderly person
		soldiers
	out of date	
state-of-the-art		
		group

Comments

Right-to-work advocate, scab, strike breaker
Public servant, bureaucrat, *government employee*
Manufacturer's representative, huckster, *salesperson*
Senior citizen, codger, *elderly person*
Freedom fighters, guerrillas, *soldiers*
Time-tested, *out of date*, old
State-of-the-art, newfangled, new
Community, mob, *group*

Assumption-Loaded Labels

In the preceding chapter we saw how labels can block critical thinking by locking us into sterile conceptual patterns and providing pseudo-justification for our views. Labels are also dangerous because they conceal assumptions that may be questionable, leading us to accept uncritically a doubtful view of things. When Hitler referred to "the Jewish problem," implied was a freight of questionable assumptions, not the least of which was that a nation's socioeconomic problems could be correctly ascribed to individuals of a particular religion or ethnic background. By systematically using the phrase "the Jewish problem," the Nazis encouraged others to consider the Jews as the source of domestic instability. "The Jewish problem" became a cover for "anti-Semitism," and Jews were made scapegoats for Germany's internal strife.

Today we speak of the "welfare problem," even the "welfare mess." "Welfare" means organized efforts to improve the living conditions of needy persons. In what sense, then, is welfare a "problem"? In fact, welfare is the *result* of many problems: unemployment, age, infirmity, racial prejudice, broken homes, limited resources, and so forth. These in turn likely are the results of fundamental problems in our political, social, and economic institutions and philosophies. The label "welfare problem" overlooks the complexity of the issue. It is loaded with the assumption that welfare is the disease, not the symptom. As a result it not only encourages us to consider welfare in isolation of its underlying causes but to blame welfare and its recipients for various social ills—for "infecting" the nation, to extend the medical metaphor.

The label "sex roles" is another term that's bandied about today. This term implies an explanation of observed sex differences; namely, that socialization and social norms, and not biology, are the origin of the behavioral differences between the sexes. Are they? Recent studies show that the brains of male and female animals differ physically and chemically. These recent findings reveal differences between the sexes in the phsysical structure of the brain regions related to reproduction and in the chemistry of nerve signal transmission. So far the differences have been found only in animals, but many scientists believe that some similar differences between the sexes probably exist in human brains as well and might someday help make clear the biological factors in personality.

On the other hand, even if you accept nature as the explanation of observed sex differences, you can, and should, ask whether role terminology is fully applicable to gender, as is implied in "sex roles." Actually, we should be careful about ascribing categories of social phenomena to biological conditions such as gender. Otherwise, we may neglect other possible explanations, such as the power differential between women and men in our society. It seems that nature *and* nurture each play a part and that they are intertwined with such complexity in humans as to defy the complete separation of their contributions. The label "sex roles" seemingly overlooks this likelihood.

By analogy, suppose that sociologists spoke in terms of "race roles" (which they don't). This label would imply that social phenomena—for example, illegitimacy, broken families, delinquency, and so forth—can be ascribed to race. But these phenomena seem due to economic factors.[3] Blacks have no greater participation in such "social problems" than their white economic counterparts. In short, if we ascribed differences in black and white behavior to "race roles" without clarifying the economic positions underlying the "roles," then we would be muddying the term "role" to the point of meaninglessness. Similarly, if we persist in explaining the differences between male and female behavior in terms of "sex roles" without flushing out the power positions underlying these "roles," then the term "role" obscures and confuses. It may even direct research on an unprofitable course.[4]

Suggestion of Inference

An inference is a conclusion drawn from observed facts. Precisely because it goes beyond known facts, an inference involves a leap from the known to the

[3]William Ryan, *Blaming the Victim* (New York: Random House, 1971).
[4]Nancy M. Henley, *Body Politics* (Englewood Cliffs, N.J.: Prentice-Hall, 1977), pp. 191–193.

unknown. Sometimes the facts don't allow us to draw the conclusion that the writer wants us to draw. Other times the writer would like the audience to feel that they are drawing their own conclusions from the facts. In this way writers make their conclusions more palatable because audiences tend to hold more tenaciously to opinions they think they themselves have formed than to those force-fed to them. In either case—whether to draw an inference from inadequate facts or to make the audience believe that they have drawn the inference—writers sometimes suggest inferences without explicitly drawing them.

At times the suggested inference may be unintentional, the result of careless syntax. The unintended humor of this news item, for example, rests not on the facts related but on the inference that the reader might make because of the writer's sloppy word order:

> Francine Wilkins of Bellevue, Washington, has been admitted to General Hospital for care and treatment after spending the last two weeks with her in-laws here in Walla Walla.

More common and dangerous to critical thinking than the unintentionally suggested inference is the intentionally suggested one. Two common devices are used to intentionally suggest inferences: rhetorical questions and innuendo.

Rhetorical Questions   *A rhetorical question is a question with a built-in answer.* Rhetorical questions *seem* to leave the conclusion up to the reader but are worded in such a way that only one answer is possible. "Would you recommend that the United States not spend every penny necessary to ensure national security?" "Can a law that is opposed to the wishes of millions of honest citizens be called fair and just?" "Since students don't know which courses will contribute to their education, should they have a strong voice in curriculum decisions?" It's hard to answer "Yes" to these questions. That's the point: The rhetorical question is intended to elicit a predetermined response. The beauty of the rhetorical question is that it makes you and me think that we are drawing inferences for ourselves. The implication of the writer's rhetorical setups is that if we took the time and made the effort to discover the answer, we would arrive at the same conclusion as the writer. Although an occasional rhetorical question can dramatize an important point, more often it is used to cover up a lack of good arguments.

To leave a more lasting impression on an audience, writers must use a less direct approach. Enter innuendo.

Innuendo   *Innuendo consists of drawing or implying a judgment, usually derogatory, on the basis of words that suggest but don't assert a conclusion.* "Has Jones been fired?" someone asks you. You may reply directly "No." Or you may say "No, as of today." By innuendo, the second response numbers Jones' days. Jones may in fact be on the proverbial block, but without further evidence the person has no logical grounds for so inferring. And without providing more evidence for your implication, you have no logical grounds for suggesting it through innuendo. Innuendo, then, is dangerous to critical thinking because it allows us to imply things or draw inferences that we are unable or unwilling to defend.

Innuendo needn't be as obvious as in the preceding example. The person who says "Most physicians are competent and altruistic health care professionals" probably isn't prepared to substantiate the charge made against the minority of physicians who by implication are incompetent and self-serving. The political candidate who distributes a brochure in which she promises to restore honesty and integrity to an office seldom is prepared to prove that her opponent is by implication a crook.

Indeed, sometimes merely by calling attention to something, we provide enough innuendo to sandbag somebody. Consider this amusing episode— amusing, that is, for everyone except the Captain in question:

> Captain L had a first mate who was at times addicted to the use of strong drink, and occasionally, as the slang has it, "got full." The ship was lying in port in China, and the mate had been on shore and had there indulged rather freely in some of the vile compounds common in Chinese ports. He came on board, "drunk as a lord," and thought he had a mortgage on the whole world. The captain, who rarely ever touched liquor himself, was greatly disturbed by the disgraceful conduct of his officer, particularly as the crew had all observed his condition. One of the duties of the first officer [i.e., the first mate] is to write up the log each day, but as that worthy was not able to do it, the captain made the proper entry, but added: "The mate was drunk all day." The ship left port the next day and the mate got "sobered off." He attended to his writing at the proper time, but was appalled when he saw what the captain had done. He went back on deck, and soon after the following colloquy took place:
> "Cap'n, why did you write in the log yesterday that I was drunk all day?"
> "It was true, wasn't it?"
> "Yes, but what will the shipowners say if they see it? It will hurt me with them."
> But the mate could get nothing more from the captain than, "It was true, wasn't it?"
> The next day, when the captain was examining the book, he found at the bottom of the mate's entry of observation, course, winds, and tides: "The captain was sober all day." [Charles E. Trow, *The Old Shipmasters of Salem* (New York: Macmillan, 1905), pp. 14–15.]

Obviously the mate is hoping that the ship's owners will interpret his entry about the Captain as more than the literal truth. Probably they will infer that the mate recorded the Captain's sobriety because it was the exception, not the rule. When they do the mate will gain his revenge.

Extreme Quantifiers and Intensifiers

Another way writers load language, and thereby communicate bias, is by using extreme quantifiers—terms like "all" or "every"—and extreme intensifiers—terms like "absolutely" or "certainly." In either case what results is an unqualified generalization.

*An unqualified generalization is a statement that asserts that something is true of **all** members of a class.* Here are some examples of unqualified generalizations that happen to be true:

All humans are mammals.
Men can't give birth.
No human can remain under water very long without air.
An object maintains its line of direction until acted upon by some outside force.
All known life needs oxygen to survive.
Herpes is communicated by skin-to-skin contact.

In each statement a property is attributed to every member of its class. Sometimes a universal quantifier— "all," "every," and "no"—is not stated but implied, as in "Humans are vertebrates," "Voters are citizens," "Men can't give birth," and "Herpes is communicated through skin-to-skin contact."

While some generalizations can be left unqualified, the vast majority cannot. They need to be qualified. *A qualified generalization is a statement that asserts that something is true of **a percentage** of a class.*

Qualified generalizations never speak of every member of a class but only of some. Thus, "*Forty-eight percent* of the voters favor the President's economic program," "*Most* of the students in this class are prelaw majors," and "*A large number* of doctors oppose national health insurance" all are qualified generalizations. Generalizations are qualified when they include a word or phrase like "many," "almost always," "sometimes," "often," "mostly," "usually," "ordinarily," "typically," "under certain circumstances," "rarely," and "at times."

Don't misunderstand. We need not qualify everything we say or write. But it is important to frame our assertions with as much accuracy and fairness as possible and to expect the same of others. Such framing is not only conducive to fruitful thinking but precludes needless disagreement, for frequently controversy is kindled through the use of an immoderate term, an intensifier.

Unfortunately, with our natural human indolence and intellectual limitations, we are eager to view questions in the simplest terms possible and will make decisions without considering all sides of an issue. As we saw in the preceding chapter, cultural conditioning encourages the tendency to oversimplify. This tendency turns up in approaches to practical problems but even more so in questions of human conduct or social policy. One cannot say with easy assurance "The environment *certainly* must be cleaned up, even if that means plant shutdowns, unemployment, and a reduced standard of living," "*Surely* the best way to insure domestic tranquility is to erect the strongest military defense possible," "Abortion should *never* be permitted," or "Drafting young men in peace time *simply* isn't justifiable." Perhaps each or some of these assertions are warranted, perhaps none is. But before any is adopted as settled conviction, the thinking person must consider its full implications. After the implications are explored, it may be found that these unqualified generalizations don't hold up, that their extreme quantifiers and intensifiers need to to be diluted. But the writer who employs these devices ordinarily wants to shut off, not open up, debate. He or she wants you not to think but to accept blindly. Don't.

Euphemism

When certain words are considered too blunt, harsh, painful, or offensive, people substitute a more acceptable term, called a "euphemism." Instead of "lying" we "fib" or "cover up" (as in the Watergate "coverup"). Rather than "fighting a war," we "engage in a conflict" (as in the "Vietnam conflict") or a "police action" (as in the "Korean police action"). Rather than "assassinating" people, the Central Intelligence Agency "terminates them with prejudice." (Lest there be any doubt, someone who is "terminated with prejudice" is just as dead as someone who is "executed," "liquidated," "exterminated," or "eradicated.") Rather than "firing" employees, bureaucrats speak of "selecting out," and instead of "rationing" gasoline, they talk of "end-use allocation." Today in some political circles it is fashionable to speak of a "tax" as a "revenue enhancement."

To be sure, euphemism sometimes is an appropriate adjustment of the language to a situation. I may be better able to deal with the death of a loved one by thinking of the person as having "passed away" rather than having "died." But euphemism can also be used to gloss over unpleasant realities that need attention or to divert us from giving an issue or event the critical inspection it warrants. In our times the rhetoric of Vietnam is the preeminent example of the use of euphemism to obscure, distort, and pollute literal meeting. Indeed, our government officials in the 1960s developed a litany of euphemisms to make the harrowing events of Vietnam palatable to the American public. Here are just a few examples with "translations":[5]

Euphemism	*Word replaced*
pacification center	concentration camp
incursion	invasion
protective reaction strike	bombing
surgical strike	precision bombing
incontinent ordnance	off-target bombs (usually used when civilians are killed)
friendly fire	shelling friendly villages or troops by mistake
specified strike zone	area where soldiers could fire at anything— replaced "free fire zone" when that became notorious
interdiction	bombing
strategic withdrawal	retreat (when the United States and its allies did it)
advisor	military officer (before the United States admitted involvement in Vietnam) or CIA agent
termination	killing
infiltrators	enemy troops moving into the battle area
reinforcements	friendly troops moving into the battle area

[5]Howard Kahane, *Logical and Contemporary Rhetoric* (Belmont, Calif.: Wadsworth, 1980), p. 127.

Bombarded by such euphemisms, our critical thinking is the first casualty. We find it hard to focus on the issues and events and to develop intelligent positions because we are encouraged to conceptualize in terms of language that is only tenuously connected to its referent.

Nevertheless, masking literal meaning through euphemism can be as psychologically persuasive as masking through exciting emotion. The psychological appeal of each lies in its capacity to win minds by capturing hearts. Watch for euphemism so used. Recognize it for what it often is: the last redoubt of those holding an untenable position.

So far we have learned about the conventional aspect of language, the various ways that language functions, the different meanings that language carries, and the ways people communicate bias through language. This discussion points to nothing if not the following warning: Be careful in using language and require care of others in their use of it. This doesn't mean that you should fall victim to nitpicking and pedantry. As indicated elsewhere the meaning of words is frequently nonproblematic. But there are times when language must be clarified to avoid confusion and aid intelligent, insightful thinking. Words frequently must be defined. It's appropriate, therefore, to bring to a close this overview of the centrality of language in effective thinking by considering word definition and techiques for defining.

Quick Check on Recognizing Bias in Language Use

Identify the bias in the way language is used in the following passages. Look for bias words, assumption-loaded labels, suggestion of inference, extreme quantifiers and intensifiers, and euphemism.

1 Certainly blacks make superb athletes.
2 President Reagan is one public servant who is a credit to the Republican party.
3 News item: "Anita Berkstrom, associate professor of psychology, addressed the local chapter of the American Association of University Women on 'Homosexuality: An Alternative Life-Style.' Not all members attended."
4 "Far more important than the press's influence on the success or failure of one President's program is the matter of its effect on the Presidency itself. Is it possible for any President to govern effectively under the circumstances that prevail today: when secret international negotiations fast become public knowledge, when Presidental actions are relayed to the public along with uninformed or misleading conjecture as to their possible success, when Presidental efforts to bolster confidence in the economy (because public attitudes have a great deal to do with the strength of the economy) are immediately countered by gratuitously pessimistic reports?" (Walter H.

Annenberg, "The Fourth Branch of Government," *TV Guide*, May 15, 1982, p. 13.)

5 Ad for 7UP: "When you're feelin' 7UP, you're only feelin' 7UP."

6 Ex-Lax contains an artificial chemical, whereas Nature's Remedy has natural active ingredients (paraphrase of an ad for Nature's Remedy laxative).

7 Former Secretary of the Treasury William Simon, commenting on inflation: "This has been here for twenty years and with every year that goes by it's going to take strong medicine to solve it. But it's been turned into a national disgrace by the demagogues who hope it will go away like some magic wand. And a hostile press has convinced the people it was a ripoff by the so-called giant oil companies. . . . It's typical of the neanderthal type of thinking on the hill [that is, in Congress]. Inflation is somebody else's fault. It's not their fault. They're trying to help the people. Well, they are putting out the programs that hurt the very people they are trying to help; that hurt the poor and the tired through insidious inflation." ("Simon: Answer 'Free Enterprise,'" *Bakersfield Californian*, September 23, 1976, p. 3.)

8 In order to unify and strengthen China, Chairman Mao used to conduct "purification" campaigns, events that in the last decade of his life became marred by violence and irrationality, especially as evidenced by the cataclysmic Cultural Revolution of 1966–1969. These campaigns meant death or imprisonment for many thousands of people. Idi Amin of Uganda also sent thousands to their deaths at the hand of the "Public Safety Unit," the dreaded murder squad during his reign. Comment on the use of the terms "purification" and "Public Safety Unit" in these contexts.

9 "Can the universe think about itself? We know that at least one part of it can: we ourselves. Is it not reasonable to conclude the whole can?" (Jose Silva, *The Silva Mind Control Method* [New York: Pocket Books, 1978], p. 116.)

10 "Ever since the defeat in 1978 of two 'targeted' Democratic U.S. senators, there has been a cacophony of debate about the import of the simplistic, venomous brand of politics practiced by assorted self-appointed apostles who epuhemistically christen themselves 'the New Right.' As one of their 'targets' in 1980, I can testify that this movement is not a harmless political curiosity. It should be taken seriously. Only then will it be appreciated for what it is—the antithesis of true American beliefs—and be stripped of its pretense of power and rejected." (Birch Bayh, "Morality and Manipulation: Which Will Wither First, the New Right or the Bill of Rights?" *Los Angeles Times*, July 19, 1981.)

11 "There is a move now to clamp down on the sexy aspects of television and return it to the purity of Ozzie and Harriet.

"Lift those necklines! Thicken those brassieres and rivet them firmly in place! Unleer those lips! Unwiggle those hips!—and watch what you say!

"The penalty? The New Puritans will reckon up the sex-points, watching narrowly for every hint of cleavage, for every parting of kissing lips, and will then lower the boom on all advertisers who fail the test. By striking at the pocket-nerve, the Puritans hope to produce a new kind of television that will

be as clean, as pink, as smooth and as plump as eunuchs usually are. . . ."
(Isaac Asimov, "Censorship: It's a 'Choking Grip,'" *TV Guide*, July 18, 1981.)

12 "The single quality of modern society that distinguishes it absolutely from
the past is this: massive, overwhelming numbers. More people, more cities,
more books, more cars, more everything. In self-defense, nation after nation
has erected vast bureaucracies—a tidal wave of administrators—to control
those numbers. There is no equivalent time in history, an age when mecha-
nized, computerized bureaucracy straddles the globe, from Moscow to
Peking to New York, all of it impossible to move or reform. Hannah Arendt
called it 'rule by Nobody.'" (Douglas Davis, "Living With Terrorism," *Newsweek*, June 14, 1976.)

13 "Only when we recognize that to abort is to interrupt the life process of an
existing person can we begin to address which factors we should properly
recognize as sufficiently compelling to legitimate that interruption. The
'human life bill' contains the potential for having us confront that question,
for moving us beyond the semantic subterfuge of deciding whether to
choose to call 'human' a life whose existence, even to opponents of the bill,
is 'incontrovertible.'" (Simon M. Lorne, "Going Beyond the Point When Life
Begins," *Los Angeles Times*, July 18, 1981.)

Comments

1. Extreme intensifier: "certainly"
2. Label: "public servant"; suggestion of the inference that some Republicans are not a
   credit to their party
3. Suggestion of the inference that some members didn't attend because of the topic
4. Suggestion of the inference, through rhetorical questions, that the President cannot
   effectively govern today
5. Extreme intensifier: "only"
6. Bias words: "artificial," "natural"
7. Labels: "demagogues," "neanderthal type of thinking"
8. Euphemism
9. Suggestion of inference, by the use of rhetorical questions, that the universe can think
   about itself
10. Word bias: "cacophony," "simplistic," "venomous"; intensifier: "only"
11. Labels: "purity of Ozzie and Harriet," "New Puritans"; word bias: "lower the boom,"
    "as clean, as pink. . . ."
12. Extreme quantifier: "single quality"; intensifier: "absolutely"
13. Quantifier: "only"; label: "semantic subterfuge"

Definition

A definition is an explanation of the meaning of a term. Definition can take a
number of short forms, depending chiefly on the purposes of the writer or
speaker. I will focus on four kinds of definition: denotative, logical, stipulative,
and persuasive.

Denotative Definition

We can define a denotative definition as we defined denotative meaning: as *the collection or class of objects to which the terms may be correctly applied.* For example, if someone didn't know what "reptile" meant, you could help that person by giving a denotative definition like this one: "Snakes, lizards, turtles, and crocodiles are reptiles." Here you are explaining the meaning of the general term by pointing out the kinds of classes of things it includes.

Although definition by denotation seems straightforward enough, sometimes a term is applied to an object to which it should not be applied or to which its application is questionable. To denote "Republican" by giving the example of Senator Edward Kennedy, a Democrat, is clearly incorrect. To denote "radical" with the example of Ronald Reagan would be highly questionable. Nevertheless writers and speakers sometimes use examples from collections of objects that are not, or at least not obviously, denoted by a term.

For example, in September 1982 President Reagan vetoed a $1-billion spending bill. The bill then returned to Congress where the veto was not upheld: It didn't get the support of two-thirds of each body. When the President heard that Congress had not upheld his veto, he termed the action a victory for "big spenders." Presumably this meant that anyone who had not supported the veto was by definition a "big spender." Many of these same legislators previously had helped pass the President's record-setting budget. But the President didn't consider them "big spenders" then. It's difficult to see, therefore, on what grounds the legislators who overrode the President's veto constituted a class of "big spenders."

It's crucial for the development of our minds not to confuse the kinds or classes of things a term includes with the subjective connotations of the term. For example, ignoring the characteristics of the extensional Mr. Smith not covered by identifying him as "a black" and attributing to Smith all the characteristics suggested by the subjective connotations of "a black," we can pass final judgment on Smith by saying "Well, a black's a black. There's no changing that." We needn't document the injustices done to "Jews," "Roman Catholics," "Republicans,""Democrats,""Southerners,""teachers,""politicians,""athletes," "liberals," "conservatives," "socialist proposals," and so on by such fixed reactions. A law requiring the registration of handguns would be denoted by the term "government regulation." Maybe the law is a good one; maybe it isn't. But writing it off simply because it is a "government regulation" is to confuse the extensional law requiring registration of handguns and the subjective connotations of "government regulation." When an editorial writer disposes of a shady business deal by writing "Business is business, after all," he confuses the denotative (the first use of "business") and cononotative (its second use) meanings of "business." What appears to be a simple statement of fact, then, is actually a directive, saying "Let's treat this transaction with complete disregard for considerations other than profit, as the word 'business' connotes."[6] In other words, the sentence is directing us to classify the transaction under discussion

[6]See S. I. Hayakawa, *Language in Thought and Action* (New York· Harcourt, 1939).

in a given way so that we can feel or act in the way suggested by the terms of the classification.

Logical Definition

Understanding what a term means involves knowing how to use it correctly. But to know how to use a term doesn't require you to know everything that it can be applied to—that is, its complete denotation.

The logical definition of a term is the collection of properties shared by all and only those objects in a term's extension. Accordingly the logical definition (or *conventional* connotation) of "spoon" is "a utensil consisting of a small shallow bowl with a handle, used in eating or stirring." Notice that, like any other logical definition, this one is constructed by using two procedures: (1) placing the term being defined in a class of similar terms and (2) showing how it differs from the other terms in the class. Thus

Term	*Class*	*Distinguishing Characteristics*
A spoon	is a utensil	consisting of a small, shallow bowl with a handle, used in eating and stirring.
A watch	is a mechanical device	for telling time and is usually carried or worn.
Ethics	is a branch of philosophy	concerned with whether an action is good or bad, right or wrong.

A logical definition, which gives the conventional connotations of a term, is a precise, economical way of identifying something. Writers have many occasions to use logical definitions. For example, if they are using an obscure term such as "tsunami," they probably would briefly define it as "an unusually large sea wave produced by an undersea earthquake or volcanic eruption." Leaving unusual or obscure terms undefined impedes communication and blocks thinking.

Over the years a number of rules have been developed for formulating logical definitions. There is nothing sacred or immutable about these rules. In fact, blind reliance on them may occasionally hamper the defining process. But if they are viewed as guidelines and not imperatives, these rules can help you detect and avoid ambiguity.

Rule 1. A good logical definition states the essential characteristics of the term being defined. As we saw earlier in our discussion of conventional connotation, "essential characteristics" are those properties of an object or concept that allow us to identify it as such. For example, people have agreed to use the property of being a closed, plane figure having three sides and three angles as the conventional criteria for calling something a "triangle." So, defining "triangle" logically requires a listing of these essential characteristics. Providing the essential characteristics of concepts such as "justice," "liberty," and "equality" is considerably more difficult. Indeed, treatises have been penned by philosophers and others in an attempt to nail down the defining characteristics of these concepts.

Rule 2. *A good logical definition is not circular.*   A definition is circular if it defines a word in terms of itself. To define "inertial" as "of or pertaining to inertia" is a circular definition. A better definition is "pertaining to the property of matter by which it retains its state of rest or its velocity along a straight line so long as it is not acted on by an external force." Again, to say that a bequest is something that has been bequeathed is to offer a circular definition. A better rendering would be "a disposition by will of property."

Be watchful of reasoning that relies on circular definition. For example, suppose someone claims:

> Professor Jones can't be considered a competent teacher because he is very biased. He is biased against all forms of modern literature. Probably he doesn't like modern literature because he doesn't read it and lacks the capacity to appreciate it.

The circularity here lies in the fact that "lacks the capacity to appreciate it" really means "incompetent" in this context. Circularity does not require a repeating of the very word but can occur when equivalent words are used. When the passage is reworded, the circularity is more apparent:

> Professor Jones is not a competent teacher because he is biased. He is biased because, given that he won't read modern literature since he dislikes it, he lacks the capacity to appreciate it (that is, because he is not competent).

Rule 3. *A good logical definition is neither too broad nor too narrow.*   This rule means that a logical definition should not denote more or fewer things than are denoted by the term itself. On the one hand, to define "pungent" as "pertaining to any taste or smell" is far too broad. Some tastes or smells are mild, whereas "pungent" means "sharp or biting tastes or smells." On the other hand, to define "shoes" as "a leather covering for the human foot" is too narrow, for a shoe can be made of wood or canvas.

Rule 4. *A good logical definition does not use obscure or figurative language.*   Obscure language, as in "a lie is an intentional terminological inexactitude," does nothing to illuminate the meaning of a term; it impedes the flow of ideas and retards clear thinking. Of course, "obscurity" is itself a relative term. What is obscure to me may be quite clear to you. A legal definition may be obscure to those not trained in the law but perfectly understandable to lawyers. In the last analysis, obscurity must be judged according to the background of the audience for whom the definition is intended.

The same cautions apply to figurative language, that is, language that is expressive or highly descriptive. To define "bread" as "the staff of life" does little to explain what bread is. Defining "discretion" as "something that comes to people after they are too old for it to do them any good" is amusing but unenlightening. Indeed, such a definition assumes that you already have some idea of what "discretion" means.

Rule 5. *A good logical definition is not negative when it can be affirmative.*   A definition should explain what a term means, not what it doesn't mean. There are countless things that "spoon," "skyscraper," and "triangle" do *not* mean. Listing all these things, even if possible, would not indicate the meaning of these terms. Of course, some words defy affirmative definition. "Orphan" means a child whose parents are *not* living; "bald" means the state of *not* having hair on one's head. Barring such terms that *must* be defined negatively, definitions should be stated in the affirmative.

Quick Check on Logical Definitions

Criticize the following definitions in terms of the criteria for a good logical definition.

1 A dinosaur is a prehistoric animal.
2 Rape is forcing a woman to have sex against her will.
3 Philosophy is the study of the classical Greek works of Plato and Aristotle.
4 Hate is an emotion.
5 A circle is a closed plane curve.
6 A bad person is one who does bad things.
7 Hell is other people.
8 Democracy is a government in which everybody may vote.
9 A cat is a domesticated animal with four legs.
10 Alimony means when two people make a mistake and one of them continues to pay for it. In contrast, palimony means when two people *knew* they would make a mistake and one of them continues to pay for it.
11 A star is a stellar body visible in the heavens at night.
12 "A cynic is one who knows the price of everything and the value of nothing." (Oscar Wilde)
13 Ornament means something not necessary for practical use.
14 "Faith is the substance of things hoped for, the evidence of things not seen." (Hebrews 11:1)
15 "Faith may be defined briefly as an illogical belief in the occurrence of the improbable." (H. L. Mencken)
16 "Economics is the science which treats of the phenomena arising out of the economic activities of men in society." (J. M. Keynes)
17 "Justice is doing one's own business, and not being a busybody." (Plato)

Comments

1. Too broad
2. Too narrow
3. Too narrow
4. Too broad
5. Essential characteristics
6. Circular
7. Figurative
8. Too broad
9. Too broad
10. Figurative
11. Circular
12. Figurative
13. Negative
14. Figurative
15. Figurative
16. Circular
17. Figurative

Stipulative Definition

Earlier I alluded to the fact that writers often depart from the standard use of a word and employ it in an unconventional way. There is nothing wrong with such departures so long as the writer stipulates how the word will be used. *A stipulative definition is one that attaches an unconventional, perhaps unique, meaning to a term*. Examples include "Murder is the prevention of a human life from coming into existence," "A trial by jury is the right that guarantees justice to all citizens by allowing them to be judged by their peers," and "Patriots stand by their country, right or wrong."

Ordinarily, writers stipulate definitions when (1) they believe that a word is ambiguous and they want to give it a more precise meaning, as with "right" or "democracy"; or (2) finding that no word exists for some meaning they have in mind, they invent one, as with "glitch" for "a brief unwanted surge of electrical power." The first use is the one you will encounter most, for good writers are sensitive to the inexactness of language, especially of abstract terms and concepts such as "loyalty," "justice," "culture," "education," "war," "love," "happiness," "right," "wrong," "good," "bad," and so forth. Since such terms are so ambiguous, look for, even demand, stipulation in what you hear and read.

Persuasive Definition

When a word has acquired a complimentary meaning, people sometimes try to use it to carry a literal meaning different from its ordinary one in order to exploit the word's favorable meaning. For example, assume that the word "sophisticated" has a logical meaning equivalent to "having or showing worldly knowledge or experience." A clever writer may now try to redefine "sophisticated" in order to take advantage of its favorable meaning. Thus "*True* sophistication is doing what's in one's own self-interests" or "If the President were *really* sophisticated, he would not be taken in by Soviet saber-rattling." Of course, there is no such thing as the "true" or "real" meaning of a word, only common or uncommon and exact or inexact meanings. But audiences seldom make these distinctions. As a result writers and speakers can use the favorable meaning of a word such as "sophisticated" to convince the audience that (1) to be sophisticated is to look out for "number one" or (2) taking Soviet threats seriously proves that the President is unsophisticated.

A persuasive definition, then, is a definition that attaches a different literal meaning to a word while preserving its original emotional impact. Persuasive definitions are sleight-of-hand tricks: Writers and speakers change the literal meaning but keep the emotive one. With luck the audience will never spot the switches and will accept the author's assertion.

Words with high emotional charges, positive or negative, are the ones most subject to persuasive definition. These words are most likely to appear in discussions of controversial issues. Often dead giveaways for a persuasive definition are intensifiers such as "real" (as in "A *real* American would never avoid the draft"), "true" ("A *true* Democrat would never support policies that result in unemployment"), "genuine" ("War is never a *genuine* option in resolving international conflict"), and "good" ("*Good* citizens always vote"). But persuasive definitions need not be so verbally telegraphed. They can come larded with emotive language, as in "Democracy is the freedom to be self-governed" or "Democracy is the tyrannical oppression of the individual by the unenlightened majority."

Don't misunderstand. Sometimes writers do clarify meaning and legitimately advance a claim. So long as they don't insist on the old positive or negative overtones of a term after they have indicated a new meaning they are, in effect, using a stipulative definition. But when they change a word's meaning while preserving its old emotive force, they're trying to pull a fast one. Don't let them.

Quick Check on Stipulative and Persuasive Definitions

Which of the following definitions are persuasive and which are stipulative?

1 The only true criminal is the one who commits crimes not in the heat of passion but calculatingly, cold-bloodedly.
2 Any good American would stand up and support the President's energy program.
3 Patriots stand by their country, right or wrong.
4 A trial by jury is the right that guarantees justice to every citizen by allowing them to be judged by their peers.
5 " 'The true,' to put it very briefly, is only the expedient in the way of our thinking, just as 'the right' is only the expedient in the way of our behaving." (William James)
6 "By good, I understand that which we certainly know is useful to us." (Baruch Spinoza)
7 "Political power, properly so called, is merely the organized power of one class for oppressing another." (Karl Marx and Friedrich Engels)
8 "Political power, then, I take to be a right of making laws with penalties of death, and consequently all less penalties, for the regulating and preserving of property, and of employing the force of the community in the execution of such laws, and in defense of the commonwealth from foreign injury, and all this only for the public good." (John Locke)
9 "We hear about constitutional rights, free speech and the free press. Every time I hear these words I say to myself, 'That man is a Red, that man is a Communist.' You never heard a real American talk in that manner." (Jersey City Mayor Frank Hague, speech before the Jersey City Chamber of Commerce, January 12, 1938)
10 "The superstar celebrity—F. Lee Bailey, Andy Warhol, Rod Stewart—is the fast-food throwaway version of a hero. To be a good goalie or dance a broken-field run with nimble abandon is really a matter of youth, coordina-

tion and television coverage. A sterling character might help, but good knees are essential. The true hero is the man or woman who changes a place or a world, makes it fitter for others. . . ." (Herbert Gold, "The Hostages Are Special, But No Heroes—Let's Not Be Cruel," *Los Angeles Times*, January 20, 1981.)

Comments

1. Persuasive
2. Persuasive
3. Persuasive
4. Stipulative
5. Persuasive
6. Stipulative
7. Persuasive
8. Stipulative
9. Persuasive
10. Persuasive

Summary

Language plays a central role in both reflecting and influencing thought. Words are conventional; that is, they are a human invention that has been adopted by users of a language. Although the conventions of language are arbitrary (i.e., they could be other than what they are), how we use and order them is not. We must follow our language's conventions if we are to communicate with other users of the language.

In general you should follow common usage, and unless otherwise indicated you can correctly assume that a speaker or writer is doing so. Common usage is a guide to meaning, not truth. This means that although some disputes can be settled by word clarification or definition, most cannot; they require the investigation of facts.

Language has several functions:

1. Informative: language used to affirm or deny statements. Example: "Washington, D.C., is the nation's capital." Only statements that purport to be informative are either true or false.

2. Expressive: language used to vent or arouse feelings. Examples: "Right on!" expresses enthusiasm; "That's too bad" expresses disappointment or sorrow.

3. Directive: language used to cause or prevent overt action. Examples: "Study for the test," "Is the overhead projector available?" "Please deliver an overhead projector to my classroom."

4. Performative: language used in certain contexts to make something so. Example: assertion by a bride during a wedding ceremony "I do."

The meaning of general words (e.g., "student," "politician," "city," and so on) can be viewed as either denotative or connotative. The denotative, or extensional, meaning of a word is the group of objects indicated by that word. For example, "building" denotes the Pan American building, the Empire State building, and so forth.

The connotation of a word can be either conventional or subjective. A term's conventional connotation is that set of properties we ordinarily accept as being shared by the objects that the term designates. Thus the conventional connotation of "circle" is a closed, plane curve, all points of which are equidistant from a point within called the center.

The subjective connotation of a word refers to its emotional impact. Thus the subjective connotation of "manipulate" or "manipulative" is derogatory; the subjective connotation of "statesperson" (as opposed to "politician") is complimentary. Words like "house," "tree," and "pencil," as well as articles, conjunctions, prepositions, and some adverbs, are neutral.

To think effectively you must be able to recognize bias in communication. Bias in communication is obvious when a direct statement of opinion is expressed (e.g., "Capital punishment deters crime") or only material that supports a claim is selected for presentation. But bias can also be communicated through various language devices, chief among which are:

1. Bias words: words with a complimentary or derogatory emotional charge. These words say more about the person's attitude to a thing than about the thing itself. Example: calling a phenomenon a "fad."

2. Assumption-loaded labels: words that carry with them questionable beliefs and taken-for-granteds. Example: As used by the Nazis, the phrase "the Jewish problem" implied that a nation's socioeconomic problems could be correctly ascribed to individuals of a given religion or ethnic background.

3. Rhetorical questions: questions with a built-in answer. Example: "Can a law that is opposed to the wishes of millions of honest citizens be called fair and just?"

4. Innuendo: drawing or implying a judgment, usually derogatory, on the basis of words that suggest but don't assert the judgment. Example: The statement "Most physicians are competent and altruistic health care professionals" implies that some are incompetent and self-serving, a charge that the speaker or writer probably isn't prepared to substantiate.

5. Extreme quantifiers or intensifiers: terms like "all" or "not" (extreme quantifiers) or "absolute" or "certainly" (extreme intensifiers). These terms result in unqualified generalizations, which are statements that assert that something is true of all members of a class. Example: "All humans are mammals." Although some generalizations need not be qualified (because they're true), most must be. A qualified generalization is a statement that asserts something is true of a percentage of a class. Example: "Most of the students in this class are business majors." Generalizations are qualified by words or phrases like "many," "almost always," "sometimes," "often," "mostly," "usually," "ordinarily," and "typically."

6. Euphemism: an acceptable term for a word that is considered too blunt, harsh, painful, or offensive. Example: "fibbing" for "lying" and "termination" for "killing." Although euphemism sometimes is an appropriate adjustment of the language to a situation, often it is used to gloss over unpleasant realities that need attention or to divert us from giving an issue or event the critical inspection it warrants (e.g., the rhetoric of the Vietnam War).

The definition of a word is an explanation of its meaning. Four kinds of definition, or techniques for defining, can be distinguished:

1. Denotative: giving the collection or class of objects to which the term may be correctly applied. Example: "Snakes, lizards, turtles, and crocodiles are reptiles." Sometimes a term is applied incorrectly to an object, as in using Senator Kennedy to denote "Republican." Be careful not to confuse the kind or class of things a term includes with the term's subjective connotations. Example: Dismissing a proposal for gun control because it's a "government regulation" is to confuse the extensional law requiring the regulation of handguns and the derogatory connotations of "government regulation."

2. Logical (conventional connotation): giving the collection of properties shared by all and only those objects in a term's extension. Example: "A spoon (term) is a utensil (class) consisting of a small, shallow bowl with a handle, used in eating and drinking (distinguishing characteristics)." A good logical definition: (1) states the essential characteristics of the term being defined, (2) is not circular, (3) is neither too broad nor too narrow, (4) does not use obscure or figurative language, and (5) is not negative when it can be affirmative.

3. Stipulative: attaching unconventional, perhaps unique, meaning to a term (e.g., "Patriots stick by their country, right or wrong.") Stipulation is crucial for abstract terms: "justice," "equality," "freedom," "loyalty," "culture," and so forth.

4. Persuasive: attaching a different literal meaning to a word while preserving its old emotional impact. Example: "A real American would never avoid the draft." Words like "real," "true," "genuine," and "good" often telegraph persuasive definition.

Applications

1 Explain why the italicized word in each of the following sentences reflects the writer's insensitivity to subjective connotations. Supply a more appropriate word.
   a Fortunately the President has made *drastic* changes in our economic policies; otherwise, inflation would be out of control.
   b Teachers don't assign homework to make students' lives miserable but *merely* to help students learn.
   c Attractive as the vice-presidency of a large U.S. corporation was, Alice decided to *spurn* the offer and seek a presidency elsewhere.

d The French painter Paul Gauguin found in Tahiti a *sensual* quality that really appealed to him as a painter.

2 Give the present subjective connotations of the following terms: "New Right," "liberal," "social worker," "censorship," "CIA," "gay" (as opposed to "homosexual"), "United Nations," "big business," "judges," "open marriage," and "virginity."

3 Assume that you have been asked to write slogans for placards to be used by the groups listed below for the causes listed in the right-hand column. Write a slogan for each, then explain why you chose the words or phrases you did and precisely what emotional effects you wanted.

Group	*Cause*
Mothers Against Drunk Drivers	demanding tough penalties for drunk driving
peace marchers	nuclear disarmament
feminists	pressing for the passage of ERA (Equal Rights Amendment)
moral majority	demanding prayer in public schools
crime victims	demanding that they qualify for public assistance
Vietnam veterans	pressing for "store-front" services and other assistance

4 The same thing can be called by different names, depending on whether one is for it or against it. For example, if you're for a proposal to outlaw retail discounts on certain merchandise, you might call it the "fair trade practices act"; if you're against it, you might call it the "price fixing law." Take a specific topic, issue, or current piece of legislation and give a favorable and an unfavorable name by which it could be designated.

5 This exercise will help you see how we sometimes confuse the kinds or classes of things a term includes with the term's subjective connotations. For each of the following persons, give three descriptive adjectives (neutral, positive, and negative) that you would associate with that person. (You might think it terms of appearance, manner, ideas, and so on.) Then ask yourself to what extent your responses are derived from your experience with actual persons included in the terms, and to what extent these responses have derived from how other people respond.

a A Texan, a Russian, a Mexican, a Californian, a New Yorker

b A physician, a construction worker, a secretary, a stewardess, a prostitute

c A Jew, a Roman Catholic, a Mormon, a Jehovah's Witness

d A member of the Rotary Club, the American Legion, the John Birch Society, the National Organization for Women, the American Civil Liberties Union, the National Association of Colored People (NAACP)

6 Tell a group of friends that you are going to read them a short list of words and ask them to indicate the feelings that each evokes: C (complimentary), D (derogatory), N (neutral). Then read this sequence of words: (a) opera singer, (b) Shakespearean actor, (c) Communist, (d) lawyer, (e) star football player, and (f) a black. Now check the responses. In fact, each of these words can be applied to one particular individual, the late Paul Robeson. Does this exercise tell you anything about how words can affect one's feelings about a given person or object?

7 Pretend that you have just attended some function or witnessed some event. Write a paragraph that contains a strictly factual account of the affair and then write one that, besides being informational, also carries a distinct bias.

8 For the following passages, show how the writer (1) has taken a word with a highly emotive charge (identify the word and its charge), (2) formulated a new meaning for it (indicate the meaning), and (3) then preserved a context that encourages the word's old emotive force (in other words changed the word's literal meaning but preserved its emotional impact).

  a I don't know why some people get so mad about companies that deceive, even jeopardize, consumers. Such practices are part of the meaning of free enterprise, which everyone knows is the foundation of our political, social, and economic institutions. Free enterprise means that all of us should do what we think is best for ourselves. That's all business is doing—looking out for itself. If consumers are deceived or damaged, then that's their fault. Let them take a page from the book of free enterprise and look out for themselves. Rather than condemning business for being ambitious, aggressive, shrewd, and resourceful, we should praise it for acting in accordance with the doctrine of free enterprise, which is the American way.

  b Murder is whatever prevents a life from coming into existence. By this account, abortion is murder. All societies have proscriptions against murder, and rightly so. There is no more heinous act than to take the innocent life of another. A society that does not stand up to murderers cannot call itself truly civilized. It's obvious, then, that if the United States is worthy of the term "civilized," it must prohibit abortion and deal harshly with those who have committed or commit abortions, since these people are murderers.

The Information
Environment

So far our study has aimed to heighten awareness of (1) the blocks to critical thinking and (2) the centrality of language in thinking and in expressing thoughts. Our awareness-raising excursion now turns to the information environment—the countless bits and pieces of data that we are regularly exposed to and that help shape how we see ourselves, others, and the world.

Think for a minute of just the myriad *verbal* messages embedded in the objects you encounter daily. Labels on food containers, cosmetics, and toiletries. Billboards. Bumper stickers. Store signs. Mellow supermarket music punctuated by sales pitches. Greeting cards. Public service announcements. Junk mail. Even skywriting. The list goes on and on. It grows gargantuan when visual messages are added to the verbal. In short, the atmosphere is alive with messages, many of which mercifully escape our consciousness but nonetheless affect how and what we think.

There are far too many sources of information in our social environment for this single chapter to cover. But three sources are so important that they warrant our scrutiny. Taken together, *advertising*, *television*, and *news* form a wellspring of information that shapes our views of reality, our values, our judgments, and even our actions. This chapter cannot begin to exhaust all that can be said about these three colossuses of the information environment, but it can flush out some of the subsurface messages that they are transmitting. Aware of these messages you will become a more critical receiver of information and a more sophisticated observer of society's mores.

Advertising

Advertising performs two functions. It provides consumers with information about the goods and services available to them, and it serves to persuade them to purchase one product rather than another. These functions are not always compatible. In their attempts to persuade, advertisers often obfuscate, misrepresent, and even lie. The array of devices that advertisers use to sell us things is far too vast to be completely covered here. Five techniques are so widespread and potentially exploitative, however, that they warrant our attention. They are false implication, ambiguity, hidden facts, exaggeration, and psychological appeals. An awareness of at least these devices is crucial for thinking intelligently about the advertising messages that bombard you daily.

False Implication

Among the devices used regularly to sell products, false implication is potentially the most dangerous. False implication consists of stating something that usually is true while implying something else that is false.

For example, a local merchant runs a sensational ad announcing "Effective immediately—50 percent off many famous brands!" The truth is that you can buy only a very few standard items for 50 percent off but will pay the same for most items as you would elsewhere.

Armour Star franks once claimed that one pound of its product was equal in nourishment to one pound of steak. True enough, but the ad implied that a meal of Armour franks was as nourishing as a steak meal. Maybe so—but only if you eat ten franks at a sitting.

In promoting to physicians a powerful tranquilizer called Haldol, McNeil Laboratories described the drug as a means of controlling "disruptive behavior in nursing home patients with minimal risk of sedation and hypotension." In a three-page ad headlined I MADE A FLOWER TODAY that ran in many health journals in 1978, McNeil pictured a smiling, alert, and wrinkle-free woman holding a cloth flower. On the facing page, it boasted of Haldol's effectiveness in keeping nursing home patients under control. The implication was clear: Not only could a nursing home keep patients under control with Haldol, it could also make them creative and able to perform delicate tasks. (Incidentally, in small print in the corner, McNeil admitted that the woman pictured had made the flower as part of a vocational group therapy project and was not a patient receiving Haldol.)

Quick Check on False Implication

What's the implication in each of the following?

1 London Fog commercials that are set in London
2 A package photo for McDonald's Cherry Pie that shows more than 100 luscious-looking cherries

3 A Bayer aspirin commercial that shows an announcer holding a bottle of Bayer while stating that doctors recommend aspirin for pain relief

Comments

1. The implication is that London Fog raincoats and jackets are made in London. Actually they're made in Baltimore, Maryland.
2. The implication is that the pie contains that many cherries. But when Consumers Union analyzed cherry pies from four McDonald's restaurants in the New York area, it found that they contained on the average five cherries each.
3. The false implication is that doctors recommend Bayer aspirin.

Ambiguity

Ads that are ambiguous can be taken to mean more than one thing. Suppose, for example, a government study found that Grit filter cigarettes were lower in tar and nicotine than its filter-tip competitors. As part of its advertising, Grit claims "The Government Supports Grit Filters." "Supports" here is ambiguous. It could mean that government research supports Grit's claim that it is lower in tar and nicotine than its competitors, but it could also mean that the government endorses the use of Grit. The Continental Baking Company was charged by the Federal Trade Commission (FTC) with displaying such ambiguity in its advertisements for Profile Bread. In these advertisements Continental implied that using the bread would lead to weight loss. The fact was that Profile had about the same number of calories per ounce as other breads but that each slice contained seven fewer calories only because it was sliced thinner than most other breads. Continental issued a corrective advertisement.

The danger of the ambiguous ad is that it is open to interpretation. We consumers are left to draw our own conclusions, and it is likely to be the incorrect one from our viewpoint but the desired one from the advertiser's. For example, for years consumers inferred from Listerine's ads that its mouthwash effectively fought bacteria and sore throats. In 1978 the FTC declared the Listerine ads extremely misleading and ordered the company to run a multi-million-dollar disclaimer. Similarly the makers of Coricidin like to advertise "At the first sign of a cold or flu—Coricidin." Although it is never explicitly stated that Coricidin can cure the common cold, that implication is rather strong. When pressed, the product's manufacturers concede that the medicine can at best only provide temporary relief from symptoms. Then why not say that, rather than couching the ad in such ambiguous language that a stronger and ultimately misleading conclusion can be inferred?

Positive Emotional Charge   Certain ambiguous words become particular favorites of advertisers, apparently because they carry a positive emotional charge. "Homemade," "locally grown," "country taste," "down-home flavor," "quality," "nutritious," "fun," "pleasure," and "good times" immediately come to mind. In recent times "natural" has surfaced as a special favorite of advertisers, as in

"It's natural for fresh breath." (ad for Wrigley's Doublemint gum)

"It's only natural." (ad for Winston cigarettes)

and

"Welcome to the pure and natural world of feminine care." (ad for a feminine deodorant spray)

The word "natural" has extremely positive connotations today. But what does it mean in these ads? That the product contains only natural ingredients? That the use of the product has become rather commonplace? That using the product is as natural, say, as eating or sleeping? In what sense are gum chewing, smoking, and using feminine deodorant sprays "natural"? In what sense did Tree Sweet's grape drink contain only "natural color"? Forced to defend this claim, Tree Sweet Products Company couldn't and thus had to pay a consumer-plaintiff $250,000 in punitive damages and an estimated seventy-five-cent refund to everybody who purchased the grape drink between 1973 and 1976. In fact the drink contained artificial flavor.

Weasel Words   Some ads give the impression of saying something they don't actually say. How do they accomplish this? By use of a "weasel," which is a word used to evade or retreat from a direct or forthright statement or position. "Help" is a weasel. "Help" means "aid" or "assist" and nothing more. Yet as one author has observed, " 'help' is the one single word which, in all the annals of advertising, has done the most to say something that couldn't be said."[1] Since "help" is used to qualify, once it is used almost anything can be said after it.

Accordingly we are exposed to ads for products that "help us keep young," "help prevent cavities," and "help keep our houses germ-free." Just think of how many times a day you hear or read pitches that say "helps stop," "helps prevent," "helps fight," "helps overcome," "helps you feel," and "helps you look." But don't think "help" is the only weasel in the advertiser's arsenal.

"Like" (as in "makes your floor look like new"), "virtual" or "virtually" (as in "virtually no cavities"), "up to" (as in "provides relief up to eight hours"), "as much as" (as in "saves as much as one gallon of gas"), and other weasels say what cannot be said. Studies indicate that on hearing or reading a weasel-containing claim, we tend to screen out the weasel and take the assertion as an unqualified statement. Thus, on hearing that a medicine *can* provide *up to* eight hours' relief," we screen out the "can" and "up to" and infer that the product will give us eight hours' relief. In fact, according to the wording of the ad, the product may give no relief at all; and if it does give relief, the relief could vary in length from a minute to just under eight hours.

---

[1]Paul Stevens, "Weasel Words: God's Little Helpers," in Paul A. Eschhol, Alfred A. Rosa, and Virginia P. Clark (eds.), *Language Awareness* (New York: St. Martin's, 1974), p. 156.

Quick Check on Ambiguity

Comment on the ambiguity in the following ads.

1 "Fleischmann's—made from 100 percent corn oil."
2 "Free gifts for every new deposit."
3 "With Real Blueberry Buds and Other Natural Flavors." (front of the package of Aunt Jemima frozen Jumbo Blueberry Waffles)
4 "Most Colgate kids got fewer cavities."
5 "In today's Army, you can earn good money, while learning a skill to make even more money. . . . If you qualify [for a number of jobs], you can enlist for one of hundreds of exciting Army skills. Or you can choose the initial area or unit you'd like to serve in, near home in the continental United States or someplace new. Your choice will be guaranteed in writing before you enlist."

Comments

1. On the other side of the package on which this claim appears, we read in fine print "Liquid Corn Oil, partially hydrogenated corn oil, water, nonfat dry milk, vegetable mono and diglicerides and lecithin, artificially flavored and colored (carotene), Vitamins A & D added." What then does the front-of-the-package claim mean? That Fleischmann's is made from 100 percent corn oil and nothing else? That the oil that is the main ingredient is 100 percent corn oil, instead of, say, partly soybean oil, as in some other brands?
2. The false implication here is that the gifts are granted to a depositor without qualification. But typically if the deposit is withdrawn before a minimum period, the gift, or an equivalent amount of money, is taken back. In what sense, then, is this a "free gift"?
3. On the other side of the package, we read in fine print "Blueberry Buds [sugar, vegetable stearine (a relase agent), blueberry solids with other natural flavors], salt, sodium carboxymethy cellulose (a thickening agent), silicon dioxide (a flow agent), citric acid, modified soy protein, artificial flavor, artificial coloring, maltol." If we take "Blueberry Buds" to mean what's included in the brackets, then it's true that the box contains *real* blueberry buds and "other natural flavors" in the blueberry buds. As for the artifical flavors, the package never said it contained none of these. This explanation notwithstanding, the claim is ambiguous and contains false implication and positively charged language ("real" is like "natural"). Many consumers will believe that the product contains whole blueberries or only natural ingredients as opposed to artificial flavors or additives.
4. The claim contains an ambiguous comparison. "Fewer" than who? The ad also contains the false implication that Colgate kids developed fewer cavities than those using other fluoride toothpastes, such as Crest. In fact the true claim is that Colgate users got fewer cavities on average than they did before using Colgate, when perhaps some of them hadn't been using a fluoride toothpaste or hadn't even been brushing their teeth.
5. False implication. The true guarantee is that you *may* qualify and that there *may* be an opening. In fact there's no guarantee for those who flunk out in training camp, and the Army's personnel needs might warrant your being sent elsewhere than your place of choice.

Hidden Facts

Advertisers regularly conceal unfavorable information about their products. As a result consumers rarely have the complete information they need to make an informed choice about product price and quality. The facts hidden from them are hard to detect because background information is required to do so—an observation that also applies to false implications. This is why it's imperative that you keep informed by reading as much consumer literature as you can.

As an example of a hidden fact, recall the old Colgate—Palmolive ad for its Rapid Shave Cream. It showed Rapid Shave being used to shave "sandpaper." We were told "Apply, soak, and off in a stroke." Certainly this was an impressive ad for any man who's ever scraped his way awake. But Colgate failed to mention that the sandpaper was actually Plexiglas and that actual sandpaper had to be soaked in Rapid Shave for about eighty minutes before it came off in a stroke.[2]

More recently Campbell's vegetable soup ads showed pictures of a thick, rich brew calculated to whet even a gourmet's appetite. What Campbell's didn't mention was that clear glass marbles had been deposited in the bowl to give the appearance of solidity.

Then there's the whole area of feminine deodorant sprays (FDS), one rife with hidden facts. Currently an industry in excess of $55 million, FDS ads not only fail to mention that such products usually are unnecessary but that they often produce negative side effects: itching, burning, blistering, and urinary infections. Now the Food and Drug Administration (FDA) requires a caution to accompany these products.

Certainly among the most dramatic cases of hidden facts is the one involving Pertussin Medicated Vaporizer, which the FDA ordered removed from market shelves on July 2, 1973, because the product was suspected to have caused the deaths of eighteen people. In the ten years the Pertussin Medicated Vaporizer had been available, shoppers who read the can's label had found nothing to make them wary of the product's contents. On the contrary, the product's manfacturers claimed it could "build a roomful of relief" from colds and hay fever. The spray's directions encouraged the spraying of the product on handkerchiefs, in rooms, and even on pillows and sheets. "Repeat as often as necessary" and "safe even in the nursery" seemed to reassure even the most skeptical of consumers. As for its ingredients, Pertussin listed the harmless menthol and oil of eucalyptus, stock ingredients in these products.

How could eighteen people possibly die after using such an innocuous substance? They apparently ingested the propellants and solvents the product contained. Evidently Pertussin's manufacturers failed to indicate the menthol and oil of eucalyptus made up only 12 percent of the total ingredients of their product. The remaining 88 percent consisted of propellants and solvents. Moreover these chemicals break down about equally between fluorocarbons

---

[2]Samm Sinclair Baker, *The Permissible Lie* (New York: World, 1968), p. 16.

and trichloroethane, which tend to upset the heartbeat and depress other vital activities such as breathing. Again no mention was made of these facts.

The conclusion we can draw from this brief discussion of hidden facts in ads is that each of us must not only be scrupulous about examining the information imparted in ads but also must read widely, especially in consumer literature. We must educate ourselves to *all* the facts, not just those a manufacturer gives us in order to sell a product.

Exaggeration

Advertisers can mislead by making claims that probably cannot be supported by the weight of evidence. In a word, they exaggerate. Here are just a few of literally hundreds of exaggerations you come across daily in reading and watching television:

"Spectacular Two-day Fur Sale!"

"Waterford: The Ultimate Gift!"

"She was the 1st and the goddess and the moon. The Mystery & the Danger . . . a closeup tribute to a beautiful woman and immortal legend." (ad for *The Last Sitting*, a photo essay of Marilyn Monroe)

"Whirlpool at Sizzling Low Prices!"

"The Amazing 'Face-Lift-in-a-Jar.' Used by Hollywood Stars who didn't want plastic surgery."

"Stand without help or pain." (ad for the Cushion-Lift chair)

"You won't believe your eyes!" (ad for *Medical Curiosities*)

"Incredible! $3.25 worth of E-A-D cream FREE!"

"Wipe away stretch marks instantly!" (ad for Fade-Out)

"Shampoo, Wave & Curls! No Permanent! No Nitely Curlers! No Teasing! No Blow Driers! Chic Salon look for permies!" (ad for Wave & Curl)

"A most incredible achievement in cosmetic science! Remove skin and discolorations forever!" (ad for Dermacure)

"Amazing new 'computerized' forehead thermometer makes oral, rectal thermometers obsolete!" (ad to Tel-A-Fever)

Sometimes the exaggeration is not this transparent. For example, various pain relievers have been claimed to provide "extra pain relief" or to "upset the stomach less frequently"; they are said to be "50 percent stronger than aspirin" or "superior to any other nonprescription pain killer on the market." While impressive, such claims fly in the face of evidence that indicates that all analgesics are about equally effective.

It is true that the FTC and the Food and Drug Administration (FDA) sometimes make advertisers defend their boasts. If they can't they are censured, as in the Profile and Listerine cases. In the tire industry, the FTC has questioned Goodyear's claim that its Double-Eagle Polysteel Tires can be driven over ax blades without suffering damage. It has also asked Sears, Roebuck and Company to prove its claim that its steel-belted radial tires can give 60,000 to 101,000 miles of service. In the auto industry, the FTC has questioned Volkswagen's claim that its squareback sedan gets about twenty-five miles per gallon and that it saves drivers two hundred gallons of gas more a year compared with the average domestic compact. In addition, the FTC has asked General Motors to verify its boast that its Vega's ground beams provide more side-impact collision protection than those of any other comparable compact. And it has questioned Chrysler's claim that its electronic system never needs tuning.

But before you conclude that government regulators are protecting you from the onslaught of exaggeration in advertising, remember that the vast majority of claims are never questioned. More important, the law permits what in the trade is termed "puffery."

Puffery Puffery is advertising or other sales representations that praise an item with subjective opinions, superlatives, or exaggerations. In his book *The Great American Blowup*, Ivan L. Preston gives a long list of examples, among which are

"When you say Budweiser, you've said it all."

"When you're out of Schlitz, you're out of beer."

"You can be sure if it's Westinghouse."

"We try harder." (Avis)

"Ford gives you better ideas."

"Toshiba—in touch with tomorrow."

"With a name like Smucker's, it has to be good."

"Come to where the flavor is." (Marlboro)

"Prudential is the strength of Gibraltar."

Lawmakers permit puffery because they have decided, on the basis of actual cases, that most puffery is not deceptive. Certainly, in some cases puffery is not deceptive. When an oil company says that you'll have a tiger in your tank when you use its gasoline, no one expects a tiger. But are most puffs so outlandish that no one takes them seriously?

If puffery were not deceptive, it wouldn't sell products. But advertising experts agree that puffs sell. What's more, a survey conducted in 1971 by R. H. Bruskin Associates supports the view that puffery deceives. In that survey a sample of citizens was asked whether they felt that various advertising claims were "completely true," "partly true," or "not true at all." Although puffery was not identified by name, a number of claims fell into that category and were rated as follows:

"State Farm is all you need to know about life insurance." (22 percent said completely true, 36 percent said partly true)

"The world's most experienced airline." (Pan Am) (23 percent said completely true, 47 percent partly true)

"Ford has a better idea." (26 percent completely true, 42 percent partly true)

"You can trust your car to the man who wears the star." (Texaco) (21 percent said completely true, 47 percent partly true)

"It's the real thing." (Coca-Cola) (35 percent said completely true, 29 percent partly true)

"Perfect rice every time." (Minute Rice) (43 percent said completely true, 30 percent partly true)

"Today, aluminum is something else." (Alcoa) (47 percent said completely true, 36 percent partly true)[3]

The conclusion seems unmistakable: Puffery does work. It must deceive, even though our lawmakers think otherwise. Since the law doesn't restrict the use of puffery, we must guard against being victimized by it.

Quick Check on Exaggeration

Comment on the use of exaggeration and puffery in the following ads and names.

1 "Pleasure is where you find it." (Viceroy cigarettes)
2 Top-Flite Golf Balls
3 Super Shell
4 *True* cigarettes
5 Wonder Bread
6 "Take the road to flavor in a low-tar cigarette." (Raleigh Lights)
7 "Ahhhhhh! Anusol."
8 "The pleasure is back. Barclay."
9 "Bud—the King of beers!"
10 "Dial—the most effective deodorant soap you can buy."

Comments

1. This ad says lots of things:"Why should you care if you smoke one of the oldest brands on the market? If you enjoy it, smoke it!" And "Maybe smoking is bad for you. But if you enjoy smoking, then smoke! Make up your own mind—and make it Viceroy."
2. The name is intended to suggest that a golfer will get the best performance (longest drives) out of this product.
3. "Super" is a superlative, tantamount to "great" or "fantastic." Thus, Super Shell is far better than other Shell gasolines and of course superior to other gasolines generally.
4. "True" implies that the product is the only real or genuine cigarette—perhaps the only cigarette that gives you a "true" smoking sensation, whatever that means.
5. "Wonder"implies something special,perhaps unique,and presumably extraordinary benefits await those who eat Wonder Bread.
6. While there are many low-tar cigarettes, supposedly only Raleigh gives you pleasure ("*the* road").

[3]From Ivan L. Preston, *The Great American Blowup* (Madison: University of Wisconsin Press, 1975). Reported in Howard Kahane, *Logic and Contemporary Rhetoric* (Belmont, Calif.: Wadsworth, 1980), p. 186.

7. "Ahhhhhh!" signals not only complete relief for hemorrhoid sufferers but immediate relief as well.
8. Presumably low-tar cigarettes don't give smokers pleasure. Barclay is special – a low-tar cigarette with pleasure.
9. "King"—a claim of preeminence. (It makes me wonder which is the "Queen" of beers, but of course that is a naive speculation. Beer, after all, is intended for men.)
10. A really insidious claim of superiority. When asked to substantiate the claim, Armour-Dial Company insisted that is was not a claim of superiority at all, but only a claim that Dial soap was "as effective" as any other soap. From which I'd conclude that Humpty Dumpty is alive and well.

Psychological Appeals

A psychological appeal is one that aims to persuade by appealing to human emotions and emotional needs, not to reason. An automobile ad that presents the product in an elitist environment peopled by members of the "in" set appeals to our need and desire for status. A life insurance ad that portrays a destitute family woefully struggling in the aftermath of a provider's death aims to persuade through pity and fear.

Ads that rely primarily on pitches to power, prestige, sex, masculinity, femininity, acceptance, approval, and so on aim to sell more than a product. They're calculated to dispense psychological satisfaction. Perhaps the best example of such appeals is the increasingly explicit and pervasive use of sexual pitches in ads.

Sexual Pitches   Consider the sexual innuendo pulsating in this ad for men's cologne:

> *Scene:* An artist's skylit studio. A young man lies nude, the bedsheets in disarray. He awakens to find a tender note on his pillow. The phone rings and he gets up to answer it.
>
> *WOMAN'S VOICE:* "You snore."
> *ARTIST [smiling]:* "And you always steal the covers."

More cozy patter between the two. Then a husky-voiced announcer intones "Paco Rabanne. A cologne for men. What is remembered is up to you."[4]

While sex has always been used to sell products, it has never before been used as explicitly in advertising as it is today. And the sexual pitches are by no means confined to products like cologne. The California Avocado Commission supplements its "Love Food from California" recipe ads with a campaign featuring leggy actress Angie Dickinson, who is sprawled across two pages of some eighteen national magazines to promote the avocado's nutritional value. The copy line reads "Would this body lie to you?" Not to be outdone, Dannon Yogurt recently ran an ad featuring a bikini-clad beauty and the message "More nonsense is written on dieting than any other subject—except possibly sex."

Some students of marketing claim that ads like these appeal to the sub-

[4]Gail Bronson, "Sexual Pitches in Ads Become More Explicit and Pervasive," *The Wall Street Journal*, November 18, 1980, p. 1.

conscious of both marketer and consumer. Purdue psychologist and marketing consultant Jacob Jacoby contends that marketers, like everyone else, carry around sexual symbols in their subconscious that, intentionally or not, they use in ads. A case in point: the widely circulated Newport cigarette "Alive with Pleasure" campaign. One campaign ad featured a woman riding the handlebars of a bicycle driven by a man. The main strut of the bike wheel stands vertically beneath her body. In Jacoby's view such symbolism needs no interpretation. In short, Newport is hawking more than a cigarette: It's selling sexual gratification.

Author Wilson Bryan Key, who has extensively researched the topic of subconscious marketing appeals, claims that many ads take a subliminal form. Subliminal advertising is advertising that communicates at a level beneath our conscious awareness, where some psychologists claim that the vast reservoir of human motivation primarily resides. Most marketing people would deny that such advertising occurs. Key demurs. In fact he claims "It is virtually impossible to pick up a newspaper or magazine, turn on a radio or television set, read a promotional pamphlet or the telephone book, shop through a supermarket without having your subconscious purposely massaged by some monstrously clever artist, photographer, writer or technician."[5]

In beginning to think critically about the messages imparted in advertising, then, keep in mind the advertiser's use of false implication, ambiguity, hidden facts, exaggeration, and psychological appeals. Truth is rarely foremost in the minds of advertisers. For the advertising agency, the first consideration in concocting a campaign is what can be said, true or not, that will sell the product best. The next consideration is how it can be said effectively and got away with so that (1) people who buy won't feel let down by too big a promise that doesn't come true and (2) the ads will avoid quick and certain censure by the FTC.

Television

A woman writes that her niece's three-year-old saw a dog lying in the street after it had been hit by a car. When the niece used the incident to warn her child about the dangers of running out into the street, the child replied "Oh, no! Momma, Wonder Woman would fly down and stop the car."[6]

This brief letter to the writer of an advice column speaks volumes about the potential impact of television on how we think and see the world. It is true that the episode recounted involves the unformed mind of a preschooler. As we mature we realize that there is no Wonder Woman to rescue us from life's perils; we learn to separate that television fantasy from real life. But television is part of the education process that makes adults out of children. How and what we think, what we value, what role models we follow, what we aspire to, how we

[5]Wilson Bryan Key, *Subliminal Seduction* (New York: New American Library, 1972), p. 11. Key is also the author of *Sexploitation* and *The Clam-Plate Orgy*, books that further explore subliminal messages.
[6]Dorothy Singer and Jerome Singer, "Today's Lesson Will Be Mork and the Fonz," *TV Guide*, June 12, 1982, p. 35.

view ourselves, other people, and the world—all are influenced by the messages that television programs transmit to viewers.

Impact on Thought and Behavior

There is some empirical basis for suggesting a connection between television and human thought and behavior. For example, research conducted by James Bryan at Northwestern University has demonstrated that children who watched a five-minute videotape in which the characters donate their prize-winning certificates to charity were influenced by the segment to later do the same. Other researchers have replicated Bryan's work. They have found that children who watch videotapes of people sharing money and candy are also influenced to share. Similarly, in one of a series of studies using "Mr. Rogers' Neighborhood"—a children's television program stressing cooperation, sharing, and friendship—a group of researchers under directors Aletha Huston and Lynette Friedrich-Cofer found that the show, in conjunction with role-playing techniques, succeeded in producing more instances of empathy and helpfulness among children who watched the show than among those who watched shows unrelated to positive social behavior. Programs such as "Lassie," "I Love Lucy, "The Brady Bunch," and "Father Knows Best" have been studied in Australia. Segments were designated as either "high" or "neutral" in positive social values. Children who watched "high" segments—which stressed concern for others, sympathy, and task persistence—were found to be more helpful and cooperative after four weeks of such viewing than children who watched the "neutral" segments of these programs.

The results of studies like these are consistent with the report issued by the National Institute for Mental Health in May 1982. The Institute reported that there exists a consensus among most of the research community that violence on television does lead to aggressive behavior by children and teenagers who watch the programs.

Fewer studies have been conducted to discover what, if any, effect television has on the adult viewer. One conducted by Dr. Rod Gurney at UCLA studied 183 married couples to see what would happen if husbands were assigned certain shows to watch. After only seven consecutive evenings, the wives (who were the observer–reporters) found that the husbands viewing highly "helpful" programs showed less "hurtful" behavior toward family members. Of course the wives didn't know what programs the husbands were watching.

Reality Warp

George Gerbner, Dean of the University of Pennsylvania's Annenberg School of Communications, is perhaps the nation's leading authority on the social impact of television. Over the past fifteen years, he and his assistants videotaped and thoroughly analyzed 1600 prime-time programs involving more than 15,000 characters. They then drew up multiple-choice questionnaires that offered correct answers about the world at large along with answers that reflected what Gerbner saw as misrepresentations and biases of the world according to television. These questions were posed to a wide sampling of citizens of all ages, educational backgrounds, and socioeconomic strata. In every survey the Annenberg team found that heavy viewers of television (those watching more than fours hours a day), who make up about one third of the population, typically chose the television-influenced answers, whereas light viewers (those watching fewer than two hours a day) selected the answers corresponding more closely to actual life. Here's a summary of some of the dimensions of reality warp.[7]

Sex: 1. Male prime-time characters outnumber females by three to one.
2. Women are usually depicted as weak, passive satellites to powerful, effective men.
3. TV males generally play a variety of roles, whereas females are portrayed as lovers or mothers.
4. Less than 20 percent of TV's married women with children work outside the home. In real life more than 50 percent do.

Conclusions: Television's distortions reinforce stereotypical attitudes and increase sexism. An Annenberg survey showed that heavy viewers are far more likely than light ones to feel that women should stay at home and leave the running of the country to men.

Age: 1. People over sixty-five are generally underrepresented on TV.
2. Old people are typically portrayed as silly, stubborn, sexually inactive, and eccentric.

Conclusions: Again stereotypes are reinforced. Heavy viewers believe that the elderly make up a smaller portion of the population today than two decades ago. In fact old people are the fastest-growing age group. Heavy viewers also believe that old people are less healthy today than twenty years ago. The opposite is true: Old people as a group are healthier than they were before.

Race: 1. The overwhelming number of television blacks are portrayed as employed in subservient, supporting roles.
2. Blacks rarely are portrayed as doing interesting and important things.
3. Blacks are typically presented as accepting minority status as inevitable and even deserved.

Conclusions: TV's distortion of blacks reinforces stereotypes and encourages racism. This conclusion is supported by Annenberg surveys that included questions like "Should white people have the right to keep blacks out of their neighborhoods?" and "Should there be laws against marriages between blacks and whites?" Heavy viewers answered "Yes" to these questions far more frequently than light viewers.

Work: 1. Only 6 to 10 percent of television characters hold blue-collar or service jobs, whereas 60 percent of the real work force are employed in such jobs.

[7] Harry F. Waters, "Life According to TV," *Newsweek*, December 6, 1982, pp. 136–142B.

    2. TV overrepresents and glamorizes the elite occupations (e.g., law, medi-
      cine, entertainment, and athletics).
    3. TV neglects to portray the occupations that most young people will end
      up in (e.g., small businesses and factory work).

Conclusions: Heavy viewers generally overstate the proportion of American workers who are physicians, lawyers, entertainers, or athletes. By glamoriz-
ing elite occupations, TV sets up unrealistic expectations. Doctors and lawyers
often find they can't measure up to the idealized image TV projects of them, and
young people's occupational aspirations are channeled in unrealistic directions. The problem is especially frustrating for adolescent girls, who are given
two conflicting views: the woman as homebody versus the woman as glamorous
professional.

Health: 1. TV characters exist almost entirely on junk food and quaff alcohol
         fifteen times more often than water.
      2. Despite such a punishing diet, video characters remain slim, healthy,
         and beautiful.
      3. Health professionals typically are portrayed as infallible.
      4. TV may be the single most pervasive source of health information.

Conclusions: The Annenberg investigators found that heavy TV watchers
eat more, drink more, and exercise less than light viewers and have unflinching
faith in the curative powers of medical science. TV's idealized image of medical
people coupled with its complacency about unhealthy life-styles leaves both
patients and doctors vulnerable to disappointment, frustration, and even litiga-
tion.

Crime: 1. On TV crime rages about ten times more than in real life.
      2. Fifty-five percent of TV's prime-time characters are involved in violent
         incidents at least once a week versus less than 1 percent in real life.
      3. Video violence imparts lessons in social power: It shows who can do
         what to whom and get away with it. Usually those at the bottom of the
         power ladder are portrayed as not getting away with what a white,
         middle-class American male can.

Conclusions: Television breeds fear of victimization. In all demographic
groups in every class of neighborhood, heavy viewers overestimated the statistical chances of violence in their own lives. They also harbored an exaggerated
distrust of strangers—what Gerbner calls the "mean world syndrome." Forty-six
percent of heavy viewers living in cities rated their fear of crime "very serious" as
opposed to 26 percent of light viewers. The fear is especially acute among TV's
most common victims: women, the elderly, nonwhites, foreigners, and poor
citizens. In short, TV gets people to think of themselves as victims.

Among other things, this study belies the television programmer's glib
claim that TV is simply a reflection of the way things are. In many important
respects, it is not. Why, then, does Hollywood offer what it does?

Explanations   One possible explanation for what Hollywood offers us is that we are being treated to what Hollywood *thinks* is real, which inevitably will be distorted as long as those ensconced in Hollywood persist in thinking that nothing lies between Beverly Hills and New York. Another possible explanation is that bathos is necessary to lure viewers jaded with limp writing. Still another is that what we are seeing on TV more accurately reflects contemporary life in Hollywood than in the nation as a whole. Probably those who work in the entertainment industry are occupationally more vulnerable than most of us. Major network executives can be fired on the spot; the women's rights movement seems more visible in the entertainment industry than in overall society; and Hollywood writers and producers seem to cultivate a morbid concern with what they view as "social issues," focusing on what may, in fact, be atypical cases that are, through the magic of television, transposed into the seemingly commonplace. As one television writer puts it:

> The closest thing you can get in real life to an anxious crippled person on the tube are the people you see at the network commissaries. The anxiety level in a meeting of the Writers Guild is about a million times greater than anything on television. [Benjamin Stein, "TV on the Couch: Why Prime-Time Characters Are So Troubled," *TV Guide*, May 15, 1982, p. 36.]

Another writer says that for the real-life prototypes of the angry women on TV shows, we should look to the wives, mothers, and daughters of the men who make most TV shows. "They're in their Mercedes convertibles but they're not happy."[8]

The most obvious explanation for TV's distortions, however, is that programmers are obsessed with demographics. Prime-time sponsors want to reach the audience that buys most of the consumer products advertised on the tube. This audience happens to be white, middle-class females between eighteen and forty-nine. Observers like Gerbner believe that TV's fictional characters are tailored to what programmers perceive to be this audience's expectations. In short, TV creates a world for its best consumers.

Whatever the explanations for what we see on television, something serious is afoot. If TV can sell dog food, toilet paper, and political candidates, then it's safe to assume that it can sell views of life, role models, and values. It can affect how we think about things. If the standard of beauty becomes Valerie Bertinelli; if J. R. Ewing is the paradigm of the "real man"; if every teenage girl would like her boyfriend to look like Eric Estrada and every teenage boy would like his girlfriend to look like Heather Locklear; if every tyke would like to talk like Gary Coleman; then TV must be influencing its viewers. Of course, the relationship between TV and reality is far from clear-cut and is difficult, perhaps impossible, to prove. It's just as difficult to establish precisely what influence TV has on us. But, in the words of television critic Benjamin Stein, it's far too late to deny that a relationship does exist.

> If TV says that the world is a deceitful, dangerous place, where nothing is as it seems and where treachery is the rule, that has to encourage a paranoid, apprehensive

[8] Stein, "TV on the Couch," p. 36.

view of the world, especially among younger viewers. When the psychological top blows off the TV Mount St. Helens, that has consequences for the real world. The most obvious is that we people who live in the real world should be aware that the alternative world of television is sending us a message that may not be healthy. We have to realize that just as TV might have been giving us a fairy tale 20 years ago, it is giving us a nightmare vision, or something close to it, today. Neither is particularly helpful as a model for daily life. Beyond that awareness, we simply may have to wait for the pendulum to swing back. In the meantime, write it down and remember it: TV is not real life.[9]

Even though TV is not real life, it has a sizable impact on how we perceive reality. Precisely how does TV accomplish this? To find out requires a close look at the content and form of television programs, which in turn will reveal that TV is teeming with ideologies.

Quick Check on Television's Reality Warp

What characters, programs, or depictions could you point to on TV to support Gerbner's observations?

Comments

Sex: "Dynasty"'s Krystal Carrington has no identity apart from husband Blake; the same holds for Sue Ellen Ewing ("Dallas"). Notice also that on "Dallas" most of the females don't do much of anything except cheer on their husbands and lovers.

Work: "Trapper John," "General Hospital," "St. Elsewhere," and so forth all focus on medical personnel.

Health: Alcohol is a mainstay on "Dallas."

Transmitter of Ideology

"Ideology" refers to the doctrines, opinions, or way of thinking of an individual or group. It is often conveyed through images of country and race, class, sexuality, individuality, and solidarity. Thus images of success through hard work may become an effective symbolic device to advance belief in rising mobility; images of happiness through domestic life may propagate belief in the value of the family.

Ideology is also spread by means of myths, which are stories that teach, explain, and justify the practices and institutions of a given society to people in that society. The "rags-to-riches" myth, for example, teaches that even the poorest of us can become wealthy and powerful. Myths profoundly shape consciousness, often influencing our thoughts and actions in subtle and unperceived ways. They deal with what is most important to us: love, death, violence, sex, work, and social conflict.

[9]Ibid., p. 36.

We're accustomed to thinking that ideology is transmitted by an elaborate apparatus or set of rituals, for example military pomp and parades, religious rites, political speeches, heady lectures given in university classes, and so on. It is true that ideology is passed on to the masses this way after being formulated, usually in print. But the centrality of the electronic media in our society has endowed them with the function of ritualistically transmitting ideology.

How does television transmit ideology? Philosophy professor Douglas Kellner, a student of television and film, thinks that TV transmits ideology in a number of ways, including three that I will consider here: images and symbols, paleosymbols, and moral instruction.[10]

Images and Symbols   A symbol is something that stands for or represents another thing. A flag can stand for country; a cross for Christianity; a heart for love; a wedding ring for union and commitment. Natural objects provide a rich source of symbolic images. The sea, for example, has a range of symbolic meanings, including change, energy, cleansing, rebirth, passion, even the female.

Although television uses traditional symbolism, it seems to create its own symbols as well, symbols that reflect and reinforce the dominant ideologies of society. Jim Anderson of "Father Knows Best," Ironside, and Ben Cartwright of "Bonanza" become father symbols. Mary Tyler Moore and Joyce Davenport ("Hill Street Blues") become symbols of the independent working woman. J. R. Ewing ("Dallas") is a symbol of evil, whereas his brother Bobby represents J. R.'s antithesis—good in neverending conflict with evil. For their part, situation comedies become symbols of domesticity and the soaps continue to generate symbols of stoic endurance through suffering. Game shows exhibit symbols of greed and money worship, and commercials try to create symbols that will get us to consume.

But not all symbols with powerful effects are easily identified and conventionally defined. Some consist of whole scenes, often repeated, in which positive or negative situations occur. Kellner calls these paleosymbols.

Paleosymbols   "Paleosymbol" means a sort of symbolism that "precedes" or "lies underneath." Freud found that certain scenic images, such as a child being beaten for masturbation, significantly affect later behavior. The images of the scenes remain as paleosymbols that influence, even control, behavior—they might for example prohibit masturbation or inhibit sexual function. According to Freud, scenic understanding is necessary to master scenic images. The mastery in turn helps one understand what the scenic images signify and how they shape behavior.[11]

Kellner thinks that paleosymbolic scenes on TV may function analogously. TV programs often crackle with such emotion that the empathic viewer becomes deeply involved in the actions presented. Kellner makes his point by

[10]Douglas Kellner, "TV, Technology and Ideology," in Larry Hickman and Azizah Al-Hibri (eds.), *Technology and Human Affairs* (St. Louis: C. V. Mosby, 1981), pp. 37–46.
[11]Kellner, "TV, Technology and Ideology," p. 39.

recounting an episode from TV's adaptation of Arthur Hailey's novel *The Mon-eychangers* :

> An up-and-coming junior executive is appealingly portrayed by Timothy Bottoms. It is easy to identify with this charming and seemingly honest and courageous figure; he is shown, for example, vigorously defending a Puerto Rican woman accused of embezzling money. It turns out, however, that the young man stole the money himself to support a life-style, including gambling, that far outstripped his income. He is apprehended by a tough black security officer, tries to get away, and is caught and beaten by the black. There are repeated episodes in which we may identify with the young man trying to escape, and then feel pain and defeat when he is caught and beaten. Some of the escape scenes take place at night in alleys, recreating primal scenes of terror and pursuit. Furthermore, to white viewers the fact that the pursuer is black may add to the power of the imagery, building on socially inculcated fear of blacks and reinforcing racism. Hence, the paleosymbolic scene is multidimensional and multifunctional. The paleosymbolism in this example carries the message that crime does not pay and that one should not transcend the bounds of one's income or position.[12]

Paleosymbolic scenes like this one are especially effective because, long after we've forgotten the story—or even that we watched the program—the image may remain. More important, the powerful image, together with others like it, may have the effect of influencing behavior—in this case dissuading us from crime, especially of the white-collar variety. If this is so, then we must wonder what other effects paleosymbols might have. Here are some possibilities, some of which tie in with Gerbner's findings.

1. **Paleosymbols may perpetuate racism** Paleosymbols may play a part in fostering racism, for images of minorities can be in part shaped by media images. For example, blacks are frequently portrayed in crime dramas as dope dealers, prostitutes, pimps, militants, and vicious killers. These negative images often are presented in dramatic scenes that can convey paleosymbolic images of blacks as evil and dangerous. "The viewer is more likely to have a strong paleosymbolic image of the black junkie shooting up dope and killing a white person to feed his habit than of the good black cop who finally apprehends him, since the paleosymbolic scenes involving the evil black were more charged with emotion and dramatic intensity."[13]

The other side of the coin is that blacks commonly are presented as strictly comic characters, often in the role of domestic. Take, for example, Nell of "Gimme a Break" and Florence of "The Jeffersons." This need-to-be-funny-if-you're-black requisite also applies to many black TV males, for example Benson and George Jefferson. Repeated enough, a stereotypically acceptable, "nice" black surfaces, which really isn't so far removed from the way blacks were portrayed in the first decades of film—as comical, foot-shuffling, eye-rolling dolts in the role of servant or clown.

[12] Kellner, "TV, Technology and Ideology," pp. 39–40.
[13] Kellner, "TV, Technology and Ideology," p. 40.

2. Paleosymbols may foster sexism   Just as it stereotypes blacks, TV also stereotypes women. Thus we're fed images of zany madcaps (such as Lucy, Edith Bunker, Laverne and Shirley, and Private Benjamin); empty-headed sex kittens, as on "Three's Company" and "Too Close for Comfort"; and greedy egotists (e.g. Alexis on "Dynasty" or Sue Ellen on "Dallas"). Most of today's TV heroines seek goods, not goodness. They use guile, not virtue, to get what they want—indeed it is not generosity and selflessness that are viewed as virtue, but cunning. And the scenes in which these women carry out their evil plots often are riveting. Thus, in one episode of "Dynasty," we're treated to a scene in which Alexis fires a hunting rifle, causing the horse on which her rival, Krystal, is riding to buck and throw the pregnant woman to the ground. The resulting miscarriage is precisely what the diabolical Alexis had intended. In another episode Alexis chooses the occasion of a hospital visit to her daughter Fallon, who has just given birth to a child she didn't want and is profoundly depressed, to tell her that Blake Carrington is not her real father. In "Dallas" more than a little of J. R. Ewing has rubbed off on his wife Sue Ellen, whose appetite for money and position would rival Lady Macbeth's and almost weekly is dramatized in high relief. And let's not forget the seemingly endless supply of beautiful playthings who, for the right price, will help J. R. blackmail some male dupe like the young son of the Ewings' lawyer.

Not all the principal females on TV are so ruthless and destructive. But those of more temperate appetites show a penchant for cunning and manipulation, albeit in the quest for love and romance. Think of all the "Love Boat" episodes that show women—and men—trying to worm their way into another's heart through deceit and manipulation. Think of the wild and crazy antics of the heroines of "Three's Company" and "Too Close for Comfort." And recall that Jennifer of "WKRP" spent her off-the-job hours relieving rich old men of their loot before they croak. You needn't be a cryptographer to decode the messages implicit in all this: The successful woman is a shrewd operator who vamps her way to fame and fortune, if not happiness. Love isn't required; it may even be an impediment. The key thing is that the man can provide her with what she needs to impress her other admirers. In short, the most popular TV heroine today no longer is interested in giving love but in being indulged by some rich male who's smitten with her.

Although these images sometimes are counterbalanced by positive ones (Mary Beth and Chris of "Cagney and Lacey" and Joyce Davenport of "Hill Street Blues"), the negative image may remain uppermost in our minds because of its place and treatment in the scenic narrative, its sheer repetition, and its consistency with long-lived stereotypes. If paleosymbols can influence how we view women and blacks, they can also affect how we view money, power, and sex.

3. Paleosymbols may help shape attitudes toward money, power, and sex   The importance of money to males in Western society unquestionably transcends the mere ability to purchase commodities. Television programs implicitly recognize this in their portrayals of male characters. Accordingly the TV male frequently flaunts his purchasing power to the female in a clear attempt to impress her. J. R. Ewing immediately comes to mind. J. R. believes that most women will be more attracted to the man with a great deal of money. His immediate rival, Cliff Barnes, does too. For both the way to Sue Ellen's heart is through ostentatious wealth. Money is for them the equivalent of sexual attractiveness; to Sue Ellen it's a sign of masculinity. Even when the view of wealth isn't as overdrawn as it is on "Dallas," it nevertheless is portrayed as a magnet to which women are drawn. Thus Jonathan Hart of "Hart to Hart" is independently wealthy. So is "Dynasty" 's Blake Carrington.

When money has the same effect as potency on the male character, it becomes a symbol of potency. Parading across our TV screens are women who are excited by the man with lots of money. He represents to her glamorous and exotic things and places. Since sexual excitement frequently accompanies and even is stimulated by general excitement, TV females such as Sue Ellen or Charlie's angels often find themselves aroused by rich men in unusual, even unique ways. A large part of the never-seen Charlie's mystique for the three sensuous and attractive angels was Charlie's fabulous wealth. Indeed, since Charlie's character was never developed, we can only assume that his sexual life, which we occasionally glimpsed, was connected with his wealth and power.

If wealth is portrayed on TV as a symbol of potency, sexual or otherwise, its loss or absence is associated with impotency and feelings of worthlessness and despair. Thus, when Cliff Barnes loses a fortune at the hands of the infinitely more scheming J. R. Ewing, he goes into an emotional nosedive that results in a suicide attempt. Of course the catalyzing event is Sue Ellen's announcement that she is returning to J. R. because he can better provide for her in the manner to which she's become accustomed. Similarly Lucy's husband, although a young physician, is overcome with feelings of inadequacy because he can't compete with Ewing wealth.

The predominance of the wealthy on television—"Dynasty," "Falcon Crest," "Flamingo Road," "Hart to Hart," and so on—reflects and reinforces the psychological meaning that money has for many of us. Social psychologists have demonstrated that we tend to perceive objects of value and importance to us as larger than neutral objects of the same size. In one experiment on this subject, people were hypnotized and alternatively told that they were either rich or poor. When asked to judge the size of coins under these conditions, the subjects perceived all coins as larger when they were "poor."[14] Another experiment produced similar results. In this one poker chips could be exchanged for objects of differing value. The subjects perceived "more valuable chips" as larger.[15] The tendency to project importance onto the different aspects of the environment, then, seems directly related to our needs. How we perceive things has more to do with our own predispositions than with any set of objective facts. The importance of money or any similar commodity, therefore, will depend more on who is viewing it than on any estimate of its intrinsic value. If it's true that we

[14]W. R. Ashley, R. S. Harper, and D. L. Runyon, "The Perceived Size of Coins in Normal and Hypnotically Induced Economic States," *American Journal of Psychology* 34 (1951):564–572.

[15]W. W. Lambert, R. L. Solomon, and P. D. Watson, "Reinforcement and Extinction Factors in Size Estimations," *Journal of Experimental Psychology* 39 (1949):637–641.

perceive things of higher value as larger, then we will be likely also to perceive the wealthy as larger or more important.[16]

A strong case could be made for the claim that TV programmers portray the wealthy just this way—as larger or more important than the rest of us. This impression is not created merely by shows like "Dallas," "Dynasty," and "Falcon Crest." Such fictional accounts are bolstered by news features and programs that profile the "beautiful people," usually the rich and famous, who are often show-business personalities. "Entertainment Tonight," for example, is a highly successful thirty-minute excursion into the lives and loves, hopes and heartaches of people in the entertainment industry. Thus TV confers VIP status not only on J. R. Ewing but also on Larry Hagman, who plays J. R., when, for example, "Entertainment Tonight" profiles him. While this bigger-than-life status reflects the programmer's view of wealth, power, and celebrity, it also has the effect of encouraging you and me to think and perceive in similar terms. It may also contribute to the deference paid to the real-life rich and powerful, to our growing preoccupation with celebrities, and to our apparently insatiable appetite for details of the lives of the "beautiful people." Of greatest concern, it may diminish our own sense of self-worth.

If TV tends to associate money with power and both with sexual attractiveness in men, it also has a decided view of what makes a woman sexually attractive. Almost without exception the sexually attractive TV female has a lovely face, perfectly coiffed hair, and a slim, alluring figure. Whether the show is a soap or has dramatic pretensions, these features are constant. The women in sitcoms still must fit this mold, as in "Three's Company," "9 to 5," "WKRP," "Alice," "Newhart," "Taxi," or "Cheers."

Of course there is nothing startling about this; sexual attractiveness is a time-honored feature of all heroes and heroines.[17] But television viewers are treated to a single, unwavering standard of female beauty and sexual attractiveness, which of course is reinforced by advertising. Implicit in this standard are a number of things. First and most obvious, TV's standard of beauty and sexual attractiveness is the one against which all women must measure themselves, just as men must judge themselves by the standard of wealth and power. By the same token, this becomes the standard against which men are to judge the beauty and sexual attractiveness of women, the prototype of which is *Playboy*'s "playmate of the month." Forget that most of the pulchritudinous females who grace our TV screens are heavily made-up, often kept on diets that would starve a bird, rarely can act, and, if their appearances on talk shows and interviews in magazines are any indication, are banal and vacuous. The fantasy is what counts.

A second implication of TV's ideal of female beauty is that sexiness is redemptive. No matter how inane or despicable the character is, she escapes censure or at least must be judged by different standards from the rest of us mere mortals because of her disarming physical attractiveness.

---

[16] Louis Benson, *Images, Heroes and Self-Perception* (Englewood Cliffs, N.J.: Prentice-Hall, 1974), pp. 128–129.

[17] Benson, *Images, Heroes, and Self-Perception*, p. 36.

Third and most important, sexual attractiveness, as defined by television, is the passport to, even the requirement of, a life filled with adventure, excitement, and glamor. In a word, if you want to live the life of a Charlie's angel, you must look like one.

Quick Check on Television's Symbols and Images

Try to identify a TV character or personality who symbolizes (1) the independent working woman, (2) father, (3) "new breed" professional, (4) authority, (5) "castrating bitch," and (6) macho-man-with-dash-of-sensitivity.

Comments

(1) Joyce Davenport ("Hill Street Blues"), (2) Walter Cronkite, (3) Gonzo Gates ("Trapper John"), (4) Trapper John (probably also a father symbol), (5) Fallon ("Dynasty"), and (6) Thomas Magnum ("Magnum, P.I.").

Moral Instruction   A large part of a group's ideology is what it believes is good and bad, right and wrong, proper and improper behavior. TV sitcoms invariably present problems that are resolved within an allotted time, usually thirty minutes (actually about twenty-three minutes, with commercials). We all know that the conflict/resolution model is unrealistic. But what we may not realize is that it subtly imparts a conventional moral framework within which moral problems can be resolved, thereby reflecting and reinforcing the popular assumption that conflicts can be resolved within the current society and way of life. Here are some moral lessons transmitted by TV.

1. **You reap what you sow**   In a 1982 episode of "Archie's Place," Harry the bartender fell for a younger woman and promptly made a fool of himself. He got a flashy new wardrobe, strung gold chains around his neck, and flitted from club to club with the woman, a divorcee. When Harry's wife discovered the affair, she was crushed. Harry, callous to her anguish, moved out of their house with his single pal Barney. Predictably enough the younger woman soon dropped Harry like a hot potato. Realizing the error of his ways, Harry tried to patch things up with his wife. But she'd have none of it. Indeed, while Harry was out having his fling, she was striking out in a new and independent direction of her own. In the touching last scene, a pathetic Harry is seen asking his wife out for dinner. She demurs, explaining that she already has a date—with a man.

The moral lesson is crystal-clear: Harry shouldn't have strayed and been so indifferent to his wife's pain. He must and does pay the price; he gets what he deserves for betraying his wife and for lapsing back into adolescence. At the same time, there is the hint of a possible later reconciliation, thus reinforcing the popular double standard that expects, if not permits, male but not female dalliance.

2. **Good is triumphant**   Television melodrama also uses the conflict/resolution paradigm, in which good is pitted against evil. In just about all action-adventure series, the regular characters are the "good guys" and the intruders

are evil, thus mirroring and promoting fear of outsiders and fostering group adhesion. The melodramas thus teach that adherents of conventional morality are good and transgressors are evil. Thus, after a spirited conflict, good inevitably triumphs and order is restored.

3. **No one is above the law**   Often TV mutilates movies first seen in theaters to make them conform to its view of conventional morality. Language thought to be offensive is deleted, scenes of violence and sex are cut, and sometimes something is even added to make the story conform to the assumed moral ideology.

For example, we like to see ourselves as a nation that has a respect for law. In theory we don't believe in taking the law into our own hands. A movie that doesn't fit this mold is sometimes altered to conform to it.

In December 1982 NBC showed *The First Deadly Sin*, a film in which Frank Sinatra plays a soon-to-retire detective facing both a complex series of street killings and the critical condition of his wife after emergency surgery. Through a keen bit of investigation, Sinatra finally tracks down the psychotic killer. When it becomes clear to Sinatra that given the killer's wealth and connections he may "beat the rap," Sinatra shoots him dead, then walks away.

Not only were 16 of the film's original 112 minutes cut for the usual "language and violence" but a voice-over was added to teach or assure us that vigilantism never is justified.

4. **Authority figures embody basic moral truths**   Some action-adventure series provide ideologies of law and order and typically idealize authority figures. A popular motif is the glorification of both the individual's dedication to law and order and his basic commonsense view of the world. These heroic champions of the man-in-the-street's view of justice take various forms—cowboy, soldier, detective. Perhaps the most common today is the cop. T. J. Hooker (played by William Shatner, the mythic hero of "Star Trek") is the latest in a long blue line of TV cops who are convinced that the world is neatly divided into decent people and thugs, that soft-hearted judges (in concert with social workers and fuzzy-headed intellectuals) are ruining this country, and that women are fragile, dependent creatures whose proper place is in the home.

5. **You should accept your lot in life**   Often the moral instruction TV imparts is a sort of homily about work, family, or sexual relations. TV accomplishes this by offering opportunities for viewers to experience ritualist solutions to everyday problems. The solutions take many forms. A popular one is submission to one's lot, as illustrated by sitcoms like "Laverne and Shirley," "Alice," and "9 to 5." The same theme shows up in "Hill Street Blues" and used to on "M*A*S*H." The long-suffering Captain Furillo of the Hill and Hawkeye Pierce of "M*A*S*H" try hard to deal with war on the street and battlefield, but in the end stoically settle for the occasional modest victory.

This analysis suggests that the form and content of TV programs teem with ideology. Sitcoms, melodramas, and adventure-action series typically use conflict/resolution models that show that all problems can be resolved within the framework of current society. These programs transmit ideologies of law and order, sex and race, sexual attractiveness, power and authority, and so on that tend to legitimate established institutions.

Quick Check on Moral Instruction

The stars of "Charlie's Angels" rarely, if ever, had lovers or erotic relationships. Neither does Thomas Magnum of "Magnum, P.I." Remington Steele and Laura ("Remington Steele"), although physically attracted to each other, haven't yet consummated their relationship. "Three's Company" celebrates the sexual attractions of two single women and a single man who live together. Every episode pulsates with sexual temptation and titillation among the three and their dates and involves eventual frustration and renunciation. What view of sexual morality do shows like these implicitly endorse?

Comment

Despite their sexy facades, these shows seemingly endorse traditional, puritanical codes of sexuality.

Mixed Messages

Because our society is undergoing profound social change, television often carries mixed messages about family, sex, authority, and law.

Consider, for example, TV's mixed messages about family life. In the 1950s the then-dominant view of family life characterized sitcoms like "Father Knows Best," "Ozzie and Harriet," and "Leave It to Beaver." These series scrupulously avoided plot complications that went beyond losing car keys, leaving golf clubs out in the rain, and forgetting to pick up a tuxedo on the night of the prom. In short, the middle-class family unit was idealized as the proper locus of sexuality, socialization, domesticity, and authority.

In the 1960s and 1970s, however, one-parent families and individuals living alone became more commonplace in society and not surprisingly began to turn up on TV with increasing frequency. Today virtually the only programs to present facsimiles of the traditional family unit on TV do so in the context of nostalgia ("Little House on the Prairie," "The Waltons," "Happy Days") or fantasy ("Mork and Mindy"). More often you'll find parents trying to make it alone ("Alice," "Gloria," and "Silver Spoons") and childless couples ("Hart to Hart" and "Tucker's Witch"). Indeed, a happy TV marriage is about as rare today as a single-car family.

In some cases TV substitutes work for marriage, as in "M*A*S*H," "Barney Miller," "WKRP," "Hill Street Blues," "Lou Grant," "Hotel," "Trapper John," and "Trauma Center." Even when a principal character is happily married, marriage and family are peripheral to work, as with Mary Beth Cagney of "Cagney and Lacey."

In other instances marriage is viewed as the end of fun and games ("The Dukes of Hazzard," "Three's Company," and "Too Close for Comfort"). In still other cases, marriage simply doesn't exist, either because it would detract from the glamorous ambience of the show ("Fantasy Island" and "Love Boat") or kill off its characters ("Laverne and Shirley," "Bosom Buddies," "Simon and Simon," and "Hardcastle and McCormick").

Of course there are shows in which marriage and family are an integral part of the lives of the characters. But consider some of them: "Dynasty," "Dallas," "Knot's Landing," "Falcon Crest," and "The Yellow Rose." These night-time soaps are sudsy with adulteries, rancorous divorces and custody fights, separations, and one-night stands.

To be sure, each of these shows has its token happy marriage. On "Dynasty" it's the Carringtons'. But this marriage is constantly imperiled by the flotsam of past liaisons, usually in the form of venomous ex-mates. Viewers of "Dallas" had hopes that Lucy Ewing's marriage would turn out well. But if they were sensitive to foreshadowing (not to mention the internal dynamics of soap operas), their hopes wouldn't have extended beyond the length of a commercial. After all, during Lucy's lovely marriage ceremony, no fewer than three spouses were graphically shown lusting after someone else's mate. Sure enough, Lucy's marriage failed. Apparently her husband-physician couldn't live with her because she was so rich. Shortly after her separation, Lucy was impregnated by a rapist. So much for young love's chances of survival, at least in Dallas.

So the single dominant ideology of the family that reigned supreme in the fifties has changed. So have other prevailing ideologies about sexuality, socialization, domesticity, and authority.

In the past thirty years, society's so-called traditional values have undergone radical change. The roles of men and women have lost sharp definition. The nuclear family has replaced the extended family and has in turn been shattered by connubial and generational strife. Sex outside marriage has become so commonplace as to be the norm, not the exception. The main concern of those having sex outside marriage seemingly is not unwanted pregnancies, feelings of guilt, or the pain caused other parties, but herpes. Self-interest and immediate gratification have largely crowded out our sense of social responsibility. Nobility seems no longer defined in terms of heroic self-sacrifice but of expediency in the cause of self-advancement. Our concept of punishment has swung from retribution to rehabilitation to a mix of the two, with retribution again in ascendancy.

The mixed messages TV today imparts reflect these sea changes. Kellner's explanation for these often contradictory TV images and messages is that they reflect the contradictions embedded in our advanced capitalistic system, which no longer has one unifying, comprehensive ideology but many, often contradictory ones. This doesn't lessen the impact of television, however. If anything it would seem to intensify it; for if he's right, then TV is probably for most of us the preeminent means of transmitting these ideologies.

News

Perhaps the most important thing to remember about news is that what eventually is reported as news is determined by what is deemed newsworthy by those who report it. Newsworthiness in turn is largely influenced by journalists' judgments of reality and value and by their news sources. These, then, are three great forces shaping the news: reality judgments, values, and sources.

Reality Judgments

Students of journalism have observed that like sociology, journalism is an empirical discipline. This means that the news consists of findings based on an investigation of the world and the people in it. But it also means that the news consists of the concepts and methods that underlie this investigation. These in turn are shaped by a set of assumptions about the nature of reality. What, then, is journalism's view of reality?

For ten years sociologist Herbert Gans spent considerable time in four television and magazine newsrooms, observing and talking to the journalists who choose most of the news stories that inform us about ourselves and our world. Gans was interested in their values, professional standards, and the external pressures that shaped their judgments. His study of the unwritten rules of American journalism help clarify how our society works and how our perceptions of it are formed.[18] Gans' findings about journalism's view of reality can be conveniently ordered according to the following categories: people in the news, activities, race, class, sex, age, political ideologies, and foreign news.

People in the News   Journalists like to say that news should be about individuals rather than groups or social issues. And they achieve this aim: Most news is indeed about individuals. But not *all* individuals, or even most individuals, or even the most influential individuals.

About three-quarters of domestic news deals with individuals who are well known: the incumbent President, presidential candidates, members of the House and Senate, state and local officials, alleged lawbreakers, and flouters of social convention. Of these probably less than fifty are repeatedly covered. Overlooked are those figures who are often thought to play important roles; military leaders, political party officials, large campaign contributors, heads of local and state political organizations, business lobbyists, and so on. About one-fifth of all news time and space is devoted to individuals who are not known: protesters, rioters, strikers, lawbreakers, voters, survey respondents, and participants in unusual activities.

Activities   The activities covered in the news are largely determined by the dominant well-known figures. Thus coverage concentrates on government conflicts and disagreements (about 15 percent of the coverage); government decisions, proposals, and ceremonies (about 14 percent); government personnel changes (about 22 percent); violent and nonviolent protests (10 percent); crimes, scandals, and investigations (about 25 percent); and actual and averted disasters (14 percent).[19]

---

[18] Herbert J. Gans, *Deciding What's News* (New York: Vintage Books, 1980.)

[19] Gans, *Deciding What's News*, p. 138.

Race   Over the past decade or so, the primary societal division in the news has been racial, although this was largely an outgrowth of the ghetto disorders of the 1960s. In general the national news features middle- and upper-middle-class blacks who have overcome racial, economic, and political obstacles. Less affluent blacks more often are noteworthy as protesters, criminals, or victims. Blacks who already have been integrated into national institutions and those who make no attempt to enter them tend to be ignored, as do poor blacks, simply because they are poor and unknown.

Class   Rarely does domestic news deal with income difference among people or with people as earners of income. This stands in sharp contrast to foreign news coverage. For example, stories over the past ten years about Chile, Nicaragua, and El Salvador regularly have described demonstrations and conflicts, among upper-, middle-, and working-class groups. Domestic events rarely are couched in these class terms. To the degree that the news has a conception of the stratification system, it recognizes four strata: poor, lower-middle class, middle class, and rich. What journalists see and refer to as "lower-middle class" sociologists would call "working class," a term journalists eschew, perhaps because of its Marxist overtones. Moreover, journalists disregard the sociologists' "lower-middle class"; that is, skilled and semi-skilled white-collar workers who, next to blue-collar workers ("working class"), are the largest economic stratification in the country. In effect, then, the news lumps the working class and upper-middle class together into "middle class." Not only does this stratification blur significant economic and cultural differences between the classes within this category, it also makes the so-called "middle-class" group appear to be more numerous than it would be by the more exacting sociological stratification. In any event, most news is about the minority affluent class (the top 1 to 5 percent of the nation's income distribution), since these tend to be the "knowns" in society. Most important, the news rarely discusses a possible connection between lack of property and powerlessness.

Sex   In the 1970s the primary national division feature in the news was that between the sexes. Although most of the people featured in the news continue to be men, both print and electronic journalism have regularly reported on the women's liberation and feminist movements, as well as on male—female relations and related issues. But a large proportion of the stories has concerned the successful entry of certain women into traditionally all-male occupations and institutions (such as banking). As a result of the emphasis on politics and professions, the activities of organized women's movements and the advances of professional women have been covered in the news far more than either the feminist activities of unorganized women or the concerns of working-class feminists. Thus comparatively little attention has been given to the wage disparity between women and their male counterparts, on-the-job sexual harassment, the way prostitution is reported, and the depiction of violence directed against women.

Age   Since most news is about politics, in which age divisions are relatively unimportant, the news takes little notice of age groups. Most people over sixty-five and under twenty-five are nearly invisible. When the elderly do get coverage, typically it's in the context of need (health care) or disaster (victims of crime), both of which fall under the rubric of "the problems of the elderly." The general impression given, then, is that the elderly are nonproductive, out-of-touch, sick, lonely, poor, and victimized. Curiously, a study conducted in 1975 by the American Council of Aging turns up quite a different portrait of the elderly in America. Only 21 percent of those interviewed who were at least sixty-five actually found themselves with health problems; only 12 percent in that age category actually felt lonely; only 15 percent felt their income was too low to live on; and only 23 percent considered themselves threatened by crime.[20]

When "middle-class" young people are given coverage, it is typically in the context of violations of social standards. Thus, over the past ten years, adolescents have appeared in the news variously as protesters, criminals, hippies, pot smokers, mystics, and lovers of music that is viewed by the general public as at best cacophonous, at worst downright inimical to morality and social stability.

Political Ideologies   The news spectrum embraces several ideological positions, ranging from "far left" to "far right." Both television and newspapers approve the moderate core, which would include both liberals and conservatives. To the degree that political groups deviate from the acceptable center, they are handled less seriously and kindly. Thus radicals on the left are portrayed as Socialists or Communists, radicals on the right as neo-Nazis. Moreover, journalism makes no distinction between democratic and revolutionary socialists, nor between those who preach revolution and those who practice or condone violence. It applies the "ultraconservative" label without distinction to those who favor aid to private enterprise and to libertarians, who advocate complete free-market enterprise and the assumption of many public services by private industry. It uses "liberal" as a catchall for those who favor the New Deal or its latter-day versions as well as for those like former California Governor Jerry Brown and former New York Governor Hugh Carey who favor cutbacks in welfare expenditures.

Foreign News   Whatever occurs on the international scene that is relevant to America's interests is generally reported; what is not immediately perceived as connected to our interests is ignored until its relevance emerges. But this observation about the news' ethnocentrism must be quickly qualified by another: Because foreign news is given less coverage than domestic, only the most dramatic foreign events receive coverage.

Sometimes the concern for drama eclipses newsworthiness. Television is particularly susceptible to this concern, as evidenced by the crash of a Russian commercial jet in Luxembourg in September 1982. Each of the networks focused on this event, replete with film.

Other times the sensational qualities of an event crowd out its significance. For example, in the winter of 1981, a popular circus performer known as "Boris the Gypsy" was arrested in Moscow for dealing in the black market. NBC covered

---

[20]See Juanita M. Kreps, "Human Values and the Elderly," in D. D. Van Tassel (ed.), *Again, Death and the Completion of Being* (Philadelphia: University of Pennsylvania Press, 1979), p. 18.

the incident, mentioning Boris' rumored friendship with Soviet President
Leonid Brezhnev's daughter and the previously reported death of Brezhnev's
longtime confidant Mikhail Suslov. NBC concluded that Brezhnev's political
power was waning. ABC went further, quoting unconfirmed reports that
Brezhnev's son was also being questioned for an unspecified wrongdoing and
that a power struggle *might* be brewing within the Kremlin. Overlooked in the
reports on these tales of high intrigue were questions of profound relevancy to
the United States: Who were the major leaders contending for Brezhnev's
position? In what ways would their ascendency affect U.S.–USSR relations?

So journalists clearly make judgments about reality that help determine
what they consider newsworthy. Since these judgments carry bias, they slant
the news, for better or worse. But like all other empirical disciplines—and for
that matter all other purposeful endeavors in general—journalism does not
limit itself to reality judgments. News gathering and news making are also
conducted within a framework of values. The daily news that you see, hear, and
read originates with values (and the biases they carry) common to (1) the daily
press as a whole, (2) the individual medium, (3) the key figures determining news
content, and (4) society generally. While not exhaustive, these four categories do
account for the chief sources of news values, a subject to which we now turn.

Values

Numerous professional values influence what is judged to be newsworthy.
Three of them warrant special attention: objectivity, the dramatic and visual,
and efficiency and economy.

Objectivity   Objectivity entails impartiality. In being objective reporters, at
least in theory, are supposed to "let the facts speak for themselves." They are not
supposed to comment on or to interpret what they report but, in the role of
disinterested party, simply to inform the public. Presumably opinions are
relegated to editorials and commentaries. Objectivity has been honored as a
news value by American journalists ever since Adolph S. Ochs took on the
languishing *New York Times* in 1896 and sought to rid it of any signs of bias on
the part of his reporters, his editors, or himself. This value endures to this day.
All reporters like to consider themselves objective; to be objective is to be
thought unbiased.

In fact, the ideal of objectivity carries with it a built-in bias favoring
acquaintance with something, a type of knowledge that the philosopher William
James, for one, distinguished from *knowledge about* that thing. Thus you may be
acquainted with the parliamentary form of government; that is, you've heard of
it and know it functions in Britain. At the same time, you may have little or no
knowledge about how a parliamentary system of government operates: what
makes it different from a democratic republic; how, when, and where it originat-
ed; and so on. Thus you have acquaintance with the parliamentary system but
not knowledge about it.

Whatever we are acquainted with is likely to be concrete and descriptive;

what we know about tends to be abstract and analytic. You and I typically become acquainted with things through personal experience or some other type of immediate apprehension. In contrast, we usually acquire knowledge about them through formal education or systematic investigation. Acquaintance emphasizes fact; knowledge stresses concepts. A newspaper announcement of a new drug to fight cancer provides acquaintance with the fact that a new cancer therapy is available rather than knowledge about how it works. The announcement of still another skirmish in the Middle East provides acquaintance with the fact rather than knowledge about why it happened and about the likely short- and long-term effects. Although acquaintance with and knowledge about something can be located on a continuum, and we can develop knowledge about matters that we earlier only were acquainted with, each kind of knowing is employed for different purposes.[21]

In the view of most students of journalism, news is largely a matter of timely acquaintance with the world. But if news is not enhanced by "knowledge about," it can provide only a superficial understanding of what is being reported; for it is then a report of events, not of their significance, their connection with other events, or relevant hidden facts. Accordingly, for most reporters the truthful reporting of, say, a speech lies in its being accurate regarding the spelling of the speaker's name, what the speaker said, the size of the audience and its responses, and other descriptive details. But the reporter is not usually expected to assess the validity of the speaker's assertions if they have not been publicly contradicted. In fact, the norms of their profession usually prevent reporters from providing what knowledge they possess about something, for this would not be "objective."[22] For example, suppose the reporter knew for certain that the speaker was lying through his teeth. To comment on this would require knowledge about the issue, which if introduced would violate the ideal of objectivity.

Thus objectivity, as understood by most reporters, carries a built-in bias favoring acquaintance with rather than knowledge about the world, the superficial rather than the in-depth, the signalizing of events rather than the analysis of their significance. The preeminent journalist Walter Lippmann said it best several decades ago:

> News and truth are not the same thing. . . . The function of news is to signalize an event, the function of truth is to bring to light the hidden facts, to set them into relations with each other, and make a picture of reality on which man can act.[23]

Readers and viewers who forget this are apt to think erroneously that in the news they have the whole picture, a sufficient knowledge about people, events, and issues.

Still it's difficult in most areas of inquiry to prevent our likes, dislikes,

---

[21] See Bernard Roscho, *Newsmaking* (Chicago: The University of Chicago Press, 1975), pp. 13–14.

[22] Roscho, *Newsmaking*, p. 14.

[23] Walter Lippmann, *Public Opinion* (New York: Free Press, 1965), p. 226.

hopes, and fears from influencing our judgments. Journalism is no exception. Reporters will be as biased by their perceptions of their news organization's and editors' preferences as by their own life histories. Don't foget that the print and electronic press are commercial enterprises whose very existence depends on a financial profit. They are competitive enterprises that are and must be concerned with ratings, sales, and growth. They are large-scale enterprises interlocked with other industries. Finally they are enterprises whose owners obviously have influence over the occupational status of their employees. These realities necessarily influence what is considered newsworthy. Recall the masthead of *The New York Times*. Emblazoned across it is the motto "All the news that's fit to print." Implied is the editor's prerogative to exercise personal judgment about what is appropriate for publication.

The Dramatic and Visual   It's no secret that in the United States many more people are killed each year in auto accidents than in airplane accidents. In fact, about four times as many deaths can be attributed to auto smashups. Yet the intensity of media attention accorded a plane crash by far outpaces that given the cumulatively greater numbers of deaths in automobile accidents. Why? Because perceptions seem affected by what we are better able to describe than explain. The dramatic quality of a singular event typically evokes popular interest. Both television and newspapers feed this popular interest by focusing on the dramatic and, in the case of television, the visual.

For example, on March 2, 1982, CBS ran two news items on the Soviet Union: one on the outcome of Poland's Gen. Wojciech Jaruzelski's visit to Moscow, the other on a young Soviet couple who crashed their car into the U.S. embassy compound in Moscow. The Jaruzelski spot was given twenty seconds; the more dramatic and visual crash, two minutes and twenty seconds.

Advances in technology have made possible, and hence imperative, reliance on the dramatic and visual in television news coverage, especially in local news. The "action-cam" or minicam is a perfect example. Since its appearance as a regular tool of TV news coverage around 1975, this portable, hand-held camera has been hailed by many news directors as the device that freed video journalism from the dreary "talking heads" era. But the short history of the action-cam doesn't bear out such pronouncements. Because no one can predict when a story will actually break, much of the so-called on-the-scene coverage consists of prearranged clichés (such as pickets, protests, press conferences) or of reporters standing at the place (such as a bank) where something significant has happened (such as a robbery) *some time ago*.

But more important, it is the action-cam and not the intrinsic value of the day's stories that influences the nightly news agenda. If you disagree, consider the opinion of Walter Jacobson, co-anchor of WBBM-TV's successful newscast in Chicago:

> The whole newscast is dictated by what the action-cam can do. We put stories on the air that are not worth anything. . . . Examples? All right. A 22-year-old man and his girl friend are in a boat on Lake Michigan near the shore. It's a windy day and their boat capsizes. They're all right, but the Coast Guard tows their boat in.

We pick up the Coast Guard call on our squawk box. We send an action-cam crew racing out to the lake. And we do a live shot: "Patrol boat bringing in sunken boat at this moment!"

My feeling is, *what the hell does this story mean?* It doesn't help the viewer get through the city's system. It doesn't help him exercise his franchise as a voter. It doesn't really tell him anything he needs to know. It drives me nuts.[24]

Don't be too hasty to write off this episode as nothing but a waste of time and resources. What you and I perceive as our community's or nation's pressing problems reflect the issues featured in the press. If the issues to be covered are determined largely by appeal to dramatic and visual content rather than intrinsic news worth, we can be left thinking that the riveting events presented are more important than they really are. A classic example of such misperception was the sudden concern about a seeming "crime wave" in New York City shortly after famed muckraker Lincoln Steffens and his fellow reporters at police headquarters engaged in some competitive sensationalizing in the 1910s. Nearly a half-century later, a study of crime news published in four Colorado newspapers showed that the amount of coverage varied independent of the actual crime rate. But—and here's the point—the public's *perception* of the level of criminality reflected not how much crime actually was committed but the amount of crime news reported.[25]

The other side of the coin is that, no matter how significant, what is not dramatic and visual often goes ignored, at least until it becomes highly visible. Festering social, sexual, racial, environmental, and economic problems can go unreported, not to say unexamined, until some dramatic event catches media attention: a demonstration, a strike, a march on Washington, a riot. For example, throughout the year one rarely sees or hears any reports about educational issues. Yet, come September, the cameras are rolling and microphones waiting to record the drama of the latest teachers' walkout or strike, the reasons for which inevitably get lost in sensationalized reports on how many thousands of students are being hurt. One of the more subtle social implications of this kind of approach to news coverage is that, feeling they lack the coverage needed to inform public opinion, groups that see themselves as victims have little recourse but to attempt to manage the news through dramatic, symbolic protests that often produce serious, if temporary, social dislocations.

Efficiency and Economy   The media operate under the economic and technological constraints that typify other mass-production processes. As a result efficiency of operations emerges as a key value in news judgment. To see why you need only consider how the mountain of material made available to a news medium (primarily by its wire services) is reduced to usable size.

Working constantly under the pressure of deadlines, editors often make split-second decisions regarding comparative newsworthiness, whether of facts to be included in a story that may be too long or of stories competing for limited

[24]Ron Powers, "Now! Live on the Action Cam! A Reporter Talking!" *TV Guide*, June 19, 1982, p. 22.
[25]F. James Davis, "Crime News in Colorado Newspapers," *American Journal of Sociology* 57 (June 1952): 325–330.

space or time. (Of course other judgments precede these, including the editor's deciding who to send on a story and the reporter's deciding which facts to include, stress, downplay, or omit.) Decisions about which stories to run and how much coverage to give them occur in rapid succession, and rarely is there time for reflection.

Besides working under the pressure of deadlines and having to process reams of potential news, editors work within structural constraints. For example, the reason that most newspapers exist is to provide what's called "straight news." But straight news fills hardly more than a quarter of most dailies.[26] So a basic constraint on news judgments is the "news hole." Whoever decides how large a newspaper will be effectively determines how much straight news it will contain. Who decides? Usually the advertising department. The editor's job, then, is not one of making the newspaper conform to the stories of the day but of fitting the stories of the day into the space allotted them by personnel whose primary function is to make money for publishers.

What about the prominence given stories? Will they go on the front page or in a less important place? Will they be given a couple of paragraphs or several columns? In fact, editors never see all the stories of the day before they make their decisions. Efficiency of operations dictates an editorial decision-making process that begins well before editors know what all the news reports will look like. This means that the later news typically has the least chance of inclusion. More important, editors usually scan five times more words and five times more individual stories than they can use. On large metropolitan dailies (over 350,000 circulation) they may see ten times more words and seven times more stories than you or I will ever see. What is discarded is never knowable to the reader or viewer. In short, the vast majority of stories that arrive in newsrooms, in a sense, never happen.[27] This is just as true of television news.

In making their news judgments, then, editors work within severe constraints of time and space. These constraints finally emerge as institutional values associated with profit. The order of the day is efficiency of operations, which means that the allotted space must be filled up in the time available. The good editor succeeds; the bad one doesn't. The result: instantaneous editorial judgments. Snap judgments are by definition unreflective, and they are profoundly influenced by the press' reality judgments. Judgment made with little or no reflection usually carries a bias and runs a high risk of inaccuracy or misrepresentation. This is especially true of television news, for which the economic and technological constraints are even greater than for print news. Thus, during the television coverage of the attempted assassination of President Reagan, viewers were told by two networks that Press Secretary James Brady had died. Indeed, they were exposed to the understandable frustration and irritation of one anchor, the late Frank Reynolds of ABC, who at one point in the coverage wondered aloud if it were known for a fact that Brady had died.

---

[26] Roscho, *Newsmaking*, p. 111.
[27] Ben H. Bagdikian, *The Information Machines: Their Impact on Man and the Media* (New York: Harper & Row, 1971), p. 90.

The values that we've just discussed are embedded in the news profession as it functions in this society. But beyond them are a whole cluster of sociocultural norms that the news parrots. Various sociologists have compiled lists of these values, and you should consult them to deepen your awareness of how the news media function. Journalist Jack Neufield, for example, speaks of "organic" values, among which he includes "beliefs in welfare capitalism, God, the West, Puritanism, the Law, the family, property, the two-party system, and perhaps most crucially . . . that violence is only defensible when employed by the state."[28] Similarly journalist Herbert J. Gans writes of "enduring" values, under which he lists ethnocentrism, altruistic democracy, responsible capitalism, small-town pastoralism, individualism, moderatism, social order, and national leadership. Value judgments in these areas influence news content and presentation as much as the professional values we have focused on.

Quick Check on News Values

Evaluate the coverage of a specific event of national importance (like the shooting down of Korean Air Lines' Flight 007 on September 1, 1983) with respect to objectivity. Look for bias in word choice, headlines, and amount of copy. Determine whether readers are acquainted with or given knowledge about the issue.

News Sources

News sources, together with reality judgments and professional values, are responsible for shaping the news. Although sources alone don't determine the news, they go far toward focusing the journalist's attention and shaping news content. Powerful, authoritative people are a primary source of news. This explains in part why the media reflect the opinions and interests of the rich and powerful. Such figures can always supply information and are both authoritative and productive, as sources need to be. As a result journalists develop a kind of institutionalized relationship with the most regular sources—high public officials and those associated with them—and at times even are assigned to them. Beat reporters in effect become almost allies of these sources, either because they develop a mutually beneficial relationship with them or because they identify with them.[29] Even when general reporters cover an especially important story, they typically consult the same sources and are effectively managed by them.

To get some idea of the predominance of high public officials as news sources, consider a decade-old analysis conducted of the origin of 2850 domestic and foreign stories that appeared in *The New York Times* and *The Washington Post*. Seventy-eight percent of the stories had public officials as their sources.[30]

---

[28]Jack Neufield, "Journalism: Old, New and Corporate," in Ronald Weber (ed.), *The Reporter as Artist: A Look at the New Journalism Controversy* (New York: Hastings House, 1974), p. 56.

[29]Roscho, *Newsmaking*, p. 83.

[30]Leon V. Sigal, *Reporters and Officials: The Organization and Politics of Newsmaking* (Lexington, Mass.: Heath, 1973).

To a large degree, this reliance on public officials both reflects and accounts for the news' reality judgments. More important for those of us who are trying to learn how to think critically about the information we get, it means that most of the information parallels the values and viewpoints of the public officials who are its primary source, a point I'll return to shortly.

By far the single most valuable public official news source is the President. As George E. Reedy, press secretary to President Lyndon Johnson, pointed out:

> There is no official of the government who can make a headline story merely by releasing a routine list of his daily activities. There is no other official of the government who can be certain of universal newspaper play by merely releasing a picture of a quiet dinner with boyhood friends. There is no other official who can attract public attention merely by granting an interview consisting of reflections, no matter how banal or mundane, on social trends in fields where he has no expertise and in which his concepts are totally irrelevant to his function as a public servant.[31]

While support for Reedy's claim is not hard to find, one of the most dramatic examples in recent times involves President Richard Nixon's trip to China in 1972. Although the visit promised little hard news and few members of the press knew enough about China to provide interpretive reporting, all the networks and every major daily sent reporters to cover that event: Forty-three commentators, cameramen, and technicians from the television networks, and forty-four reporters and photographers from the print media made the trip.[32] Commenting on the press entourage accompanying Nixon to Peking, *The New York Times'* Russell Baker observed:

> When President Nixon goes to China he will take most of the American television industry with him. Harry Reasoner, Walter Cronkite, John Chancellor, Barbara Walters, Dan Rather, Herb Kaplan, Bernard Kalb, Eric Sevareid and many more. . . . We already know that the President could make it very difficult for anyone else to get attention on television, but until the Peking trip we did not realize that he had the power to pack the entire television industry into an airplane and transport it lock, stock, and Sevareid out of the country. This is not entirely due to Presidential power, let it be hurriedly said, but rather a disclosure of how thoroughly absorbed television has become with the Presidency. . . . Television is exceedingly Presidential. It is at its best with the bold, simple stories about strong men in familiar situations and this is the kind of story the White House, of all America's institutions, is most likely to provide consistently.[33]

As Baker intimates, through its automatic coverage of the words and deeds of the President, public officials, and other high-ranking sources, the news often gives coverage that is disproportionate to the significance of what is being reported. Further evidence of this appeared in *The Washington Post* after the 1970 congressional elections. *Post* writer Robert Harwood called our attention to a study of the front page of *The Washington Post* in the seventeen days preceding the November elections, and specifically to coverage that seemed to indicate a decided Republican bias. During that period the *Post* printed thirty

[31]George E. Reedy, *The Twilight of the Presidency* (New York: Mentor Books, 1971), pp. 101–102.
[32]"Made for Television," *Newsweek*, February 21, 1972, p. 100.
[33]Russell Baker, *New York Times*, February 10, 1972, p. 43.

page-one stories about the GOP campaign, which took up 268 inches of front-page space. In contrast only six front-page stories about the Democrats were printed, and these stories took up 35 inches of space. Along with the stories, the *Post* printed fifteen front-page pictures of Republican campaigners, which took up 306 inches of space and only one picture of a Democrat, which took up 10 inches. In short, the Republicans received twelve times more space on the front page of *The Washington Post* during those seventeen days than Democrats did. It's almost irresistible to conclude that the *Post* favors Republicans, that it's a one-party paper. The inaccuracy of this inference would stem from ignorance about the degree to which high-ranking sources can influence, even determine, news media. As Harwood puts it:

> . . . like most American newspapers, we [i.e., the *Post*] are vulnerable to a syndrome that might be called Pavlovian journalism after the Russian who taught dogs to salivate when bells ring.
>
> We salivated over the Republicans last fall for one reason only—the President was out campaigning for them. No matter that he had very little to *say* that was significant or unpredictable at the whistlestops along the way. No matter that he *did* very little beyond waving at crowds. No matter that there was very little or no evidence that what he said or did affected a single voter. The mere fact that he was out there was Page One news in *The Washington Post*. What he was doing was "important," we told ourselves, because Presidents are "important" men.
>
> That kind of circular reasoning frequently affects our news judgment and results in statistical imbalances. . . . It says something about our sense of values and about our perspectives on the world.[34]

Presidents and other people and events are covered, then, not necessarily because they are newsworthy but because they *could be.* As a result sources with a track record for newsworthiness—typically because they hold high stations in the social structure—are covered routinely. What they or others associated with them say or do dominates the news, even though the specific events in which they're involved aren't very important. Over-reliance on such sources can give credence to rumors, hearsay, speculation, and all manner of stories for which there is no hard evidence.

A good example of this occurred in the winter of 1981 when Libyan leader Muammar Kaddafi supposedly sent a "hit team" to the United States to assassinate President Reagan and other high officials in the U.S. government. Even though there was no hard evidence for the suspected plot, the press ran it as a working story, primarily because administration officials, including the President himself, gave it importance and credibility. Running with this story, television and newspapers variously relied on "informed" and "reliable" —though rarely identified—sources at home and abroad to keep this dramatic and sensational story on the front burner of news coverage for at least a month. As a result, between November 25 and Christmas Day, 1981, viewers were told that

1. The number of hit men being searched for was three (ABC), five (CBS), six (ABC), ten (ABC, CBS), twelve (CBS), and thirteen (NBC).

[34] Robert Harwood, "Pavolvian Journalism: Different Standards for Presidents," in *Of the Press, by the Press, for the Press (And Others, too)* (Washington, D.C.: Washington Post Co., 1974), pp. 91–92.

2. The would-be assassins had entered the United States from Canada (ABC, CBS); were in Mexico (NBC).
3. Carlos "the Jackal" was a possible hit team member (CBS, NBC).
4. The personal habits of various hit team members involved wearing cowboy boots and Adidas jogging shoes and smoking English cigarettes.
5. The hit team was composed of (a) three Libyans (ABC, NBC), (b) three Iranians (CBS, NBC), (c) two Iranians (ABC), (d) one East German (NBC, CBS, ABC), (e) one Palestinian (ABC, CBS, NBC), and (f) one Lebanese (ABC, CBS, NBC).
6. One hit team member visited Phoenix, Arizona (ABC).

All this information came from off-camera interviews with sources— "officials," "security officials," "Capitol Hill sources"—unwilling to be identified and thus were introduced by such phrases as "It's been learned," "ABC has learned," and the like. On the evening news of November 26, ABC anchor Frank Reynolds announced that it was *known* that Libyan agents were in this country to assassinate the highest officials of the U.S. government. Neither Reagan, CIA Director William Casey, nor Secretary of State Alexander Haig had confirmed this. In fact William Webster, the head of the FBI, told ABC's Sam Donaldson on January 3, 1982 "We've never confirmed any hard evidence about a hit team inside the United States."[35] And ABC senior correspondent John Scali, who first broadcast reports about the Libyan plot on ABC, insists "No one ever told me there was hard evidence."[36]

   In fact, the only thing the press knew for sure was that security around Reagan and his top aides had been increased and that Reagan had been briefed about a possible plot. That the expressed concern of administration officials was well founded was strictly the opinion of the press. It's entirely possible that Muammar Kaddafi exploited the American press' reliance on "official sources" for information and on television's penchant for the sensational to influence events in the United States. At least that's the thesis of *Time* magazine's David Halevy. Halevy was able to check a number of purported hit team names on a Tel Aviv—based computerized system listing of 55,000 to 60,000 terrorists and came up empty. His conclusions:

> While the threat was perceived as serious, too few in the American media looked at the possibilities of Kaddafi playing the disinformation game. Send squads to Europe. Send Libyans to the North American continent. Just get the word out. Kaddafi is no madman—he's a shrewd Bedouin who understands the demands of his society, and also how Western society works. Take that supposed voice intercept of Kaddafi threatening Reagan's life. In the Middle East, everybody who ever makes a phone call assumes the call can be intercepted by somebody.[37]

   Besides giving disproportionate coverage to events that often are not significant and lending credence to the speculative, over-reliance on high officials for news produces managed news; that is, news that sources cut to fit

[35] John Weisman, "Why American TV Is Vulnerable to Foreign Propaganda," *TV Guide*, June 12, 1982, p. 12.
[36] Weisman, "Why American TV Is Vulnerable to Foreign Propaganda," p. 12.
[37] Weisman, "Why American TV Is Vulnerable to Foreign Propaganda," p. 121.

their own purposes. Because more news occurs than a journalist could begin to cover, news people must rely on surrogate observers—on "briefings"—to acquaint themselves with the day's events. But these sources are continually deciding what information to provide; what details to stress, downplay or suppress; and when the story should be given the press, if at all. By the account of journalist Richard Rorchler, "Scores of American newspapers give their readers no hint that the 'news' they are reading has been 'generated,' 'leaked,' provided not by journalistic legwork and thought but by a government handout which is 'not for attribution.'" [38] When the events being covered happen to be highly technical, the reporter's reliance on canned copy can become total.

Case in point: the press' coverage of the first moonwalk. Here's a snippet from an article describing how the National Aeronautics and Space Administration (NASA) coddled the press during the coverage of that historic event:

> ... Dr. Wernher von Braun held a microphone in the big golden auditorium of the Manned Spacecraft center....
> "I would like to thank you for all of the fine support you have already given the program ... because without good public relations and good representations of these programs to the public, we would have been unable to do it." ...
> NASA has assembled scores of publicists into one of the most effective and accommodating public relations machines in the history of press agentry ...
> The press kit ... 250 pages is forbidding. The NASA press men ... accept with equanimity the odds that of the 3,700 people who get press credentials for Apollo 11, maybe a couple dozen were intimately conversant with the press kit....
> The next superhandout from NASA is the 350-page flight plan. With it, you can make a timetable for your leads and bulletins, and naps and lunches....
> There was life on the moon and his name was Armstrong. He said ...
> Get the NASA man. Get the tape. Get the transcript. Get it right. NASA quoted it: "That's one small step for man, one giant leap for mankind."
> Okay. That's official. We go with that and we stick with that.[39]

In responding to news, then—in using it to understand, think about, and form judgments about the world—remember that news carries a number of built-in biases. These result chiefly from the reality judgments journalists make, the professional and sociocultural values they hold, and the sources they rely on.

Summary

Central to learning how to think critically is an awareness of the information environment. Three key forces shape how and what we think: advertising, television, and news.

Advertising does more than inform; it tries to persuade. In an attempt to persuade, advertisers often confuse, distort, and make undeliverable promises.

---

[38] Richard Rorchler, "Managing the News," *Commonwealth*, March 22, 1963, p. 659.

[39] Charles K. Siner, Jr., "How the Moonwalk was Reported from Houston: YOU AND NEIL AND BUZZ—YOU MADE IT," *The Quill* 57 (September 1969): 8–12.

Five advertising devices are particularly noteworthy:

1. False implication (the Haldol ad picturing a smiling, alert woman who was not taking the tranquilizer)
2. Ambiguity (Coricidin's ad: "At the first sign of a cold or flu—Coricidin"). Emotionally charged words ("natural") and weasels ("up to" or "helps") result in ambiguity.
3. Hidden facts (the Pertussin label that didn't list harmful chemicals as ingredients of the medication)
4. Exaggeration ("Dial is the most effective deodorant soap you can buy.") Although puffery is legal, it is deceptive.
5. Psychological appeals (Newport's "Alive with Pleasure" campaign)

Studies indicate that television influences how we see things. George Gerbner has conducted extensive studies on TV's impact on heavy viewers. He has found that

1. TV reinforces stereotypes toward sex, race, and age.
2. TV gives a distorted view of elite occupations.
3. TV gives the misimpression that one can thrive on junk food.
4. TV breeds fear of victimization.

For the most part, this reality warp can be explained by TV's preoccupation with ratings and hence with advertising dollars.

TV is a preeminent transmitter of ideologies—the doctrines, opinions, or ways of thinking of an individual or group. TV transmits ideologies through

1. Its symbols and images (Joyce Davenport as the independent working woman or J. R. Ewing as the symbol of evil)
2. Paleosymbols, which are emotionally charged scenes, often repeated, in which positive or negative situations occur (the scene in "The Money-changers," which might have the effect of dissuading one from stealing). Paleosymbols may perpetuate racism and sexism and help shape attitudes toward money, sex, and power.
3. Moral indoctrination through the conflict/resolution model. Some lessons possibly taught by TV that correspond with conventional morality include (1) you reap what you sow; (2) good is triumphant; (3) no one is above the law; (4) authority figures embody basic moral truths; and (5) you should accept your lot in life.

TV also contains mixed messages, which reflect society's current ambivalence toward sex, authority, law, and acceptable life-styles. A good example is the conflicting TV messages about family.

The most important thing to remember about news is that what is reported as news is determined by what is deemed newsworthy by those reporting the news. Newsworthiness in turn is shaped by journalists' reality judgments, professional values, and news sources and by the dictates of time and space as determined by advertisers.

Journalism's view of reality results in the following:

1. **People:** Usually only well-known figures are regarded as newsworthy; the less well-known are infrequently reported or ignored.

2. **Activities:** Usually only the activities of the well known are considered newsworthy.

3. **Race:** Typically the national news considers newsworthy only middle- and upper-class blacks who have overcome racial, economic, and political obstacles.

4. **Class:** Rarely does domestic news consider as newsworthy the income differences among people and the connection between property and power.

5. **Sex:** The successful entry of certain women into traditionally all-male occupations and institutions usually is considered newsworthy, as are the efforts of organized women's movements. The activities of unorganized women and the concerns of working-class women are largely ignored.

6. **Age:** The elderly are considered newsworthy usually in the context of social problems (as recipients of health care or as victims of crime); young people typically are covered in the context of protest, crime, or the flouting of social convention.

7. **Political ideologies:** Both television and print news favorably report on the moderate core of the political spectrum and handle critically extremes to the right or left; they also tend to overlook differences among politicians and group them under a single heading (as when they describe both Jerry Brown and Hugh Carey as "liberals").

8. **Foreign news:** What affects America's interests is considered newsworthy; what doesn't, or what is not immediately perceived as doing so, is usually ignored. Drama sometimes eclipses news significance (reporting the crash of a Soviet jet). Just as often the sensational crowds out stories of news significance (the arrest in Moscow of Boris the Gypsy).

Journalism's professional values of striving for objectivity, the dramatic and visual, and efficiency and economy result in the following:

1. Objectivity carries a built-in bias favoring acquaintance with rather than knowledge about things when reporting. Reporters are influenced by their perceptions of their news organizations' and editors' preferences as much as by their own life histories.

2. The dramatic and visual often are given top priority, as for example in giving twenty seconds to a story covering a Polish official's visit to Moscow but two minutes and twenty seconds to a story about a young Soviet couple's crashing their car into the U.S. embassy compound in Moscow. Advances in technology (the action-cam) encourage news choices that favor the dramatic and visual.

3. The news media operate within institutional constraints of ratings, circulation, and profit. Efficiency of operations is of overriding concern.

News sources are a third force shaping the news. Powerful, authoritative people like the President are a primary source of news. Preoccupation with these sources can give significance to a story with little intrinsic news value. It also can make the press susceptible to rumor, hearsay, and speculation, as for example in coverage of the alleged Kaddafi plot to assassinate President Reagan and other high government officials.

Applications

1 Keeping in mind the devices advertisers use to sell products, comment on the following pitches:
   a Four bars of Ivory cost about the same as three bars of most other soaps. So buy four bars of Ivory and "it's like getting one bar free."
   b "Alka Seltzer: the best antacid you can buy without a prescription."
   c RELUCTANT AUTO BUYER: I don't know. The sticker price doesn't seem like such a deal to me.
   SALESPERSON: Okay, tell you what I'm going to do. I'm going to slash three hundred bucks off the sticker price. How's that?
   RAB: Now you're talking!
   d "Incredible. Almost 50 percent of America's children don't get their recommended daily allowance of vitamin C. That's why I'm glad my whole family loves the fresh taste of Tang Instant Breakfast drink. It gives us a full day's supply of vitamin C." (Florence Henderson for Tang)
   e "Here's 7 cents to try a cereal that's big with kids. Save 7 cents when you buy Post Honeycomb cereal. It's a big, nutritious cereal kids love to eat. . . . Fortified with 8 essential vitamins." (Ad for Post Honeycomb)
   f "*Fact:* Ready-to-eat cereals do not increase tooth decay in children.
   Fact: Ready-sweetened cereals are highly nutritious.
   Fact: There is no more sugar in a one-ounce serving of a ready-sweetened cereal than in an apple or banana or in a serving of orange juice.
   Fact: The per capita sugar consumption in the United States has remained practically unchanged for the last 50 years." (Excerpt from a two-page ad entitled: "A Statement from Kellogg Company on the Nutritional Value of Ready-Sweetened Cereals")
   g "At Phillips 66, it's performance that counts."
   h "Wisk puts its strength where the dirt is."
   i "At Bird's Eye, we've got quality in our corner."
   j "Of America's best-tasting gums, Trident is sugar-free."
2 Report to the class on five ads that make use of psychological appeals.
3 Identify and document three ads that hide facts.
4 Watch and listen closely to several episodes of some television program. Determine what world view is illustrated. (For example " 'Trapper John'

presents a world in which doctors are competent, caring, and successful; have a good sense of humor; and often get intimately involved in the personal lives of their patients.") Then decide whether this world view corresponds with your own experience.

5 Use the following chart to record the coverage of an entire local newscast with respect to (1) order of stories, (2) subject of story (such as crime or natural disaster), (3) time given to each story, (4) whether the coverage acquaints you with or gives you knowledge about the subject, and (5) the nature of the visuals accompanying each story, if any (such as mini-cam coverage of bank where robbery occurred or on-the-street coverage of burning building).

STORY ORDER	SUBJECT	TIME (IN SECONDS)	ACQUAINTANCE WITH OR KNOWLEDGE ABOUT	VISUALS
1.				
2.				
3.				
etc.				

Based on your log, draw some tentative conclusions about the story priorities of your local newscast. What considerations about television news coverage help explain these priorities?

6 How would you account for these two seeming contradictions to the money/ratings explanation of the TV reality warp? (a) If female viewers are so dear to the hearts of sponsors, then why are female characters cast in such unflattering light? (b) Since the corporate world provides network TV with all of its financial support, why are businesspeople on TV portrayed in such a sinister light ("Dallas," "Falcon Crest," "Dynasty," and the like)?

PART TWO

Analysis

The Anatomy of Arguments

So far our study of critical thinking has been a kind of logical consciousness-raising. I have tried to make you aware of (1) the nature of critical thinking and blocks to its exercise, (2) the crucial role of language in thinking, and (3) the impact of the mass media on how we view things.

While such awareness is a good beginning on the long road to more effective thinking, it is only a beginning. You must also be able to recognize, understand, inspect, and assess what you hear, read, and write. You must have analytical skills.

This part of the book deals with the analytical skills you need to improve your thinking. It focuses on argument, which is at once a product of critical thinking and an object to which critical thinking is applied.

The study of argument can be divided into three main areas: argument identification, argument evaluation, and argument generation. Among other things argument identification shows us how to recognize arguments and portray their structures; argument evaluation shows us how to criticize them; and argument generation shows us how to construct them.

We start with argument identification. In order to identify an argument, you must know something about its anatomy, which is the subject of this chapter.

Argument

An argument is any group of statements one of which is claimed to follow from the others. Here's a simple example: "Mothers are females. Joan's a mother. Therefore Joan's a female." "Joan is a female" is the statement that is claimed to follow from the others. In other words, the first two statements are claimed to entail the third. If we wanted we could combine all three statements into a single sentence and still have an argument. "Since (1) mothers are females and (2) Joan is a mother, (3) Joan is a female." So an argument can take the form either of individual assertions or of a single sentence that embodies those assertions.

We often assert things without arguing: "Baseball is a popular sport in the United States. Football generally is played in winter. Basketball can be played inside or outside. Soccer is played throughout the world." These statements are nonargumentative. None of them is intended to follow from the others; so, taken as a group, they do not produce an argument.

We also use statements to explain things: "The class on the history of music has been canceled for lack of enrollment"; "The horse was frightened by a snake in the grass"; "Marie looks better since her vacation." These are explanatory statements. They help explain something: the cancellation of the class, the fright of the horse, Marie's improved look.

The basic difference between such nonargumentative statements and arguments is one of interest or purpose. If people are interested in establishing the truth of a claim and offer evidence intended to do that, then they are arguing, and what they are offering is an argument. But if they regard the truth of a claim as nonproblematic and are interested in explaining why it is the case (rather than demonstrating that it is in fact the case), then they are explaining. Thus, when I say "Marie looks better since her vacation," I'm not trying to establish that Marie does in fact look better. I am taking that as an established truth and am offering an explanation for why I think it is the case. But if I said "Marie deserves to be hired, since she is the most qualified," I am trying to establish the truth of the statement "Marie deserves to be hired." I am not taking this statement as an established truth but trying to show how it follows from the other statement. Thus I am setting forth an argument.

Quick Check on Argument Recognition

Determine which of these passages are arguments.

1 Most people I know prefer foods with no preservatives added. So I imagine such foods are good for you.
2 Since the President has expressed a view, the issue is closed.
3 Of course Vitamin C helps prevent colds. A Nobel laureate has said so.
4 "Even the most productive writers are expert dawdlers, doers of unnecessary errands, seekers of interruptions—trials to their wives or husbands, associates, and themselves. They sharpen well-pointed pencils and go out to buy

more blank paper, rearrange their office, wander through libraries and book-stores, change words, walk, drive, make unnecessary calls, nap, day dream, and try not 'consciously' to think about what they are going to write so they can think subconsciously about it." (Donald M. Murray, "Write before Writing," quoted in Morton A. Miller (ed.), *Reading and Writing Short Essays* [New York: Random House, 1980], p. 275.)

5 "It is worth saying something about the social position of beggars, for when one has consorted with them, and found that they are ordinary human beings, one cannot help being struck by the curious attitude that society takes toward them." (George Orwell, *Down and Out in Paris and London* [New York: Berkley, 1967], p. 125.)

Comments

1, 2, 3, and 5 are arguments.

Premises and Conclusions

Arguments consist of premises and a conclusion. The premises of arguments are those statements that are claimed to entail the conclusion. The conclusion is the statement that is claimed to be entailed by the premises. Thus far we have considered two simple arguments:

1. All mothers are females.
   Joan is a mother.

   _____

   Joan is a female.

2. Marie is the most qualified.

   _____

   Marie deserves to be hired.

The statements above the solid line are premises; the statements below the line are conclusions.

Identifying the premises and conclusion of an argument isn't easy, especially when they are embedded in longer passages. If you learn to read and listen carefully, however, you can pick up clues to the presence of arguments in written or spoken discourse. One of the most important clues is the *signal word*.

A signal word is a word that indicates the presence of a premise or conclusion. There are three main kinds of signal words: (1) words or phrases that signal conclusions, (2) words or phrases that help locate the general area where premises are to be found, and (3) words or phrases that help locate particular premises.[1]

_____

[1] Barrie A. Wilson, *The Anatomy of Argument* (Washington, D.C.: University Press of America, 1980), pp. 18–19.

Conclusion Signals

The English language has a rich store of clue words and phrases that often indicate conclusions; that is, what is being argued for. They include

so
thus
therefore
consequently
it follows that
as a result
hence
finally
in conclusion
we see, then, that
one can conclude that
shows that

On first reading a passage, you should underline its conclusion indicators. You will thereby alert yourself to an important part of the argument's structure: the conclusion. Consider for example the following passage:

> Capital punishment deters crime. It also ensures that a killer can never strike again. <u>It follows that</u> capital punishment should be permitted.

"It follows that" in the last sentence helps locate the argument's conclusion: "Capital punishment should be permitted." The first two assertions are reasons or premises used to support that conclusion.

Here's another example, followed by a comment:

Example: "A teacher who asks a question is tuned to the right answer, ready to hear it, eager to hear it. . . . He will assume that anything that sounds close to the right answer is meant to be the right answer. *So*, for a student who is not sure of the answer, a mumble may be the best bet." [John Holt, *Why Children Fail* (New York: Delacorte, 1982), p. 82. Italics added.]

Comment: The word "so" in the last sentence helps locate the conclusion: "for a student who is not sure of the answer, a mumble may be the best bet." The author offers two reasons to support this conclusion: (1) "a teacher who asks a question is tuned to the right answer, ready to hear it, eager to hear it" and (2) the teacher "will assume that anything that sounds close to the right answer is meant to be the right answer."

General Area Premise Signals

General area premise signals are words or phrases that indicate the general area of the passage within which you will likely find a premise. Conclusion signals function as general area premise signals, since they not only indicate that conclusions follow but that premises likely precede. But there are other general area premise signals, and premises typically are found after them. Such expressions include the following:

since
because
for
for the reason that
this follows from
consider the following
the following reasons
inasmuch as
insofar as

Again, in reading a passage, underline such expressions in order to discover another important part of an argument's anatomy: its premises. Consider the following example:

> Capital punishment should not be permitted <u>because</u> it allows the possibility of executing an innocent person. Indeed, people have been executed who have been proved innocent later.

In this passage the word "because" indicates that what follows it are the reasons for the arguer's opposition to capital punishment. It helps locate the general area in which the premises are to be found.

Here is another example, followed by a comment.

Example: "It is worth saying something about the social position of beggars, <u>for</u> when one has consorted with them, and found that they are ordinary human beings, one cannot help being struck by the curious attitude that society takes toward them." [George Orwell, *Down and Out in Paris and London* (New York: Berkley, 1967), p. 125; underscore added]

Comment: In this passage the word "for" indicates the general area in which the premise can be found. It signals the author's reasons for asserting "It is worth saying something about the social position of beggars."

Before turning to other premise signals, I should caution you to distinguish between the argumentative and nonargumentative functions of some premise signals. For example, if we compare

> Marie ought to be hired, since she is the best qualified

with

> Marie looks better since her vacation,

we see that the first is an argument in which "since" indicates a premise but that the second is not an argument at all. In the second "since" has a temporal, not logical, function: It merely connects two events in time. "Since" and other such terms (like "because" and "for") have both nonargumentative and argumentative functions.

Specific Premise Signals

Besides expressions that indicate generally where premises or conclusions are likely to be found, there are words and phrases that help point out specific individual premises in a passage. Such expressions may be termed specific premise signals. They include

1. Devices used for numbering premises, such as "first . . . , second . . . , third . . ."; "in the first place . . . , in the second place . . . , finally . . ."

2. Devices used for indicating the accumulation of different considerations related to the same conclusion, such as "for one thing . . . for another . . ."; ". . . furthermore . . ."; ". . . moreover . . ."; ". . . in addition . . ."; ". . . also . . ."; "consider this . . . and this . . . and finally this . . ."

3. Devices used to contrast considerations related to the same conclusion, such as "however . . ."; "despite this, . . ."; "nevertheless . . ."; but . . ."

Underlining such expressions will help you focus on the premises of an argument, as illustrated in this passage:

> Prisons in the United States are an abysmal failure. <u>First</u>, they don't rehabilitate anyone. <u>Second</u>, they don't so much punish as provide free room and board. <u>Third</u>, they further alienate those with well-established antisocial tendencies. <u>Fourth</u>, they bring criminals together, thereby allowing them to swap information and refine their unseemly crafts. <u>Finally</u>, those who do time are far more likely to commit additional crimes than those who have never been in prison.

In this passage the arguer uses "first . . . second . . . third . . . finally . . ." to indicate the accumulation of reasons that support the conclusion that prisons in the United States are an abysmal failure. Here's an additional example, followed by a comment.

> **Example:** "There is nothing in the biorhythm theory that contradicts scientific knowledge. Biorhythm theory is totally consistent with the fundamental thesis of biology, which holds that all life consists of discharge and creation of energy, or, in biorhythmic terms, an alternation of positive and negative phases. <u>In addition</u>, given that we are subject to a host of smaller but nonetheless finely regulated biological rhythms, it seems reasonable that longer rhythms will also come with play." [Bernard Gittelson, *Biorhythms: A Personal Science* (New York: Basic Books, 1977), p. 146; underscore added.]
>
> **Comment:** In this passage the arguer uses "in addition" to indicate the accumulation of two premises: (1) "biorhythm theory is totally consistent with the fundamental thesis of biology" and (2) "given that we are subjects to a host of smaller but nonetheless finely regulated biological rhythms, it seems reasonable that larger rhythms will come with play." These premises support the conclusion stated in the opening sentence: "There is nothing in the biorhythm theory that contradicts scientific knowledge."

The preceding remarks suggest the following three-step strategy for argument identification:

Step 1: Underline all signal words on first reading a passage.
Step 2: Locate the conclusion.
Step 3: Locate the premises.

Arguments with No Signal Words

Many of the arguments you encounter and express contain no signal words. Take this one, for example:

> When we cheat impersonal corporations, we indirectly cheat our friends—and ourselves. Department of Commerce data show that marketplace theft raises the cost of what we buy by more than 2 percent. Doctors who collect Medicare and Medicaid money for unnecessary treatments cost the average taxpayer several hundred dollars a year. The same applies to veterans who collect education money but who do not attend school.

This passage contains four sentences but not a single word clue. Yet the assertions are related; the passage is an argument.

The passage opens with the general claim that when we cheat impersonal corporations we are really cheating our friends and ourselves. This claim is what the arguer is advancing; it's the conclusion. Why does the arguer make this claim? What reasons support it? The next three sentences in the passage cite several pieces of evidence: (1) Department of Commerce data that show that marketplace theft raises the cost of what we buy by more than 2 percent; (2) federal estimates that indicate that doctors who collect Medicare and Medicaid money for unnecessary treatments cost the average taxpayer several hundred dollars a year; and (3) veterans who collect education money but who do not attend school further inflate the taxpayer's bill. These three assertions are the argument's premises.

In arguments with no signal words, you must first ask, What is being advocated? What claims is the arguer attempting to establish as true? What is the arguer trying to convince me of or get me to do? By asking these questions, you will locate the argument's conclusion. Having done that, you must then locate the premises by asking questions like these: Why is the arguer's conclusion so? What reasons, data, or evidence does the arguer give for advancing the conclusion? In short, identifying arguments with no signal words requires close contextual analysis. Contextual analysis is not something you can develop from doing a set of exercises or two. It's a painstaking process that requires careful reading and often much reflection. But it is a skill that you can master, and when you do you will be poised for argument analysis and evaluation.

Here are some additional arguments with no signal words:

> **Example:** "Names are far more than mere identity tags. They are charged with hidden meanings and unspoken overtones that profoundly help or hinder you in your relationships and your life." [Christopher A. Anderson, *The Name Game* (New York: Simon & Schuster, 1977), p. 1.]

> **Comment:** The arguer advances the claim that "names are far more than mere identity tags." This is the conclusion. He believes this is so because names "are charged with hidden meanings and unspoken overtones that profoundly help or hinder you in your relationships and your life." This is the premise.

> **Example:** "Belief in the existence of God is as groundless as it is useless. The world will never be happy until atheism is universal." [J. O. La Metterie, *L'Homme Machine*]

Comment: What claim is the author advocating? That "the world will never be happy until atheism is universal." The second sentence, then, is the conclusion. Why does the author hold such a view? Because he thinks that "belief in the existence of God is as groundless as it is useless." The first sentence, therefore, is the premise.

Example: " 'An unhappy alternative is before you, Elizabeth. Your mother will never see you again if you do *not* marry Mr. Collins, and I will never see you again if you *do*.'" [Jane Austen, *Pride and Prejudice*]

Comment: The speaker is attempting to show Elizabeth that an unhappy alternative faces her. The alternative is unhappy because should Elizabeth not marry Mr. Collins, her mother will never see her again; if she does marry Mr. Collins, then the speaker, who happens to be her father, will never see her again. Thus the first sentence is the conclusion, the second the premise.

Quick Check on Argument Identification

Analyze the following arguments by applying the three-step strategy for argument identification: (1) underline all signal words, (2) locate the conclusion, and (3) locate the premises.

1 TV shows like "Dallas" and "Dynasty" portray marriage in a most unflattering light. First, the partners are always quarreling. Second, they are always lusting after someone they're not married to.

2 Two out of three people interviewed preferred Zest to another soap. Therefore Zest is the best soap available.

3 In the 1980s more and more people will turn to solar heating to heat their homes because the price of gas and oil will become prohibitive for most consumers and the price of installing solar panels will decline.

4 People who smoke cigarettes should be forced to pay for their own health insurance. They know smoking is bad for their health. They have no right to expect others to pay for their addiction.

5 It's no wonder that government aid to the poor fails. Poor people can't manage their money.

Comments

1. Conclusion: TV shows like . . . light.
   Premises: <u>First</u>, . . . quarreling.
            <u>Secondly</u>, . . married to.
2. Conclusion: <u>Therefore</u> Zest . . . available.
   Premise: Two out of three . . . soap.
3. Conclusion: In the 1980s . . . homes . . .
   Premises: <u>because</u> the price . . . consumers
            <u>and</u> the price . . . decline.
4. Conclusion: People who . . . insurance.
   Premises: They know . . . health.
            They have . . . addiction.

5. Conclusion: It's no wonder . . . fails.
   Premise: Poor people . . . money.

Unexpressed Premises

In argument we attempt to demonstrate the truth of an assertion. We do this by providing reasons (the premises) that lend logical support to that assertion (the conclusion). Sometimes the support offered is conclusive; other times it is not.

We have all come across, and composed, arguments whose reasons are so strong that no sensible person could or would doubt their conclusions. Take for example this simple argument, which we met earlier:

> Joan is a mother. Therefore Joan is a female.

Any person who understands and accepts the premise of this argument logically must accept the conclusion: One cannot endorse the former and reject the latter. The same applies to this simple argument:

> Jack is an officer of the National Rifle Association (NRA). So Jack must be an NRA member.

But sometimes the reasons expressed, the explicit premises given as evidence, do not offer conclusive support for the conclusion. Consider this passage, for example:

> Joan is a mother. Therefore Joan must be a member of Mothers Against Drunk Drivers (MADD).

Or

> Jack is an officer of the National Rifle Association. So Jack must be opposed to gun-control legislation.

Even if the premises of these arguments are true, the support they offer is not conclusive. In each case an additional premise is needed to entail the conclusion. In the first argument, the missing premise is "All mothers are members of MADD." In the second argument, the missing premise is "Officers of NRA are opposed to gun-control legislation." The truth of these additional premises aside, we can say that they complete the arguments. Together with the stated premises, they give conclusive support to the conclusions; for if the premises are accepted as true, they logically entail the conclusions.

When we argue we frequently leave premises unexpressed. These unexpressed premises are an important part of the structure of some arguments because they, as much as the explicit premises, are the evidence that we are using to support a conclusion. Consider for example this argument:

> Most working women don't complain of sexual harassment on the job. Therefore sexual harassment on the job must not be a widespread problem.

The stated premise is "Most working women don't complain of sexual harassment on the job." This premise does not provide conclusive support for the conclusion. In fact, nothing in the premise covers the issue of how widespread sexual harassment on the job is. The arguer must be assuming something that, together with the stated premise, is thought to entail the conclusion. The unexpressed premise apparently is "Only that which is complained about by most people is a widespread problem." The complete argument, then, can be expressed as follows:

> **Unexpressed premise:** Only that which is complained about by most people is a widespread problem.
> **Expressed premise:** Most working women don't complain of sexual harassment on the job.
> **Conclusion:** Sexual harassment on the job must not be widespread.

Here are two additional examples of arguments with unexpressed premises:

> **Argument:** Bill must be a poor student, for he spends most of his time watching television.
> **Unexpressed premise:** Any student who spends most of his time watching television must be a poor student.
> **Expressed premise:** Bill spends most of his time watching television.
> **Conclusion:** Bill must be a poor student.

> **Argument:** Few people can appreciate Jackson Pollock's painting "Convergence," for it's a work of modern art.
> **Unexpressed premise:** Few people can appreciate modern art.
> **Expressed premise:** Jackson Pollock's painting "Convergence" is a work of modern art.
> **Conclusion:** Few people can appreciate Jackson Pollock's painting "Convergence."

> **Argument:** Since Smith married largely for sexual reasons, his marriage won't last long.
> **Unexpressed premise:** Marriages entered into largely for sexual reasons don't last long.
> **Expressed premise:** Smith married largely for sexual reasons.
> **Conclusion:** Smith's marriage won't last long.

I have intentionally kept these examples simple. But filling in the missing premises of an argument is a difficult and crucial task that requires considerable skill. I will say more about this subject in a later chapter. Suffice it here to point out that unexpressed premises are part of the structure of many arguments.

Premise Support

Consider the structural features of these two arguments, which deal with censorship:

> **Argument 1:** Censorship would be acceptable if it could be easily enforced. <u>But</u> censorship cannot be easily enforced. <u>Therefore</u> censorship is not acceptable.

> **Argument 2:** Censorship would be acceptable if it could be easily enforced. <u>But</u> censorship cannot be easily enforced. The main problem with enforce-

ment is determining which works will not be censored. <u>Therefore</u> censorship is not acceptable.

The argument contained in the two examples is identical:

> **Premise:** Censorship would be acceptable if it could be easily enforced.
> **Premise:** Censorship cannot be easily enforced.
> **Conclusion:** Censorship is not acceptable.

However, argument 2 differs from argument 1 in offering some support for the second premise. The argument states that if we consider the problems of identifying which works need not be censored, there is good reason to regard censorship as unacceptable. Offering support for one of several premises is another structural feature of some arguments.

Sometimes the support offered for a premise is necessarily lengthy, especially when the argument is complex. For example, consider the same argument with more developed support, as represented by the italicized portion of the following passage:

> Censorship would be acceptable if it could be easily enforced. But censorship is not easily enforced. The main problem is determining which works will not be censored. *For example, some have said that the "classics" will and should be exempt from censorship. But what is a "classic"? Any traditional definition probably would exclude new works, since a work usually cannot be recognized as a classic until some time after its release. That means that the censor must determine which works will become classics, surely an impossible task. As a result censors will have little choice but to ban those "nonclassics" that smack of smut. If you think this is an idle fear, recall that plenty of works of art and literature that today are considered classics were once banned. Works by Chaucer, Shakespeare, Swift, and Twain are just a few. More recently William Faulkner, Ernest Hemingway, and James Joyce found their works banned.* There is no question, then, that determining which works will not be censored is a major, perhaps insurmountable, problem in enforcing censorship. Therefore censorship is not acceptable.

There is no simple way to determine how much support is needed to substantiate a premise and by implication an argument's conclusion. But surely the more controversial the conclusion, the more support it needs. Premise support is especially important in extended arguments; that is, the multiparagraph arguments that we commonly encounter in editorials, reviews, and essays and that we are called on to write. Since the following chapters deal with refining analytical and evaluative skills, they take up the challenge of determining adequate premise support. It's enough here, therefore, simply to acknowledge premise support as an integral part of the structure of many arguments.

Unexpressed Conclusions

Just as some arguments leave premises unexpressed, others leave conclusions unexpressed. Here's a simple example taken from Shakespeare's play *Julius Caesar:*

> Yond Cassius has a lean and hungry look. . . . Such men are dangerous.

In this passage the conclusion is missing. But one needn't ponder long to supply it: Cassius is a dangerous man.

Consider this argument:

Citizens can vote. But Jones isn't a citizen.

The implied conclusion of these two premises is that Jones cannot vote.

Here are two more arguments whose conclusions are unexpressed:

Argument: "Only demonstrative proof should be able to make you abandon the theory of Creation; but such a proof does not exist in nature." [Moses Maimonides, *The Guide for the Perplexed*]

Unexpressed conclusion: Nothing in Nature should be able to make you abandon the theory of Creation.

Argument: "When we regard a man as morally responsible for an act, we regard him as a legitimate object of moral praise or blame in respect of it. But it seems plain that a man cannot be a legitimate object of moral praise or blame for an act unless in willing the act he is in some important sense a 'free' agent." [C. Arthur Campbell, "Is 'Freewill' a Pseudo-Problem?," *Mind*, LX, No. 240 (1951), 447.]

Unexpressed conclusion: Free will is a precondition of moral responsibility.

Summary

An argument is a group of statements, one of which is claimed to follow from the others. The argument is attempting to establish the truth of this statement. In contrast, explanations take the truth of a statement for granted and give reasons that account for it.

Example of an argument: Marie deserves to be hired, since she is the most qualified for the job.

Example of an explanation: Marie looks better since her vacation.

Arguments contain premises and conclusions. The premises of an argument are those statements that are claimed to entail the conclusion; the conclusion is the statement that is claimed to be entailed by the premises.

Example with conclusion italicized: *Marie deserves to be hired,* since she is the most qualified for the job.

Signal words, which are terms and phrases that indicate the presence of premises and conclusions, are helpful in recognizing arguments.

Some conclusion signals: so, thus, therefore, consequently, it follows that
Some general area premise signals: since, because, for, insofar as
Some specific premise signals: first ... second ... third; for one thing ... for another; on the one hand ... on the other

A useful strategy for identifying arguments consists of these three steps:

Step 1: Underline all signal words on first reading a passage.

Step 2: Locate the conclusion.
Step 3: Locate the premises.

When faced with an argument that contains no signals, you should first ask, What is being advocated? What claim is the arguer attempting to establish as true? Answering questions like these will help you locate the argument's conclusion. Having done that, you can locate the premises by asking questions like these: Why is this conclusion so? What reasons, data, or evidence does the arguer give for advancing the conclusion?

Some arguments leave premises unexpressed.

> **Example:** Since Smith married largely for sexual reasons, his marriage won't last long.
>
> **Unexpressed premise:** Marriages entered into largely for sexual reasons don't last long.

An additional feature of the anatomy of many arguments is premise support. There is no simple way to determine how much support a premise needs, but generally the more controversial the claim the more support needed.

Finally, just as some arguments leave premises unexpressed, others leave conclusions unexpressed.

> **Example:** "Yond Cassius has a lean and hungry look. . . . Such men are dangerous."
>
> **Unexpressed conclusion:** Cassius is a dangerous man.

Applications

1 Decide which passages are arguments and which are not. If they are arguments, apply the three-step strategy for argument identification: (1) underline all signal words, if any; (2) locate the conclusion; and (3) locate the premises.

   a The game has been delayed because of rain.

   b We must maintain a strong defense; otherwise we will invite war.

   c Most teachers want better pay. It follows that most teachers are in favor of unions.

   d Anyone who criticizes and disrupts society is a threat to social stability. That's why civil disobedience should have no place in society.

   e Because students come to school to learn, they should have no say in curriculum decisions.

   f "The shad, perhaps, or any fish that runs upriver [would be ideal for sea ranching]. . . . They range out to sea, using their own energies, grow, and then come back." (John D. Isaacs, "Interview," *Omni*, August 1979, p. 122.)

   g "In bureaucratic logic, bad judgment is any decision that can lead to embarrassing questions, even if the decision was itself right. Therefore . . . no man with an eye on a career can afford to be right when he can manage to be safe." (John Ciardi, "Bureaucracy and Frank Ellis," in *Manner of Speaking* [New Brunswick, N.J.: Rutgers University Press, 1972], p. 250.)

h "An arctic mirage is caused by a temperature inversion created when the air immediately above the earth's surface is cooler than air at a higher elevation. Under these conditions, light rays are bent around the curvature of the earth. The stronger the inversion, the more bending. With a high degree of bending, the earth's surface looks like a saucer, and the landscape and ship normally out of sight below the horizon are raised into view on the saucer's rim. The effect can last for days and cover thousands of kilometers." (Barbara Ford, "Mirage," *Omni*, August 1979, p. 38.)

i "And the tragic history of human thought is simply the history of a struggle between reason and life—reason bent on rationalizing life and forcing it to submit to the inevitable, to mortality; life bent on vitalizing reason and forcing it to serve as a support for its own vital desires." (Miguel de Unamuno, *The Tragic Sense of Life* [New York: Dover, 1921], p. 63.)

j "Vitamin E is an essential part of the whole circulation mechanism of the body, since it affects our use of oxygen." (Ruth Adams and Frank Murray, *Vitamin E: Wonder Worker of the 70's* [New York: Larchmont Books, 1972], p. 17.)

2 Identify the unexpressed premises in b, c, d, and e.

3 Identify the conclusions, premises, and premise support in these arguments.

a "Nor is there anything smart about smoking. A woman who smokes is far more likely than her nonsmoking counterpart to suffer from a host of disabling conditions, any of which can interfere with her ability to perform at home or on the job. . . . Women who smoke have more spontaneous abortions, stillbirths, and premature babies than do nonsmokers, and their children's later health may be affected." (Jane E. Brody and Richard Engquist, "Women and Smoking," *Public Affairs Pamphlet 475* [New York: Public Affairs Committee, 1972], p. 2.)

b "Since the mid '50s, for example, scientists have observed the same characteristics in what they thought were different cancer cells and concluded that these traits must be common to all cancers. All cancer cells had certain nutritional needs, all could grow in soft agar cultures, all could seed new solid tumors when transplanted into experimental animals, and all contained drastically abnormal chromosomes—the 'mark cancer.'" (Michael Gold, "The Cells That Would Not Die" in "This World," *San Francisco Chronicle*, May 17, 1981, p. 9.)

c "One woman told me that brown spots, a bugaboo to older women, were twice as numerous on the left side of her face and arm due to daily use of her car. The right, or interior, side of her face and right arm showed far fewer brown spots. Since these unattractive marks seem to be promoted by exposure to the sun, either cover up or use a good sunscreen." (Virginia Castleton, "Bring Out Your Beauty," *Prevention*, September 1981, p. 108.)

d "It also appears that suicide no longer repels us. The suicide rate is climbing, especially among blacks and young people. What's more, suicide has been appearing in an increasingly favorable light in the nation's press. When Paul Cameron surveyed all articles on suicide indexed over the past

50 years in the *Reader's Guide to Periodical Literature*, he found that voluntary death, once portrayed as a brutal waste, now generally appears in a neutral light. Some recent articles even present suicide as a good thing to do and are written in a manner that might encourage the reader to take his own life under certain circumstances. Last year, a majority of Americans under 30 told Gallup pollsters that incurable disease or continual pain confer on a person the moral right to end his life." (Elizabeth Hall with Paul Cameron, "Our Failing Reverence for Life," *Psychology Today*, April 1976, p. 108.)

e "If there were clear boundaries between the animals and the people, each side having its own territory, friction would be minimized. But that is not the case. Although some of the 5,000 square miles of ecosystem that lie outside the park are protected areas—including neighboring Ngorongoro Conservation Unit and Masai Mara Game Reserve in Kenya—sizable sectors have no conservation status. Consequently, the migratory herds spend a good part of their annual cycle competing with humans for food." (Norman Myers, "The Canning of Africa," *Science Digest*, August 1981, p. 74.)

4 The following statements represent conclusions of arguments. For each conclusion state a premise, one piece of evidence that supports it, and the missing premise. For example:

> Conclusion: Drunk drivers should be severely punished.
> Premise: Drunk drivers threaten the public safety.
> Support: Statistics indicate that the automobile accidents that result in deaths involve at least one drunk driver.
> Missing
> premise: Whoever threatens the public safety should be severely punished.

a Conclusion: Children should (should not) be given allowances.
b Conclusion: The best medical care available should be provided all Americans regardless of their ability to pay for it.
c Conclusion: Individuals should (should not) be allowed to grow marijuana for personal use.
d Conclusion: Unmarried female adolescents should (should not) be allowed to obtain birth control devices without being reported to their parents.

5 Examine the premises, unexpressed premises, and support material you constructed for the preceding conclusions. Can you account for any of them in terms of cultural conditioning, reliance on authority, hasty moral judgment, black-and-white thinking, labels, or frame of reference? For example, in the sample, the missing premise—"Whoever threatens the public safety should be severely punished"—stems from several cultural assumptions. One is that any threat to the general welfare is undesirable. A second is that as soon as any aspect of a person's conduct affects prejudicially the interests of others, society has jurisdiction over it. A probable third is that physical punishment deters crime.

Casting Arguments

5

In the last chapter you learned that an argument consists of one or more premises and a conclusion and that many arguments also contain support for their premises as well as unexpressed premises or conclusions. Before you can critically examine an argument, you must be able to identify its structure: You must pick out the premises and conclusion, see what support is offered for the premises, and determine whether there are any missing premises or conclusions. If the argument is very simple, identification presents little problem, and you may proceed with your critical analysis. But when the argument is a long one (as in an editorial or essay), then you need some method of portraying its structure before you can criticize it.

This chapter teaches you how to cast arguments; that is, how to portray their structure. It gives you a simple three-step procedure for cutting through the verbiage in a passage, detecting the argument, and diagramming it. Casting is a useful skill for several reasons.

First, it helps you zero in on arguments. In longer passages it's not always easy to spot arguments and follow the author's line of thought. Casting reduces the chances that you'll be overwhelmed by a piece of writing or a speech.

Second, casting lets you look beyond the asides, the fluff, and the other rhetorical devices that writers and speakers often use in arguing. Such flourishes, though sometimes enlivening, can distract (indeed, sometimes they are intended to). You must be able to penetrate these rhetorical colorings to reach the arguments they camouflage. Casting helps you do this.

Third, evaluating longer arguments can become unwieldly, for you may have to reproduce or refer to them continuously. Casting, as you will see, greatly reduces if not eliminates this tedious task.

One final and important word about casting before we begin. You will soon discover that portraying an argument's structure demands careful judgment. But when any two people are casting an argument, they don't always agree. You might consider a statement to be merely a single assertion, I might see two assertions in it; you might consider an example integral to an argument, I might not. Except for the very simplest arguments, there is almost always room for alternative castings. Don't be unduly concerned or confused by this. Keep in mind that casting is a means to an end, not an end in itself. You are learning to cast an argument so that by better understanding it, by following its line of thought, you are able to assess it critically. Ultimately casting allows you to offer substantive criticism of an argument, not trivial, irrelevant, or unfair criticism.

Argument Organization: Series and Chain

Before learning to cast, it's helpful to know something about the organization of arguments. Basically arguments present one or both of two structures: (1) the series structure and (2) the chain structure. In a series structure, the argument offers a series of independent reasons, each of which is given in support of the conclusion. Consider, for example, the following passage written in opposition to the legalization of voluntary euthanasia, which as you probably know refers to the practice of allowing terminally ill patients to elect to die.

> Our traditional religious and cultural opposition to euthanasia is a good reason for not liberalizing euthanasia laws. Also, permitting a patient to make a death decision would greatly add to the person's suffering and anguish. Additionally, once a death decision has been carried out, there is no chance of correcting a mistaken diagnosis. Therefore voluntary euthanasia should not be legalized.

This passage presents a series of three reasons in support of the view that voluntary euthanasia should not be legalized. Although these reasons are related to the conclusion, they are not dependent on one another. Any of them can be deleted without undermining the others, although the argument itself probably would be weakened. In short, each is a separate reason for opposing the legalization of voluntary euthanasia. In presenting independent reasons such as these, arguers are not concerned with tight linkage between them, since one reason need not logically entail any of the others.

Arguers use the chain structure when they are making a number of interdependent points. The following argument is of this kind:

> Voluntary decisions about death by definition presuppose freedom of choice. But freedom of choice entails the absence of freedom-limiting constraints. Such constraints almost always are present in cases of the terminally ill. Therefore terminally ill patients cannot make a voluntary decision about death.

The assertions in this passage are interdependent. No one of the points by itself supports the conclusion that the terminally ill should not make a voluntary death decision. Rather each assertion is linked in a chain of assertions that constitute the argument.

With these preliminary remarks behind us, let's develop a method of casting arguments that among other things portrays these organizational patterns.

Quick Check on Argument Organization

Identify the organizational structure (series or chain) of the following arguments:

1 "Why are youngsters rediscovering booze? One reason is pressure from other kids to be one of the gang. Another is the ever-present urge to act grown up. . . . Perhaps the main reason is that parents don't seem to mind. . . ." (Carl T. Rowan, "Teenagers and Booze," in *Just Between Us Blacks* [New York: Random House, 1974], pp. 95–96.)
2 "What, after all, is the foundation of the nurse's obligation to follow the physician's orders? Presumably, the nurse's obligation to follow the physician's order is grounded on the nurse's obligation to act in the medical interest of the patient. The point is that the nurse has an obligation to follow physician's orders because, ordinarily, patient welfare (interest) thereby is ensured. Thus when a nurse's obligation to follow a physician's order comes into *direct* conflict with the nurse's obligation to act in the medical interest of the patient, it would seem to follow that the patient's interests should always take precedence." (E. Joy Kroeger Mappes, "Ethical Dilemmas for Nurses: Physicians' Orders versus Patients' Rights," in T. A. Mappes and J. S. Zembatty [eds.], *Biomedical Ethics* [New York: McGraw-Hill, 1981], p. 100.)
3 Getting unbiased information about troublesome students may be impossible. Public officials, who owe us detailed and accurate reports, often give in to their fear of incessant questioning and potential lawsuits. They may become experts at covering, rationalizing, minimizing, and denying what is going on. Many clinicians are afraid of losing their jobs, such as they are. Teachers may seek relief from difficult children no matter what the cost. Parents seem to see the whole scene from the sole viewpoint of their particular child. . . .

Comments

1. Series
2. Chain
3. Series

A Casting Method

Professor of philosophy Michael S. Scriven has formulated a lucid and concise method of casting arguments that is especially useful for our purposes.[1] It consists of three steps:

[1]Michael S. Scriven, *Reasoning* (New York: McGraw-Hill, 1976).

1. Putting brackets at the beginning and end of each assertion
2. Numbering assertions consecutively in the margin or above the line of type
3. Setting out the relationships between the relevant assertions in a tree diagram to be read down the page

To see how this method works, we will reconsider the two arguments about euthanasia just presented. Let's try casting the first, which uses a series structure.

Steps 1 & 2: [Our traditional religious ^{1}and cultural opposition to euthanasia is a good reason for not liberalizing euthanasia laws.] Also [permitting a patient^{2}to make a death decision would greatly add to the person's suffering and anguish.] Additionally, [once a death decision^{3}is carried out, there is no chance of correcting a mistaken diagnosis.] Therefore [voluntary euthanasia^{4}should not be legalized.]

Step 3:

The tree diagram shows (a) the number of assertions in the argument, (b) the order of their appearance, and (c) which are the premises and which the conclusion. It also indicates that each of the premises is an independent reason offered in support of the conclusion.

Now let's apply the procedure to the second argument, which uses a chain structure.

Steps 1 & 2: [Voluntary decisions^{1}about death by definition presuppose freedom of choice.] But [freedom of choice entails the^{2}absence of freedom-limiting constraints.] [Such constraints almost always are present in cases^{3}of the terminally ill.] Therefore [terminally ill patients^{4}cannot make a voluntary decision about death.]

Step 3:

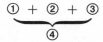

Again the diagram shows the number of assertions in the argument, their order of appearance, and which are the premises and which the conclusion. By means of a plus sign and brace, it also shows that the premises are interdependent. For a "balance of considerations" argument, where, say, assertions 1, 2, and 3 support the conclusion, assertion 4, but some assertion 5 does not, a minus sign can be used.

Here are some additional examples of casting arguments that contain the series or chain structure.

Example: Capital punishment deters crime. It also ensures that the killer will never strike again. Reasons enough, then, to legalize capital punishment.

Comment: Each of the two reasons is an independent point asserted in favor of the legalization of capital punishment.

The argument can be cast as follows:

Steps 1 & 2: [Capital punishment deters crime.]¹ [It <u>also</u> ensures that the killer² will never strike again.] Reasons enough, <u>then</u>, to [legalize³ capital punishment.]

Step 3:

Example: Capital punishment does ensure that a killer can never strike again. But it consists of killing human beings, and killing human beings should never be allowed. Therefore capital punishment should not be permitted.

Comment: In this argument two interdependent points are offered in support of the conclusion that capital punishment should not be permitted. These points are thought to be convincing despite the fact that capital punishment does ensure that a killer can never strike again (first assertion), which points to an opposite conclusion. The argument can be cast as follows:

Steps 1 & 2: [Capital punishment does¹ ensure that a killer can never strike again.] <u>But</u> [it consists² of killing human beings] <u>and</u> [killing human beings³ should never be allowed.] <u>Therefore</u> [capital punishment should not be permitted.]⁴

Step 3:

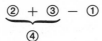

Example: A college education increases your earning potential. In addition, it makes you aware of interests you didn't know you had. Most important, it teaches one the inherent value of knowledge. It is true, of course, that a college education is very expensive. Nevertheless, a college education is of inestimable worth.

Comment: This argument presents a series of reasons, each of which taken independently offers support for the conclusion that a college education is worthwhile. At the same time, the arguer concedes a fact that points away from this conclusion: "A college education is very expensive." Notice that "nevertheless," although appearing in the conclusion, is being used to contrast this concession. The argument can be cast as follows:

Steps 1 & 2: [A college education¹ increases your earning potential.] <u>In addition</u>, [it makes you aware² of interests you didn't know you had.] <u>Most important</u>, [it teaches³ you the inherent value of knowledge.] [It is true, of course, that a college⁴ education is very expensive.] <u>Nevertheless</u>, [a college education⁵ is of inestimable worth.]

Step 3:

Example: A college education makes you aware of interests you didn't know you had. This helps you choose a satisfying job. Job satisfaction is itself your best assurance of personal well-being. Certainly personal well-being is a goal worth pursuing. Therefore a college education is a worthy goal.

Comment: The points of this argument are arranged in a chain. No one of them taken independently supports the conclusion. Only when they are taken together, in their logical sequence, do they support the claim that a college education is valuable. The argument can be cast as follows:

Steps 1 & 2: [A college education makes you aware of interests you didn't know you had.]¹ [This helps you choose a satisfying job.]² [Job satisfaction is itself your best assurance of personal well-being.]³ [Certainly personal well-being is a goal worth pursuing.]⁴ Therefore [a college education is a worthy goal.]⁵

Step 3: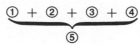

   In each of the preceding arguments the conclusion happened to appear at the end of the passage. Just as often, however, a conclusion can appear at the beginning of a passage:

   Capital punishment should not be permitted <u>because</u> it in fact consists of killing human beings, <u>and</u> killing human beings should never be permitted by society.

Bracketing and numbering this version of the argument, we get

   [Capital punishment should not be permitted]¹ <u>because</u> [it in fact consists of killing human beings,]² <u>and</u> [killing human beings should never be permitted by society.]³

The tree diagram for this argument would be

$$\underbrace{② \ + \ ③}_{①}$$

   Of course, conclusions also can come sandwiched between premises, as in the following version of the same argument:

   <u>Because</u> killing human beings should never be permitted by society, capital punishment should not be permitted; <u>for</u> it in fact consists of killing human beings.

Bracketing and numbering this version of the argument, we get:

   <u>Because</u> [killing human beings should never be permitted by society,]¹ [capital

punishment should not be permitted;] _for_ [it in fact consists of killing human beings.]

Diagrammed:

So far we have cast arguments containing only premises and conclusions. But, as you know, some arguments also contain support for premises as well as unexpressed premises and conclusions. You must learn how to cast these additional structural features.

Quick Check on Casting

Cast the following arguments.

1 "This phenomenon [of the mobile employee seeking fulfillment] reflects a sudden change in societal and personal values. It also threatens industrial reliance on trade secrets for the protection of certain forms of intellectual property. ... The formulation of management responses ... is one which must be undertaken." (Michael S. Baram, "Trade Secrets: What Price Loyalty?" _Harvard Business Review_, November–December 1968.)

2 "The diet works because it specifically mobilizes fat. [It] also stimulates the release of ketones and fat mobilizers. [It] causes a disproportionately greater loss of fat. It helps eliminate excess water. It stabilizes blood sugar. It lowers insulin levels and cortisol levels. And it delivers a metabolic advantage." (Robert C. Atkins and Shirley Linde, _Dr. Atkins' Super-Energy Diet_ [New York: Bantam, 1977], p. 130.)

3 "... the development of a human being from conception through birth into childhood is continuous. [Then] it is said that to draw a line, to choose a point in this development and say 'before this point the thing is not a person, after this point it is a person' is to make an arbitrary choice. [It is further said that this is] a choice for which in the nature of things no good reason can be given. It is concluded that the fetus is ... a person from the moment of conception. ..." (Judith Jarvis Thomson, "A Defense of Abortion," _Philosophy and Public Affairs_, 1:1 [Fall 1971].)

4 "'You have been at your club all day. ... A gentleman goes forth on a showery and miry day. He returns immaculate in the evening with the gloss still on his hat and boots. ... He is not a man with intimate friends.'" (Sherlock Holmes to Dr. Watson in Arthur Conan Doyle, _The Hound of the Baskervilles._)

Comments

1. [This phenomenon of the mobile employee seeking fulfillment reflects a sudden change in societal and personal values.] [It _also_ threatens industrial reliance on trade

secrets[2] for the protection of certain forms of intellectual property.] [The formulation of management[3] responses . . . is one which must be undertaken."]

2. ["The diet works[1]] <u>because</u> [it specifically mobilizes[2] fat.] [It <u>also</u> stimulates the release[3] of ketones and fat mobilizers.] [It causes a disproportionately greater[4] loss of fat.] [It helps eliminate[5] excess water.] [It stabilizes[6] blood sugar.] [It lowers insulin[7] levels and cortisol levels.] [And it delivers a metabolic[8] advantage."]

3. [". . . the development of a human being[1] from conception through birth into childhood is continuous.] Then [it is said to draw a line, to choose a point in this development and say[2] 'before this point the thing is not a person, after this point it is a person' is to make an arbitrary choice.] It is <u>further</u> said that [this is a choice[3] for which in the nature of things no good reason can be given.] <u>It is concluded that</u> [the fetus is .[4]. a person from the moment of conception.]

$$\underbrace{① + ② + ③}_{④}$$

4. ["'You have been at[1] your club all day. . . .] [A gentleman goes[2] forth on a showery and miry day.] [He returns immaculate in the evening[3] with the gloss still on his hat and his boots.] . . . [He is not a man[4] with intimate friends. . . .'"]

$$\underbrace{② + ③ + ④}_{①}$$

Casting Support Premises

Let's reconsider two arguments we discussed in Chapter 4:

Argument 1: Censorship would be acceptable if it could be easily enforced. <u>But</u> censorship cannot be easily enforced. <u>Therefore</u> censorship is not acceptable.

Argument 2: Censorship would be acceptable if it could be easily enforced. <u>But</u> censorship cannot be easily enforced. The main problem with enforcement is determining which works will not be censored. <u>Therefore</u> censorship is not acceptable.

Following the three-step procedure, we can cast argument 1 as follows:

Steps 1 & 2: [Censorship would be acceptable^1 if it could be easily enforced.] <u>But</u> [censorship cannot be^2 easily enforced.] <u>Therefore</u> [censorship is^3 not acceptable.]

Step 3:
$$\underbrace{① + ②}_{③}$$

    Argument 2 differs from argument 1 in providing support for its second premise. The assertion "The main problem with enforcement is determining which works will not be censored" presumably supports the premise "But censorship cannot be easily enforced." In casting this argument, then, you must show the proper relationship between these two assertions. You must portray the structure of this argument in a way that makes it clear that one assertion is supporting another. This may be done in the following way:

Steps 1 & 2: [Censorship would be acceptable^1 if it could be easily enforced.] <u>But</u> [censorship cannot be^2 easily enforced.] [The main problem with enforcement is determining^3 which works will not be censored.] <u>Therefore</u> [censorship^4 is not acceptable.]

Step 3:

The solid line between 3 and 2 means that assertion 3 implies assertion 2. The arguer believes that 2 can be inferred from assertion 3.

    Suppose that the same argument contained additional support material, as in the following passage:

Argument 3: [Censorship would be acceptable^1 if it could be easily enforced.] <u>But</u> [censorship is^2 not easily enforced.] [The main problem is determining^3 which work will not be censored.] [<u>Another</u> problem concerns^4 who will do the censoring.] [<u>Still another</u> problem^5 pertains to the standards that will be used.] <u>Therefore</u> [censorship is^6 not acceptable.]

    In this passage assertions 3, 4, and 5 are offered as support for assertion 2. The arguer believes that assertion 2 can be inferred from assertions 3, 4, and 5. Therefore the argument can be diagrammed as follows:

The diagram indicates that assertions 3, 4, and 5 are independent reasons offered in support of assertion 2 and that assertions 1 and 2 entail assertion 6, the conclusion.

It should be evident from these examples that in supporting an individual premise, the arguer is actually presenting an argument. Such arguments can be termed "mini-arguments" as opposed to the main argument of a passage.

The mini-argument in argument 2 has as its premise "The main problem with enforcement is determining which works will not be censored." The conclusion of this mini-argument is "Censorship cannot be easily enforced."

In argument 3 the mini-argument has three premises: "The main problem is determining which works will not be censored"; "Another problem concerns who will do the censoring"; and "Still another problem pertains to the standards that will be used." The conclusion of this mini-argument is "Censorship cannot be easily enforced."

In relation to the main argument, then, assertion 2 functions as a premise in both arguments, for it supports the conclusion of each. In relation to the mini-arguments, however, assertion 2 is a conclusion, for it itself is supported by a single premise in argument 2 and three premises in argument 3. The tree diagrams provide a visual representation of these relationships. For argument 2 the diagram indicates a main argument containing two main premises and one mini-argument containing one mini-premise:

$$
\underbrace{① \ + \ ②}_{④} \quad \overset{\textstyle ③}{\textstyle |} \ .
$$

And for argument 3, the diagram indicates a main argument containing two main premises and one mini-argument containing three mini-premises:

A complex argument may have several mini-arguments embedded in the main argument. A good deal of getting the point of a passage, then, depends on sorting out what roles the assertions are playing in relation to other assertions in the passage. Following the three-step casting procedure helps you do this.

Here are some further examples of arguments with premise support (mini-arguments).

Example: [Most marriages between people under twenty end in divorce.]¹ [This should be enough to²discourage teenage marriages.] <u>But</u> there is <u>also</u> the fact that [marrying young³reduces one's life options.] [Married teenagers must forget⁴about adventure and play.] [They can't afford to spend⁵time "finding themselves."] [They must⁶concentrate almost exclusively on earning a living.] <u>What's more,</u> [early marriages can make parents of young⁷people, who can hardly take care of themselves, let alone an infant.]

Comment: This passage offers three assertions—1, 3, and 7—in opposition to teenage marriages (assertion 2). Assertions 1, 3, and 7 thus function as main premises in the main argument. In addition, assertion 3 is further supported by reasons given in assertions 4, 5, and 6. Taken together, assertions 3, 4, 5, and 6 form a mini-argument that can be diagrammed as follows:

The entire argument in turn can be diagrammed as follows:

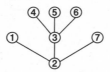

Example: ["... suicide no longer¹repels us.] [The suicide rate is climbing,² especially among blacks and young people.] <u>What's more,</u> [suicide has³been appearing in an increasingly favorable light in the nation's press.] [When Paul Cameron surveyed⁴all articles on suicide indexed over the past 50 years in the *Reader's Guide to Periodical Literature,* he found that voluntary deaths . . . generally appear in a neutral light.] [Some recent articles even present suicide as⁵a good thing to do. . . .] [They are written in a manner that might⁶encourage the reader to take his own life under certain circumstances. . . ."] [Elizabeth Hall with Paul Cameron, "Our Failing Reverence for Life," *Psychology Today,* April 1976, p. 108.]

Comment: This passage offers assertions 2 and 3 as premises for the conclusion that suicide no longer repels us (assertion 1). In support of assertion 3, the arguer offers assertions 4 and 5, which is supported by 6. Therefore assertions 3, 4, 5, and 6 make up a mini-argument within the main argument. These mini-arguments can be diagrammed as follows:

The entire argument can be diagrammed this way:

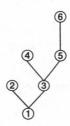

Example: [" ... more and more silent evidence is being turned into loudly damning testimony.] [Over the past ten years, no area has developed faster than the examination of blood stains.] [Before we used to be satisfied with identifying a blood sample as type A, B, AB or O.] [Now we have three or more different antigen and enzyme systems.] ... [The probability that any two people will share the same assessment of their blood variables is .1% or less.] ... [The size, shape, and distribution of blood spatters tells much about the location and position of a person involved in a crime.] ... [The use of bite-mark evidence has skyrocketed.] ... [Even anthropology is making a courtroom contribution. . . .] [Some anthropologists can identify barefoot prints as well as match a shoe to its wearer. . . ."] [Bennett H. Beach, "Mr. Wizard Comes to Court," *Time,* March 1, 1982, p. 90.]

Comment: In this passage assertions 2, 7, and 8 are the premises of the main argument in support of the claim that "more and more silent evidence is being turned into loudly damning testimony" (assertion 1). Taken together, the chain of assertions 3, 4, and 5 provides one piece of evidence for assertion 2. So one mini-argument in the passage consists of the relationship between assertions 3, 4, 5, and 2. This relationship can be diagrammed as follows:

$$\underbrace{③ \; + \; ④ \; + \; ⑤}_{②}$$

Assertion 6 provides additional support for assertion 2, thus yielding a second mini-argument:

Assertion 9 supports assertion 8, yielding a third mini-argument:

We can represent the relationships among these various assertions in the argument by means of the following diagram:

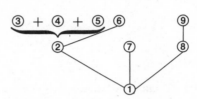

Quick Check on Casting Premise Support

Cast the following arguments, all of which contain premise support.

1 "A recent five year study at a major electronics company indicates that getting fired may have a lot to do with overreaching. Among 2,000 technical, sales and managerial employees who were followed during their first five years with the company, the 173 people who eventually were fired started out with much higher expectations of advancement than either the 200 people who left voluntarily or the people who remained. On a questionnaire given during their first week on the job, more than half the people who were fired within the first two years ranked themselves among the top 5 percent of typical people in their job category. Only 38 percent of those who stayed with the company ranked themselves that highly." (Berkeley Rice, "Aspiring to a Fall," *Psychology Today*, March 1980, p. 25.)

2 We must stop treating juveniles differently from adult offenders. Justice demands it. Justice implies that people should be treated equally. Besides, the social effects of pampering juvenile offenders has sinister social consequences. The record shows that juveniles who have been treated leniently for offenses have subsequently committed serious crimes.

3 It's high time we seriously investigated the impact of television on children. Children spend much of their free time watching television. The average American child by age eighteen has watched thousands of hours of televi-

sion. The same average viewer has watched thousands of hours of inane situation comedy, fantasy, soap operas, and acts of violence.

4. "... the tax cuts will result in higher deficits than would have occurred had the Democrats stayed in office. The result will be blistering inflation. The federal deficits for the last half of the 1970s totalled $310 billion. Without the tax cuts, they would have totalled at least twice that amount for the first half of the 1980s. With the cuts, they will probably total $800 billion for that period. ..." (John Pugsley, "The Deficits Deepen: An Economic Program Disintegrates," *Common Sense*, December 13, 1981, p. 4.)

5 "Such crises [of employees departing with a firm's trade secrets] are not surprising. ... The highly educated employees of R&D [research and development] organizations place primary emphasis on their own development, interests and satisfaction. Graduates of major scientific and technological institutions readily admit that they accept their first jobs primarily for money. [They also want] the early and brief experience they feel is a prerequisite for seeking more satisfying futures with smaller companies. ... Employee mobility and high personnel turnover rates are also due to the placement of new large federal contracts and the termination of others. One need only look to the Sunday newspaper employment advertisements for evidence as to the manner in which such programs are used to attract highly educated R&D personnel." (Michael S. Baram, "Trade Secrets: What Price Loyalty?" *Harvard Business Review*, November–December 1968.)

Comments

1. ["A recent five year study at a major electronics company indicates that getting fired may have a lot to do with overreaching.] [Among 2,000 technical, sales and managerial employees who were followed during their first five years with the company, the 173 people who eventually were fired started out with much higher expectations of advancement than either the 200 people who left voluntarily or the people who remained.] [On a questionnaire given during their first week on the job, more than half the people who were fired within the first two years ranked themselves among the top 5 percent of typical people in their job category.] [Only 38 percent of those who stayed with the company ranked themselves that highly.]

Comments: I'm inclined to see 3 and 4 as interdependent reasons for 2, since neither is statistically meaningful without the other. It's unimportant for later evaluation of the argument that you may view them as independent reasons. But we should agree that 3 and 4 are supporting 2.

2. [We must stop treating juveniles^1 differently from adult offenders.] [Justice demands^2 it.] [Justice implies that people^3 should be treated equally.] <u>Besides</u>, [the social effects of pampering juvenile offenders^4 has sinister social consequences.] [The record shows that juveniles who have^5 been treated leniently for offenses have subsequently committed serious crimes.]

3. [It's high time we seriously investigated the impact^1 of television on children.] [Children spend most of their free time^2 watching television.] [The average American child by age eighteen^3 has watched thousands of hours of television.] [The same average viewer has watched thousands of hours of inane situation comedy,^{4} fantasy, soap operas, and acts of violence.]

4. ["... the tax cuts will result in higher deficits^1 than would have occurred had the Democrats stayed in office.] [<u>The result</u> will^2 be blistering inflation.] [The federal deficits for^3 the last half of the 1970s totalled \$310 billion.] [Without the tax cuts,^{4} they would have totalled at least twice that amount for the first half of the 1980s.] [With the cuts, they will probably^5 total \$800 billion for that period. ...."]

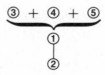

5. ["Such crises [of employees departing with a^1 firm's trade secrets] are not surprising. ...] [The highly educated employees of R&D [research and development] organizations place primary^2 emphasis on their own development, interests and satisfaction.]

[Graduates of major scientific and technological institutions readily admit[3] that they accept their first jobs primarily for money.] [They <u>also</u> want the early and brief experience they feel is a prerequisite for seeking[4] more satisfying futures with smaller companies. . . .] [Employee mobility and high personnel turnover rates are <u>also</u> due to the placement of new[5] large federal contracts and the termination of others.] [One need only look to the Sunday newspaper employment advertisements for evidence as[6] to the manner in which such programs are used to attract highly educated R&D personnel."]

Casting Unexpressed Premises and Conclusions

As you learned in the preceding chapter, unexpressed premises and conclusions are a structural feature of many arguments. Consider this simple example:

<u>Since</u> [Smith is a police officer,][1] [he's probably in favor of gun-control[2] legislation.]

The stated premise, assertion 1, does not provide conclusive support for the conclusion, assertion 2. The arguer is assuming something that together with the stated premise entails the conclusion. The missing premise is "Most police officers are in favor of gun-control legislation." Because this unexpressed premise is needed to complete the argument, it is an essential part of the argument's structure and therefore must be cast.

A convenient way to show an unexpressed premise is by a letter: a, b, c, and so forth. The preceding argument, then, can be cast as follows:

$$\frac{① + ⓐ}{②}$$

Here's another simple argument:

[Phyllis must be a college graduate,][1] <u>for</u> [she's a member of the American[2] Association of University Women (AAUW).]

This argument has a single stated premise, assertion 2, and a conclusion, assertion 1. But the inference to assertion 1 from assertion 2 is not obvious because nothing in the premise covers the conditions for membership in the AAUW. The argument assumes that only female college graduates can be members of the AAUW. Once this premise is flushed out, the conclusion becomes perfectly obvious, and the argument is complete. We can now diagram the argument as follows:

$$\frac{② + ⓐ}{①}$$

Filling in missing premises correctly is perhaps the most challenging aspect of argument analysis. Since we consider this subject in the next chapter we needn't say anything more about it here.

Unexpressed conclusions can be handled like unexpressed premises. For example recall this argument from *Julius Caesar:*

["Yond Cassius has a lean and hungry look. . . .]¹ [Such men are dangerous."]²

Although missing, the conclusion of this argument is obvious: Cassius is a dangerous man. It would appear in the diagram as follows:

$$\frac{① + ②}{ⓐ}$$

Recall this argument:

[Citizens can vote.]¹ *But* [Jones isn't a citizen.]²

The expressed premises entail the unexpressed conclusion: Jones can't vote. The argument therefore yields this diagram:

$$\frac{① + ②}{ⓐ}$$

Of course, the arguments you come across and compose often are far richer in rhetorical devices than the specimens we've been dealing with. As a result they can raise problems in casting. You need guidelines to handle these kinds of arguments.

Quick Check on Casting Unexpressed Premises and Conclusions

Fill in the missing premises or conclusions of the following simple arguments, then cast them.

1 Cows are ruminants because they chew the cud.
2 Liberty means responsibility. That is why most men dread it.
3 Whatever isn't an evil must be a good. Wealth isn't an evil.
4 The American government leaves business on its own. A government that lets business alone is said to be a laissez-faire government.
5 There are no strong philosophical bents on the Supreme Court. Each of the justices is a pragmatist who takes each case as it comes. The philosophical inconsistencies in their rulings is proof of this. Besides, most of the justices themselves have said that they must judge each case on its own merits.

Comments

1. Missing premise: Whatever animal chews[a] the cud is a ruminant.

   [Cows are ruminants][1] because [they chew[2] the cud.]

2. Missing premise: Most men dread[a] responsibility.

   [Liberty means[1] responsibility.] That is why [most men dread[2] it.]

3. Missing conclusion: Wealth must[a] be a good.

   [Whatever isn't evil[1] must be a good.] [Wealth isn't an[2] evil.]

$$\frac{① + ②}{ⓐ}$$

4. Missing conclusion: The American government is[a] a laissez-faire government.

   [The American government leaves[1] business on its own.] [A government that lets business alone is said[2] to be a laissez-faire government.]

5. Missing premise: Being a pragmatist is incompatible with having strong philosophical bents.

[There are no strong philosophical bents on the Supreme Court.] [Each of the justices is a pragmatist who takes each case as it comes.] [The philosophical inconsistencies in their rulings are proof of this.] Besides, [most of the justices themselves have said that they must judge each case on its own merits.]

$$
\begin{array}{c}
\text{③ ④} \\
\text{② + ⓐ} \\
\hline
\text{①}
\end{array}
$$

Guidelines for Casting Rhetorical Features

We use a variety of rhetorical devices in argument, including examples, asides, background information, and repetition. The following guidelines tell you how to handle these features, which are common to longer arguments.

1. **Cast each assertion separately.** Sometimes a sentence makes a single assertion: "All cancer cells have nutritional needs." But a single sentence may contain several assertions: "All cancer cells have certain nutritional needs, all can grow in soft agar cultures, all can seed new solid tumors when transplanted into experimental animals, and all contain drastically abnormal chromosomes." This sentence contains four separate assertions. If it were part of the following argument, then, it would be portrayed as follows:

[All cancer cells have certain nutritional needs,] [all grow in soft agar cultures.] [all can seed new solid tumors when transplanted into experimental animals,] and [all contain drastically abnormal chromosomes.] It follows that [these traits must be common to all cancers.]

2. **Don't cast repetitions of the same assertion.** When we argue we often repeat assertions for emphasis or clarity. In fact it's not uncommon in long arguments for a main premise or a conclusion to be repeated several times. Notice for example how the arguer repeats the conclusion in this argument:

> Capital punishment is a legitimate punishment. For one thing it deters crime. For another it ensures that a killer can never strike again. Therefore the death penalty is a permissible form of punishment.

In this passage the conclusion is stated in the first sentence, and repeated in other words in the last. When premises or conclusions are repeated, they needn't be numbered or portrayed in the argument's structure. The preceding argument, then, can be cast as follows:

[Capital punishment¹ is a legitimate punishment.] <u>For one thing</u> [it deters crime.]² <u>For another</u> [it ensures that the³ killer can never strike again.] Therefore the death penalty is a permissible form of punishment.

3. **Don't cast asides.**   Often in written and especially in oral discourse, arguers introduce matters that are not relevant to the issue under discussion. Or they may change the subject or interrupt the line of argument. Consider for example this argument:

> Women still don't get a fair shake in the work place. For one thing they're not paid the same as their male counterparts. This, by the way, is also true of black males in relation to white males. For another thing women are not as often promoted to upper-level executive positions as men are, which is really unfortunate because women have qualities desperately needed by American business. But beyond this women continue to be plagued by stereotyping.

The first sentence of this argument is the conclusion. The second, fourth, and fifth are premises. The third sentence and the clause beginning with "which" in the fourth sentence are irrelevant. The argument, then, can be cast as follows:

[Women still don't get a fair¹ shake in the work place.] <u>For one thing</u> [they're not paid the same² as their male counterparts.] This, by the way, is also true of black males in relation to white males. <u>For another thing</u> [women are not as often³ promoted to upper level executive positions as men are,] which is really unfortunate because women have qualities desperately needed by American business. <u>But beyond this</u> [women continue⁴ to be plagued by stereotyping.]

   4. **Don't cast background information.**   In longer arguments arguers sometimes indicate how they became interested in an issue or controversy. They tell the audience what prompted them to address the topic, what the central concerns are, or who the participants are. While such information is useful in placing the argument in context, it is not part of the argument and therefore should not be cast. For example, consider the following argument, which deals with abortions:

> The most fundamental question involved in the long history of thought on abortion is: When is the unborn a human? To phrase the question that way is to put in comprehensive humanistic terms what theologians either dealt with as an explicitly theological question under the heading of "ensoulment" or dealt with implicitly in their treatment of abortion. The answer to the question of when the unborn is a human is simple: at conception. The reason is that at conception the new being receives the genetic code.

The first two sentences of this passage provide background information. While informative, they are not a part of the argument, which is to be found in the last two sentences. Accordingly the argument may be cast as follows:

. . . . [The answer to the question¹ of when the unborn is a human is simple: at conception.] The reason is that [at conception the new being receives² the genetic code.]

Here's another example, followed by a comment:

Example: "In recent years government policies intended to ensure fairer employment and educational opportunities for women and minority groups have engendered alarm. Although I shall in this paper argue in support of enlightened versions of these policies, I nevertheless think there is much to be said for the opposition arguments. In general I would argue that the world of business is now overregulated by federal government, and I therefore hesitate to support an extension of the regulative arm of government into the arena of hiring and firing. Moreover, policies that would eventuate in reverse discrimination in present North American society have a heavy presumption against them, for both justice-regarding and utilitarian reasons. . . . [Tom Beauchamp, "The Justification of Reverse Discrimination," in William T. Blackstone and Robert Heslep (eds.), *Social Justice and Preferential Treatment* (Athens, Ga.: University of Georgia Press, 1977).]

Comment: The first two sentences of this paragraph provide background information. The author's argument is contained in the third and fourth sentences, in which he provides support for his reluctance to extend further the "regulative arm of government into the arena of hiring and firing." Thus the argument can be cast as follows:

. . . . In general I would argue that [the world of business is now overregulated by federal government,] and [I therefore hesitate to support an extension of the regulative arm of government into the arena of hiring and firing.] Moreover, [policies that would eventuate in reverse discrimination in present North American society have a heavy presumption against them, for both justice-regarding] and [utilitarian reasons.]

5. Do not cast examples that merely illustrate or clarify a point. We often use examples to illustrate or clarify a point when we argue. Examples used like this should not be considered a formal part of the argument. The following passage contains such strictly illustrative examples. You can use a broken bracket ($\lceil \ \ \rceil$) to show a break in or interruption of an assertion.

[The average athlete begins to wonder when his career is going to end almost as soon as he starts.] [He knows that it either can be shortened with devastating swiftness by an injury,] or [eventually reach the point at which the great skill begins to erode.] As time goes on . . . [the player has to decide whether to cut it clean and retire at the top—⌈as Rocky Marciano, the heavyweight champion, did⌉—or wait for some sad moment—⌈Willie Mays stumbling around in the outfield reaches of Candlestick Park⌉—when the evidence is clear not only to oneself but one's peers that the time is up.] [George Plimpton, "The Final Season," *Harper's*, January 1972, p. 62.]

In this passage the author uses Rocky Marciano and Willie Mays as outstanding familiar illustrations of the dilemma athletes inevitably face: "retire at the top" or "wait for some sad moment." Because these examples have been used strictly for illustration, they are excluded from bracketing and numbering. The argument can be diagrammed as follows:

That such illustrations or clarifying examples are not a formal part of an argument does not mean that they shouldn't appear in arguments. When well chosen, as in the preceding passage, such examples both elucidate and enliven an argument. They provide a common ground of understanding between arguer and audience. They can thus be most effective rhetorical devices. But for purposes of casting an argument they are irrelevant.

6. **Cast examples used to support a point being made; that is, examples that indicate why the point is so.** Besides using examples strictly to clarify and illustrate, arguers also use them as support for their claims:

[The ethical code of ancient Greece did not[1] extend to human chattel, as this example shows.] [When godlike Odysseus returned from the war in Troy, he hanged on one rope some[2] dozen slave girls whom he suspected of misbehaving during his absence.]

The example cited in this passage does more than graphically illustrate the author's point. It also provides support for the claim made about the ethical code of ancient Greece. Thus the example can be considered a premise in the argument. The argument therefore consists of two assertions. The first assertion is the conclusion, the second the premise. The argument may be diagrammed as follows:

Here is another instance in which examples are used to support a claim:

Example: "... We go out for coffee, invite friends over for drinks, celebrate special occasions with cakes or big meals. We can't think of baseball without thinking of hot dogs and beer, and eating is so often an accompaniment to watching TV that we talk of TV snacks and TV dinners ... the activities we associate with food can become signals to eat...." [Michael J. Mahoney and Kathryn Mahoney, "Fight Fat with Behavior Control," *Psychology Today*, May 1976, p. 43.]

Comment: This passage uses a series of pithy examples to establish the point that activities we associate with food can become signals to eat. Therefore these examples can be considered premises in the argument, which can be cast as follows:

... [We go out for[1] coffee], [invite friends[2] over for drinks], [celebrate special occasions[3] with cakes or big meals.] [We can't think of baseball[4] without thinking of hot dogs and beer], and [eating is so often an accompaniment[5] to watching TV that we talk of TV snacks and TV dinners] ... [the activities we associate with[6] food can become signals to eat.]

7. **Do not cast as a separate assertion information that follows a colon.** In general, information that follows a colon simply extends the point being made in the part of the sentence that precedes the colon. The entire sentence should be treated as a single assertion.

To illustrate, consider this passage:

[There is no scientific proof for the assumption that reading about sexual matters or about violence and brutality leads to antisocial actions, particularly to juvenile delinquency.] <u>In the absence of such evidence,</u> [two lines of psychological approach to the examination of this assumption are possible:] (1) a review of what is known about the cause of juvenile delinquency and (2) a review of what is known about the effects of literature on the mind of the reader.

This passage consists of two assertions. The first is the premise, the second the conclusion. The information following the colon simply extends the conclusion; it specifies the "two lines of psychological approach" possible.

8. **Cast as separate assertions information separated by a semicolon.** The semicolon typically separates different pieces of information. Each piece of information must be considered an individual assertion and cast as such. The following passage, for example, contains three premises separated by two semicolons:

Jones is the best-qualified candidate. He is experienced in domestic and foreign affairs, having held positions in both fields; he is extremely dedicated; and he has demonstrated the imagination and creativity that this office requires.

The first sentence of this passage is the conclusion. The second sentence contains three premises, the first of which is supported. The argument can be cast as follows:

[Jones is the best-qualified candidate.] [He is experienced in both domestic and foreign affairs,] [having held positions in both fields;] [he is extremely dedicated;] <u>and</u> [he has demonstrated the imagination and creativity that this office requires.]

Quick Check on Casting Rhetorical Features

Apply the guidelines you have just learned in casting the following arguments. Ignore unexpressed premises.

1 "Evolution is a scientific fairy-tale just as the 'flat earth theory' was in the 12th century. Evolution directly contradicts the Second Law of Thermodynamics, which states that unless an intelligent planner is directing a system, it will always go in the direction of disorder and deterioration. . . . Evolution requires a faith that is incomprehensible! . . ." (Dr. Edward Blic, *21 Scientists Who Believe in Creation* [Harrisonburg, Va.: Christian Light Publications, 1977].)

2 "Contrary to popular assumption, volcanoes are anything but rare. The Smithsonian Scientific Event Alert Network often reports several dozen [volcanic eruptions] per quarter. America's slice of the volcanic 'ring of fire' includes the Cascades, a mountain range that arcs across the Pacific Northwest. When peaceful, shimmering Mt. St. Helens exploded this past spring, blasting 1.3 billion cubic yards of rock into powder, the people of Washington state received a rude lesson about nature's penchant for change. Bathed in ash every few weeks over the summer, the Washingtonians queasily came to the realization that the mountain might stay belligerent for years, that they had, in a sense, been living on borrowed time between inevitable eruptions. 'There are potential volcanoes all over the Cascade Range where Mt. St. Helens stands,' says geologist Alfred Anderson of the University of Chicago. 'There's still a lot of change, a lot of formations, going on in that area of the world.'" (Edward M. Hart, "The Shape of Things to Come," *Next: A Look into the Future*, December 1980, pp. 69–70.)

3 "A scientific colleague of mine, who holds a professorial post in the department of sociology and anthropology at one of our leading universities, recently asked me about my stand on the question of human beings having sex relations without love. Although I have taken something of a position on this issue in my book, *The American Sexual Tragedy*, I have never quite considered the problem in sufficient detail. So here goes. . . . In general, I feel that affectional, as against nonaffectional, sex relations are *desirable*. . . . It is usually desirable that an association between coitus and affection exist— particularly in marriage, because it is often difficult for two individuals to keep finely tuned to each other over a period of years. . . ." (Albert Ellis, *Sex Without Guilt* [New York: Lyle Stuart, Inc., 1966].)

4 "Scientists are human beings with their full complement of emotions and prejudices, and their emotions and prejudices often influence the way they do their science. This was first clearly brought out in a study by Professor Nicholas Pastore . . . in 1949. In this study Professor Pastore showed that the scientist's political beliefs were highly correlated with what he believed about the roles played by nature and nurture in the development of the person. Those holding conservative political views strongly tended to believe in the power of genes over environment. Those subscribing to more liberal views tended to believe in the power of environment over genes. One distinguished scientist (who happened to be a teacher of mine) when young was a socialist and environmentalist, but toward middle age he became politically conservative and a firm believer in the supremacy of genes!" (Ashley Montagu, *Sociobiology Examined* [Oxford: Oxford University Press, 1980], p. 4.)

Comments

1. ["Evolution is a scientific fairy-tale[1]] just as the 'flat earth theory' was in the 12th century. [Evolution directly contradicts the Second Law of Thermodynamics,[2]] which states that unless an intelligent planner is directing a system, it will always go in the direction of disorder and deterioration. ... Evolution requires a faith that is incomprehensible! ..."

2. "Contrary to popular assumption, [volcanoes are anything but rare.[1]] [The Smithsonian Scientific Event Alert Network[2] often reports several dozen [volcanic eruptions] per quarter.] [America's slice of the volcanic[3] 'ring of fire' includes the Cascades, a mountain range that arcs across the Pacific Northwest.] When peaceful, shimmering Mt. St. Helens exploded this past spring, blasting 1.3 billion cubic yards of rock into powder, the people of Washington state received a rude lesson about nature's penchant for change. Bathed in ash every few weeks over the summer, the Washingtonians queasily came to the realization that the mountain might stay belligerent for years, that they had, in a sense, been living on borrowed time between inevitable eruptions. ['There are potential volcanoes[4] all over the Cascade Range where Mt. St. Helens stands,'] says geologist Alfred Anderson of the University of Washington, 'There's still a lot of change, a lot of formations, going on in that area of the world.'"

3. "A scientific colleague of mine, who holds a professorial post in the department of sociology and anthropology at one of our leading universities, recently asked me about my stand on the question of human beings having sex relations without love. Although I have taken something of a position on this issue in my book, *The American Sexual Tragedy*, I have never quite considered the problem in sufficient detail. So here goes.... In general, I feel that [affectional, as against nonaffectional,[1] sex relations are desirable. ...] It is usually desirable that an association between coitus and affection exist— particularly in marriage <u>because</u> [it is often difficult for two[2] individuals to keep finely tuned to each other over a period of years...."]

4. "Scientists are human beings with their full complement of emotions and prejudices, and [their emotions and prejudices[1] often influence the way they do their science.] [This was first clearly brought out[2] in a study by Professor Nicholas Pastore . . . in 1949.] In this study [Professor Pastore showed that the scientist's[3] political beliefs were highly correlated with what he believed about the roles played by nature and nurture in the development of the person.] [Those holding conservative political views strongly tended[4] to believe in the power of genes over environment.] [Those subscribing to more liberal views tended[5] to believe in the power of environment over genes.] One distinguished scientist (who happened to be a teacher of mine) when young was a socialist and environmentalist, but toward middle age he became politically conservative and a firm believer in the supremacy of genes!"

Comment : You may not have cast assertions 4 and 5. I did because in assertion 2 the author states that Pastore's study "clearly brought out" the point that emotions and prejudices often influence the way scientists do science. In order to evaluate that claim, I need as much pertinent information about the study as possible. Assertions 4 and 5 provide at least some of it. If this information is inadequate to support assertion 3 (which I think is the case, given the absence of data that establish a causal and not just a statistical correlation between scientists' political beliefs and their scientific beliefs), then the author has no basis for inferring assertion 2 and therefore none for inferring assertion 1. As for the last sentence, while amusing, it says no more than was previously said in assertions 4 and 5.

Summary

Casting refers to portraying the structure of arguments. Casting is an important skill because (1) it helps you zero in on arguments, which is not always easy to do in longer passages; (2) it trains you to penetrate a passage's rhetorical flourishes; and (3) it minimizes the need to reproduce or keep referring to previous passages when evaluating an argument.

In learning to cast, it's useful to remember how arguments are organized. Arguments typically are organized in series or chains. In a series structure, the argument presents a series of independent reasons, each of which is offered in support of a conclusion. In a chain structure, the argument presents a number of interdependent points.

The casting method presented in this chapter consists of three steps:

1. Putting brackets at the beginning and end of each assertion
2. Numbering assertions consecutively in the margin or above the line of type
3. Setting out the relationship between the relevant assertions in a tree diagram to be read down the page

When diagramming an argument, drawing a single line between assertions means that one assertion implies the other. Here, assertion 1 implies assertion 2:

In this diagram

assertions 1 and 2 imply assertion 3, which in turn implies assertion 4. A plus sign and brace mean that two or more assertions, taken together, imply a third.

$$① + ②$$
$$③$$

Unexpressed premises or conclusions are represented by letters: a, b, c, and so forth. Here, assertion a is an unexpressed premise:

$$① + ⓐ$$
$$②$$

Similarly, in this diagram

$$① + ②$$
$$ⓐ$$

assertion a is the unexpressed conclusion.

Writers and speakers often use a variety of rhetorical devices in arguing. The following guidelines are useful in casting arguments with such rhetorical flourishes:

1. Cast each separate assertion.
2. Don't cast repetitions of the same assertion.
3. Don't cast asides.
4. Don't cast background information.
5. Don't cast examples that merely illustrate or clarify a point.
6. Cast examples used to support a point being made; that is, examples that indicate why the point is so.
7. Don't cast as separate assertions information that follows a colon.
8. Cast as separate assertions information separated by a semicolon.

Casting calls for interpretations. This means that two people may differ in how they cast the same argument. The key point to remember is that casting is a means to an end. You cast to familiarize yourself with an argument so that you can raise substantive criticisms of it.

Applications

1 Cast the following arguments.
   a "Many a reader will raise the question whether findings won by the observation of individuals can be applied to the psychological understanding of groups. Our answer to this question is an emphatic affirmation. Any group consists of individuals and nothing but individuals, and psychological mechanisms which we find operating in a group can therefore only be mechanisms that operate in individuals. In studying individual psychology as a basis for the understanding of social psychology, we do something which might be compared with studying an object under the microscope. This enables us to discover the very details of psychological mechanisms which we find operating on a large scale in the social process. If our analysis of socio-psychological phenomena is not based on the detailed study of human behavior, it lacks empirical character and, therefore, validity." (Eric Fromm, *Escape From Freedom* [New York: Avon Books, 1965], p. 158.)
   b "Flextime (Flexible Working Hours) often makes workers more productive because being treated as responsible adults gives them greater commitment to their jobs. As a result it decreases absenteeism, sick leave, tardiness and overtime, and generally produces significant increases in productivity for the work group as a whole. For example, in trial periods in three different departments, the U.S. Social Security Administration measured productivity increases averaging about 20 percent. Many companies that have tried flextime have recorded increases of at least five to ten percent and none has reported a decline." (Barry Stein et al., "Flextime," *Psychology Today*, June 1976, p. 43.)

c "The medical community has long debated the effects of tobacco smoke on non-smokers. Now recent studies have bolstered the contention of many physicians that, apart from the clear health hazard to smokers, tobacco smoke has harmful effects on non-smokers as well. In fact, in 1972 the U.S. Surgeon-General devoted fully a quarter of his 226-page report, "The Health Consequences of Smoking," to the other effects of smoke on non-smokers. Other people's smoking, says the report, is retarding fetal growth and increasing the incidence of premature birth; is exacerbating respiratory allergies in children and adults; and is causing acute irritation and taxing hearts and lungs of non-smokers by filling the air in smoky rooms with carbon monoxide, the deadly poison found in automobile exhaust." *(Reader's Digest,* July 1974, pp. 102, 104.)

d "Government control of ideas or personal preferences is alien to a democracy. And the yearning to use governmental censorship of any kind is infectious. It may spread insidiously. Commencing with suppression of books as obscene, it is not unlikely to develop into official lust for the power of thought-control in the areas of religion, politics, and elsewhere. Milton observed that 'licensing of books ... necessarily pulls along with it so many other kinds of licensing.' Mill notes that the 'bounds of what may be called moral police' may easily extend 'until it encroaches on the most unquestionably legitimate liberty of the individual.' We should beware of a recrudescence of the undemocratic doctrine uttered in the seventeenth century by Berkeley, Governor of Virginia: 'Thank God there are no free schools or preaching, for learning has brought disobedience into the world, and printing has divulged them. God keep us from both.'" (Jerome Frank, dissenting opinion in *United States* v. *Roth,* 354 U.S. 476, 1957.)

e "While the networks are among the staunchest defenders of free expression ... they will compromise principles in order to enhance their audience ratings. In an astonishing article *The New York Times* described how ABC subordinated its news division's integrity to an outside influence. Soviet officials were permitted to censor and monitor ABC news stories about life in Russia. Some Soviet officials actually sat in ABC's New York offices reviewing its network reporting. The *Times* article contended that these startling concessions to the Russians were part of the network's effort to secure coverage rights for the 1980 Olympics...." (Marvin Maurer in *Point-Counterpoint: Readings in American Government,* Herbert M. Levine, ed. [Glenview, Ill.: Scott, Foresman, 1977].)

f "Well, is it true that the black community is edging into the middle class? Let's look at income, the handiest guide and certainly the most generally agreed-upon measurement. What income level amounts to middle-class status? Median family income is often used, since that places a family at the exact midpoint in our society. In 1972 the median family income of whites amounted to $11,549, but black median family income was a mere $6,864.

"That won't work. Let's take another guide. The Bureau of Labor Statistics says it takes an urban family of four $12,600 to maintain an 'intermediate' living standard. Using that measure, the average black family not only is *not* middle class, but it earns far less than the 'lower, non-poverty' level of $8,200. Four out of five black families earn less than the 'intermediate' standard." (Vernon E. Jordan, Jr., "The Truth about the Black Middle Class," *Newsweek*, July 8, 1974.)

g "American institutions were fashioned in an era of vast unoccupied spaces and preindustrial technology. In those days, collisions between public needs and individual rights may have been minimal. But increased density, scarcity of resources, and interlocking technologies have now heightened the concern for 'public goods,' which belong to no one in particular but to all of us jointly. Polluting a lake or river or the air may not directly damage any one person's private property or living space. But it destroys a good that all of us—including future generations—benefit from and have a title to. Our public goods are entitled to a measure of protection." (Amitai Etzioni, "When Rights Collide," *Psychology Today* XI, no. 5 [October 1977].)

2 Find two arguments with premise support in a newspaper, magazine, or book. Cast these arguments.

3 Compose five arguments, each of which contains at least three premises and support for at least one premise. Then cast the arguments.

4 Construct arguments for the following castings:

a

b $\dfrac{② + ⓐ}{①}$

c

d

e

5 Construct arguments that illustrate each of the following guidelines. Then cast your arguments.
  a Cast each separate assertion.
  b Don't cast repetitions of the same assertion.
  c Don't cast asides.
  d Don't cast background information.
  e Don't cast examples that merely illustrate or clarify a point.
  f Cast examples used to support a point; that is, examples that indicate why the point is so.
  g Don't cast as separate assertions information that follows a colon.
  h Cast as separate assertions information separated by a semicolon.

Missing Premises

So far you've learned about the structure of arguments and how to cast them. Many of the arguments you will read, hear, and compose will be rather lengthy and complex. Such arguments typically leave premises, and even conclusions, unexpressed. To understand, to cast, and to evaluate the structure of an argument, you first must be able to fill in the missing premises in your arguments and those of others. In short, (1) if you can't fill in missing premises, you can't understand how the arguer proceeds from the evidence to the conclusion; (2) if you don't understand how the arguer proceeds from the evidence to the conclusion, you can't understand the structure of the argument; and (3) if you don't understand the argument's structure, you can't evaluate it. Thus the art of critical thinking hinges largely upon your ability to fill in missing premises correctly, which is the subject of this chapter.

The Importance of Filling in Premises

Here's a simple, familiar argument, which I'll use to emphasize further the importance of filling in missing premises:

Since [Smith is a police officer,[1]] [he's probably in[2] favor of gun-control legislation.]

150

Taken by itself, assertion 1 does not entail assertion 2. Inferring Smith's position on gun-control legislation *solely* from the fact that Smith is a police officer is simply wrong-headed. After all, the expressed premise does not even mention the issue of gun-control legislation. To make such an inference based only on the expressed premise would be the same as inferring from the assertion "B is greater than C" that "A is greater than C." If an arguer made such an inference, you'd rightly ask "How can you infer anything about A's relation to C when you don't even mention A in your premise?" The arguer might reply "Oh, I'm assuming that A is greater than B." With this additional premise, the connection between conclusion and stated premise is clear. You would then see how the arguer proceeded from the premise that B is greater than C to the conclusion that A is greater than C, namely, with the help of the unexpressed premise "A is greater than B." You would also understand the structure of the argument: It doesn't consist of a single premise and a conclusion but of *two* premises and a conclusion. You would realize that the argument should *not* be cast

$$\begin{array}{c} \textcircled{1} \\ | \\ \textcircled{2} \end{array}$$

but

$$\underbrace{\textcircled{1} \ + \ \textcircled{a}}_{\textcircled{2}}$$

It is this latter form that you will eventually evaluate in determining the worth of the argument.

Of course you rarely can query an arguer about his or her unexpressed premises. The task of filling in missing premises therefore falls to you, the critical thinker: You must reconstruct the assumed premises. When an argument is incomplete, you must determine the premises assumed by the arguer that, together with the expressed premise or premises, entail the arguer's conclusion.

Let's return to the argument about police officer Smith:

<u>Since</u> [Smith is a police officer,]¹ [he's probably in favor of gun-control legislation.]²

This argument appears to have only one premise and a conclusion. Actually it consists of two premises, one expressed, the other unexpressed. The unexpressed premise is "Most police officers are in favor of gun-control legislation" or "Police officers generally are in favor of gun-control legislation" or "The majority of police officers are in favor of gun-control legislation" or something to that effect. The structure of this argument, then, should be cast as follows:

$$\underbrace{\textcircled{1} \ + \ \textcircled{a}}_{\textcircled{2}}$$

Certainly these premises entail the conclusion: The reasoning process is as legitimate here as it was in "A is greater than B, and B is greater than C. Therefore A is greater than C."

Whether an argument is a good one depends, of course, on more than correct reasoning. It also requires true premises. Is it true that most police officers are in favor of gun-control legislation? The legitimacy of the argument's conclusion—that Smith is probably in favor of gun-control legislation—depends on the truth of the unexpressed premise. But if you never detect this assumed premise, you cannot evaluate it to determine whether it is true. Therefore you cannot evaluate the argument.

Filling in missing premises is important for another reason. Suppose you take the argument we're discussing at face value. You assume that it has only one premise: "Smith is a police officer." You therefore cast the argument as follows:

You then call the argument unsound because the single premise does not entail the conclusion: That Smith is a police officer doesn't necessarily mean that he's probably in favor of gun-control legislation.

But what have you really done? You've misrepresented the argument. The argument doesn't consist of a single premise but of two. When the unexpressed premise is filled in—"Most police officers are in favor of gun-control legislation"—the argument makes perfect sense. The expressed premise, when taken together with the unexpressed one, does imply the conclusion. Of course, the argument may still be faulty: It may not be true or may at least be doubtful that most police officers favor gun-control legislation. But in that case the fault would lie not in the reasoning procedure but in the false content on which the reasoning is based.

Thinking correctly calls for right assessments for the right reasons. Calling an argument faulty for the wrong reason is like a physician's describing a patient as ill for the wrong reason. Without a proper diagnosis of the problem, both critical thinker and physician are ineffectual.

At this point you may be wondering "Why should I, the reader or listener, have to fill in missing premises? Isn't that the job of the arguer? I have enough to do sorting out what the argument says without having to worry about what it doesn't say." Certainly it would be less trouble for critical thinkers if all arguments came complete. But they don't. If they did, writing, reading, and listening would be dishwater-dull. After all, sometimes premises are too obvious to be stated. For example, when I say

> Since you're planning to go to medical school, you'd better get good grades in college

what I'm assuming is obvious: "Anyone planning to go to medical school must get good grades in college." And when you say to me "I try to avoid unhealthful habits. That's why I don't smoke," I realize you're assuming that "Smoking is an unhealthful habit." Often premises are just too obvious to be stated.

Sometimes arguers simply overlook premises. This is especially common in oral arguments. Although failing to express premises may impede communication, there is nothing logically objectionable about an argument with missing premises. It can be as good as one with no missing premises.

Finally, arguers don't always realize what they're assuming and in fact often would prefer to leave their assumptions uninspected. Indeed, concealing questionable assumptions is a common and effective ploy in argument, as we'll see in a later chapter. If you and I don't take pains to fill in missing premises, we invite our own exploitation; we make ourselves easy marks for every huckster who comes down the pike.

These preliminary observations should impress on you the importance of filling in missing premises. Of course, it's one thing to realize that thinking critically requires you to fill in missing premises; it's another to do so correctly. In fact, accurate reconstruction of missing premises is the most challenging aspect of critical thinking and argument analysis. It can also be the most rewarding. To do it well you must be attentive, thoughtful, and clever. In the process you likely will uncover weaknesses in an argument, for falsehoods typically lie more in what is unsaid than in what is said. Discovering these flaws can be an exhilarating problem-solving exercise. Even when filling in premises is more exercising than exhilarating, it still is useful, for when done well, it allows you to focus on the essential weaknesses of an argument. An ability to fill in missing premises makes you an incisive and formidable critic; it helps you get on top of the mountain of argumentative material that looms large in your personal and professional life.

When to Fill in Premises

In general, you should fill in missing premises whenever an argument is incomplete and its missing premises are not obvious. In an incomplete argument, the stated premise does not entail the argument's conclusion. Before you can fill in its premises, however, you must be able to recognize an argument as incomplete. There are two strategies you can use to identify incomplete arguments: (1) the "what if" strategy and (2) the topic coverage strategy.

"What if" Strategy

Let's begin with the simple argument "Bill must be a man because he's a father." If you want to determine whether this argument is complete or incomplete, you could ask *"What if* it's true that Bill is a father? Must it follow that he's a man?" By definition a father is a male parent. Therefore, if Bill is a father, then he must be a male. The single premise in this argument thus entails the conclusion. The argument is complete as it appears.

In contrast, reconsider the argument "Since Smith is a police officer, he's probably in favor of gun-control legislation." If you wanted to determine whether this argument was complete, you could ask *"What if* it's true that Smith is a police officer? Must it follow that he's probably in favor of gun-control legislation?" Not necessarily, for most police officers may be opposed to such legislation. Nothing in the stated premise disallows that possibility. If in fact most police officers are not in favor of such laws, then the conclusion would not follow from the expressed premise. Thus the conclusion may not be inferred from this premise. Something is missing; the argument is incomplete.

These simple examples should illustrate how the "what if" strategy works. Notice that in applying it you needn't know whether the expressed premise is true to determine whether it implies the conclusion. All you have to do is ask *"What if* it was true? Would the conclusion then have to be true?" Thus the "what if" strategy consists of *assuming* that the expressed premise (or premises) is true and asking whether the conclusion therefore would have to be true. If the answer is yes, the argument is complete; if it is no, the argument is incomplete.

You can look at the "what if" strategy as placing you in the role of a detective who might be testing someone's alibi.

ALIBIING

SUSPECT: My girlfriend will testify that I was with her in her apartment when the crime was committed. So I couldn't have committed the crime.

SKEPTICAL

DETECTIVE: *What if* the suspect's girlfriend testifies that he was with her in her apartment at the time of the crime? Must it be true that he couldn't have committed the crime?

The detective needn't be a Sherlock Holmes to see that if the girlfriend does so testify, the suspect still could have committed the crime, for she could be lying. On the other hand, let's say that it was established indisputably that the suspect was not at the scene of the crime when it was committed. Then the detective would have to formulate the "what if" question differently. *"What if* the suspect was not at the scene of the crime when it was committed? Must it be true that he couldn't have committed the crime?" In this case the alibi given in the expressed premise would warrant the conclusion.

Counterexamples   In applying the "what if" strategy, you are in effect performing two operations:

1. You are imagining a situation in which all the premises are accepted.
2. You are trying to imagine a loophole that will allow you to reject the conclusion while still accepting the premises.

The second operation really consists of trying to come up with a counterexample to the argument.

A counterexample is an example that is consistent with the expressed premise but is inconsistent with the conclusion. Again consider the argument about the police officer. Let's suppose that most police officers are opposed to gun-control legislation. This imagined situation is perfectly consistent with the argument's expressed premise "Smith is a police officer." But it is inconsistent with its conclusion. In fact, if most police officers are opposed to gun-control legislation, then Police Officer Smith probably is *not* in favor of gun-control legislation. The effect of this counterexample is to show that the argument is incomplete. For when an argument is complete, it disallows counterexamples by ruling out all alternatives to the conclusion.

Suppose that the original argument had been stated this way: Most police officers are in favor of gun-control legislation. Since Smith is a police officer, he's probably in favor of gun-control legislation.

Now try testing this argument with my counterexample and watch what happens. To say that most police officers are opposed to gun-control legislation is inconsistent with one of the expressed premises: "Most police officers are in favor of gun-control legislation." Thus it isn't a counterexample at all. Now try saying that "My friend Officer Jones is opposed to gun-control legislation." Since this is consistent with the premises, *and* with the conclusion, it too fails as a counterexample. In fact, no counterexample is possible because stated this way the argument is complete.

The detective in our example could use a counterexample to point out the weakness in the suspect's alibi. Thus, suppose the girlfriend is lying. This supposition allows the detective to reject the suspect's claim of innocence while accepting the suspect's reason for the claim. It is consistent with the premise but inconsistent with the conclusion; therefore it's an effective counterexample. On the other hand, if it is established indisputably that the suspect was not at the scene of the crime when it was committed, then no counterexample is possible.

The "what if" strategy for identifying incomplete arguments thus consists of imagining a situation in which all the premises are accepted and then trying to devise a counterexample that is compatible with the premises but incompatible with the conclusion. If such a counterexample is possible, then the argument is incomplete.

A word of caution. Devising counterexamples requires imagination and creativity as well as a keen sense of what is relevant. Failing to come up with a counterexample does not necessarily prove that an argument is complete. It may simply mean that you weren't imaginative enough in concocting your counterexample.

Quick Check on "What if" Strategy

Using the "what if" strategy, determine whether the following arguments are incomplete. Make use of counterexamples.

1 Because prisons do not rehabilitate inmates, they are an ineffective form of punishment for criminal behavior.
2 The United States should develop solar energy on a widespread basis because it must become energy-independent.
3 Abortion involves the taking of a life. Therefore it should be discouraged.

4 Jane's probably married. She's wearing a wedding ring.
5 Men are not innately superior to women. If they were they wouldn't establish caste systems to ensure their preferred positions, and they wouldn't work so hard to maintain these systems. But obviously men do both.

Comments

1. Incomplete: Prisons effectively remove from the streets threats to society. They also help deter crime. Both these premises are consistent with the stated premise but inconsistent with the conclusion.
2. Incomplete: The development of nuclear power presumably could make the United States energy-independent, but so could mining our vast coal reserves.
3. Incomplete: Killing in self-defense involves the taking of a life. Should that be discouraged?
4. Incomplete: Some divorced women still wear their wedding rings.
5. Complete: No counterexample is possible.

Topic Coverage Strategy

Conclusions relate topics that are covered in the premises. "Smith is probably in favor of gun-control legislation" relates Smith and his opposition to gun-control legislation. "A is greater than C" relates the sizes of A and C. "The suspect could not have committed the crime" relates the suspect and his lack of involvement in the crime. Because the conclusion relates topics, you can tell what topics must be covered in the premises by examining an argument's conclusion.

To better understand this strategy, let's look at the table below. If we assume that the assertion in the left-hand column is a conclusion, then the two topics in the right-hand column must be covered in the argument's premises, whatever they may be. Notice how in each case the second topic is introduced by an interrogative word (e.g., "why") suggestive of the relationship.

Conclusion	Topics to Be Covered
1. Capital punishment should be legalized for certain serious crimes	capital punishment and why it should be legalized for certain serious crimes
2. Foods containing sugar should not be sold in elementary schools	foods containing sugar and why they shouldn't be sold in elementary schools
3. Television violence contributes to real-life violence	television violence and why it contributes to real-life violence
4. The United States should start constructing commercial nuclear power plants	the United States and why it should start constructing commercial nuclear power plants
5. Living at home while attending college makes for the best living arrangement while at college	living at home while attending college and why it makes for the best living arrangement

6. Young people should complete college
7. People who want to lose weight need regular exercise

young people and why they should complete college
people who want to lose weight and why they need regular exercise

Whatever the arguments that led to these conclusions, their premises must relate the topics in the right-hand column.

An incomplete argument by definition is an argument whose conclusion covers topics that are uncovered in the expressed premises. Consider the simple example we've been examining:

Since Smith is a police officer, he's probably in favor of gun-control legislation.

The conclusion relates Smith and his position on gun-control legislation. But the expressed premise of itself provides no basis for saying anything about his position on gun-control legislation. Thus the argument is incomplete.

The topic coverage strategy thus consists of determining whether the conclusion contains topics that are uncovered in the premises. If it does then the argument is incomplete. In applying this strategy, you must perform two steps: (1) identify the topics covered in the conclusion and their relationship and (2) determine whether the topics and their relationship are covered in the premises. If a topic and/or the relationship has been left uncovered in the premises, then the argument is incomplete. The chart on pages 158–159 shows how the strategy can be applied. In each instance assume that the original argument appeared as I have stated it. Pay special attention to the note.

There are, then, two strategies for determining whether or not an argument is complete: the "what if" strategy, which makes use of counterexamples; and the topic coverage strategy. When an argument is incomplete and its missing premise or premises is not obvious, you should apply one or more that, taken together with the explicit premise, provides conclusive logical support for the conclusion.

Quick Check on Topic Coverage Strategy

Indicate the topic that was left uncovered in the expressed premises of the four incomplete arguments in the preceding Quick Check, page 155.

Comments

1. Why prisons are an ineffective form of punishment for criminal behavior
2. Why the United States should develop solar energy on a widespread basis
3. Why abortion should be discouraged
4. Why Jane is probably married

Argument	Conclusion	Topics Covered in Conclusion and Their Relationship	Topics Missing in Premises	Complete or Incomplete
1. [Capital punishment should be legalized for certain serious crimes,]¹ because it's a deterrent.²	1	Capital punishment and why it should be legalized for certain serious crimes.	Why capital punishment should be legalized for certain serious crimes.	Incomplete
2. [Sugar promotes disease.]¹ That's why [foods containing sugar² shouldn't be sold in elementary schools.]	2	Foods containing sugar and why they should not be sold in elementary schools.	Why foods containing sugar shouldn't be sold in elementary schools.	Incomplete
3. Because [television violence is¹ portrayed in graphic detail], [it² contributes to real-life violence.]	2	Television violence and why it contributes to real-life violence.	Why TV violence contributes to real-life violence.	Incomplete
4. Since [the United States should¹ do whatever it takes to become energy-independent], [the United States should start² constructing commercial nuclear power plants]; for [only they will³ make us energy-independent.]	2	The United States and why it should start constructing commercial nuclear power plants.	None	Complete

5. [Living at home while attending college is the best living arrangement]¹ because [it's the² cheapest.]	Living at home while attending college and why it makes for the best living arrangement while at college.	1	Why living at home while attending college makes for the best living arrangement.	Incomplete
6. [Young people should try to maximize their earning potential.] Therefore [they should² complete college.]¹	Young people and why they should complete college.	2	Why young people should complete college.	Incomplete
7. [People who want to lose weight need regular exercise]¹, for [increasing the metabolic rate² contributes to weight loss.]	People who want to lose weight and why they need regular exercise.	1	Why people who want to lose weight need regular exercise.	Incomplete

NOTE: It's tempting to think that the "why" query of the missing premise has in fact been addressed in the stated premise. For example, in argument 1 the missing topic concerns why capital punishment should be legalized for certain serious crimes. The stated premise, "It's a deterrent," appears to state why. But one can still ask "Even if capital punishment is a deterrent, why should it be legalized?" The arguer must be assuming something which, together with the claim that capital punishment is a deterrent, entails the conclusion that capital punishment must be legalized for certain serious crimes. When the missing premise is provided, then the premises provide a *complete* answer to the question of why capital punishment should be legalized.

Guidelines for Filling in Missing Premises

There is no surefire way to fill in missing premises properly. But some of the observations just made provide us with useful guidelines.

   1. **Apply the topic coverage strategy.**   The topic coverage strategy for identifying incomplete arguments also can be useful in reconstructing premises. The reason is that premise reconstruction requires you to formulate a premise that covers what is covered in the conclusion but not in the expressed premise. Since the topic coverage strategy aims to pinpoint the missing topic and its relationship to other topics, it identifies the very component of the argument that you must fill in.

   Take for example argument 1. The topic covered in the conclusion but not in the premise is, Why capital punishment should be legalized for certain serious crimes. You know, therefore, that any reconstructed premise, *in conjunction with the expressed premise*, must address this topic. Similarly, in argument 2 some assertion about why foods containing sugar should not be sold in elementary schools is missing. Any premise reconstructed to complete this argument must cover this topic.

   Being aware of topic coverage helps you avoid reconstructing irrelevant premises; that is, ones that do not help entail the conclusion. For example, suppose you filled in the missing premise of argument 1 by saying "Capital punishment is the most inexpensive form of punishment" or "Capital punishment ensures that the killer will never strike again." Although these statements are true and the arguer may agree with them, neither of them, *together with the expressed premise* ("Capital punishment is a deterrent"), provides conclusive support for the conclusion "Capital punishment should be legalized for certain serious crimes." These suggested premises are irrelevant to the conclusion. *Taken together with the expressed premise*, neither covers the topic of why capital punishment should be legalized.

   Now suppose that for argument 2 you think that the missing premise is "Sugar contributes to tooth decay" or "Consuming great amounts of sugar can make one hyperactive." While true, these assertions do not help the expressed premise provide conclusive support for the conclusion, although they certainly support the premise itself. So these reconstructions would be irrelevant.

   If you can correctly isolate the topics that are covered in the conclusions of arguments 1 and 2 but not in their premises, you will never make the mistake of reconstructing irrelevant premises for these arguments. Recognizing that the arguments are incomplete because these topics have been left uncovered, you'll realize that the topics must be addressed in any reconstruction that will help the expressed premises conclusively support their conclusions. In short, you'd realize that a properly reconstructed premise for argument 1 must help the expressed premise cover the topic of why capital punishment should be legalized. A properly reconstructed premise for argument 2 must help the expressed premise cover the topic of why foods containing sugar should not be sold in elementary schools. So you can use the topic coverage strategy not only to identify incomplete arguments but also to reconstruct missing premises properly by pinpointing the topic of the premise and its relationship to other topics in the argument.

2. **Reconstruct a premise that is just strong enough to help support the conclusion.** Identifying the topics that must be covered in the missing premise doesn't of itself guarantee a proper reconstruction. Consider once again this argument: "Since Smith is a police officer, he's probably in favor of gun-control legislation." Having determined that the missing topic concerns why he supports gun-control legislation, you can make a number of possible reconstructions, a:

Reconstruction 1a: All police officers favor gun-control legislation.
Reconstruction 2a: Most police officers favor gun-control legislation.
Reconstruction 3a: Some police officers favor gun-control legislation.

Because each of these premises, in conjunction with the stated premise, covers the uncovered topic, each is a candidate for the missing premise. Which one should you choose?

Notice that these reconstructions can be distinguished by their degree of generality. Reconstruction 1a speaks of every single police officer (*All* police officers); reconstruction 2a speaks of a consensus, or some unspecified number above the majority (*Most* police officers); reconstruction 3a speaks of an unspecified number below a majority (*Some* police officers). *In deciding which of the three reconstructions is the real missing premise, you should choose the one that is strong enough to help entail the conclusion but no stronger.* Strong enough but not too strong—there are good reasons for this advice. If the reconstruction is not strong or general enough, then it won't help provide conclusive support for the conclusion. But if it's too strong, then it will misrepresent the argument; it will say more than the arguer intended. Such an overstatement might be too strong to be true and thus you would have succeeded only in distorting the argument, thereby making it a target for unfair criticism. Now let's apply these points to the three candidates for the missing premise.

Reconstruction 1a is the strongest of the three. Certainly if "All police officers favor gun-control legislation," then the conclusion can be inferred: "Smith is probably in favor of gun-control legislation." In fact, reconstruction 1a would allow the even stronger conclusion "Smith *must be* in favor of gun-control legislation." That the arguer did not make this strong an inference is itself convincing evidence that reconstruction 1a is stronger than the missing premise needs to be to help support the conclusion. This argument doesn't need a sweeping generalization about *all* police officers to entail a conclusion that asserts what is only probably the case. If you insisted on reconstruction 1a, then, you'd be turning the argument into a sitting duck. All you'd have to do to discredit the argument would be to cite a single example of a police officer opposed to gun-control legislation. That single example would disprove the assertion that all police officers favor gun-control legislation, which in turn would prove the argument faulty.

Let's skip over reconstruction 2a for a moment and consider reconstruction 3a: "Some police officers favor gun-control legislation." If "some" is taken to mean at least one but less than a majority, then this premise does not help support the conclusion, which states that Smith is *probably* in favor of gun-control legislation. If he's *probably* in favor, then he's *more likely* in favor of it than opposed or indifferent to it. But if less than a majority of police officers favors the legislation, then the arguer has no basis for inferring Smith's *probable* support of it. The inference of probability would only follow if a majority favored gun-control legislation. But "some" does not imply that. So whereas reconstruction 1a is too strong, reconstruction 3a is too weak.

Reconstruction 2a falls between these extremes. In referring to the position of *most* police officers, it avoids the overstatement of reconstruction 1a and the understatement of reconstruction 3a. It is strong enough to help provide grounds for the conclusion, for "most" means a majority, which in turn helps give conclusive support to the inference that Smith is *probably* in favor of gun-control legislation.

In reconstructing premises, then, pay attention to the strength of the reconstruction. An appropriate missing premise is strong enough to help support the conclusion but not so strong that it overstates the arguer's assumption.

3. Reconstruct a premise that illuminates the argument instead of just repeating it. This third guideline relates to the second. Consider argument 3:

Because [television violence is portrayed in graphic detail,]^1 [it contributes to real-life violence.]^2

Assertion 1 is the premise, assertion 2 the conclusion. That TV violence is portrayed in graphic detail does not of itself demonstrate that TV violence contributes to real-life violence. A missing premise is needed to link the idea of TV violence portrayed in graphic detail (1) with TV's contribution to real-life violence; that is, the premise must concern *why TV violence contributes to real-life violence.* The missing premise (a) can be formulated in at least two ways:

Reconstruction 1a: Whatever portrays violence in graphic detail contributes to
    real-life violence.
Reconstruction 2a: If television violence is portrayed in graphic detail, it contrib-
    utes to real-life violence.

Both of these reconstructions, in conjunction with the expressed premise, link the idea of television violence portrayed in graphic detail with television's contribution to real-life violence. Each helps the expressed premise provide conclusive support for the conclusion. Which is the better reconstruction?

While both premises are relevant and do help entail the conclusion, they clearly differ in the breadth of their claims. Reconstruction 1a in effect asserts that *anything* that portrays violence in graphic detail contributes to real-life violence. In contrast reconstruction 2a speaks only of the connection between television violence and real-life violence. Although reconstruction 2a sticks closer to the argument's topics, it really just repeats the argument without illuminating it. Anyone who argues "Because television violence is portrayed in graphic detail, it contributes to real-life violence" obviously must believe that the expressed premise leads to the expressed conclusion. After all, that's how arguments and reasoning work: One point presumably entails another. All reconstruction 2a does, then, is to make the assumption about the nature of arguments and the reasoning process explicit. Reconstruction 2a is in effect an expression of the general principle that leads an arguer from premise to conclusion: If you accept my premise, you must accept my conclusion. But it does not tell anything about the reasoning behind the argument; it doesn't show how the arguer moved from premise to conclusion. If we fill in the missing premise with reconstruction 2a, we can still ask "But <u>why</u> does television violence contribute to real-life violence?"

Of these two possibilities, then, reconstruction 1a is preferable. It does not repeat what is already explicit in the argument but illuminates it. It shows how the arguer moved from the expressed premise to the conclusion. After filling in the missing premise with reconstruction 1a, we cannot logically ask "But why does television violence contribute to real-life violence?" Reconstruction 1a provides the answer: *"Whatever portrays violence in graphic detail contributes to real-life violence."*

In reconstructing missing premises, then, you should follow these three guidelines: First, apply the topic coverage strategy. Second, ensure that the premise is just strong enough to help support the conclusion but not too strong. Third, ensure that the premise illuminates the argument and doesn't merely repeat it.

Quick Check on Filling in Missing Premises

1 Fill in the missing premises of the incomplete arguments in the Quick Check on "what if" strategy, page 155.

Comments

1. Rehabilitation is a necessary part of any effective form of punishment for criminal behavior.
2. Only the development of solar energy on a widespread basis can make the United States energy-independent.
3. Any life-taking action should be discouraged.
4. Women who wear wedding rings probably are married.

2 Select the best reconstructed premise from the alternatives offered for each of the following arguments:

    a Some of these people can't be golfers. They're not carrying clubs.

        Reconstruction 1a: Some golfers are carrying clubs.
        Reconstruction 2a: Everyone carrying a club is a golfer.
        Reconstruction 3a: All golfers are carrying clubs.

Comment: 3a. 1a is too weak. 2a provides no basis for drawing the conclusion, for simply because everyone carrying a club is a golfer doesn't exclude the possibility that those not carrying clubs are also golfers.

b Many prison inmates simply aren't cooperative. That's precisely why they cannot be rehabilitated.

Reconstruction 1a: If prison inmates are cooperative, they can be rehabilitated.
Reconstruction 2a: Any prison inmate who isn't cooperative can't be rehabilitated.
Reconstruction 3a: Cooperation on the part of prison inmates is necessary for rehabilitation.
Comment: 3a. 1a is too strong. The arguer isn't necessarily asserting that cooperation is a sufficient condition for rehabilitation. Other things may also be necessary (hard work, a reassessment of values, change of life style, for instance). 2a adds nothing to the argument that isn't already asserted. 3a asserts that a prison inmate *must be* cooperative to be rehabilitated. In short, no cooperation, no rehabilitation. This reconstruction, or some logical equivalent, expresses the precise relationship between willingness and rehabilitation that the arguer assumes in drawing the conclusion.

c If capital punishment isn't a deterrent to crime, then why has the rate of violent crimes increased since capital punishment was outlawed?

Reconstruction 1a: Because the rate of violent crime has increased since capital punishment was outlawed, it must be a deterrent to crime.
Reconstruction 2a: An increase in the rate of crime following the abolition of a punishment proves that the punishment is a crime deterrent.
Reconstruction 3a: An increase in the rate of crime following the abolition of a punishment usually indicates that the punishment is a crime deterrent.
Comment: 2a. 1a merely repeats what's already stated. 3a is too weak, given its use of "usually."

d Constitutionally only the House of Representatives may initiate a money-raising bill. Thus when the Senate drafted the recent tax bill, it acted unconstitutionally. Therefore the proposed tax bill should not be made law.

Reconstruction 1a: Any bill the Senate drafts should not be made law.
Reconstruction 2a: Any bill that is unconstitutional should not be made law.
Reconstruction 3a: Any tax bill originating in the Senate should not be made law.
Comment: 2a. 1a is far too strong. 3a does not cite the reason why a tax bill originating in the Senate should not be made law, whereas 2a does.

e All aspirin are equal quality. You should therefore buy the cheapest brand.

Reconstruction set 1: 1a: The quality of an aspirin depends solely on its pain-relieving capacity.
1b: The point of buying aspirin is to get pain relief.
Reconstruction set 2: 2a: The quality of an aspirin depends solely on its pain-relieving capacity.
2b: You want a quality aspirin at the lowest price.

> **Comment:** Set 2. Set 1 doesn't say why you should buy the cheapest brand, only that all brands relieve pain equally.

f For the past forty years, the U.S. government has wantonly interfered with business to regulate business activity. At the same time, we've seen government increasingly assume roles traditionally assigned to private enterprise. It's no wonder capitalism isn't working.

> **Reconstruction set 1:** 1a: Capitalism will work in the absence of government interference with private enterprise.
> 1b: Capitalism will work if government doesn't assume the roles traditionally assigned to business.
> **Reconstruction set 2:** 2a: If the U.S. government wantonly regulates business, capitalism can't work.
> 2b: If government assumes roles traditiionally assigned to business, capitalism can't work.
> **Reconstruction set 3:** 3a: Capitalism can work only in the absence of wanton government interference to regulate business.
> 3b: Capitalism can work only if government does not assume roles traditionally assigned to business.
> **Comment:** Set 3. Set 1 is too strong: Other things may be necessary for capitalism to work. Set 2 repeats the argument. We can still wonder, Why won't capitalism work in the presence of those conditions? Set 3 focuses on the assumptions that government noninterference and separation of roles are necessary for capitalism to work. It expresses precisely the relationship between noninterference and separation of roles on the one hand, and the workability of capitalism on the other, that the arguer must be assuming to draw the conclusion.

3 Fill in the missing premises of the following incomplete arguments, and cast them. Some may have *more than one* premise missing.

a All successful politicians are self-serving, for only ambitious people succeed in politics.

b Whatever invades privacy threatens justice. That's why subjecting people to polygraph tests as a condition of employment is so serious.

c Resident reacting against a mobile home park's becoming part of the neighborhood: "I have nothing against mobile homes as a way of living, but it's unthinkable to put a mobile-home park right in the middle of a residential area. After all they're usually in outlying areas."

d Because they see it as a hedge against malpractice suits, doctors typically welcome a patient's informed consent.

e "Imperialist is a dirty word all right, but it hardly fits a nation like the United States which, with all our faults, is ready to give millions of dollars to help starving and dying Cambodians." (William Randolph Hearst, Jr., "Editor's Report," *Los Angeles Herald Examiner*, November 4, 1979, p. F3.)

f Former Michigan Governor George Romney in describing the Equal Rights Amendment as a "moral perversion": "Surely this resolution and its supporting statements are designed to legitimize sex and social relationships other than those that form the basis of divinely ordained marriage, parenthood and home." (AP release, January 2, 1980)

Comments:

a. **Missing premise:** All ambitious people are^a self-serving.

[All successful politicians are^1 self-serving,] <u>for</u> [only ambitious people succeed^2 in politics.]

$$\underbrace{② + ⓐ}_{①}$$

b. **Missing premises:** Whatever threatens justice^a is serious.

Subjecting people to polygraph^b tests as a condition of employment invades privacy.
[Whatever invades privacy threatens justice.] <u>That's why</u> [subjecting people^2 to polygraph tests as a precondition of employment is so serious.]

$$\underbrace{① + ⓐ + ⓑ}_{②}$$

c. **Missing premise:** To alter the traditional location^a of a mobile-home park is unthinkable.

["I have nothing against mobile homes^1 as a way of living,] <u>but</u> [it's unthinkable to put a mobile-home park^2 right in the middle of a residential area.] <u>After all</u> [they're usually^3 in outlying areas."]

$$\underbrace{③ + ⓐ - ①}_{②}$$

d. **Missing premise:** Doctors generally welcome any^a hedge against malpractice suits.

Because [they see it as a hedge against^1 malpractice suits,] [doctors typically welcome^2 a patient's informed consent.]

$$\underbrace{① + ⓐ}_{②}$$

e. **Missing premise:** A country that gives millions of dollars^a to help the starving and dying people of another country can't be imperialist.

"Imperialist is a dirty word all right, <u>but</u> [it hardly fits a nation like the U.S.]^1 [which, [with all our faults,] is ready to give millions of dollars to help starving and dying Cambodians."]^2

f. *Missing premises:* Violating what is divinely ordained^a is a moral perversion. ["Surely this resolution and its supporting statements^1 are designed to legitimize sex and social relationships other than those that form the basis of divinely ordained marriage, parenthood and home.] <u>From which it follows that</u> [this resolution is a moral perversion.]^2

Comment: The speaker makes other assumptions that I have not made explicit; for example, that a God exists and that God ordains certain institutions and prescribes human behavior. You could examine these other assumptions when evaluating the argument. Also I have expressed the conclusion as if it were a part of the argument. You might prefer to treat it as unexpressed, in which case you would make it explicit and signify it with a letter.

Longer Arguments

So far I have restricted our discussion of missing premises to short arguments. But as you know, long arguments can contain many intermediate mini-arguments. Such subarguments require more than filling in a single missing premise. Nevertheless the strategies for identifying incomplete arguments and the guidelines for reconstruction of missing premises apply with equal force to longer arguments.

Consider for example this longer argument, which connects the increase in premarital sex with a reduction in teenage marriages and a subsequent reduction in the divorce rate.

[Premarital sex is on the rise.]^1 [One study shows that sexual intercourse is initiated at a younger age]^2 <u>and that</u> [its occurrence among teenagers is^3

increasing.] <u>Another shows that</u> [the percent of married persons between the ages of eighteen and twenty-four who had sexual experience prior to marriage was 95 percent for males and 81 percent for females.] <u>Still another</u> [survey shows that of the sampled adolescents between ages thirteen and nineteen, 52 percent had had some premarital intercourse.] [This increase in the prevalence of premarital sex is bound to reduce the number of teenage marriages.] <u>Thus</u> [there will probably be a substantial decline in the divorce rate.]

This argument consists of seven explicit assertions. (I am taking sentence 2 as two separate assertions.) The main conclusion is assertion 7, which the arguer feels is implied by assertion 6. This assertion is supported by assertion 1, which in turn is supported by assertions 2, 3, 4, and 5. The argument, then, has two mini-arguments, which can be diagrammed as follows:

and

Taken on face, the entire argument may be diagrammed

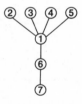

Is this argument incomplete? It is if *any* of its conclusions 1, 6, or 7 is not warranted by the support expressed. To see if there are any unwarranted inferences, we can apply the "what if" and topic coverage strategies.

Mini-conclusion 1 is inferred from a series of independent statistical references expressed in mini-premises 2, 3, 4, and 5. What if the data are true? Must it then be true that "Premarital sex is on the rise"? If we concede that the data are up-to-date and typify the results of research in the field, then they do entail the inference. There is no point in reconstructing these concessions as assumptions because they merely repeat the argument. After all, the arguer presumably believes that these data are typical and current and that they support the mini-conclusion about the increasing incidence of premarital sex.

So we can take the data presented in mini-premises 2, 3, 4, and 5 as providing conclusive support for mini-conclusion 1. (Obviously, if we have reason to dispute the data as atypical or dated, then in evaluating the argument, we'd criticize them.)

Applying the topic coverage strategy to this same mini-argument yields an identical judgment. The mini-conclusion relates premarital sex and the fact that it's increasing. The expressed mini-premises for this mini-conclusion cover premarital sex and give statistical evidence for its increase. In short, what is covered in the mini-conclusion is covered in the expressed mini-premise.

Let's now turn to the second mini-argument, in which mini-conclusion 6 is inferred from mini-premise 1. *What if* it's true that premarital sex is on the rise? Must it then be true that teenage marriages will be reduced (that is, the age of the average couple at marriage will be older than it was, say, in the immediately preceding generation)? Not necessarily. Why couldn't premarital sex just as likely encourage teenagers to marry *earlier?* It's possible that, having satisfied themselves that they are sexually compatible, a couple might be more inclined to marry than if they hadn't. Or because they are having premarital sex, a couple might be inclined to marry rather than risk having a baby or facing an abortion decision outside marriage. Thus the mini-premise that premarital sex is on the rise doesn't of itself lead to the mini-conclusion that teenage marriages will decline.

An application of the topic coverage strategy turns up the same assessment. Notice that the mini-conclusion covers teenage marriages and their decline. The mini-premise, however, says nothing of either topic. What, then, led the arguer from mini-premise 1 to mini-conclusion 6? It must have been an unexpressed mini-premise.

Our next job is to decide what mini-premise a together with the expressed mini-premise 1 leads to the mini-conclusion 6. What must the arguer be assuming that will complete the mini-argument "Premarital sex is on the rise. . . . This . . . is bound to reduce the number of teenage marriages"?

The reconstruction must connect premarital sex and how it reduces the number of teen marriages. It must be strong enough to support the conclusion but not so strong that it overstates the case. And it must not merely repeat the argument.

Here are three possible reconstructions:

Reconstruction 1a: Whenever premarital sex is on the rise, marriages are bound
  to be delayed.
Reconstruction 2a: Premarital sex discourages people from marrying.
Reconstruction 3a: Premarital sex discourages teenagers from marrying.

  Reconstruction 1a merely repeats the argument. We are still left wondering why premarital sex is bound to delay marriage. Reconstruction 2a looks better, but it's too strong. Taken together with mini-premise 1, it would yield the conclusion that there will be fewer marriages, or something to that effect. But the arguer infers only that *teenage* marriages will be reduced. Young people may marry later; they won't stop marrying altogether. Reconstruction 3a expresses what needs to be covered. It connects premarital sex and teenage marriages. It is strong enough to help produce the conclusion without overstating the issue. And, unlike reconstruction 1a, it illuminates rather than repeats. With the help of reconstruction 3a, we see how the arguer was led to mini-conclusion 6 from the expressed mini-premise 1.

The second mini-argument, therefore, can be diagrammed as follows:

$$\underbrace{① + ⓐ}_{⑥}$$

where a is taken to mean reconstruction 3a in our list of candidates.

The arguer then moves from premise 6 to conclusion 7, from the assertion that "the prevalence of premarital sex is bound to reduce the number of teenage marriages" to the argument's main conclusion: "There will be a substantial decline in the divorce rate."

You needn't be a professional logician to sense a considerable leap of logic between assertions 6 and 7. The conclusion covers a decline in the divorce rate but the premise mentions nothing of this. Why will a reduction in teenage marriages produce a substantial reduction in the number of divorces? Clearly the arguer must be making at least one other assumption b, which together with premise 6, helps provide support for conclusion 7.

Here are four possible reconstructions for the missing premise b:

1b: If the number of teenage marriages is reduced, the divorce rate likely will decline substantially.
2b: Teenage marriages end in divorce.
3b: A substantial number of teenage marriages end in divorce.
4b: A substantial number of divorces involve teenage marriages.

Reconstruction 1b merely repeats the argument; it doesn't illuminate it. We're still left wondering "But why will a reduction in teenage marriages likely lead to a substantial decline in divorce?" Reconstruction 2b supplies an answer: Teenage marriages result in divorce. The problem, however, is that this reconstruction is a sweeping generalization. It overstates the case. Not all teenage marriages end in divorce. And even if they did, a reduction in teenage marriages wouldn't necessarily produce a *substantial* decline in the number of divorces. This last observation applies equally to reconstruction 3b.

To illustrate this point, let's say that 75 percent of teenage marriages fail; that is, a substantial number of teenage marriages end in divorce (3b). Let's further say that these divorces account for only 2 percent of the total number of divorces; the other 98 percent involves nonteenage marriages. If this were the case, then reducing the number of teenage marriages would not produce a *substantial* decline in the divorce rate. But the conclusion of this argument implies that a substantial percentage of the total divorce rate involves teenage marriages. Reconstruction 3b misses this point; it merely asserts that a lot of teenage marriages end in divorce. Thus, if the number of such marriages can be reduced, then the number of divorces will decline, assuming that everything else remains constant. But will they decline *substantially?* They will do so only if teenage marriages contribute *substantially* to the total number of divorces.

Reconstruction 4b covers this point. It rightly focuses on the contribution teenage marriages make to the total divorce picture and not on the number of teenage marriages ending in divorce, as reconstructions 3b and 2b do. In addition it is strong enough to help support the conclusion but not so strong that it overstates the case, as does reconstruction 3a. If it's true that a substantial number of divorces involve teenage marriages (4b) and that the number of teenage marriages will decline (6), it must then be true that the divorce rate probably will decline (7). The diagram for this mini-argument, therefore, would be

$$\underbrace{⑥ \;+\; ⓑ}_{⑦}$$

where b is now taken to mean reconstruction 4b in our list of candidates. The diagram for the entire argument would be

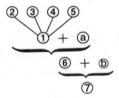

Summary

If you are unable to fill in an argument's missing premises, you cannot understand how the argument proceeds from evidence to conclusion; you cannot understand its structure and flow. If you are ignorant of its structure and flow, you can't evaluate it. So filling in missing premises is crucial to understanding, structuring, and evaluating arguments.

Fill in missing premises whenever an argument is incomplete and its missing premise(s) not obvious. There are two strategies you can use:

1. The "what if" strategy: Ask "what if" the stated premise(s) is true? Would the conclusion have to be true? If the answer is yes, the argument is complete; if it is no, the argument is incomplete. This strategy typically employs counterexamples, which are imagined situations that are consistent with the stated premise(s) but inconsistent with the conclusion. If an argument is complete, no counterexample is possible; if it is incomplete, a counterexample is possible. Failure to come up with a counterexample does not necessarily prove that an argument is incomplete. It may be that the critic has not been imaginative enough.

2. Topic coverage strategy: Determine whether the conclusion contains topics that are not covered in the stated premise(s). If so, the argument is incomplete.

In filling in missing premises, observe the following guidelines:

1. Apply the topic coverage strategy. The reconstructed premise, *taken together with the expressed premise*, should yield the conclusion.

2. Reconstruct a premise that is just strong enough to help support the conclusion. A reconstruction that overstates the missing premise misrepresents the argument, thereby making it easy to refute. One that understates the missing premise will be too weak to help support the conclusion.

3. Reconstruct a premise that illuminates, and doesn't just repeat, the argument.

Longer arguments generally can be handled like shorter ones. But be sure to unearth *all* missing premises that are not obvious. In other words, take care to uncover the longer argument's many mini-arguments.

Applications

The following arguments contain at least one missing premise and possibly more. Fill in the missing premise (or premises) and cast the argument.

1 Prime-time television encourages sexism by stereotyping women.

2 Television news has a penchant for portraying the visual and sensational. As a result it overlooks many newsworthy stories.

3 It's little wonder that many ads are misleading. They are geared primarily to selling us something.

4 Most news gives us an acquaintance with issues. That's why it's dangerous to assume that we gain knowledge about issues from viewing the evening news.

5 "Even though they'll rarely admit it, little boys do like little girls. . . . A little boy, the acknowledged 'tough guy' in the class, found a dead snake on the playground. To the accompaniment of cheers and jeers from the other boys, he picked it up and slung it carelessly around his neck. Then he marched purposefully across the playground to where the girls were huddled, shrieking and squealing. Unerringly he sought her out, the loudest squealer of them all, and stopped in front of her. In the silence that followed, the young lover cast his trophy at the feet of his beloved. Secure in the knowledge that he had bestowed a gift of inestimable value, he turned and strode away, while behind him the shrieks and squeals of outraged femininity broke out anew. . . ." (Joan C. Roloff and Virginia Brosseit, *Paragraphs* [Encino, Calif.: Glencoe, 1979], pp. 109–110.)

6 "After thirteen years in universities, trying to teach writing and literature, I

am convinced it is impossible to teach anyone to write, compose, paint, sculpture, or innovate creatively. With luck, you might get across minor techniques, or perhaps elementary craftsmanship suitable for low skill level commercial production. And, of course, you can teach about art and creativity and perhaps inspire self-confidence in individuals who already possess innate creative abilities. You can also teach individuals to recognize and appreciate perceptual innovation and significance. And, of course, you can teach about the importance of creativity in our cultural heritage. But no one can be taught to create a significant human experience in any media form." (Wilson Bryan Key, *The Clam-Plate Orgy and Other Subliminal Techniques for Manipulating Your Behavior* [New York: New American Library, 1980], p. 69.)

7 "In spite of the menacing developments (nuclear weapons, overpopulation, biological and psycho-pharmacological engineering, hybernation, changes in the environment), we remain unable to forecast the social consequences of technology. . . . Scientists are aware of the technological possibilities but are not sufficiently sensitive to their social implications. Some of the scientists care only about the success of their favorite projects. Some apply to these problems a personal pseudo-sociology made useless by its arrogance or naivete. And still others dodge responsibility by arguing that technology itself is neither good nor bad, that its virtues are determined by its uses. . . ." (D. N. Michael, "Science, Scientists, and Politics," in Willis H. Truitt and T. W. Graham Solomons, eds., *Science, Technology and Freedom* [Boston: Houghton Mifflin, 1974], p. 180.)

8 "The medical professional undoubtedly has special skills for determining and applying the specific criteria that measure whether particular body functions have irreversibly ceased. Whether the Harvard criteria [i.e., criteria that define death largely in terms of the absence of brain activity] taken together accurately divide those who are in irreversible coma from those who are not is clearly an empirical question (although the important consideration of just how sure we want to be takes us once again into matters that cannot be answered scientifically). But the crucial policy question is at the conceptual level: should the individual in irreversible coma be treated as dead? . . . If I am to be pronounced dead by the use of a philosophical or theological concept that I do not share, I at least have a right to careful due process. Physicians in the states that do not authorize brain-oriented criteria for pronouncing death who take it upon themselves to use those criteria . . . should be . . . prosecuted. . . ." (Robert M. Veatch, *Death, Dying and the Biological Revolution* [Englewood Cliffs, N.J.: Prentice-Hall, 1978], p. 75.)

9 "At its heart, the question of whether the sane can be distinguished from the insane (and whether degrees of insanity can be distinguished from each other) is a simple matter: do the salient characteristics that lead to diagnoses reside in the patients themselves or in the environments and contexts in which observers find them. . . . Gains can be made in deciding which of these is more nearly accurate by getting normal people (that is, people who do not have, and have never suffered, symptoms of serious psychiatric

disorders) admitted to psychiatric hospitals and then determining whether they were discovered to be sane and, if so, how. If the sanity of such pseudo-patients were always detected, there would be prima facie evidence that a sane individual can be distinguished from the insane context in which he is found. . . . If, on the other hand, the sanity of the pseudo-patients were never discovered, . . . this would support the view that psychiatric diagnosis betrays little about the patient but much about the environment in which an observer finds him." (D. L. Rosenhan, "On Being Sane in Insane Places," *Science* 179 [January 19, 1973]: 251.)

10 "No matter what my conviction may be as to the advisability of abortion for a given patient, it is overruled by my adherence to the principle of autonomy. By this I mean that we should support the adolescent patient in her autonomous decision making. [We must ask] questions in an unbiased fashion. (If we can't do this, our obligation is to refer the patient to someone else.) This approach may increase the anxiety and suffering of the patient. . . . The increased anxiety . . . may lead to further exploration, reading of material on abortion, talking to people who agree or disagree with her, etc. She will then make a decision with more understanding. . . . By guiding the adolescent not to avoid stressful questions, . . . a counselor also is preparing her for a better future. The tragedy of the adolescent facing the abortion decision is that she has to choose between the 'sin of aborting' and the 'sin of harming one's life.' In her dilemma the adolescent might have to 'sin boldly.'" (Thomas Silber, "Abortion in Adolescence: The Ethical Dimension," *Adolescence* 15 [Summer 1980]: 467.)

11 "Let us now examine the Golden Rule ["Do unto others as you would have them do unto you"] in terms of its clarity. . . . We might begin by asking about the unit of action. Are the actions implied in the rule [those of] a person or persons, groups or some larger social [unit]? Are you and the others in the Golden Rule to be seen as representatives of various social units or as independent citizens or persons in their own right, or does it make a difference? Of course the word 'do' in the Golden Rule can mean many things too, and as usually interpreted all behaviors are included. Another thing which is not too clear has to do with the adequacy of resources. In most human situations there is a scarcity of resources. . . . We know from the research in psychology that emotional and situational factors, among others, can alter and distort what is perceived to be done to oneself, this seemingly inviting considerable distortion and error. And of course the Golden Rule is not very clear as to how one measures the consequences which arise by using it. Do we look at both mental and physical consequences, how does the time dimension come in, and so on? . . . I believe that we have demonstrated that the Golden Rule cannot be taken as a categorical imperative. . . ." (Craig C. Lundberg, "The Golden Rule and Business Management: *Quo Vadis?" Economic and Business Bulletin* 20 [January 1968]: 39 — 40.)

PART THREE

Evaluation

Criticizing Arguments

You have just learned how to identify arguments, cast them, and fill in their missing premises. You are now poised, ready to evaluate arguments.

As I mentioned in the first chapter, many of us don't quite know what to make of the myriad messages that bombard us daily. This is especially true of claims designed to win our assent. On what basis can we intelligently evaluate the arguments we come across daily? What should we accept? What should we reject or reserve judgment about? Furthermore, when can we feel confident that our own arguments are good ones? We take up these questions in this part of our study.

Books have been written about argument evaluation, so what we cover in the next four chapters will hardly exhaust the subject. But it will give you the essentials you need to evaluate your arguments and those of others.

You will notice that this part comprises Chapters 7 through 10. In Chapter 8 you will learn how to detect argument bias. In Chapter 9 you will learn a simple, brief format for evaluating arguments. And in Chapter 10 you will learn how to handle the argumentative essay.

Before tackling any of these subjects, however, you must learn how to criticize arguments. This requires a familiarity with certain key terms and concepts: cogency, validity, truth, and justification. The present chapter provides you with this necessary background.

A final word before starting. Throughout this chapter I use the word "criticize" or some variation of it. Indeed, the title of the chapter is "Criticizing Arguments." In the context of argument evaluation, "to criticize" does not mean "to find fault with" but to make judgments regarding the merits of an argument, and "criticism" refers to the act of judging the quality of an argument. In criticizing an argument, then, we inspect it to determine whether it is good or bad, whether it is what I will term "cogent" or "not cogent."

Cogency

When we criticize an argument, we are trying to find out whether it's cogent. Broadly speaking, a cogent argument is one that convinces because of its clear, forcible presentation. But I want to use "cogent" more specifically to signify the two properties essential to a good argument, namely: (1) that its conclusion correctly follows from its premises and (2) that its premises are acceptable. Put in other, more technical words: A cogent argument is one whose conclusion is *validly* drawn from *true*, or *justified*, premises.

Validity

In every argument an inference is drawn from the premises given. When the inference correctly follows from the premises, it is said to be valid—and so is the argument. There are two basic kinds of valid argument: deductive and inductive.

Valid Deductive Arguments   The essential property of a valid deductive argument is this: If its premises are taken to be true, then its conclusion must also be true. In other words, if the premises of a valid deductive argument are assumed true, then its conclusion cannot be false.

Here's a simple example of a valid deductive argument:

Because [all humans are[1] vertebrates] and [Fred is[2] a human,] [Fred must be a vertebrate.[3]]

When premises 1 and 2 are taken to be true, then the conclusion, assertion 3, must follow. To accept these premises and reject the conclusion would be contradictory; the conclusion cannot be false if these premises are true.

Notice that validity does not depend on the premises' actually being true. Take for example this silly but illustrative valid deductive argument:

[All four-legged creatures are humans.[1]] [Chickens have[2] four legs.] Therefore [chickens[3] are humans.]

The premises of this argument, assertions 1 and 2, are absurdly false. But if they are *assumed* true, the conclusion must also be true. If you don't see why, apply the "what if" strategy we discussed in the preceding chapter. *What if* it's true that all four-legged creatures are humans and *what if* chickens have four legs?

Must it then be true that chickens are humans? Yes, for no counterexample is possible. Therefore this is a *valid* deductive argument, although it's obviously not *cogent* because its premises are untrue.

Similarly, it's possible for an invalid deductive argument to have *true* premises:

$$\left[\text{All mothers are}^1 \text{females.}\right] \left[\text{Lisa is}^2 \text{a female.}\right] \underline{\text{Thus}} \left[\text{Lisa is}^3 \text{a mother.}\right]$$

To see why this deductive argument is invalid, ask yourself *"What if* it's true that all mothers are females and that Lisa is a female? Must it then also be true that Lisa is a mother? No, for Lisa could be a female who is *not* a mother." Such an imagined situation is consistent with the premises but obviously inconsistent with the conclusion. The counterexample therefore shows that we are dealing with an *invalid* deductive argument.

Quick Check on Valid Deductive Arguments

1 Determine which are valid deductive arguments. Then cast the valid ones.
   a Most corporation lawyers are political conservatives. Bill Morrison is a corporation lawyer. Therefore Bill Morrison is probably a political conservative.
   b Marty must be a real male chauvinist. After all, he's an athlete, isn't he?
   c Some reference books are textbooks, for all textbooks are books intended for careful study and some reference books are intended for the same purpose.
   d Since snakes are reptiles, clearly some dangerous animals aren't reptiles.

Comments

a. ***Valid:*** $\left[\text{Most corporation lawyers are}^1 \text{political conservatives.}\right]$ $\left[\text{Bill Morrison}^2 \text{is a}\right.$
   corporation lawyer.$\left.\right]$ $\underline{\text{Therefore}}$ $\left[\text{Bill Morrison is probably}^3 \text{a political conservative.}\right]$

$$\frac{① + ②}{③}$$

b. ***Valid:*** missing premise: All athletes are male^a chauvinists. $\left[\text{Marty must be a}^1 \text{real male}\right.$
   chauvinist.$\left.\right]$ $\underline{\text{After all,}}$ $\left[\text{he's an}^2 \text{athlete,}\right]$ isn't he?

$$\frac{② + ⓐ}{①}$$

c. ***Invalid***
d. ***Invalid:*** missing premise: Some snakes are not dangerous animals, or some dangerous animals are not snakes. Neither possibility helps entail the conclusion.

Valid Inductive Arguments   Of course many arguments that are cogent do not provide *conclusive* grounds for the acceptance of their conclusions. The premises of valid inductive arguments, for example, provide grounds—but not conclusive grounds—for their conclusions. The truth of the premises of a valid inductive argument do not guarantee the truth of its conclusion, but they do make this conclusion probable or likely.

Here's an example of a valid inductive argument:

[Professor Jones has never missed a class.] So [chances are she'll be in class today.]

If the premise, assertion 1, is accepted as true, then it would be reasonable to accept the argument's conclusion, assertion 2. Of course, even if the premise is true, the conclusion may prove false: Jones may not show up for class. Perhaps she's ill or had an accident or an important conflicting appointment.

Here's another example of a valid inductive argument:

[It's highly unlikely that any female will play football in the National Football League in the near future,] for [none has so far.]

Again, if the premise is accepted as true, it provides good grounds—though not conclusive ones—for accepting the conclusion.

Given this brief analysis of valid deductive and valid inductive arguments, you should be able to recognize the essential difference between deductive and inductive reasoning. It is this: The conclusion of a valid deduction is just as certain as its premises, while the conclusion of a valid induction is not. Even when valid, an inductive argument always contains an element of doubt because its inference is not already made by its premises. In contrast, the premises of a valid deductive argument provide conclusive grounds for the acceptance of its conclusion.

We have considered one basic ingredient of a cogent argument: the validity, or correctness, of its inference. In determining an argument's validity, we have seen that it isn't necessary to know whether its premises are true. We need only hypothesize that they are true and then determine whether they provide conclusive or probable grounds for the conclusion. If they do, the argument is valid. But though it isn't necessary to know that the premises are true to determine an argument's validity, we need to know that they are true to determine whether the argument is cogent.

Quick Check on Valid Inductive Arguments

By relating each of the following sets of terms, compose first a valid deductive argument, then a valid inductive argument.

> **Sample:** jobs, college education, personal fulfillment
> **Valid Deductive Argument:** College education is necessary to get a good job.

Without a good job, a person stands no chance of attaining personal fulfillment. It follows that a college education is necessary to attain personal fulfillment.

Valid Inductive Argument: College education typically qualifies one for a good job, which is an essential ingredient of personal fulfillment. So, with a college education, I'll probably attain personal fulfillment.

1 Students, homework, teachers
2 Love, sex, marriage
3 Television, entertainment, relaxation
4 Reading, thinking, arguing

Truth

As a concept truth doesn't present much of a problem. *An assertion is true if it reports an actual state of affairs* (that is, some present, past, or future event, condition, or circumstance). Obviously there are many states of affairs in the world. If you're over five feet tall, that's a state of affairs; if the current air temperature is sixty degrees Fahrenheit, that's a state of affairs. States of affairs needn't exist only in the present; they may already have occurred or will be occurring: "George Washington was the first President of the United States," "Water will boil at 212 degrees Fahrenheit at sea level," and "A spirochete causes syphilis" are true statements that report actual states of affairs in the past or future.

In contrast, a false statement is one that does not report an actual state of affairs, present, past, or future. Just negate the three preceding examples and you'll get false statements.

Although truth is a straightforward enough concept, determining what is true can be troublesome. One reason is that truth is often confused with opinion or belief; another is that truth sometimes is considered relative.

1. **Truth is not opinion or belief.** Whereas a true assertion reports an actual state of affairs, a belief or opinion portrays a person's attitude toward a particular assertion. For example, the astronomer Carl Sagan *believes* that extraterrestrial life exists and the chemist Linus Pauling *believes* that vitamin C can prevent the common cold.

Here the word "believes" can be understood in at least two ways. It may mean that Sagan regards the statement "Extraterrestrial life exists" as true. It may also mean that Sagan has a high degree of confidence in the truth of the assertion "Extraterrestrial life exists." Either way of understanding statements of belief is fine for our purposes. For us the key point is that belief refers to the attitude that someone has toward an assertion. Since an attitude may be correct or incorrect, belief may be erroneous. Maybe extraterrestrial life doesn't exist; perhaps vitamin C doesn't cure the common cold.

2. **Truth is not relative.** When we ignore the difference between belief and truth, we make the mistake of assuming that truth is relative. We assume that persons themselves determine at least some truths and that these truths

may vary from individual to individual. The error of this position lies in a misunderstanding of what truth is.

Remember that truth is a characteristic of an assertion that is reporting an actual state of affairs. Thus "Humans have visited the moon" reports an actual state of affairs. That state of affairs is *independent* of what any one of us thinks or believes about it. Humans have either visited the moon or they have not. In this instance they have. That's a fact, and facts are not relative, although beliefs certainly are.

What if the statement "Humans have visited the moon" had been made prior to the summer of 1969, when the first person visited the moon? Then the statement would be false. But be careful. This doesn't mean that truth changes, that what was not true yesterday may be true today or tomorrow. The error in thinking that truth changes arises from a failure to see that we must evaluate each statement within its context. This means in part that we must take into account *when* a statement is made. The assertion that humans have visited the moon, when made prior to July 20, 1969, is a separate and distinct assertion from the one uttered today: We're really speaking about two different statements. What makes them different is the time context in which each is asserted. Failing to realize this, we fall into the error of thinking that what is true today may be false tomorrow, or that what's false today may be true tomorrow.

Testing for Truth   Although distinguishing truth from belief and realizing that truth is not relative helps us understand the nature of truth, it doesn't help us test the truth of premises. For example, consider this common argument:

[The death penalty should be legalized^1 for certain serious crimes] because [it is a^{2}deterrent.]

In criticizing this or any other argument, we can rightly assume that the arguer is doing more than just asserting belief in its premises. For an argument to be cogent, its premises must be true; they must be reporting an actual state of affairs. In this argument the arguer obviously *believes* that the death penalty is a deterrent. Our job in criticizing the argument is not to determine whether the person truly believes this assertion but whether or not this premise is true. Does the death penalty actually deter crime?

Answering this question probably would require some research. If the research turns up conclusive evidence, then you can accept the premise as true. But what constitutes *conclusive* evidence? How much evidence do we need to accept a statement as true? There is no simple or certain answer, for assertions vary in breadth, and consequently the amount and quality of the evidence needed to support them will vary. For example, if I said "Washington D.C., is the nation's capital," you'd readily agree. But if I said "Cancer is caused by a virus," you'd likely ask my reasons for making such a claim. The truth of the first assertion, if in doubt, can be determined readily enough by consulting an encyclopedia, for example. But the truth of the second assertion requires considerable scientific support. How much? As already indicated, that's impossible to say. But familiarity with the concept of justification helps clarify this important question.

Before turning to the subject of justification, let's return to the argument on capital punishment to make a related point. Suppose that your research left no reasonable doubt that capital punishment does in fact deter crime. You would still have to test the truth of the argument's missing premise: Whatever deters crime should be a legal punishment for certain serious crimes. This assertion poses unique problems because it's a value judgment; that is, an assessment of worth. To find out whether the death penalty deters crime, you can introduce all sorts of data discovered in your research. But what can you do to determine the truth of the assertion "Whatever deters crime should be a legal punishment for certain serious crimes"?

Value judgments like this one figure prominently in everyday arguments. To discover whether they are true, you must be familiar with the concept of justification.

Quick Check on Testing for Truth

1 Which premises of the arguments in the Quick Check on Valid Deductive Arguments (page 179) would you accept as true?
2 Which arguments would you consider cogent; that is, valid and true?

Comments

1. In a, the statement "Most corporation lawyers are political conservatives," is at least doubtful. Without supporting evidence, I'd reserve judgment about its truth. Reserving judgment isn't the same as judging it to be false. In fact, the assertion may be true. But until its truth is no longer in reasonable doubt, it must be considered as *possibly* false. In b, the unexpressed premise "All athletes are male chauvinists" is patently false. In c, the premises are true. In d, the premises are true. (Note: Be sure to test for truth the premises of the arguments you constructed.)

2. When an argument's conclusion does not follow validly from its premises or if any of its premises is false or in doubt, the argument is not cogent. Thus none of the arguments—a, b, c, or d—is cogent. Notice, however, why they fail the test of cogency. Arguments a and b are not cogent because of faulty premises, even though the arguments are valid. Arguments c and d are not cogent because they are invalid, even though their premises (and conclusions) are true.

Justification

Justification refers to the reasonableness of the evidence used to support an assertion. When you're testing the truth of premises, you are trying to discover if the premises are justified; that is, if there is reasonable evidence to support them. If so, they can be considered true; if not, they can't be considered true.

But what constitutes *reasonable* evidence? Evidence is reasonable when there is enough of the right kind of evidence to make a claim. *Enough* and the *right kind*—the justification of premises clearly depends on both the *quantity* and *quality* of evidence. How much and what kind of evidence need be given will in turn depend largely on the kind of assertion the premise happens to be.

Types of Assertions

Premises can be any of the various types of assertions we can make. Consider for example the following types of assertions:

1. *X* is not non-*X*.
2. *X* is either *Y* or non-*Y*.
3. All humans are vertebrates.
4. No circle is a square.
5. The sum of the interior angles of a triangle is equal to two right angles.
6. $C^2 = A^2 + B^2$
7. This candy is sweet.
8. That leaf is green.
9. The bird on that limb is a robin.
10. Sacramento is the capital of California.

While we would be justified in making any of these assertions, the justification would not always be the same. In other words, the reasons that these assertions are true are not identical.

For example, assertions 1 and 2 are justified because their denial paralyzes all thought. If they are not justified, we can forget about ever thinking intelligently. Put in more technical terms, their denial is self-contradictory. Philosophers often call these statements *laws of logic*. A law of logic is a principle presupposed in all human thought and discourse. Its justification is found in reason, not in the things of the world.

The justification for assertions 3 and 4 also is found in reason. Specifically it's found in the meaning of the terms themselves. Assertion 3 is justified because the meaning of "vertebrates" is included in the meaning of "humans," and the utterance merely asserts this inclusion. Similarly, in assertion 4 the meaning of "circle" excludes the meaning of "square," and the utterance merely asserts this exclusion. Such assertions are sometimes said to have *semantic justification*, which means that their justification is given in the meaning of the terms or in their syntactical combinations.

Assertions 5 and 6 find justification in their being theorems that we can infer from the postulates and definitions of geometry and algebra. They are examples of what is termed *systemic justification*. Systemic justification refers to types of assertions that derive their justification from the logical interdependence of all integral parts in a deductive system. Again, they find their justification strictly in reason.

Rather than appealing strictly to reason, as the previous assertions have, assertions 7 through 10 appeal to the world of sense experience. Assertions such as 7 and 8 are sometimes termed *basic*. A basic assertion is one that finds justification in first-person experience; qualities immediately experienced by the individual confirm the claim being made. Thus the justification of such statements (similar to those preceded by "I believe" or "I think" or "It seems to me") is found in the person making the assertion: You cannot argue with my assertion that I see green any more than you can argue that I don't believe in capital punishment when I assert that I do, though you could challenge the belief itself.

Assertions 9 and 10 essentially are *hypotheses*. As with all hypotheses, their confirmation rests on the other statements they entail. Thus the assertion "The bird on the limb is a robin" entails a variety of assertions that pertain to this type of bird, to birds as a whole, and to animals generally—assertions regarding flight, color, plumage, and so on. If all these entailed assertions can be accepted, then the original assertion is justified. The same analysis applies to "Sacramento is the capital of California."

Assertions 7 through 10, then, are cases of *empirical justification*. This means that their justification requires the confirmation of sense experience. Sometimes, as with assertions 7 and 8, the confirmation may be sought strictly within the self. Other times, as with assertions 9 and 10, confirmation must be sought outside the self; that is, in the world. It is assertions like these—empirical assertions that need justification in the world—that raise the most serious questions about sufficiency of evidence.

Thus the justification of assertions 1 through 8 presents no problem. The justification of assertions 9 and 10, however, does. This type of assertion raises the question, How much evidence do we need to make an assertion whose justification lies in some state of affairs? It's impossible to say precisely. But although some philosophers would require it, we will assume that we don't need *all the evidence there could ever be*. If we did it is doubtful that any empirical statement needing confirmation in the world could ever be justified, and critical thinking in the practical realm would stop dead in the water.

Justification for assertions like 9 and 10 requires evidence so strong in quantity and quality that, in a manner in speaking, it amounts to certainty. But, I admit, it's still possible to ask, On what basis do I judge evidence to be so strong in quantity and quality that it amounts to certainty? Notice that I have moved the question from "How much and what kind of evidence are needed for justifying a premise?" to "On what grounds can we determine that there's enough of the right kind of evidence for a premise to conclude that it is justified?" In other words, in assessing the truth of empirical statements like 9 and 10, what counts as justification, as reasonable evidence in support of the premise? Answering this question, which concerns criteria for evaluating evidence, will take us far in verifying the premises of ordinary arguments. Before proceeding to the subject of evidence evaluation, study the chart on page 186, which sums up what we've been discussing.

Type of Assertion	Example	Justifica-tion	Problem-atic
1. law of logic	X is either Y or not Y, as in "A human being is either a verte-brate or not a vertebrate."	reason	no
2. semantic	"All humans are vertebrates."	reason	no
3. systemic	"No circle is a square."	reason	no
4. empirical			
a. basic	"This candy is delicious."	sense experience within self	
	"I believe capital punishment deters crime."		no
b. hypothetical	"Capital punishment deters crime."		
	"Cancer is caused by a virus."	sense experience	
	"Extraterrestrial life exists."	outside self; that is,	yes
	"Compared with men, women don't get equal pay for equal work."	in the world	

Note: One important type of assertion not covered here is the value assertion. This type of assertion is considered in depth later in this chapter.

Quick Check on Types of Assertions

What type of assertion—law of logic, semantic, systemic, basic, or hypotheti-cal—is each of these statements? Which do you think are justified? Explain.

1 This dog before me is an English shepherd.
2 Lee Harvey Oswald could not have fired three times—hitting President Ken-nedy twice and Governor Connally once—in 5.6 seconds or less.
3 Three times two is six.
4 A robin is a bird.
5 If the battery in my car is dead, the car won't start.
6 There's intelligent life in outer space.
7 I've got a hunch that there's life somewhere else in the universe.
8 Beta-blockers like the drug Inderal can help prevent second heart attacks.
9 If I release this piece of chalk and it's unsupported, it will fall.

Comments

1. A hypothetical statement whose justification depends on whether the dog does, in fact, fall into the category of canines termed "English shepherds."
2. A hypothetical statement whose justification hinges upon considerable confirmatory data. One datum is that tests indicated that it took at least 2.3 seconds to operate the bolt on Oswald's rifle. Presumably, then, it would have taken Oswald at least 6.9 seconds to fire three shots. This fact alone, however, is insufficient to establish that Oswald *could not* have fired three times in 5.6 seconds or less. But it would go far toward justifying a weaker statement, such as "Oswald *probably* didn't fire three times in 5.6 seconds or less."
3. A systemic statement that is justified.
4. A semantic statement that is justified: A robin is, by definition, a bird.

5. A hypothetical statement that is justified.
6. A hypothetical statement that is not justified.
7. A basic statement that is justified. Notice *what* is justified here: that *the person has a hunch* that there's life somewhere else in the universe and *not* that there is, in fact, life somewhere else in the universe.
8. A hypothetical statement that is probably justified, given the considerable evidence that shows the efficacy of beta-blockers in reducing the chances of a *second* heart attack.
9. A systemic statement that is justified by appeal to the law of gravitation. Note that the law of gravitation, and other scientific laws, are not laws of logic but descriptions of nature as we understand it. Thus, if the chalk didn't fall, or even rose, this wouldn't confound logic but our understanding of the physical universe.

Evaluating Evidence: Observations

Before proceeding let's summarize what we've learned so far. In criticizing arguments we are basically trying to determine whether they are cogent. A cogent argument is both valid and true. A valid argument is one whose premises, expressed and unexpressed, provide conclusive (in the case of deduction) or probable (in the case of induction) grounds for its conclusion. A true statement reports an actual state of affairs. In testing a premise for truth, we must determine whether the assertion is justified; that is, whether there is reasonable evidence to support it. In general, a premise is justified (and hence is considered true) when there is enough of the right kind of evidence to support it. In the case of empirical assertions whose confirmation must be sought in the world (such as assertions 9 and 10 on the list on page 184), the issue of justification is problematic. Instead of trying to determine precisely how much and what kind of evidence is needed for their justification, we are better served by trying to establish the grounds on which we can satisfy ourselves that a premise has sufficient evidence supporting it, in both quantity and quality.

When determining the grounds for the justification of premises, it's helpful to recognize that what is essential as evidence is what scientists call "observations." Whenever scientists weigh, measure, or take the temperature of something and then record their findings, they are making observations. These observations frequently serve as a basis for the premises of a subsequent argument. For example, your family doctor inductively concludes that you have a flu because you have certain flulike symptoms. Thus

> **Premises:** Symptom A: runny nose
> Symptom B: fever
> Symptom C: bodily aches and pains
> **Conclusion:** You probably have the flu.

Underlying this diagnosis and its legitimacy are observations the doctor has made. Similarly, Carl Sagan would conclude that extraterrestrial life exists, and Linus Pauling would conclude that vitamin C can prevent the common cold, on the basis of observations they have made. So the question of sufficiency of evidence for a claim to knowledge is bound up with observations.

When can we accept an observation as correct? We can do so when we are satisfied with the conditions under which the observation was made and with the ability of the observer. Specifically, there are five key points to consider in evaluating observations: (1) the physical conditions, (2) the sensory acuity of the observer, (3) the background knowledge of the observer, (4) the objectivity of the observer, and (5) the supporting testimony of other observers.

1. Physical conditions. *Physical conditions refer to the conditions under which the observations were made.* If your doctor diagnoses your condition solely on the basis of a telephone conversation with you, then her diagnosis would be in serious doubt. But suppose she made her observations during a complete physical examination. In this case the conditions under which she made the observations were conducive to obtaining correct information on the basis of which a diagnosis could be made.

2. Sensory acuity. *Sensory acuity refers to the sensory abilities of the observer.* Some people can see and hear better than others; some have a more sharply developed sense of smell and taste, and even of touch. Observations always must be evaluated in light of the observer's ability to have made the observations.

In science, where precise measurements are crucial, instruments heighten the observer's sensory acuity. As a result, in evaluating the reliability of scientific investigations where exact measurements of height, weight, volume, and temperature are crucial, we must evaluate the accuracy of the instruments as well as the sensory abilities of the persons making the observations.

The technological extension of the human senses can be decisive in providing enough of the right kind of evidence to justify a conclusion. A classic example is the invention of the telescope, which allowed so many claims of the so-called Copernican revolution to be confirmed. Today we can point to such things as the Pioneer XI spacecraft, which journeyed into outer space and, with the aid of marvelously sophisticated cameras, confirmed among other things that Saturn is surrounded by radiation.

3. Necessary background knowledge. *Necessary background knowledge refers to what an observer must already know to make a reliable observation.* To observe a lump in your thyroid gland is one thing. To infer that the lump is malignant is entirely different. Such a claim requires evidence collected by someone with a medical background, for example a pathologist.

You needn't look far today to see how often this criterion for evaluating the reliability of observations is violated. For example, celebrities are paid handsomely for endorsing anything from toothpaste to a dazzling computer. More often than not, however, these endorsers lack the necessary background knowledge to make their endorsements credible. Yet the endorsements seem to persuade, and they certainly provide a nice living for those making them.

4. Objectivity. *Objectivity refers to the ability to view ourselves and the world without distortion.* None of us can be totally objective, for as hard as we try, we will always view things according to our own frames of reference. But we can become aware of these biases and minimize their impact on our observations. We can expect the same of others.

Be aware of people's frames of reference, their "taken-for-granteds." This doesn't mean that you should automatically dismiss the views of those who have vested interests. But you should realize that their loyalties—and hence their built-in biases—may be coloring their observations and thus coloring the evidence they present as justification for a claim. Failing to do this, you will end up swallowing and formulating all sorts of bogus arguments.

5. *Supporting testimony.* *Supporting testimony refers to the observations of other observers that tend to support the evidence presented.* In general, the greater the number of corroborative observations, the greater the evidence.

For example, suppose that one morning a friend tells you that your English professor won't be in class that day. "If he won't," you think to yourself, "there probably won't be any class." You'd prefer not to wait for several hours until class time to find out but then again you don't want to miss class either. So you seek out several other class members to corroborate your friend's assertion. No one does. Still, maybe your friend knows something your classmates don't. You go to the professor's secretary, who tells you that as far as he knows, the professor will be in class. Lacking corroborations for your friend's claim, you shouldn't accept it; you have no justification for inferring that there will be no class.

Even if an observation meets all the other criteria, it is unreliable if it lacks supporting testimony. What's more, the corroborative evidence itself must meet these criteria. The greater the number of corroborative observations, the more reliable the observation at issue. Although it's impossible to say how many corroborations are needed, surely the more controversial the claim the more the corroborations needed.

These five criteria, whose relationship to observations and the hypothetical statements they support is illustrated in the chart below, are extremely helpful in evaluating empirical assertions that need confirmation in the world. Although an observation that passes these tests may prove erroneous, these criteria together provide a quick and immediate way of deciding whether you have enough of the right kind of evidence for accepting a premise or asserting it. They are also useful in criticizing still another kind of common assertion, the value assertion.

Hypothetical Statements				
OBSERVATIONS				
Physical Conditions	Sensory Acuity	Necessary Background Knowledge	Objectivity	Supporting Testimony

Value Assertions

In addition to the types of assertions already mentioned, there is still another—the value assertion—that is so common and so misunderstood as to warrant depth coverage.

Value assertions are judgments of worth. Ordinarily we think of them as expressing our values in ethics, art, and social and political philosophy. Thus, regarding ethics someone might claim "You *shouldn't* lie" or "Murder is *immoral*" or "Abortion is *wrong*." Regarding art: "Beethoven's Fifth Symphony is his *best*"; "Neil Simon's latest plays are *flawed*"; "Steven Spielberg is a *great* film director." Regarding social and political philosophy: "Democracy is the *best* form of government"; "Capital punishment *should be* legalized"; "The United States *should* evenly distribute its wealth among its citizenry."

Sometimes value assertions become premises in arguments. Here's an example:

[Selling illicit drugs to children is reprehensible.]^1 Since [Frank sells children illicit drugs,]^2 [he's doing something reprehensible.]^3

I will call this type of argument a value argument because one of its premises, assertion 1, is a value assertion. Here's another example of a value argument.

[If democracy is the best form of government, then all nations should strive to be democratic.]^1 [Democracy is the best form of government.]^2 Therefore [all nations should strive to be democratic.]^3

Assertion 2 expresses a value.

Here's one final example:

[The film *Stardust Memories* must be worth seeing]^1 because [it's written and directed by Woody Allen.]^2

Here the unexpressed premise is a value assertion: "Any film written and directed by Woody Allen is worth seeing."

As with any argument, the cogency of a value argument depends in part on the truth of its premises. Determining the justification of value assertions raises problems.

Quick Check on Value Assertions

1 Identify whether these are value or nonvalue statements.
  a Stealing is wrong.
  b Shakespeare is the most effective dramatist in the English language.
  c Shakespeare wrote comedies, histories, and tragedies.

  d Oxygen starvation can result in brain damage.
  e Education is the surest ticket to occupational success.
  f Sexism is a function of acculturation.
  g American foreign policy since World War II has been based on a narrow
       and short-term view of national interest.
  h Sex without love is sin.
  i Honesty is the best policy.
  j A man who defends himself has a fool for a client.
  k Polygamy is illegal in California.
  l If two candidates are equally qualified for a job and one is a woman or a
       member of a minority group, the job should be given to the woman or
       minority member.
  m Photography isn't really art.
  n Our criminal justice system is a national disgrace.
  o In part, philosophy studies issues that science cannot fully answer.
  p Drunk driving is the cause of about half of all traffic fatalities.
  q The pill shouldn't be taken over a long period of time without medical
       supervision.
  r The best government is the one that governs least.
  s The cooler the light, the less energy it wastes.

Comments

Value assertions: a, b, e, g, h, i, j, l, m, n, r.
Nonvalue assertions: c, d, f, k, o, p, q, s.

2. Write two statements about each subject, one expressing a value judgment, the other
   not. Then write a third statement that combines a value and a nonvalue assertion in
   one sentence.

   Sample: sex education

   value assertion: Sex education *should not* be taught in public schools.
   nonvalue assertion: Some public schools teach sex education.
   combination: Sex education, *which is an evil plot devised by our enemies to weaken
              our nation's moral fiber,* is now being taught in some public schools. [value
              assertion italicized]

   a. Political parties   d. Pornography
   b. Legalization of marijuana   e. Premarital cohabitation
   c. Advertising   f. The military draft

Justification of Value Assertions

[Selling illicit drugs to children is reprehensible.]¹ <u>Since</u> [Frank sells children²
illicit drugs,] [he's doing something reprehensible.]³

We can easily ascertain the truth of assertion 2 by determining whether this assertion reports an actual state of affairs. But what about assertion 1? What must be the case for the statement "Selling drugs to children is reprehensible" to be true? Just what state of affairs do we measure this or any other value assertion against to test its truth?

Such a question does more than stimulate philosophical contemplation of the nature of truth and value assertions. It also gets at practical problems that often come up in criticizing arguments. To determine whether a value-laden argument is cogent, we must be able to verify its value-asserting premises. But how can we do this?

Some people believe that value assertions are essentially meaningless. Others hold that they make sense but that they can't be justified. Still others believe that value assertions make sense and can be justified but that their justification does not extend beyond the society in which the individual making the assertion lives. Since so many important arguments you come across or devise contain value assertions, you must know how to deal with them.

Before discussing some strategies for evaluating value assertions, I should explain one personal assumption about such assertions. I believe that value assertions can be evaluated. That doesn't sound like much of a claim, I know. But without getting into all the philosophical subtleties that enshroud it, rest assured that the claim is far from being obvious in a philosophical sense. For example, some individuals insist that only things that can be "counted" or "measured" can be evaluated. Since value assertions apparently cannot be so quantified, according to this view they cannot be evaluated.

Now, it's undoubtedly true that value judgments can't be weighed or measured with scientific precision. But it doesn't necessarily follow that they cannot be evaluated at all. The fact is, as we have just seen, people can, do, and must evaluate value assertions. Simply because we can't count on laboratory precision in our evaluations doesn't make our task any less trivial or meaningless. Indeed, it could be argued that the inevitable inexactness of our evaluations makes it even more urgent that we carefully consider just how we go about our evaluation.

For our purposes it probably is most important to acknowledge that values and value judgments crowd in on us. Like it or not, we must accept some, reject others, and keep an open mind about most. And this presupposes evaluation. We must weigh the reasons for accepting a value claim against those for rejecting it, just as we must for nonvalue assertions. When there are more of the right kinds of reasons for accepting it, we consider it justified. When there are more of the right kinds of reasons for rejecting it, we consider it unjustified.

It is in the sense of justification, then—of having more reasons for accepting a value claim than rejecting it—that I am connecting truth with value assertions. In short, when I speak of evaluating value assertions, I have in mind a rational process that aims to determine whether there is reasonable evidence for accepting such an assertion. This process consists of at least two steps: clarifying language and ensuring that the assertion meets minimum adequacy requirements.

Clarifying Language

To determine whether a value assertion is justified, the most important thing to do is to clarify the language used. Value words such as "good," "ought," "wrong," "superb," "should not," "best," and "inferior" are vague; they invite myriad interpretations. Before evaluating a value assertion, then, you must determine the meaning the arguer is attaching to these terms. Thus the italicized value words in these assertions must be clarified before you can tell whether the assertions are justified: "Abortion is *wrong*"; "Mercy killing *should be* permitted"; "Capital punishment *should not be* legalized"; "Steven Spielberg is a *great* film director"; "Capitalism is the *best* economic system"; "Socialism is *inferior* to capitalism"; "Democracy is the *best* form of government."

Value words can have several meanings, only some of which will be covered here. Generally the ordinary value arguments you read and hear have meanings that can be translated into empirical form and then evaluated. Specifically, when appearing in ordinary value arguments, value words typically indicate (1) personal preference, (2) social preference, or (3) conformity to principle, standard, or law.

   1. **Personal preference.**   Value words often are intended as expressions of personal approval or disapproval; that is, as forms of basic assertions. Take for example the assertion "Abortion is wrong." It's possible that people asserting this are expressing only personal disapproval of abortion. Thus "Abortion is wrong" is equivalent to "*I disapprove* of abortion." Likewise "Steven Spielberg is a *great* film director" translates into "*I like* or *I think highly of* the directorial talent of Spielberg." And "Everyone *should* get a college education" would mean "*I'm in favor of* everyone's getting a college education." In each instance the value word is intended as an expression of personal preference. This allows a translation into a basic form whose justification lies in the person making the assertion (as in "This candy tastes sweet" or "The leaf is green"). Such a translation is legitimate, of course, only if the person is not commenting about the nature or quality of the act or thing itself, but merely is expressing a belief.

   Regarding the justification of such assertions, you need only ensure that they accurately report the person's feelings. Once you realize that the value word is carrying this autobiographical meaning, you can save yourself much time and frustration in fruitless debates over value issues. Even more important, you can direct the discussion to a more constructive plane.

   For example, suppose someone argues "Abortion on demand should be legalized because it will help to minimize the number of unwanted children." Any argument with a conclusion that expresses a value must have at least one value assertion as a premise. Here the value premise is unexpressed. Presumably the arguer is assuming "Whatever will help minimize the number of births of unwanted children should be legalized." You find out that by "should be" the person intends "I approve." So this premise simply says "I approve of legalizing abortion to help minimize the number of births of unwanted children." Now you can ask the person why he or she approves of such an assertion. The arguer proceeds to draw some equation between being unwanted and being unloved, suggests that an unloved baby will turn out to be an antisocial adult, and points out that antisocial adults spell big problems for society. With this additional information, you're in a position to question the inevitable chain of events assumed by the arguer. Is an unwanted baby always an unloved one? Haven't people learned to love offspring whom they didn't want or think they wanted? While it's true that a loving atmosphere helps a child become a well-adjusted adult, it isn't at all inevitable that an unloving atmosphere will produce an antisocial adult. Besides, what is a "loving atmosphere" to begin with, or a "well-adjusted adult" for that matter? These terms are themselves loaded with value judgments.

The point is that once you have established an autobiographical interpretation of a value word, you're in a position to pin down the arguer on what generated the preference. This is crucial, for as we earlier said, we are ultimately interested in how much counts for accepting the assertion, how much for rejecting it. Once you've established that the arguer is expressing a personal preference, then you can get on with the business of seeking justification for the belief.

One other point, this one on a philosophical level, should be made. The issue of personal preference raises a number of philosophical questions that you are justified in asking. First, since value assertions presumably express only personal preference, does that mean that no acts are right or wrong in themselves, that no things are good or bad in themselves? Second, does this stance imply that something can be "right" for you and "wrong" for me under identical circumstances? Is this sensible?

Such questions may seem irrelevant to argument criticism. But they are most relevant. After all, anyone who assumes that a value word is only the equivalent of an expression of personal preference takes a lot for granted. Surely the "taken-for-granted" can and should be introduced in evaluating whether more counts for accepting the value assertion than not.

2. **Social preference.**   Frequently people don't mean that only they approve or disapprove of something when they use a value word but that society does. In other words, value words can be used to indicate social preference. "Whatever will help minimize the number of births of unwanted children *should be* legalized" may be interpreted as "*Society approves* of the legalization of whatever will help minimize the number of births of unwanted babies."

If a value assertion indicates social preference, then your job of verifying it is simplified. All you need do is verify that a majority of society approves or disapproves the view. Determine the majority view and you determine the truth of the statement.

But as with personal preference, having established a sociological bias, you can then ask trenchant questions about its implied assumptions. Is nothing inherently right or wrong, good or bad? Can't the individual be right and the majority wrong? The German theologian Dietrich Bonhoffer, having spoken out against Hitler, was imprisoned and later hanged. Was he wrong and the majority right? The nineteenth-century American writer and naturalist Henry David

Thoreau refused to pay taxes to a government that, supported by the majority, sanctioned slavery. Legend has it that one day his friend and fellow artist Ralph Waldo Emerson came to visit him in jail. "What are you doing in there?" Emerson asked. "What are you doing out there?" Thoreau answered. Was Thoreau wrong? Or was Emerson? Were Socrates and Jesus wrong? Is popular view to determine what is "good" and "bad" music, poetry, painting, sculpture, and film? And just what "majority" view do we have in mind anyway—the community, state, nation, world? Maybe the majority is within one's own ethnic group, sex, profession, or economic stratum.

These questions are not trivial. In equating value words with social preference, arguers invite profound questions about the highly controversial assumptions that underlie that equation. In criticizing arguments that make these assumptions, you are at liberty to raise these and other questions.

3. **Conformity to principle, standard, or law.** Besides translating value words into expressions of personal or social preference, arguers sometimes identify them with conformity to a principle, standard, or law. For example, someone may argue "Because sexism is *objectionable*, paying women less than their male counterparts simply because they are women is wrong." By "objectionable" the arguer may not intend either personal or social disapproval but nonconformity to the principle of justice as fair play and giving to others what they deserve. Similarly an arguer who uses "Abortion is *immoral*" as a premise might mean that abortion doesn't square with the law of God. Likewise someone might assert that Spielberg is a *great* film director because Spielberg's skills and talent conform to the artistic standards that define the expert director. When value words are used this way, you must determine whether the assertion actually does conform to the principle, law, or standard.

But having ascertained that a value word is being used to indicate conformity to law, principle, or standard, you can raise important philosophical questions about its underlying assumptions. For example, what makes the particular standard or principle itself doubtless? Take justice. In a preceding argument justice was used to mean a principle of fair play or just desert. On this basis the arguer called sexism "wrong." But why not consider justice as a principle of utility? Lots of people do. They consider fair whatever produces the most happiness for the most people, even if certain individuals suffer. Perhaps paying women less than their male counterparts produces the greatest social benefit. Elsewhere we supposed that someone asserted "Abortion is *immoral*" because abortion doesn't conform to the law of God. If "moral" and "immoral" are to be determined by conformity to the law of God, what can be said of people who don't believe in God, or at least not in the God whose law is intended? Can such people ever act morally?

Faced with questions like these, arguers sometimes call their critics "nitpickers." Don't be cowed by such name-calling. There is nothing trivial about such questions. They cut to the bedrock assumptions of value arguments. After all, if there's serious doubt about the legitimacy of the principle, law, or standard endorsed, then conformity to it might be irrelevant.

As indicated earlier, these are only a few of the interpretations people put on value words. Reading in such specialized areas as ethics and aesthetics will reveal more. The key point to remember is that the meaning of the value words used in value assertions will affect your assessment of the justification of those assertions and ultimately of the arguments in which they appear. Faced with any argument that contains an expressed or unexpressed value assertion, find out what interpretation of the value word is intended. Having done this, you should then determine whether the assertion meets minimum adequacy requirements.

Quick Check on Clarifying Language

Pick out the value words in these statements and indicate what possible interpretations could be put on them. In terms of each meaning, show how the truth of each assertion would be assessed.

1 Needlessly inflicting pain is wrong.
2 Infanticide is evil.
3 A doctor ought never operate on people without their informed consent.
4 Poetry is the higheset artistic form.
5 Hypocrisy is immoral.
6 The best form of government is the one that allows the most personal freedom compatible with a like freedom for all.
7 Einstein's theory of relativity is the greatest scientific development of the twentieth century.
8 A government should not underwrite research dealing with in vitro fertilization.
9 No war is ever morally justifiable.
10 You should never disobey those in authority over you.
11 Communism is godless.
12 The women's liberation movement threatens the survival of the family as we've traditionally known it.

Comments

1. "wrong"	7. "greatest"
2. "evil"	8. "should not"
3. "ought not"	9. "morally justifiable"
4. "highest"	10. "should never"
5. "immoral"	11. "godless"
6. "best"	12. "threatens"

All these value words can be interpreted in terms of personal preference, social preference, and conformity to principle. Once the interpretation is ascertained and translated into empirical form, the justification of each assertion can be assessed. For example, "Needlessly inflicting pain is wrong" may mean "*I disapprove* of needlessly inflicting pain." Or "*Society disapproves* of needlessly inflicting pain." Or "needlessly inflicting pain is inconsistent with how people should treat each other." Regarding the autobiographical interpretation, you could ask: "On what grounds do you base your disapproval?" Regarding the sociological: "What makes society's view correct?" Regarding conformity to principle: "On what grounds can you state how people ought to treat each other?"

Ensuring Minimum Adequacy Requirements

To see what's meant by "minimum adequacy requirements," consider this simple example. Suppose renowned astronomer Dr. McGee insisted that the expanding universe could be accounted for by something other than the big bang theory. Now Dr. McGee wouldn't be much of a thinker or scientist if she hadn't assembled as much factual support for her claim as she could. And her fellow scientists (not to mention we ourselves) wouldn't be very intelligent if they didn't insist on such factual support. Indeed, those in and outside science take for granted the need to support empirical assertions with factual data culled from observation of the world.

But along comes an argument containing value assertions, and rationality is often put on the back burner. For some reason many of us act as if this kind of assertion is exempt from any such minimal requirements, that it doesn't need to be supported by evidence that lies outside the self in the world. But they do. We need as much factual support for assertions like "Prostitution is bad" and "The government should take over the oil industry" as we need for assertions like "Vitamin C can prevent the common cold" and "Something other than a big bang caused the universe to start expanding."

Let's take a close look at these last two empirical assertions. Suppose you asked the claimant "Why do you think that vitamin C can prevent the common cold?" and the person responded "I just think so, that's all." Or suppose, regarding the second assertion, the claimant tried to justify the assertion by saying "I just know that something other than a big bang caused the universe to start expanding." Surely you'd tell these people to go peddle their papers elsewhere. Or, feeling kinder, you might point out to these people that they aren't really answering your question; you might then press them to tell you *why* they feel as they do. If they persisted in offering no more evidence than what they think or suspect or believe, you'd rightly dismiss their arguments as absurd.

When it comes to value arguments, however, it's amazing how tolerant we are. In fact we often endorse arguments on a no firmer basis than personal whim, prejudice, feeling, hunch, or fancy. Although it's true that value assertions and arguments differ somewhat from empirical ones, they don't differ so radically that what they assert can be justified on such flimsy bases. Remember, belief differs from truth and justification. Simply because I believe something doesn't mean the belief is justified and hence true. In criticizing an argument, we are interested in determining truth and justification. If the only support a person can give to an assertion is that he or she believes it, then the person hasn't given any support at all. The person may have given an explanation for the belief, but not a reason.

It is true, as I noted, that when a person expresses a value judgment, the person may be intending it strictly as an expression of personal preference. Thus "Abortion is wrong" could be interpreted as "I disapprove of abortion"; "Steven Spielberg is a great film director" may mean "I really like Spielberg's direction." But *meaning* isn't justification. Persons making these assertions still must justify why they feel as they do if their claims are to be taken seriously.

In a great many cases, arguers simply don't have the supporting facts to substantiate their value assertions. Rather than getting the facts, they allow opinion to pass as justification: "Euthanasia is good [or bad] because I feel it is"; "Premarital sex is desirable [or undesirable] because I think it is"; "*Star Trek* is the best science fiction film ever made because I prefer it to the others." Arguers may not express themselves in these unvarnished terms, but look and listen closely and you'll find countless examples of opinion masquerading as justification.

There generally is available to anyone taking the time to consult it a vast array of intelligent, insightful, and often profound scholarship in any field. Moreover, whatever the field—psychology, economics, history, nutrition, political science—there are basic assumptions, standards, and criteria that together with ongoing scholarship provide a rich source of data for criticizing value assertions. To disregard what in many cases is the distilled wisdom of civilized thought insults both the spirit and process of critical thinking. Thus an essential part of thinking critically, especially when forming and evaluating value assertions, is familiarization with myriad fields: political philosophy, economics, psychology, ethics, poetry, music, literature, painting. This doesn't mean that you need be an expert before expressing a value claim or responding intelligently to one. But surely you must be informed, and you have a right to expect the same of others who want to be taken seriously. If you lack appropriate information, you stand no chance of meeting the minimum adequacy requirements appropriate in a field or of detecting when the arguments of others don't.

In examining value arguments for minimum adequacy requirements, look especially for two things: appeal to principle and to consequences. These are the primary though not exclusive ways that value assertions are supported. Let's briefly consider each.

Appeal to Principle   Value assertions often involve evaluations of individual actions or practices in terms of some general principle. It is then necessary to express the general principle and show why the specific case is covered by it. Arguers who don't do this leave their arguments open to criticism; critics who don't watch for this lose an opportunity to illuminate an issue and perhaps move it to a higher, more fruitful plane of debate.

For example, Adrian is writing a paper in which she argues that it would be *wrong* to disconnect a particular person from a life-support system. In making her case, she should indicate the principle on which she is basing her opinion: "It is always wrong to kill someone intentionally" or "Only voluntary acts of euthanasia are permissible," for instance. She should then show that the case being considered was a type covered by the principle. To do this she might show, given the first principle, that the person was in fact not dead before being removed from the system or, given the second principle, that neither the consent of the person nor the person's surrogates had been obtained. Additionally, she might want to spend time supporting the principles themselves, explaining why she thinks they are worth endorsing. As individuals thinking critically about Adrian's position, we have a right to expect these things of her. Should she not meet our expectations, we are entitled to raise them in our criticism.

Adrian can take the same approach to a social policy question. Suppose she is writing a paper in support of the Equal Rights Amendment (ERA). She could appeal to some principle of equality: "Women deserve to be treated equally" or "All people should be treated equally," for instance. Having established the principle, she could then show that women in fact are not treated equally (and how the ERA presumably would right this situation).

Applied to an artistic judgment, the approach works the same way. Thus, in arguing that the classical Greek drama *Oedipus the King* is a good play, Adrian might apply the classical ideal of unity and catharsis and then show how the play is covered by this ideal.

Appeal to Consequences   Another common way to lend factual support to value assertions is by appealing to the purported consequences of an action or practice and providing data to justify this forecast. For example, were Adrian arguing that handguns should be prohibited, she might try to show that violent crime would decline if appropriate gun-control legislation were adopted. Of course she would have to provide information to back up her prediction. If she were arguing that married couples should be required to undergo genetic counseling before having a child, she might show that fewer defective babies would be born if that were the case. Again she would have to back up her contention.

So providing factual support is as important in expressing value assertions as it is in expressing nonvalue assertions, or what we previously called hypothetical assertions ("Life exists in outer space"; "Cancer is caused by a virus"; "John F. Kennedy was not killed by a sole assassin"). Two good ways to provide this support are (1) to take a general principle and show that some specific individual, action, or practice is a type covered by that principle and (2) to predict the consequences of an action or practice and then provide data to support the forecast made. In the best value arguments, these strategies are and should be integrated. For example, arguing against the sale of handguns, Adrian could express a principle (for example, "Society has an obligation to protect the lives of its citizens"). Then, by predicting the consequences of handgun control, she could show how the prohibition is covered by the principle. Similarly, in arguing for genetic counseling, she might appeal to the principle that parents have a right to know as much about the health of their unborn as possible. Then, by showing the kind of information prospective parents can glean from genetic counseling and the range of alternatives that counseling thereby opens to them, she could show how genetic counseling is covered by her principle.

The relationship between value assertions, language clarification, and minimum adequacy requirements is portrayed in the chart on the next page.

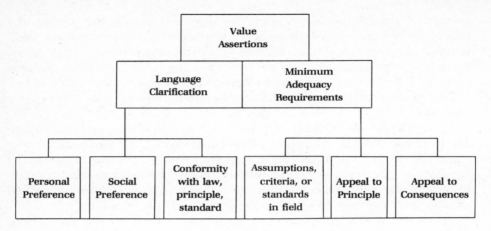

Summary

In criticizing arguments you are evaluating them for cogency. A cogent argument is valid and has true premises. A valid argument is one whose premises provide conclusive (in deduction) or probable (in induction) grounds for its conclusion. A true premise is a statement that describes an actual state of affairs, present, past, or future.

> **Example of a cogent deductive argument:** Because all humans are vertebrates, and Fred is a human, Fred must be a vertebrate.
>
> **Example of a cogent inductive argument:** Fred will probably get into the graduate school of his choice because he has a 4.0 G.P.A.

Always distinguish truth from belief and opinion. Remember that truth is not relative, although beliefs and opinions certainly are.

An argument's premises can be considered true when they are justified; that is, when there is reasonable evidence to support them. For some types of assertions, the reasonableness of the evidence is not a problem. Often these assertions, including those based on laws of logic and semantic and systemic assertions, can be justified by an appeal to reason. Basic assertions, though they require an appeal to sense experience, fall into this nonproblematic category as well.

In contrast, the truth of hypothetical statements is problematic. A hypothetical statement is one whose truth must be confirmed by sense experience outside the self in the world.

Examples of hypothetical statements:

Capital punishment deters crime.
Cancer is caused by a virus.
Compared with men, women don't get equal pay for equal work.

Instead of trying to say exactly how much and what kind of evidence is needed to justify such statements, it's more fruitful to establish on what grounds we can satisfy ourselves that, in both quantity and quality, sufficient evidence has been given. Accordingly, it's very helpful to recognize that what is essential as evidence is observations. Hypothetical assertions must be backed up by observations that are expressed or implied in the argument. Five key points must be considered when evaluating observations: (1) the physical conditions under which the observations were made, (2) the sensory acuity of the observer, (3) the necessary background knowledge, (4) the objectivity of the observer, and (5) supporting testimony.

Value assertions are another type of statement whose truth is problematic. Value assertions are judgments of worth: "Murder is *immoral*"; "Capital punishment *should be* legalized for certain serious crimes"; "Steven Spielberg is a *great* film director"; "Democracy is the *best* form of government." In determining the truth of a value assertion, first clarify the value words contained in the assertion, deciding whether (1) personal preference, (2) social preference, or (3) conformity to law, principle, or standard is indicated by their use. Then determine whether the claim meets minimum adequacy requirements. In general, minimum adequacy requirements are embodied by the basic assumptions, standards, criteria, and scholarship of a particular field. More specifically, they can be met by appeals to principle and/or to the consequences by which value assertions are supported.

Applications

Identify the following as value or nonvalue arguments. Then cast them and criticize them for validity of inference and justification of premises; that is, for cogency. Be sure to fill in missing premises if necessary.

1   Fred must be a Republican because he voted for Reagan in the 1980 presidential election.
2   There's no question that Sarah's a Christian. She believes in a personal God, doesn't she?
3   Not all moneymaking films are made by the Hollywood studios. After all, some pornographic movies are moneymakers.
4   Reverse discrimination should be allowed, for it can promote social justice.
5   Reverse discrimination sometimes occurs in the workplace. If you think not, just read the results of a study recently conducted by the *Harvard Business Review.* Ten percent of the personnel managers polled admitted that their companies did sometimes engage in reverse discrimination. So it's clear that at least in some instances people are judged on criteria not directly related to the job.
6   "... according to modern physics, radio is our only hope of picking up an intelligent signal from space. Sending an interstellar probe would take too

long—roughly 50 years even for nearby Alpha Centauri—even if we had the technology and funds to accomplish it. But radio is too slow for much dialogue. The most we can hope from it is to establish the existence (or, more accurately, the former existence) of another civilization." (Patrick Moore, "Speaking English in Space: Stars," *Omni*, November 1979, p. 26.)

7 "If a being suffers, there can be no moral justification for refusing to take that suffering into consideration, and, indeed, to count it equally with the like suffering (if rough comparisons can be made) of another being. So the only question is: Do animals other than man suffer? Most people agree unhesitatingly that animals like cats and dogs can and do suffer, and this seems also to be assumed by those laws that prohibit wanton cruelty to such animals." (Peter Singer, "Animal Liberation," in James Rachels (ed.), *Moral Problems*, 2d ed. [New York: Harper & Row, 1975], p. 166.)

Detecting Bias: Intensify/Downplay

Many arguments contain weaknesses in the quantity or quality of the premises or in the reasoning. Typically these weaknesses occur in the form of fallacies.

A fallacy is a type of argument that may seem to be correct but is not. The fallacies that most people commit result from careless language usage or inattention to subject matter. These lapses in turn stem from the human tendency to intensify or downplay as we communicate. In brief, in stating their cases people regularly load them to win over the intended audience. This is especially true of professional persuaders (such as advertisers and politicians) who have more training, technology, money, and media access than the rest of us. To evaluate the information and arguments that come your way, therefore, you must be able to recognize how communication commonly is intensified and downplayed, which is the concern of this chapter.

Communication can be intensified in several ways. One is through repetition. The political slogan or advertising jingle that is repeated until it imprints itself on the memory of the audience, making it identify, recognize, and respond in a set way, is an example of intensifying by repetition. Another way to intensify communication is by pattern and arrangement. This technique uses both design and variations in sequences and in proportion to augment the force of words, images, and movements. For example, the clause "When you know what counts" doesn't mean much alone. But when superimposed over a cigarette-puffing, ruggedly handsome middle-aged male, clad only in shorts and sitting on a locker room bench after a workout, it becomes a pitch for Kent cigarettes that cleverly identifies smoking with health, well-being, and sex appeal.

Undoubtedly these two ways of intensifying communication have many variations that we could consider. But in the following section, we will instead focus on a third that is the breeding ground for many fallacies: intensifying by association.

People who want to downplay communication rather than intensify it seemingly have even more persuasive devices at their disposal. These can be conveniently grouped as devices of omission, diversion, and confusion. We will examine each of these ways to downplay messages.

You should keep in mind that these classifications are arbitrary. The intensifying and downplaying techniques we will study could just as easily be grouped otherwise, and indeed they are differently grouped by some authors. What's more, even under the categories I've identified, it is by no means certain that a device belongs exclusively to that group or that a device typically used to intensify can't also be used to downplay. The particular classifications, then, simply are means of helping you to understand and consequently to spot and avoid the various ways that people bias communication and argument. They also will serve as the cornerstone of the evaluative procedure that will be developed in the next chapter.

Intensifying by Association

When people intensify by association, they link an idea, person, or product with what already is loved, desired, or approved of; or is hated, feared, or disapproved of by the intended audience. The aim is to win over the audience by identifying what is under discussion with something that the audience already has strong feelings about, favorable or unfavorable. Some of the more common ways to do this are through testimonials; statistics, studies, and polls; popularity; tradition; jumping to conclusions; guilt by association; positioning; provincialism; and mob appeal.

Testimonials

Intensifying by testimonal consists of invoking some well-known figure to support a claim or course of action. Examples of testimonials abound in advertising, where celebrities are used to endorse everything from aspirin to presidential candidates. Here are just a few:

Take it from Bruce Jenner: "You need a good start to get in shape. And I can't think of a better start than a complete breakfast with Wheaties."

Elke Sommer knows watching her nutrition counts as much as watching her weight. So she's starting her day with a Special K breakfast. That's good for Elke, and good for you, too.

Don Meredith for Lipton Tea: "What makes me a Lipton Tea Lover? Lipton tastes so damn good."

Robert Young for Sanka: "I think it's important that we take care of ourselves. [Remember he used to play Marcus Welby, M.D.?] That's why doctors have advised millions of caffeine-concerned Americans, like me, to drink delicious Sanka Decaffeinated Coffee."

That last ad, with its reference to doctors, also illustrates how the prestige of a profession can be used as a testimonial. Here's another from Anacin: "Doctors recommend one pain reliever most: the one you get in Anacin." Of course you get the same pain reliever, aspirin, in a smorgasbord of other analgesics. But many consumers will likely overlook this fact, which is exactly how the testimonial intensifier is designed to work. Celebrity endorsements effectively short-circuit the reasoning process: They are meant to substitute for the scrutiny you should give a product before purchasing, a candidate before voting, or a cause before supporting it. The advertiser hawks the product by linking it to an admired, trusted, or simply well-known public figure. Similarly, political strategists sell candidates by linking them to celebrities.

Of course, the use of testimonials is not always fallacious. So long as (1) the endorsing figure is truly an expert in the field, (2) there is a consensus of expert opinion to corroborate the claim, and (3) one could in theory verify the claim for oneself, then the use of testimonial is legitimate. For example, suppose someone claimed that smoking was harmful and based that judgment on the opinion of the Surgeon General. The testimonial here is legitimate because (1) the Surgeon General is an expert witness, (2) there is agreement among the medical experts that smoking is indeed harmful, and (3) in theory one could verify the claim for oneself if one took the time to conduct scientifically valid experiments.

Statistics, Studies, and Polls

Intensifying by statistics, studies, or polls consists of invoking these sources to give authority to what one says. Here are a few guidelines for evaluating these bases of opinion.

Statistics   The first thing to ask regarding statistics is *Does the statistic make any difference?* Statistics are useful when they tell us something worth knowing, and they tell us something worth knowing when they make a difference. For example, if the U.S. Department of Health and Human Services released figures showing that herpes infects about 10 percent of the population and 25 percent of those under twenty-five, these figures surely would alert government, the medical community, and the general public to an alarming health problem in need of corrective measures. The figures would make a difference to anyone concerned about disease control.

But when the U.S. postal service tells prospective buyers of its used delivery trucks that "this vehicle has met all [i.e., 100 percent] applicable safety standards," that statistical claim is meaningless because few safety standards apply to this government vehicle compared with those applying to civilian vehicles. Thus the vehicle is permitted to have a dangerously high center of gravity, which may lead to its rolling over; an unupholstered dashboard with protruding knobs and switches; and a steering column that has been likened to an iron pipe pointed at the chest of the driver. That the vehicle has met "all applicable safety standards" therefore means nothing.

The second question to ask of statistics is *Are they complete?* Incomplete statistics are as meaningless as ones that make no difference. For example, suppose that in justifying an increase in its premium rates, an insurance company argued that it had paid out $3 billion more in claims than it had collected in premiums over the past eight years. Although these figures might be accurate, the profit picture of an insurance company is hardly summed up by subtracting claims from premiums. What must also be considered is the money made by investing the premiums.

A third question to ask is *Are the statistics knowable?* It's amazing how often people bandy about statistics that are in principle or in fact unknowable. For example, if someone told you how many snowflakes fell during a particular blizzard, you wouldn't put much stock in the figure because in principle no one can know how many snowflakes fall during a storm. But sometimes we're taken in by statistics that in principle are knowable but in all likelihood are not known by the person using them. For example, the makers of Fleischmann's margarine have claimed: "Every fifteen seconds a doctor recommends Fleischmann's margarine." Even if this claim is knowable in principle, it's unlikely that the makers of Fleischmann's knows it for a fact. Just think of how much money, time, and personnel would be needed to determine it. Lacking support for the claim, we'd best treat it as unknowable.

Studies   Reports of studies and research findings warrant the same scrutiny as statistical claims. Before accepting the results of any study, find out as much as possible about it. Specifically you should determine

1. *The subjects involved.* Subtle individual differences can bias results. The age, general health, emotional state, diet, and possibly even the sex of the subjects are just some of the things that might shape the effects, say, of a drug.

2. *How long the research was conducted.* Sometimes a product that shows great early promise proves disappointing, or even dangerous, later.

3. *Who conducted the testing.* In general the research of impartial parties is more reliable than those of parties with a vested interest. (Recall what was said earlier about the need for objectivity in making observations.)

4. *Which stage of research the assertion refers to.* This guideline refers especially to claims made about drugs, which typically are subjected to three stages of study: test-tube, animal, and human. If we do not know to which stage the research refers, we cannot intelligently assess it.

5. *How the study was conducted.* What method of research was used? Specifically, what was done to control variables; that is, factors that, left uncontrolled, could bias the results? Not long ago, for example, a company boasted of the positive effects of its dishwashing detergent on hands. It neglected to mention, however, that the subjects involved in the tests had worn rubber gloves while washing dishes!

6. *How extensive the testing was.* Small or nonrepresentative samples can lead to premature conclusions.

Polls and Surveys Polls and surveys increasingly are being used to intensify claims. Like studies and statistics, polls and surveys call for cautious inspection. In particular you should always determine

1. *The sponsor's or survey's name.* If a poll has been commissioned by a party with a vested interest in the outcome, it could easily be biased.

2. *The date of contact.* The date of contact refers to when the poll or survey was conducted, which is important to know because it can lead to a wholly different interpretation of the results. For example, a poll may report that the President is enjoying unprecedented popularity. But this finding doesn't mean much if the poll was taken just before some major international or domestic blunder.

3. *The method of contact.* The method of contact is the procedure used to take the sample. A poll or survey must approximate the ideal of *randomness*, which means that each member of the population to be sampled has an equal chance of being sampled. To illustrate, suppose that you wanted to find out what students in your college thought of the school newspaper. In the next issue you include a questionnaire asking readers to respond. The sample you draw would not be random because only readers of that issue of the paper would have a chance of being sampled. Remember, you want to find out what the students as a whole think. One way to ensure randomness in this case would be to place the names of all students in a drum and then select names, one at a time, until you had a sample of sufficient size. Professional pollsters—Gallup, Harris, Roper—all use what is called a stratified random sample, which is a reliable method of contact.

4. *The sample size.* Before accepting or using a poll's or survey's results, find out how large the sample was. This is important in order to determine the margin of error. For example, a random sample of 1500 yields a margin of error of plus or minus 3 percent. This means that if a properly conducted poll of 1500 voters indicates that candidate A will receive 51 percent of the vote and candidate B 49 percent of it, candidate A could get as much as 54 percent or as little as 48 percent and candidate B could get as much as 52 percent or as little as 46 percent. Thus candidate B actually could win the election and the pollster could claim accuracy. But unless you know how large the sample is and what margin of error that implies, the poll results mean very little.

5. *What kind of questions were asked.* Often it isn't the way the sample is taken but the nature of the questions asked that bias the results. Like any other form of disclosure, questions can be ambiguous (for example, "Do you think it's a *good practice* for employers to seek out minority members and women for jobs?") or loaded (for example, *"Given that the future of the free world depends on U.S. military strength,* do you think it's wise to reduce defense spending?"). Where questions are ambiguous or biased, the answers they elicit will be an inaccurate measure of opinion.

When used properly, statistics, studies, and polls can provide effective and legitimate support for a claim. But often they are misused. So guard against being taken in by statistics, studies, and polls by following these guidelines.

Popularity

Intensifying by popularity consists of relying exclusively on numbers to support a claim. "Five million people have already seen this movie. Shouldn't you?"; "Why do I think that the President's program is sound? Because the polls indicate that the vast majority supports it"; "By a margin of two to one, shoppers prefer Brand X to any of the leading competitors. Reason enough to buy Brand X." In the appeal to popularity, sheer numbers are substituted for individual testimonial. But the intention is similar: to link something with wide approval and use that as the basis for winning over others.

Tradition

Intensifying by tradition consists of appealing to feelings of reverence or respect for some custom that supports the view being advanced. For example, Jane's friend tells her "I don't think you should keep your maiden name after marrying. In this culture the woman always takes her husband's name. That's what distinguishes a married woman from a single one." Although there may be good reasons for a woman's not keeping her maiden name after marrying, this isn't one of them. Jane is trying to link her opinion to a long-standing custom; that is, to what has been historically approved by society. But why must custom necessarily dictate present behavior? It needn't, and that's the point.

Recall the frequent appeals to tradition during the attempt to impeach President Richard Nixon in 1974. Many insisted that Nixon should not be impeached because a U.S. President never before had been successfully impeached. In a word, they tried to protect Nixon by invoking a tradition that points up understandable reluctance to impeach Presidents. But merely because a President never had been impeached was not reason enough to conclude that Nixon, or any subsequent President for that matter, should not be impeached.

Certain phrases often signal an attempt to intensify an argument by summoning tradition. Among them are "Founding Fathers," "the earliest set-tlers," "from time immemorial," "tried and true," "the lessons of history," "it says so in . . . ," "look at the record," "in the past," "customarily," "traditionally," and "historically." Of course the appeal to tradition can legitimately advance an argument when it is backed up by other facts and reasons. But such appeals are illegitimate when used exclusively to intensify by association with the past.

Novelty

In contrast to the appeal to tradition, but as deadly to correct reasoning, is the pitch to novelty. *Intensifying by novelty consists of assuming that something is good or desirable simply because it's new.* "New! Clairol Short and Sassy

Shampoo. The shampoo Dorothy Hamill uses." This ad capitalizes on the widespread tendency to equate the newest, the latest, or most advanced with the best. Thus presumably because Clairol Short and Sassy Shampoo is new, we should buy it. Just in case that line doesn't hook us, Clairol casts another—the Hamill testimonial.

In the election of 1980, a number of candidates argued "It's time for a change" and "Let's try something different." To many this meant a change in economic and social philosophy. There may have been solid reasons for so altering the nation's course, but change for the sake of change was not one of them. Every policy, law, idea, program, or action requires justification independent of its novel character. That a politician represents a "new face" or a proposal offers a "new approach" is not a logical defense, though it sometimes is an appealing one.

Consider the copy for an advertisement featuring Leonard Nimoy (the never-nodding logician "Mr. Spock") pictured beside an hourglass in a painting reminiscent of one by surrealist Salvador Dali:

> The picture of reliability. To Magnavox it's the idea that every time you turn on one of our color television sets, you know it's going to do what you bought it to do. Our Star® System color television sets combine advanced design concepts, high technology and new manufacturing systems to deliver the highest level of reliability in Magnavox history. Magnavox. For a picture as reliable as it is bright and clear. Time after time. Magnavox—the bright ideas in the world are here today.

The beauty of this kind of ad is that it trades on the reasonable assumption that industry spends time, money, and energy developing new products because of a desire to make them better and thus sell more than the competition. But although it's true that many new things are better, not *every* new thing is better. The only way to tell whether a new product is better than the old one is to examine the specifics. But don't look for specifics in the preceding ad; they're not there. Indeed, even the television set that was shown carried the following disclaimer in tiny print beneath it: "Model 4265, 19-inch diagonal measurement with remote control. TV picture and wood-grain cabinet simulated."

Jumping to Conclusions

Intensifying by jumping to conclusions consists of forming a judgment based on insufficient evidence or atypical cases. Sometimes the insufficient evidence used to form a hasty conclusion is an isolated case. For example, on the basis of one sour romance, a man concludes "No woman can be trusted." Other times several specific cases are used, but not enough to warrant the conclusion: Discovering that a few members of the National Organization of Women are lesbians, a man concludes "NOW is made up mostly of lesbians."

Just as common is leaping to a conclusion on the basis of unusual or atypical cases. Thus someone argues that the United States isn't really committed to the principle of unobstructed travel because prisoners are not permitted to go where they want. Or someone infers that narcotics really aren't habit-forming because patients taking them under medical supervision rarely become addicted. In each case the person tries to form a conclusion based on atypical cases, on exceptions to the general rule.

Guilt by Association

Intensifying through guilt by association consists of making judgments about people solely on the basis of their relationships with others. For example, during the congressional campaigns of 1982, many Democratic candidates tried to defeat their Republican opponents by identifying them with President Ronald Reagan's economic programs, which in part had contributed to widespread unemployment, even though many of the Republican candidates were trying to dissociate themselves from Reagan's policies and many of these same Democratic candidates had supported Reagan's policies. Some Republican candidates used the same tack to discredit Democrats. In the California race for the Senate, for example, Republican Pete Wilson took every opportunity to identify Democratic candidate Jerry Brown with Farm Union Leader Cesar Chavez, who is unpopular among California farmers.

Positioning

If people discredit others through associations, they can just as effectively promote themselves and others by positioning. *Intensifying through positioning consists of capitalizing on the earned reputation of a leader in a field to sell a product, candidate, or idea.* Here's how it works.

Suppose a car-rental agency such as Avis advertises "We're the world's second largest car-rental agency. Since we're second, we must try harder." Avis successfully positions itself next to the leader, Hertz, thereby creating through transference a position in the consumer's mind. Goodrich has used this technique masterfully. When it reminds us "We're the ones without the blimp," it positions itself beside the well-known tire manufacturer Goodyear.

In advertising, positioning creates a spot for a company in the prospective buyer's mind, allowing the buyer to consider not only the company's image but its competitor's as well. It's based on the assumption that the mind has become an advertising battleground. To be successful a manufacturer must relate to what's already in the mind, what is fixed as authoritative. Thus, although RCA and General Electric failed in trying to buck IBM directly in the computer industry, the smaller Honeywell succeeded by using the theme of "the other computer company."

Of course, positioning isn't confined to advertising. In politics, part of waging a successful campaign often means trading on the reputation of well-known, popular politicians. Thus, during the congressional campaign of 1982, President Reagan seemed to be everywhere at once. Reason: Local politicians wanted to be seen and photographed with the President, thereby hoping that Reagan's personal popularity would rub off on them.

Provincialism

Intensifying through provincialism consists of viewing things exclusively in terms of group loyalty. People who use this appeal are such products of cultural conditioning that they insist on seeing the world exclusively through the eyes of the group with which they identify. Whatever the issue, they attempt to win over the audience by associating that issue with what they believe to be the audience's group interests. The salesperson who argues that you should buy a domestic car rather than an import simply because "It's the American thing to do" is appealing to provincialism.

During the heated debate in 1980 over the treaty that would transfer responsibility for maintaining the Panama Canal from the United States to Panama, provincialism resounded throughout the land. Most of the arguments against the treaty assumed that (1) the United States had some kind of proprietary claim over the canal or (2) Americans were uniquely qualified to run the canal. Typical was this letter penned by a congressional representative a few years before the treaty was signed. Notice how it appeals both to provincialism and traditional wisdom.

> Our forefathers at the turn of the century built the waterways through hazardous and hard work for the security and well being of future generations. I refuse to stand on the sidelines and watch this resolve be destroyed. Consequently, you can be assured that I will do everything possible to see that the Congress defeats any bill which seeks to relinquish U.S. rights to the Canal.[1]

The fallacy of provincialism need not be confined to examples of national loyalty. Sometimes the group identified with is considerably smaller, perhaps a profession, occupation, religion, team, or school. An educator might argue "The present administration deserves very low marks because it's quite clear it knows little about educational problems." Here an opinion is formed about competence exclusively in terms of the author's field, education. Similarly, an educator might favor the reinstitution of the military draft because it would help sagging college enrollments, or police officers might favor a relaxation of search-and-seizure regulations because it would simplify their jobs.

Mob Appeal

Intensifying by mob appeal consists of attempting to persuade by arousing a group's deepest feelings and enthusiasms, by playing to its culturally conditioned prejudices.

The mob appeal is a standard tool of propagandists. Recall the famous "Cross of Gold" speech delivered to a political convention at the turn of the century by William Jennings Bryan. Bryan's address opposed gold as a monetary standard and favored bimetalism:

> We care not upon what lines the battle is fought. If they say bimetalism is good, but that we cannot have it until other nations help us, we reply that, instead of having a

[1]The late William Ketchum (R-Calif.), in a form-letter response to a constituent.

gold standard because England has, we will restore bimetalism, and then let England have bimetalism because the United States has it. If they dare to come out in the open field and defend the gold standard as a good thing, we will fight them to the uttermost. Having behind us the producing masses of this nation and the world, supported by the commercial interests, the laboring interests and the toilers everywhere, we will answer their demand for a gold standard by saying to them: You shall not press down upon the brow of labor this crown of thorns, you shall not crucify mankind upon a cross of gold.

Bryan's speech so transfixed the audience that they sat spellbound for some seconds before breaking into wild applause. The following day the convention nominated Bryan for president.

But mob appeal need not come only from the mouths or pens of propagandists and demagogues. In fact, it's a staple in advertising, where heroic efforts are made to associate the product with whatever the public can be expected to approve of strongly—for example, patriotism, status, or sexual gratification. Thus Virginia Slims advertises:

> In 1904, Julie Kelly of the famous dance team of Kelly and Kelly lit up a cigarette in the wings of the Palace Theatre in Atlantic City, New Jersey. 30 seconds later Kelly & Kelly became Kelly and Schwartz [presumably, Ms. Kelly was fired for smoking]. . . . You've come a long way, baby. Virginia Slims. Slimmer than the fat cigarettes men smoke.

Tapping into the enormous female market for cigarettes, the advertiser associates the product with sexual liberation. Smoking is portrayed as a symbol of the new, liberated woman. And Virginia Slims, differing as they do from the "fat cigarettes men smoke," are presumably distinctively feminine. Ironically, although slanted toward the liberated woman, the ad uses the sexist word "baby." Thus the liberated female smokes Virginia slims but does not relinquish her femininity. By appealing to women's deep feelings of sexual identity, this ad sells more than a smoke.

Quick Check on Intensifying

1 Identify the type of intensifying—testimonial; statistics, surveys, and polls; popularity; tradition; novelty; jumping to conclusions; guilt by association; positioning; provincialism; or mob appeal—used in these passages.

  a "We started flying four years ahead of the world's most experienced airline." (ad for Sabena Airline)

  b The Golden Rule is a sound moral principle because it is part of every ethical system ever devised.

  c STAN: I wouldn't trust any more union leaders, Ollie.

     OLLIE: My sentiments exactly, Stanley. Why, our last two union heads were put in jail for embezzling union funds.

  d FRED: I don't think Reagan's New Federalism is working.

     FRAN: The trouble with you, Fred, is that you're afraid to try anything different.

    FRED: Well, frankly, I prefer what's tried and true.

    FRAN: Tried and true? Don't you realize that economist Arthur Laffer has demonstrated that Keynesian economics just doesn't work?

e "In that melancholy book, *The Future of Illusion*, Dr. Freud, easily one of the last great theorists of the European capitalist class, has stated with simple clarity the impossibility of religious belief for the educated man today." (John Strachey, *The Coming Struggle for Power* [New York: Random House, 1950], p. 645.)

f   **JAN:** I always thought the Pope was a great spiritual and moral leader.

    JEFF: Isn't he?

    JAN: Not since he had an audience with PLO leader Yassir Arafat.

g   **GENERAL:** War has always been with us, Captain, and will continue to be.

    CAPTAIN: Sad but true, sir.

    GENERAL: Sad! The hell you say! Why, without the threat of war, you and I would be out of work.

h "The great Declaration of Independence begins 'When in the course of human events . . .' and for the first time in man's history announced that all rights come from a sovereign, not from a government but from God." (Henry J. Taylor, *Topeka Daily Capital*, July 1970. Quoted by Howard Kahane in *Logic and Contemporary Rhetoric* [Belmont, Calif.: Wadsworth, 1980], p. 28.)

i "According to folk wisdom in many cultures, redheaded people tend to be a bit temperamental. An Israeli researcher believes that there may be something to the ancient prejudice. At the Honolulu conference, psychiatrist Michael Bar of Israel's Shalvata Psychiatric Center, reported a study showing that redheaded children are three or four times more likely than others to develop 'hyperactive syndrome'—whose symptoms include over-excitability, short attention span, and feelings of frustration, and usually, excessive aggressiveness.

    "Bar arrives at his conclusion after matching the behavior of 45 redheaded boys and girls between the ages of six and twelve against that of a control group of nonredheaded kids. . . ." *(Time*, September 12, 1977, p. 97.)

j Superimposed over a picture of model Cheryl Tiegs, provocatively attired in a black velvet dress: "Isn't Black Velvet smooth? Just the thought of it can give you a good feeling. Black Velvet. Canadian Whiskey. The smooth Canadian."

k Humans have engaged in 452,783 wars since the beginning of recorded history.

2. Find an example in a newspaper or magazine of each of the devices used to intensify by association.

Comments

1. a. Positioning: Pan American is "the world's most experienced airline."

    b. Popularity

c. Jumping to a conclusion; also provincialism, for Stan and Ollie use only their own union's experience to draw the conclusion.
d. Novelty, tradition, testimonial
e. Testimonial
f. Guilt by association
g. Provincialism
h. Provincialism: French and English philosophers of the seventeenth and eighteenth centuries held similar political views, which in turn can be traced to the classical Greek formulation of democracy.
i. Jumping to a conclusion based on insufficient evidence
j. Mob appeal: sex
k. Unknowable statistic

Downplaying by Omission

Since the basic selection/omission process necessarily omits more than can be presented, downplaying by omission is common. Recall the many personal, professional, and sociocultural constraints on so-called objective news reporting. But it isn't only news reporting that is slanted; all communication is limited, edited, or biased to include and exclude items. Sometimes the omission is deliberate, made to conceal or hide. Whether deliberate or not, arguments that downplay by omission leave out important and relevant information. While there are many ways of downplaying by omission, the following fallacies are among the most commonly used devices: half-truth, invincible ignorance, faulty comparison, false analogy, questionable cause, neglect of a common cause, causal oversimplification, slippery slope, and post hoc.

Half-Truth

Downplaying by half-truth consists of ignoring, suppressing, or unfairly minimizing evidence that is unfavorable to a claim. For example, an investment counselor may tell you that municipal bonds, or mutual funds that invest exclusively in them, are good investments because they reduce one's income taxes. Before concluding that your money is best invested in municipal bonds or mutual funds, you should consider the following facts omitted by your counselor. Fact 1: Interest from municipal bonds is less than that from treasury or corporate bonds. Fact 2: The interest is not necessarily tax-free, since some or all of it may be taxable by the state. Fact 3: Municipal bonds carry risks; potential defaults by New York City and other cities have scared off some investors. Fact 4: Municipal bonds can be heavily discounted; that is, prices are often less than their face value. Before investing in municipal bonds, then, consider *all* the evidence. What your counselor said was true but incomplete.

As another example of half-truth, consider the Soviet Union's 1978 campaign against neutron weapons in which the Kremlin said that it had the capacity to build a similar weapon but for the time being would not. Presumably this act of self-restraint was to demonstrate Soviet commitment to arms limitation and convince the United States to end its flirtation with the neutron bomb. But the Soviets omitted mention that they had no use for such a weapon, for it is designed to be used against overwhelming Soviet tank forces in Europe.

Similarly, in 1981, when the United States decided to start producing and stockpiling neutron warheads, the Kremlin portrayed neutron weapons as "colonial" and "capitalistic" because they were designed to kill people while sparing property. The Kremlin failed to mention, however, that the people against whom the United States intended to use its weapons were Soviet and Warsaw Pact tank crews, and the property it hoped to spare consisted of European cities, including their civilian inhabitants. When the State Department announced U.S. intentions to build neutron bombs, it tried to reassure war-worried Europeans that the weapon would be produced and stockpiled in the United States. True enough, but State failed to mention that the bombs ultimately were to be deployed in *Europe*.

Invincible Ignorance

Downplaying by invincible ignorance consists of defending the legitimacy of an idea or principle despite contradicting facts. For example, in response to the President's economic program, someone says "I don't care what you say, the program won't help curb inflation." The speaker is closed to any facts inconsistent with his or her presuppositions. "Don't confuse me by giving me facts," he is in effect saying, "my mind is already made up." Such ignorance is unconquerable—thus the term *invincible* ignorance.

People who think and argue this way often tip their hand with phrases like "I don't care what you say, "All that is well and good, *but.* . . ," "or "Be that as it may, the fact remains. . . ." What follows the phrase is not a reasoned rejection but an insistence that contradicting facts be omitted.

Faulty Comparison

Comparisons are used to show similarities between like things, or things drawn from the same category. For example, living at home or living on campus while at college can be compared. A good comparison must show that the things compared have at least several significant points in common. If they don't then any conclusion based on the comparison is hasty and, therefore, questionable. *Downplaying by faulty comparison consists of making a comparison on too few points or only on those points that advance one's claim while ignoring other significant points.*

For example, it would be unwarranted to conclude that living at home while at college is better than living on campus on the basis of just one point of comparison: cost. What about about access to the various enrichment programs offered on campus? Or the opportunities for broadening one's outlook by living with people of diverse backgrounds, interests, and outlooks? To be complete the comparison can't omit these and other points.

Again, it would be premature to infer that solar energy is preferable to nuclear energy simply because the former may be safer. Although it's certainly one's prerogative to weigh safety more heavily in any comparison of the two, it's unfair to ignore other points of comparison, for example, feasibility and cost.

Sometimes comparisons include several significant, common points but the points chosen are biased. Overzealous to make a point, writers and speakers select only points of comparison that establish their assertions while omitting or suppressing points that detract from them. For example, suppose you were comparing the relative merits of two automobiles, A and B. Knowing you need several points of comparison to make your case, you choose safety, style, price, and power. By these criteria, car A beats car B. But missing from your bases of comparison are such significant categories as fuel efficiency, maintenance costs, performance, and engineering. Should comparison on these points weaken your conclusion, you would be arguing erroneously by omitting them.

False Analogy

Comparisons show similarities between like things, or things drawn from the same general category. Sometimes, however, we don't compare like but unlike things, as in "Football is war," "The human brain is like a computer," or "Business is like poker." Such comparisons generally are termed "analogies." Analogy, then, is a special kind of comparison involving two basically unlike things, and it is made to highlight properties in one that already are obvious in the other. Usually one of the subjects in an analogy is familiar and the other is unfamiliar. When both subjects are familiar, then a familiar property of one is used to make explicit an unfamiliar property of the other, as when the lens of an eye is used to explain the workings of a camera.

Analogy sometimes is used in argument. Through it we infer possible similarities between two things on the basis of established similarities. For example, Fred infers that he will do well on the next math test because he did well on the last three. This simple argument by analogy, and every one like it, proceeds from the observation that two or more things are similar in one or more respects to the conclusion that the things are similar in some other respect. Fred believes that his previous math tests and the current one have so much in common that they will have one more aspect in common: He will do as well on the next test as on the past ones. Schematically, where a, b, c, and d are any entities and P, Q, and R are any properties or respects, an analogical argument can be represented thus:

> a, b, c, and d all have the properties P and Q.
> a, b, and c all have the additional property R.
> Therefore d has the property R.

or

> Tests 1, 2, and 3, and test 4 (the next one) all have these properties: They deal with quadratic equations and are based on end-of-chapter exercises.
>
> Tests 1, 2, and 3 all have the property of having been successfully completed.
>
> Therefore test 4 (the next one) also will be successfully completed.

Analogy can be a potent argumentative tool. But arguments by analogy usually are bad ones because they omit significant differences between the things being compared. *Downplaying by false analogy, then, consists of overlooking significant differences in comparison and therefore assuming incorrectly that because two things are alike in one or more respects, they must be alike in some other respect.* For example, a student may argue that students should be allowed to use their texts during examinations since lawyers can use their law books in preparing cases and doctors can check their medical books in making diagnoses. Although the cases compared are similar—in each information is sought—the similarity is trivial compared with the omitted outstanding difference: Doctors and lawyers are *not* taking tests to see what they have learned, but students are.

Similarly, someone may argue analogically that people shouldn't allow pornographic material into their homes any more than they should serve their families contaminated foods. Presumably the reason for not serving contaminated food is that it makes people physically ill. But there's no evidence that reading or viewing pornographic material makes a person ill, physically or even mentally.

As one final example of a false analogy, consider this statement, made by Iran's Ayatollah Khomeini in defending state executions of those convicted of adultery, prostitution, or homosexuality:

> If your finger suffers from gangrene, what do you do? Let the whole hand and then the body become filled with gangrene, or cut the finger off? . . . Corruption, corruption. We have to eliminate corruption.[2]

The analogy is this: Physical disease is to an individual body as moral corruption is to the state. Since the diseased parts of the body sometimes must be removed to preserve the life of the body, so moral corruption must sometimes be rooted out to preserve the integrity of the state.

But Khomeini overlooks many differences that make the analogy false, and dangerously so. First, physical disease and moral corruption differ in nature and form. Whereas people can easily agree that a hand is gangrenous and must be removed, rarely can they as easily agree about what constitutes moral corruption. Second, people don't agree that moral corruption warrants execution. Third, an individual is not part of the state in the same way that a member of the body is a part of that body. The fundamental difference is that a body member has no life or integrity, not even meaning, except in reference to the whole body. But an individual has meaning, substance, and worth independent of any relationship to the state.

Assuming a Causal Relationship

People often downplay by omission when arguing that a causal relationship exists between two things by using the following devices: questionable

---

[2]*Time*, October 22, 1979, p. 57.

cause, neglect of a common cause, causal oversimplification, slippery slope and post hoc. We will examine each in turn.

Questionable Cause   *Downplaying by questionable cause consists of asserting a causal relationship where there is no evidence for one, or where the evidence provided is only a statistical correlation.* For example, when the Borana tribe in Kenya witnessed the solar eclipse of June 30, 1973, it claimed that the eclipse had been caused by the white man who, having landed on the moon, learned the secrets of the heavenly bodies and was now tampering with them. Similarly, after a tornado ripped through sections of Louisville, Kentucky, in 1973, an evangelist marched through town warning passersby to mend their evil ways or expect another devastating storm. In both cases the natural causes of the phenomena were ignored. Fortunately, these kinds of eye-popping causal inferences are rare. Far more common, even epidemic, are causal inferences based on some statistical correlation between two things.

A correlation is a connection between the properties shared by members of a group. For example, a study may indicate that users of a particular toothpaste had far fewer cavities than nonusers. It is tempting to infer—indeed, advertisers would have us do precisely that—that this toothpaste prevents cavities. But such statistical correlations are of themselves insufficient to establish a causal connection between the use of the toothpaste and reduced cavities. The difference in the number of cavities could be explained by data that have been omitted, such as proper dental hygiene, diet, and genetics.

Of course, a high degree of correlation between two sets of data may *suggest* causal connection. For example, medical scientists knew for some time of a statistical correlation between cigarette smoking and lung cancer: The incidence of lung cancer in the smoking population was higher than in the nonsmoking population. Although this suggested a causal connection, researchers had to investigate the smoking process, with special attention to its impact on the lungs, before they could establish with certainty that such a connection existed. Carefully controlled studies involving animals and humans revealed that smoking not only injures lung tissue but also produces malignant lesions. Using this hard evidence, researchers could demonstrate a causal connection between smoking and lung cancer and thus had a basis for accepting the statistical correlation as a causal one. But the point is that statistical correlations of themselves were not enough to establish the causal connection.

Neglect of a Common Cause   *Downplaying by neglect of a common cause consists of failing to recognize that two seemingly related events may not be causally related at all but rather are effects of a common cause.* For example, suppose a person suffers from both depression and alcoholism. It's tempting to infer that one is causing the other—the depression causes the drinking or the drinking causes the depression. But both may be the effects of some underlying cause, such as a profound emotional disturbance.

Causal Oversimplification   *Downplaying by causal oversimplification consists of assuming that what merely contributes to a phenomenon is enough to produce* *it.* For example, intense debates are waged over the wisdom of increased defense spending. Very often those in favor of more military spending assume that such expenditures of themselves ensure national security. Although defense expenditures may contribute to a nation's security, they certainly don't guarantee it. Those who think they do omit other important considerations, for example that the money must be wisely spent, that armies must be made up of knowledgeable, enthusiastic personnel, and that the nation as a whole must have the will to defend itself. Others may insist that huge military budgets ensure war. Not necessarily. While big military spending may predispose a nation to solving international disputes by war, they don't of themselves necessitate that approach.

Slippery Slope   *Downplaying by slippery slope consists of objecting to a particular action because it supposedly will lead inevitably to a similar but less desirable action, which in turn will lead to an even less desirable action, and so on down the "slippery slope" to some ultimate horror.* "Don't take the first drink, my boy," a father tells his son, "you'll end up a drunk." Will the first drink necessarily lead to alcoholism? No. The father omits or is ignorant of the fact that the vast majority of people who take the first, second, third, and many other drinks do not become alcoholics.

Similarly someone says "I'm opposed to national health insurance because, if enacted, it won't be long before the government will take over other aspects of our lives, and pretty soon we'll be living in a socialist state." Here the speaker uses a chain of events on the basis of whose final, undesirable link she rejects the first link. If the first does in fact entail the last, then the claim is sound. But it doesn't. The speaker overlooks the fact that the chain can be broken at any point between the first link, national health insurance, and the last, a socialist state. Granted, national health insurance might predispose us to other socialist solutions, but it would not necessarily lead us to these solutions. Each is a separate and distinct issue that could, should, and probably would be debated on its merits.

Post Hoc   *Downplaying by post hoc consists of asserting that one event is the cause of another merely because the first preceded the second.*[3] For example, someone observes that crime among youth has increased in the United States since the arrival of punk rock from England. The person concludes, therefore, that punk rock is causing an increase in juvenile crime. Similarly someone observes that every war in this century has followed the election of a Democratic president. The person therefore concludes that the Democrats are the war party. In each case the arguer assumes that one event caused another simply because it immediately preceded it. Overlooked are the complex causes of both juvenile crime and of war.

---

[3]The full Latin phrase is *post hoc, ergo propter hoc,* which means literally "after this, therefore because of this." In other words, those arguing post hoc assume that since event B followed event A, A must be the cause of B.

Quick Check on Downplaying by Omission

1 Identify the type of downplaying by omission — half-truth, invincible ignorance, faulty comparison, false analogy, questionable cause, causal oversimplification, neglect of a common cause, slippery slope, or post hoc — that
occurs in these passages.

   a While Ulysses S. Grant was handily winning battles in the West, President
   Lincoln was receiving lots of complaints about the general's drinking.
   Legend has it that one day a delegation told Lincoln "Mr. President, the
   general is hopelessly addicted to whiskey." To which Lincoln reportedly
   replied, "I wish General Grant would send a barrel of his whiskey to each of
   my other generals."

   b " 'Before he took B_{15} he [her husband] could barely get up for his meals
   because of a severe heart condition,' said Jayne Link, a 51-year-old Glen
   Cove, New York, widow. 'Two weeks after he started taking the vitamin pill
   he was completely changed.' Then Bill stopped taking the vitamin. Three
   months later he was dead — victim of a fifth heart attack. . . . Now Mrs. Link
   takes B_{15} herself for arthritis. 'I take it constantly, three 50 milligram tablets
   a day,' she said. 'I have a slipped disc in addition to the arthritis. I tried
   everything under the sun to relieve the pain. But nothing else has worked.' " (*Globe,* September 11, 1979, p. 22.)

   c Colleges should start paying students for getting high grades. After all,
   business handsomely rewards its top people with bonuses and commis-
   sions, and everybody can see the beneficial effect of that practice on
   worker productivity.

   d "Arthritics: Arthritis Strength Bufferin provides more complete help than
   Anacin, Bayer, and Tylenol. Greater amount of pain reliever than Bayer or
   even Anacin for hours of relief from minor arthritis pain. Stomach protection ingredients Bayer and other Aspirin do not have. More anti-inflamma-
   tory and antiswelling ingredients than Anacin."

   e Most women have a penchant for child care. Since the sick and infirm
   resemble children in many ways, women also are well qualified to care for
   the ill.

   f MOTHER: I really think you should major in nursing rather than philosophy, dear.
   DAUGHTER: But why?
   MOTHER: Well, because you're good at science. And also because it'll be
   easier for you to find a job in nursing.

   g Argument for a bill restricting the giving of discount prices on beer to large
   wholesale purchasers: Discount prices to large retailers drive out of business "mom-and-pop" stores that so often depend on beer sales for part of
   their earnings. These stores aren't eligible for the volume discounts, which
   enable supermarkets to sell beer at lower prices.

   h MAY: We've wasted a lot of money on space exploration.
   MEG: But what about all the things the space program has given us?
   MAY: Name one.

MEG: Weather satellites.

MAY: Name another.

MEG: Transistor technology.

MAY: Well, whatever it may have given us doesn't make any difference. As far as I'm concerned, it's still a waste of money.

i CARRIE: You know, Don, you should get married.

DON: Really?

CARRIE: Sure, married men on the average live longer than single men.

DON: So what?

CARRIE: So that proves that for men marriage is more conducive to a longer life than bachelorhood.

DON: Okay, you've talked me into it. Let's get hitched.

CARRIE: Are you nuts? Why, within a month we'd be fighting, within a year we'd be separated, and within two years I'd have all your money.

DON: Wow! I'm glad you mentioned that. I'd rather die young and rich than live to be old and poor.

j "If you could get rid of drugs [in the work place], we'd be far ahead of other countries in productivity." (Ira Lipman, quoted in Stanley Penn, "Losses Grow From Drug Use at the Office," *Wall Street Journal*, July 29, 1981, p. 27.)

k Presidential counselor Edwin Meese III explaining why the United States was considering hiding 200 MX missles among 4600 shelters scattered across the Utah and Nevada desert: ". . . a bad idea dictated only because of the Carter administration's slavish adherence to Salt II . . . and that was the only reason for 4600 holes in the ground."

l "Are interior decorators really necessary? Yes. . . . Since one cannot set one's own broken leg one relies on a doctor. Without a formidable knowl-edge of legal intricacies one depends on a barrister. Likewise, unless the individual is well versed in the home furnishing field the services of an interior decorator are a distinct advantage." (Helen-Janet Bonelli, *The Status Merchants: The Trade of Interior Decoration* [Cranbury, N.J.: Barnes, 1972], p. 36.)

m Letter to the media by a public-relations firm trying to promote the sale of a drug: "After 12 years of successful use by people in 21 countries around the world, American asthma sufferers can now legally obtain and use the drug known as Ventolin (albuterol). The remarkable therapeutic effects of Ven-tolin finally have been recognized by the U.S. Food and Drug Administra-tion. The significance of this new drug and its potential impact on their life style should be good news to 9 million Americans suffering from asthma." (Alan Parachin, "The Medical Community Ponders a 'Touchy Subject,'" *Los Angeles Times*, July 9, 1981, part 5, p. 1.)

2 Find an example of a half-truth, a false analogy, and one of the six variations of faulty causation in a magazine or newspaper.

Comments

1. a. Neglect of common cause
   b. Post hoc

c. False analogy

d. Selective comparison and half-truth: No mention is made of cost. The analgesic effect of any of these products comes from its aspirin content. To the degree that aspirin in this "arthritic product" happens to meet the requirements of the arthritic's condition, it may bring a measure of relief. But the price of relief is greater, compared with plain aspirin, which costs much less and does the job. The typical patient suffering from rheumatoid arthritis who can tolerate aspirin may be maintained on as many as twenty five-grain tablets of aspirin a day. Arthritis Strength Bufferin contains 7.5 grains, or 50 percent more than the typical patient would need. So why pay the extra money? And why choose any of these name brands when plain aspirin may prove just as effective?

e. False analogy

f. Faulty comparison, incomplete

g. Half-truth: The argument conceals at least three significant unfavorable points: (1) small stores could form cooperatives for volume purchase; (2) small stores have not gone under because of similar deregulation of wine and liquor sales; (3) small stores often survive more because of their location, hours, and general convenience than because of their prices.

h. Invincible ignorance

i. Questionable cause, slippery slope

j. Causal oversimplification

k. Neglect of a common cause: The primary reason was to give the Soviet Union an uncertain target in any surprise attack, which supposedly was important because of the vulnerability of existing U.S. Minuteman missle silos to increasingly accurate Soviet weapons.

l. False analogy

m. Half-truth: omits that (1) a competitor simultaneously had been authorized to sell a version of the same drug and (2) the FDA had classified albuterol as a new drug with *little or no* advantage in therapeutic benefit over asthma drugs already on sale. You wouldn't be likely to know any of this, a fact that underscores the insidiousness of half-truth.

Downplaying by Diversion

When people downplay by diversion, they attempt to blur or distract from key issues or important considerations. Typically this is accomplished by raising side issues, the irrelevant, and the trivial. Among the more common devices used to downplay are the following: genetic appeal, ad hominem, poisoning the well, humor and ridicule, fear or force, two wrongs make a right, straw man, and red herring.

Genetic Appeal

A number of diversionary devices take the form of personal attacks. One of them is called the genetic appeal. *Downplaying by means of genetic appeal consists of trying to discredit a conclusion by condemning its source or genesis.* Since how an idea originates or who holds it is irrelevant to its worth, rejecting a conclusion by condemning its source is always fallacious.

For example, suppose Grey opposes national health insurance because it smacks of socialism. True, guaranteeing all people access to medical care despite their ability to pay may be socialistic. But of itself that doesn't prove that the United States shouldn't have such a program.

Again, Grey summarily dismisses an argument against gun control because it is put forth by the National Rifle Association (NRA). Yes, the NRA has a vested interest in opposing gun-control laws. But that in itself doesn't discredit its argument against control. Certainly it would be wise to withhold judgment pending further consideration of the facts and the views of more objective sources, but it would be erroneous to reject the argument outright simply because the NRA drafted it.

Ad Hominem

Ad hominem is the Latin phrase for "to the man." When people argue ad hominem, they argue to the person, not the person's argument; that is, they attack the person rather than what the person is saying. *Downplaying by ad hominem, then, consists of attacking the person making an assertion rather than his or her position.* A most persuasive way of diverting attention from the real issue, ad hominem takes two forms: abusive, which consists of attacking a person's character; and circumstantial, which consists of attacking the circumstances of the person's life.

Like the genetic appeal, the abusive ad hominem attacks the source of origin. But it also heaps abuse on that source. For example, suppose that in rejecting a charge of malfeasance of office, comptroller White replies "My accusers are blackguards whose connections to organized crime are a matter of record. What's more, it's common knowledge that they have been out to get me for years." In damning the source of the charge, White would discredit them with allegations of underworld connections and ulterior motives.

Similarly, in responding to a proposal to limit the use of nuclear power, energy expert Black says "The people behind this proposal are wild-eyed environmentalists and fanatics." Like White, Black not only condemns the source, but through name-calling heaps abuse on them as well.

You should remember that not every argument that introduces the character and motives of the parties to that argument is fallacious. Personal considerations are certainly relevant when deciding whether a person is reliable and willing to tell the whole truth. If people have proved unreliable, we surely have a basis for holding what they say suspect. But suspecting their words is different from rejecting them. Weighing the reliability of a witness differs from assuming that personalities dispose of issues.

When an argument ad hominem is circumstantial, an attack is made on the facts of a person's life. For example, someone may disparage Jane Fonda's position on nuclear energy because she happens to be an actress. Someone else may disregard Richard Nixon's view on U.S.–China relations because he was forced to resign the presidency. These critics are not assassinating Fonda's or Nixon's characters but diverting attention from the issues by focusing on aspects of their lives that supposedly invalidate their positions. That Fonda is an actress or has socialist leanings and Nixon was forced out of office in disgrace have no bearing on the merit of their positions.

Poisoning the Well

Downplaying by poisoning the well, still another personal attack, *consists of trying to place one's opponents in a position from which they cannot reply.* Metaphorically, someone "poisons the well" before anyone can drink from it. For example, just before his election opponent is about to speak, Brown tells the audience "Don't believe a word my opponent is about to say. She's a born liar!" Some introduction! Whatever Brown's opponent now says probably will be suspect. Of course, Brown might have been more subtle and simply said "Don't be taken in by my opponent's get-tough-on-crime rhetoric. It's become fashionable for even the most permissive of lawmakers to assume this pose, now that they know the public no longer will tolerate the coddling of criminals." Brown's opponent will find it very difficult to convince her audience that she means what she says about crime because Brown has shrewdly polluted the waters before anyone can drink from them.

Humor or Ridicule

A common variation on downplaying by diversion is the appeal to humor and ridicule. *Downplaying by humor and ridicule consists of relying strictly on whimsy or contempt to discredit an argument.* For example, a member of the British Parliament named Thomas Massey-Massey once introduced a bill to change the name of Christmas to Christide. He reasoned thus: Since "mass" is a Catholic term and since Britons are largely Protestant, they should avoid the suffix "mass" in Chris*tmas*. On hearing the proposal another member suggested that Christmas might not want its name changed. "How would you like it," he asked Thomas Massey-Massey, "if we changed your name to Thotide Tidey-Tidey?" The bill died in the ensuing laughter.[4]

Similarly, a story is told of an incident that occurred at the Yalta meeting of Franklin D. Roosevelt, Winston Churchill, and Joseph Stalin. Churchill reportedly mentioned that the Pope had suggested a particular course of action as right, whereupon Stalin is said to have replied "And how many divisions did you say the Pope had available for combat duty?" Stalin diverted attention from the issues through ridicule.

Fear or Force

Downplaying by fear or force consists of using a threat of harm to make someone accept a position. Also known as "swinging the big stick," this fallacy is

---

[4]Reported in S. Morris Engel, *With Good Reason* (New York: St. Martin's Press, 1976), p. 109.

summed up in the adage "Might makes right." Of course it doesn't; but it does divert from a cool, calm reflection of the issue.

Lobbyists like to remind legislators of the many voters that they, the lobbyists, represent. The message is clear: "Disregard the merits of the bill; vote my way or you'll be looking for work after the next election." An employer "counsels" a worker that joining a union would be "imprudent." Translation: "Forget the pros and cons of union membership; if you join the union, you'll be fired." A male supervisor suggests to a female subordinate that she might "go further faster" if she were a "bit more cooperative." That is to say "Go to bed with me or else!" A member of a law-and-order group tells a judge that "being soft on crime" could prove "most unwise." In other words, "Don't get caught up in the petty details of dispensing justice. Get tough on criminals or we'll hound you out of office." Appeals to fear and force, all.

Two Wrongs Make a Right

Downplaying by means of a two-wrongs-make-a-right appeal consists of attempting to justify what is considered objectionable by appealing to other instances of the same objectionable action. For example, a police officer stops a speeding motorist. "Why stop me?" the driver asks. "Didn't you see that Jaguar fly by at eighty miles an hour?" The motorist tries to divert attention from his own infraction and to justify it by citing the wrongdoing of another. But the speed of the other motorist is irrelevant; the issue is whether he himself was speeding.

Sometimes, rather than appealing to a single instance of similar wrongdoing, people appeal to a widely accepted practice to divert attention from and justify their behavior. Caught using company stationery for personal use, a worker may say "Why, everybody else does it." In other words, helping themselves to company stationary is a common practice of workers in this office. Similarly, faced with criticism over the appointment of longtime Reagan friend and personal lawyer William French Smith as Attorney General, Reagan defenders pointed out that the office commonly is held by a close legal associate of the President. Although their observation was true, the common-practice appeal was irrelevant to whether Smith was qualified for the office. A nondiversionary defense would have begun by pointing out that association with a President, though valuable, is not of itself sufficient to disqualify a candidate for office and ended by listing Smith's qualifications.

Straw Man

Downplaying by straw man consists of so altering a position that the altered version is easier to attack than the original. The name of this fallacy bespeaks what it accomplishes: It sets up a "straw" that is easy to "blow over." Of course the straw version is not the original, but that's exactly the point. The altered version makes a far more inviting target. As a result an unthinking audience can easily infer that the original argument is demolished when the straw is blown over.

See if you can spot the straw man in this dialogue:

> TOM: The theory of creationism should be taught in the public schools right along with biological evolution.
>
> TRISH: Why do you say that?
>
> TOM: Prohibiting the teaching of creationism is precisely what is done in Communist countries.
>
> TRISH: Well, I certainly don't want our public schools acting like Communist schools.
>
> TOM: Precisely.
>
> TRISH: You know, Tom, I never thought of it that way. I'm going to write my legislators right away and have them look into this.

The real issue here is the teaching of creationism; the straw issue is communism. It is certainly much easier to get Americans to support a position *against* communism than *for* teaching creationism. Simply because Communist countries prohibit the teaching of creationism doesn't mean that any system that does not include instruction in creationism is Communist or shares communism's motives. Anticreationists typically invoke the doctrine of church/state separation to keep creationism out of the classroom; so do many religionists who believe in creationism. Or both sometimes assert that creationism properly falls under instruction in religion, not science. But such relevant points are obscured once the failure to teach creationism is identified with communism.

The dean of a prestigious school of business recently objected to the inclusion of a course on business ethics in the business curriculum. He claimed that by the time students entered graduate business schools their ethical standards had long been set. Moreover, he thought it presumptuous to tell them what was right and wrong.

The argument has great psychological appeal because it associates courses in business ethics with dictating morality to students. The implication is that since we don't want moral dogma taught in the classroom, we shouldn't want courses in business ethics. But such courses needn't indoctrinate. They can investigate the possible bases for a just economic system, explore the relationship between business and various claimants (such as employees, stockholders, consumers, and government), and consider a variety of business issues within the framework of diverse ethical theories. The real issue, then, is whether such topics warrant a place in the business curriculum. If not, the reasons should be thoroughly investigated. But it's far easier to undercut coverage of these topics by identifying business ethics with dogma than by demonstrating that these issues are not worthy of study in a graduate school, or elsewhere for that matter.

Red Herring

Downplaying by red herring consists of presenting facts that do not support the stated position but a position that may vaguely resemble it. This colorful name derives from the habit of some prison escapees of smearing themselves with herring (which turns brown or red when it spoils) to throw dogs off their track. For example, in charging an executive with embezzlement, a prosecutor quotes harrowing statistics about white-collar crime. Although her statistical appeal may influence the jury, it is irrelevant to establishing the guilt of the defendant. The alarming statistics only support the assertion that white-collar crime is a serious social problem. They give no support to the charge that the defendant is guilty of embezzlement and in fact divert attention from it.

Let's say that Frank argues that the courts have treated newspaper reporters unfairly by imprisoning them for not revealing their sources of information. "Reporters help keep people informed and public officials honest," he contends. True enough, but such evidence only shows that reporters perform a useful public service. It does not demonstrate that the courts have been unfair to them. To establish that point Frank might show that reporters cannot function without being permitted to protect their sources and that freedom of the press presupposes this right.

Quick Check on Downplaying by Diversion

1 Identify the kind of downplaying by diversion—genetic appeal, ad hominem, poisoning the well, humor or ridicule, fear or force, two wrongs make a right, straw man, and red herring—evident in these passages.
   a "Mr. North, a fascist flunkey, wishes by means of his semantics to make meaningless not only the sacred deed of heroism of the fighters against fascism, but the whole past and future struggle for liberty. But he only exposes his reactionary guts, his hatred for liberty and social progress. . . . Stuart Chase, the petty bourgeois American economist, who writes prescriptions for the disease of capitalism, having read the writing of semantics has lost the last remnants of common sense and has come forward with a fanatical sermon of the new faith, a belief in the magical power of words." (Bernard Emmanuilovich Bykhovsky, *The Decay of Bourgeois Philosophy* [Moscow: Mysl, 1947], p. 173.)
   b "Name calling, derogatory articles, and adverse propaganda are other methods used to belittle persons refusing to recommend refined foods. We have long been called crackpots and faddists regardless of training or of accuracy in reporting research. The words 'quack' and 'quackery' are now such favorites that any one using them is receiving benefits from the food processors." (Adele Davis, *Let's Eat Right to Keep Fit* [Los Angeles: Cancer Control Society, 1970], p. 21.)
   c "Every criminal, every gambler, every thug, every libertine, every girl ruiner, every home wrecker, every wife beater, every dope peddler, every moonshiner, every crooked politician, every pagan Papist priest, every shyster lawyer, every K. of C. [Knights of Columbus, a Roman Catholic organization of laymen], every white slaver, every brothel madam, every Rome controlled newspaper, every black spider—is fighting the Klan. Think it over. Which side are you on?" (From a Ku Klux Klan circular)

d "Remember the plot to dose up Cuban Premier Fidel Castro so his beard would fall out? the contract with Mafia hit men to knock him off? the CIA agent who plugged in a lie detector machine and blew out all the lights in a dingy Sinapore hotel? the clandestine military operations that backfired in Cuba, Laos and Iraq?

"The James Bonds responsible for those slapstick misadventures are back in business. A few weeks ago, for example, a report appeared in print that the CIA was plotting a multiphase operation to rid the world of Libya's radical ruler, Moammar Khadafy. . . ." (Jack Anderson, "Slapstick Plots," *San Francisco Chronicle*, August 25, 1981, p. 41.)

e "If your planet is subjected one day to the unimaginable horrors of a third world war, 1977 [the year in which the B-1 bomber project was scrapped] might be recorded as the year in which the seeds of defeat for the Western powers were sown." (John W. R. Taylor, in *Preface to Jane's All the World Aircraft* [London: Jane's Year Book, 1977]. The B-1 bomber project was resurrected in 1981.)

f A Soviet official, commenting on the Reagan administration's apparent unwillingness to negotiate key issues, such as the location of the Soviet Union's SS-20 missiles and a new Strategic Arms Limitation Treaty: "We shall continue to urge real negotiations but our patience is not unlimited. This does not mean, of course, that we would start a war, but ultimately if there is no change we will have to counter measures being taken by your administration with measures of our own. We don't want to do this. It can only result in a dangerous spiral. This would be a very dangerous development." (Fred Warner Neal, "America Frustrates Soviets—And That's Dangerous," *Los Angeles Times*, July 31, 1981, part 2, p. 7.)

g A Duke University historian, arguing for a controversial proposal to locate Nixon's presidential archives library at Duke University: " 'Whether one approves or disapproves of Richard Nixon himself seems quite beside the point.' The Nixon documents 'are of critical importance for the study of the political and diplomatic history of the United States.' " (Barry Jacobs, "Duke Academicians up in Arms over Nixon Library Plans," *Christian Science Monitor*, September 4, 1981, p. 5.)

h A spokesperson for Regimen weight-reducing tablets, in responding to Justice Department charges of deliberate misrepresentation and falsehood in advertising the product: "Thousands of other advertisers and agencies are doing the same thing." (Samm Sinclair Baker, *The Permissible Lie* [New York: World, 1968], p. 24.)

i "Everybody complains about the U.S. mail these days—prices going up and service down. But our Postal Service seems like a winner compared with the Canadian one. In fact, our neighbors to the north have elevated post-office bashing into a national sport." ("The World," *San Francisco Chronicle*, July 26, 1981, p. 5. The article went on to catalogue deficiencies in the Canadian postal system.)

j "There is a move now to clamp down on the sexy aspects of television and return it to the purity of Ozzie and Harriet. *Lift* those necklines! Thicken those brassieres and rivet them firmly in place! And watch what you say! The penalty! The New Puritans will reckon up the sex-points, watching narrowly for every hint of cleavage, for every parting of kissing lips, and will then lower the boom on all advertisers who fail the test. By striking at the pocket-nerves, the Puritans hope to produce a new kind of television that will be as clean, as pink, as smooth and as plump as eunuchs usually are." (Isaac Asimov, "Censorship: It's 'a Choking Grip,'" *TV Guide*, July 18–24, 1981, p. 13.)

k In the fall of 1970 Princeton University adopted a plan under which the university would schedule no classes for a short period before the congressional elections of 1970, thus enabling students to campaign for candidates *if* they so wished. The proposal came in the aftermath of the U.S. invasion of Cambodia in June 1970, which touched off a number of campus demonstrations. The Princeton administration thought its plan would help defuse any further unrest and violence that might result during the campaign among students who believed that they had no voice in their electoral process. The immediate reaction to the plan among other colleges was quite favorable. But learning of the plan, Senator Strom Thurmond attacked it by asking the Internal Revenue Service to investigate how it might affect the tax-exempt status of institutions adopting it. In the aftermath of Thurmond's warning, the American Council of Education cautioned member institutions to be careful about engaging in any "political campaign on behalf of any candidate for public office." Under tax laws an institution can lose its tax-exempt status for engaging in partisan political activity. As a result very few institutions adopted the Princeton plan. (Reported in Howard Kahane, *Logic and Contemporary Rhetoric* [Belmont, Calif.: Wadsworth, 1976], pp. 53–55.)

2 From your reading and television viewing, find one example of each of the downplaying by omission devices discussed.

Comments

1. a. Abusive ad hominen
   b. Circumstantial ad hominem and genetic appeal
   c. Genetic appeal and abusive ad hominem (lumping Catholics into such an unsavory crowd)
   d. Poisoning the well: Before the analysis of the CIA's alleged plot even begins, the author discredits it.
   e. Fear
   f. Fear and force
   g. Red herring: The issue is not the preservation of the Nixon documents but housing them at Duke.
   h. Two wrongs of the common-practice variety
   i. Red herring: Lambasting the Canadian postal system is irrelevant to whether the U.S. system is inadequate.
   j. Humor and ridicule, abusive ad hominen ("Puritans")

k. Straw man: The institutions were not engaged in *partisan* politics as Thurmond suggested. Therefore there was no real threat to their tax-exempt status.

Downplaying by Confusion

A third way of downplaying issues is to make things so complex or chaotic that the audience gives up, grows weary, or gets overloaded. Chaos can be the accidental result of a disorganized mind or the intentional flimflam of a con man. One great source of confusion is ambiguous language, including jargon and weasel words. Recall what we said in Chapter 2 about the need for (though not obsession with) clear and precise language usage. There are in addition several specific ways that people confuse their audience: equivocation, accent, composition, division, inconsistency, and begging the question.

Equivocation

Downplaying by equivocation consists of drawing an unwarranted conclusion by using a word or phrase to mean two different things in the same argument. In equivocation the meaning of a word actually has shifted in the course of an argument, thereby entailing the conclusion. Here's an absurd though illustrative example of equivocation: "John is a weird man, because he does math problems in a weird way." "Weird" as used in the expressed premise refers to an unusual way of doing arithmetic. But "weird" in the unexpressed premise ("People who do math problems in a weird way are *weird*") refers to an odd or peculiar personality. Thus, two different meanings of the same word are used in the same argument to entail the conclusion.

A more serious instance of equivocation is seen in this sometimes-invoked argument for the existence of a divine being:

> The laws of gravitation and motion must have a lawmaker for the simple reason that they are laws, and all laws have a lawmaker.

Here the word "laws" is given various meanings. In the sense that laws are humanmade statutes that proscribe certain behavior, all laws do have a lawmaker. But the laws of gravitation and motion are scientific descriptions of how the physical universe operates and as such don't presuppose lawmakers. Therefore the conclusion is unwarranted.

Accent

Downplaying by accent consists of drawing an unwarranted conclusion, or suggesting one, by the use of improper emphasis. The improper emphasis in the accent downplay may fall on a word, phrase, or aspect of the argument. In any event the confusion results from the emphasis.

Том: I'm not going to contribute any more to your charity.
Liz: Great! I'll just put you down for the same amount as last year.
Том: What!

Liz draws the faulty conclusion that Tom wants to contribute the same as he did the year before because she erroneously accents "more." Without that accent the colloquial "any more" means "any longer."

The news media and ad writers commonly use accent to ensnare us. PRESIDENT DECLARES WAR, a headline screams in bold print. Concerned that the United States is embroiled in combat somewhere, you buy the paper and anxiously read the article. The "war," you discover, is a "war on inflation." Television uses this tack ad nauseam. How many times have you been teased by the promise of "details at eleven"? "Air crash!" a so-called news brief or update announces and then adds "Details at eleven!" Rarely is the 11:00 report of the incident as significant as the teaser made it appear. In fact, often as not it isn't even the lead story. The editor intentionally used accent to confuse you about the significance and coverage of the story.

The accent fallacy has several variations. One is giving the impression that something is special or unique. For example, for years the firm C and H has advertised its sugar as "pure cane granulated from Hawaii!" The manufacturer proudly proclaims

> Warm tropical sunshine—gentle tropical rains—rich and fertile soil, born of vol-canoes. In Hawaii, there is this happy combination of climate and setting—the perfect place for growing fine sugar cane. We grow it for eighteen months, then harvest and refine it for you to enjoy. C and H—the pure cane sugar from Hawaii!

This ad makes Hawaii-grown sugar sound special, doesn't it? It isn't. The Federal Trade Commission claims that there is no difference in granulated sugars. Sugar from beets or sugar grown elsewhere than Hawaii is not inferior to C and H's.

Another common variation of the accent fallacy is the out-of-context quote, used pervasively to advertise films. Thus

> *"Revenge of the Reptilians* . . . a masterpiece of . . . filmmaking!" (Rodd of the *Times)*

The ellipses indicate that something has been left out of the review excerpt. In fact, the review might have read *"Revenge of the Reptilians* is without doubt a masterpiece of the gut-turning, mindless tripe that has become sickeningly commonplace among graduates of the school of inanely adolescent filmmak-ing!" Beware the out-of-context quote in news reporting and political campaign literature.

Composition

Downplaying by composition consists of reasoning improperly from a prop-erty of a member of a group to a property of the group itself. For example, a man observes that every member of a local club is wealthy and therefore infers that the club itself must be wealthy. Not necessarily. The confusion results from assuming that what is true of the part must also be true of the whole. In fact, the whole represents something different from simply the sum or the combination of its parts. The whole either takes on a new character because of its composi-tion or at least does not need to maintain the particular character of its parts.

Each chapter of a book considered individually may be a masterpiece, but the book, considered as a whole, may not be. Each member of an orchestra may be an outstanding musician, but that doesn't imply that the orchestra as a whole is outstanding.

Division

Downplaying by division, the converse of downplaying by composition, consists of reasoning improperly from a quality of the group to a quality of a member of the group. Observing that a club is wealthy, a man infers that each club member must be wealthy or that a particular member must be wealthy. But just as a property of the part does not imply a property of the whole, so a property of the whole doesn't imply a property of the part. That a book is a masterpiece doesn't mean that each chapter is one; that an orchestra is out- standing doesn't imply that each member is a great musician.

Inconsistency

Downplaying by inconsistency consists of using contradictory premises in an argument. If two premises contradict each other, one must be false. So even if an argument in which they appear is valid, we should not accept the argument because it is inconsistent.

The fallacy of inconsistency has several variations. First, arguers may contradict themselves in the same statement. For example, in the summer of 1981 Israel's Prime Minister Menachem Begin ordered the bombing of Beirut, Lebanon. As a result the United States decided to withhold shipment of F-16 fighter planes to Israel. Commenting on the delay, Deputy Secretary of State William Clark said "Mr. Begin is without question making it difficult to assist Israel. Our commitment is not to Mr. Begin but to the nation he represents."[5] But if the U.S. commitment was to Israel, why should any action of Begin's have made it difficult to assist Israel? Of course, it's impossible to make a simple distinction between a nation and its leader, as Clark himself later admitted by disavowing any intention of drawing such a distinction between Begin and Israel.

Second, arguers may contradict themselves at different times without attempting to justify the change of mind. For example, at first Secretary of State Alexander Haig was reported to be opposed to Clark's appointment as Deputy Secretary of State. Later he enthusiastically backed him. Similarly, in July 1981 a flap developed over Central Intelligence Agency head William Casey's appoint- ment of the inexperienced Max Hugel as chief of U.S. clandestine intelligence. When Hugel resigned under fire, Senator Barry Goldwater said that Casey should continue as CIA chief. A week later, however, Goldwater said that Casey should resign or be fired for having made the Hugel appointment. Shortly

---

[5]Oswald Johnston and George Skelton, "Weinberger Puts Blame on Israelis," *Los Angeles Times*, July 23, 1981, part 5, p. 1.

thereafter, Goldwater reasserted his support of Casey. Why all the turnabouts? Goldwater didn't say.

Third, arguers may contradict the positions of their institutional affiliation. During his 1980 campaign Reagan declared that the United States had become second in military power to the Soviet Union. About six months after the inauguration, however, Secretary of Defense Caspar Weinberger was warning Congress that the Russians *might* achieve "clear superiority" if they kept building their forces at current rates and if the United States didn't do more. He went on to say "We will clearly be second in military power to the Soviet Union if the U.S. strategic forces are not improved."[6] Weinberger's views were consistent with neither the preelection nor the postelection position of Ronald Reagan.

Fourth, words and actions can be contradictory. For example, many times during his campaign and after his election President Reagan underscored the need for competition and deregulation. But his actions as President sometimes belied his commitment to either. Thus, in its first year the Reagan administration pressured Japan to adopt "voluntary" quotas on automobile imports. The President also appointed Riese H. Taylor to head the Interstate Commerce Commission. By his own admission Taylor was no devotee of deregulation, and in fact he was supported by the Teamsters union, which opposed deregulation.

Begging the Question

Downplaying by begging the question consists of asserting in the premises what is asserted in the conclusion. Sometimes begging the question is transparent, as when the premise is merely a restatement of the conclusion. For example, Myra asserts that pornographic films are "objectionable" because they are "immoral." But by definition what is immoral is objectionable. Thus, Myra's premise says exactly what her conclusion does. It's as if she had said "Pornographic films are immoral because they are immoral."

Similarly, Ted insists "User's fees should be tacked onto the purchases of certain goods and services because that would generate tax revenue." But a user's fee is a tax. So Ted's premise, like Myra's, is asserting what the conclusion asserts. It's as if he had said "Taxes should be tacked onto the purchase of certain goods and services because that would generate tax revenue."

Such arguments, which involve *circular reasoning*, say nothing more than "A is true because A is true." Although circular arguments may be formally valid (that is, the premises may logically entail the conclusion), they are not cogent because at least one of the premises is as doubtful as the conclusion. That premise cannot logically support the conclusion, although the arguer presumes that it does.

Not all cases of begging the question involve circularity. Often arguers will use evaluative terms or phrases as if they were purely descriptive ones to sway an audience about an issue or situation. For example, in arguing against abor-

---

[6]"Reagan Defense Buildup," *San Francisco Sunday Examiner and Chronicle,* July 26, 1981, p. A10.

tion someone says, "A baby shouldn't have to suffer and die at the mother's convenience." By calling the fetus a "baby," the arguer implies that it is a human being, the very assumption that is hotly contested in abortion debates. Similarly, another person asserts that the student-loan program should be continued, even expanded, because "the right to higher education should not be denied a person for financial reasons." But is the opportunity for higher education a "right"? The speaker in effect is asking the audience to accept without proof that higher education is a right.

Quick Check on Downplaying by Confusion

1 Identify the kind of downplaying by confusion—equivocation, accent, composition, division, inconsistency, and begging the question—used in these passages.

 a Shortly after his appointment as Secretary of Health and Human Services, Richard S. Schweiker called prevention of disease the nation's highest health priority. In response to research findings about salt, Schweiker used his office to propagandize against it and prod manufacturers to cut their use of salt and list sodium content on their labels. Schweiker also defended cutting $2 million from the $3 million a year that his department had spent to counter the tobacco industry's $1-billion-a-year advertising budget.

 b HARRY: "How do you account for the Senator's dramatic come-from-behind victory?"
     HILDA: One big factor is that his campaign was on the rise.
     HARRY: You mean it had momentum?
     HILDA: Exactly.

 c "Should we not assume that just as the eye, the hand, the foot, and in general each part of the body clearly has its own proper function, so man too has some function over and above the function of his parts?" (Aristotle, *Nicomachean Ethics*, trans. Martin Oswald [Indianapolis: Bobbs-Merrill, 1962], p. 16.)

 d "Most Calvinists were theological determinists. Most New England Puritans were Calvinists. Therefore, most New England Puritans were theological determinists. . . . The fortunes of the Federalists decayed after 1980. Joseph Dennie was a Federalist. Therefore, the fortunes of Joseph Dennie decayed after 1800." (Paraphrase of historian Vernon Parrington in "Main Currents of American Thought," in David Hackett Fischer (ed.), *Historians' Fallacies* [New York: Harper & Row, 1970], p. 222.)

 e People object to sexism and racism on the ground of discrimination. But what is objectionable about discrimination? We discriminate all the time—in the cars we buy, the foods we eat, the books we read, the friends we choose. The fact is that there's nothing wrong with discrimination. So there's nothing wrong with discrimination against people on the basis of color or sex.

f **TOD:** Why do you dislike Frank so much, when the Bible says, "Love thy neighbor"?

   TED: But Frank's not my neighbor. He doesn't live anywhere near me.

g Certainly death is the perfection of life. After all, the end of anything is its perfection. And since death is the end of life, death must be the perfection of life.

2 Find in a newspaper and a magazine one example of each device used to downplay by confusion.

Comments

1. a. Inconsistency
    b. Begging the question: A "come-from-behind" victory presupposes a campaign that was "on the rise" and had "momentum." So to explain such a victory in those terms is to assert what a "come-from-behind" victory itself asserts.
    c. Composition
    d. Division
    e. Equivocation: When applied to racism and sexism, "discrimination" means making a distinction in favor of or against a person on the basis of color or sex alone. As such, racial and sexual discrimination raise questions of social justice. When people object to racism and sexism on the ground of discrimination, then, "discrimination" is understood to mean *unfair* selection. When applied to cars, foods, books, and friends, "discrimination" merely means distinguishing among items on the basis of some standard and carries no overtones of social injustice.
    f. Accent
    g. Equivocation on "end"

Summary

In arguing their cases, people typically slant them by intensifying certain facts and downplaying others. Specifically, people intensify by association—linking an idea, person, or product with what already is strongly approved of or disapproved of by the intended audience. In downplaying by omission, people exclude data that don't support their conclusions. When they downplay by diversion, they try to blur or distract from key issues. And when people downplay by confusion, they make terms so complex or chaotic that the audience gives up, grows weary, or gets overloaded. The following common devices frequently are used to intensify or downplay communication:

Intensifying by Association

1. Testimonials: endorsements of a person, product, or position, usually by some well-known figure. When the testimonial represents expert opinion and there is agreement among the experts, it is legitimate; otherwise it isn't. Examples: using the Surgeon General's opinion as a reason to avoid smoking (legitimate testimonial); invoking Florence Henderson's endorsement of Tang as a reason for using that product (illegitimate testimonial).

2. Statistics, studies, and polls: Before accepting any statistic, you should ask yourself (a) Does it make any difference? (b) Is it complete? (c) Is it knowable? Before accepting the results of any study, you should determine (a) the subjects involved, (b) how long the research was conducted, (c) who conducted the testing, (d) which stage of research the assertion refers to, (e) how the study was conducted, and (f) how extensive the testing was. Before accepting the results of any poll or survey, you should find out (a) the sponsor's or survey's name, (b) the date of contact, (c) the method of contact, (d) the sample size, and (e) the kinds of questions that were asked.

3. Popularity: relying exclusively on numbers to support a claim. Example: claiming that the President's economic program is unsound because a recent poll indicates that the vast majority of Americans disapprove of it.

4. Tradition: appealing to feelings of respect for some custom that supports the view being advanced. Example: arguing that a woman shouldn't keep her maiden name after marrying because in this culture the woman always takes her husband's name.

5. Novelty: assuming that something is good or desirable simply because it's new. Example: voting on the basis of the claim "It's time for a change!"

6. Jumping to a conclusion: forming a judgment based on insufficient evidence or atypical cases. Example: inferring that NOW is made up mostly of lesbians on the basis of a few known lesbian members of NOW (insufficient evidence); claiming that the U.S. does not support the principle of free travel because prisoners aren't allowed to go where they want (atypical case).

7. Guilt by association: making judgments about people solely on the basis of their relationship with others. Example: Pete Wilson's attempt to discredit Jerry Brown by identifying him with Cesar Chavez, the farm union leader unpopular among California farm owners.

8. Positioning: capitalizing on the earned reputation of a leader in the field to sell a product, candidate, or idea. Example: Goodrich's claim "We're the ones without the blimp."

9. Provincialism: viewing things exclusively in terms of group loyalty. Example: an educator's claim that the administration deserves low marks because it knows little about educational problems.

10. Mob appeal: attempting to persuade by arousing a group's deepest feelings and enthusiasms by playing to its culturally conditioned prejudices. Example: William Jennings Bryan's "Cross of Gold" speech.

Downplaying by Omission

1. Half-truth: ignoring, suppressing, or unfairly minimizing evidence that is unfavorable to a claim. Example: claiming that municipal bonds are a good investment because they reduce one's income taxes.

2. Invincible ignorance: defending the legitimacy of an idea or principle despite contradictory facts. Example: insisting that no matter what good has resulted from the space program, it is a waste of money.

3. Faulty comparison: making a comparison on too few points or only on those points that advance one's claim while ignoring other significant points. Example: Claiming that solar energy is preferable to nuclear energy simply because the former is cheaper (too few points); claiming that nuclear is preferable to other energy alternatives because it is cleaner, efficient, and more economical (overlooking a significant point, namely, safety).

4. False analogy: overlooking significant differences in a comparison and assuming that because two things are alike in one or more respects they must be alike in some other respect. Example: claiming that people shouldn't allow pornographic materials into their homes any more than they should serve their families contaminated food.

5. Questionable cause: asserting a causal relation when there is no evidence for one or when the evidence is only a statistical correlation. Example: inferring that a toothpaste prevents cavities because a study indicates that its users have fewer cavities than nonusers.

6. Neglect of common cause: failing to recognize that two seemingly related events may not be causally related at all but the effect of a common cause. Example: inferring in the case of a person suffering from both alcoholism and depression that one must be the cause of the other.

7. Causal oversimplication: assuming that what merely contributes to a phenomenon is enough to produce it. Example: insisting that military spending is enough to ensure national security.

8. Slippery slope: objecting to a particular action because it supposedly will lead inevitably to a similar but less desirable action, which in turn will lead to an even less desirable action, and so on down the "slippery slope" to some ultimate horror. Example: opposing national health insurance because it will supposedly lead inevitably to a socialist state.

9. Post hoc: asserting that one event is the cause of another simply because the first precedes the second. Example: claiming that because juvenile crime in America increased after the arrival of punk rock from England punk rock must have caused the increase in juvenile crime.

Downplaying by Diversion

1. Genetic appeal: trying to discredit a conclusion by condemning its source or genesis. Example: dismissing an argument against gun control because it is put forth by the National Rifle Association.

2. Ad hominem: attacking the person making an assertion rather than the person's position. Example: calling people who want to limit the use of nuclear power "wild-eyed environmentalists and fanatics" (abusive); rejecting Nixon's views on U.S.–China relations because he was drummed out of office (circumstantial).

3. Poisoning the well: trying to place one's opponents in a position from which they cannot reply. Example: introducing an opponent by saying "Don't be taken in by my opponent's get-tough-on-crime rhetoric. It's become fashionable for even the most permissive of lawmakers to assume this pose."

4. Humor or ridicule: relying strictly on whimsy or contempt to dismiss an argument. Example: Stalin's replying to the Pope's peace plan "And how many divisions did you say the Pope had available for combat?"

5. Fear or force: using a threat of harm to make someone accept a position. Example: lobbyists' reminding legislators how many voters they, the lobbyists, represent.

6. Two wrongs make a right: attempting to justify what is considered objectionable by appealing to other instances of similar action. Example: a motorist's trying to defend speeding by pointing to another motorist driving even faster; Reagan's supporters defending his appointment of a long-time friend and personal lawyer as Attorney General by pointing out that the office is commonly held by a close legal associate of the President (common practice).

7. Straw man: so altering a position that the altered version is easier to attack than the original. Example: arguing that creationism should be taught in public schools because doing so is forbidden in countries under communism, which all good Americans presumably oppose.

8. Red herring: presenting facts that do not support the stated position but a position that may vaguely resemble it. Example: a prosecutor's quoting harrowing statistics about white-collar crime when charging an executive with embezzlement.

Downplaying by Confusion

1. Equivocation: drawing an unwarranted conclusion by using a word or phrase to mean two different things in the same argument. Example: claiming that the laws of gravitation and motion must have a lawmaker for the reason that they are laws and all laws have a lawmaker.

2. Accent: drawing or suggesting an unwarranted conclusion by the use of improper emphasis. Example: C & H's touting its sugar as "pure cane granulated from Hawaii!"

3. Composition: reasoning improperly from a property of a member of a group to a property of the group itself. Example: inferring that a local club must be wealthy because every member is.

4. Division: reasoning improperly from a property of the group to a property of a member of the group. Example: inferring that the individual members of a club must be wealthy because the club itself is.

5. Inconsistency: using contradictory premises in an argument. People can contradict themselves in four ways.

First, they can contradict themselves in the same argument. Example: Deputy Secretary of State Clark's claiming that Begin's actions were making it difficult to continue assistance to Israel while at the same time claiming that U.S. commitment was not to Begin but to Israel.

Second, people can contradict themselves at different times without attempting to justify the change of mind. Example: Senator Goldwater's insistence that CIA director Casey should resign, then his unexplained turnaround in support of Casey's continuance.

Third, people contradict themselves when their positions are incompatible with those of their institutional affiliations. Example: Reagan's campaign claim that the United States was militarily second to the USSR and Defense Secretary Weinberger's implied claim of U.S. superiority, made six months after the inauguration of Reagan.

Fourth, people contradict themselves when their actions don't parallel their words. Example: Reagan's campaign and postelection insistence on the need for competition and deregulation versus his pressure on Japan to adopt "voluntary" quotas and his appointment of Riese Taylor, no friend of deregulation, to head the Interstate Commerce Commission.

6. Begging the question: asserting in the premise what is asserted in the conclusion. Example: Claiming that user's fees should be tacked onto the purchase of certain goods and services because that would generate tax revenue.

Applications

Application 1. Identify the devices—testimonial, popularity, tradition, novelty, jumping to conclusions, guilt by association, positioning, provincialism, and mob appeal—used in these passages to intensify by association.

1 MORT: No matter what office Andrew Young ever runs for, I'll never vote for him.
   MOLLY: Why's that?
   MORT: He's an antisemite.
   MOLLY: Really?
   MORT: Don't you remember that when he was the U.S. ambassador to the U.N. he attended that party where there were members of the PLO?
   MOLLY: Right, I'd forgotten that.

2 Los Angeles Police Chief Daryl F. Gates, reacting to criticism of his department by a retiring Deputy Police Chief: "For police department officials to talk to reporters, people from the CAO [City Administrative Office], the board of commissioners, people in the mayor's office, council members— that is serious. There is a theme of disloyalty about that kind of thing." (David Johnston, "LAPD's Problems Serious, Retiring Top Officer Says," *Los Angeles Times*, June 29, 1981, part 1, p. 3.)

3 Owner of a San Francisco restaurant, reacting against a proposed truth-in-advertising ordinance to require restaurant owners to identify food prepared off the premises and then frozen: "Three quarters or seven-eighths of the people who come into my place ... don't give a good goddamn." (*Los Angeles Times*, July 4, 1974, part 1, p. 11.)

4 "The elegant Lord Shafesbury somewhere objects to telling too much truth, by which it may be fairly inferred that, in some cases, to lie is not only excusable but commendable." (Henry Fielding, *Tom Jones* [New York: Random House, 1950], p. 645.)

5 Sherlock Holmes drawing conclusions about Dr. Watson, on first meeting:

"Here is a gentleman of a medical type but with the air of a military man. Clearly an army officer, then. He has just come from the Tropics, for his face is dark and that is not the natural tint of his skin, for his wrists are fair. He has undergone hardship and sickness, as his haggard face says clearly. His left arm has been injured. He holds it in a stiff and unnatural manner. Where in the Tropics could an English doctor have seen much hardship and got his arm wounded? Clearly in Afghanistan." (Arthur Conan Doyle, "A Study in Scarlet," *The Adventures of Sherlock Holmes* [New York: Berkley Publications, 1963], pt. 1, ch. 7.)

6 "Subaru and Mercedes, two of the finest engineered cars around. One sells for eight times the price of the other. The choice is yours." (Ad for Subaru)

7 Written below a 1950-vintage picture of a father helping his son with his homework: "NOBODY ELSE LIKE YOU SERVICE. We stole the idea from your father." (Ad for Equitable Life Assurance Society. Oh yes, Equitable ran another ad that was identical except that Mom replaced Pop.)

8 "Winston Churchill, the archbishop of torydom, came to tell us how we shall live. And what is the life he maps for us? An Anglo-American tyranny to ride roughshod over the globe. He said that it was against Communism that he wanted the armies and navies combined. The words are Churchill's but the plan is Hitler's. Churchill's own domain of plunder is ripping at the seams and he asks Americans to save it for him. We are to be the trigger men, we are to provide him billions in money to regain what the robber barons are losing." (From the Communist publication *New Masses*, March 19, 1946.)

9 RON: Smoking pot definitely leads to heroin addiction.
ROY: Oh, I don't know.
RON: Figures don't lie. A report by the U.S. Commission of Narcotics on a study of 2000 narcotics addicts in a prison shows that well over two-thirds smoked marijuana before using heroin.
ROY: Hmm, I guess I can't argue with that.

10 MORTON: Did you know that it's safer to make a trip across country than to drive into town for a movie?
MEL: Really?
MORTON: Amazing but true. Half of all auto accidents occur within five miles of the driver's home.

11 Criticize the following Gallup Poll questions:
"How would you describe yourself—as very conservative, fairly conservative, middle of the road, fairly liberal, or very liberal?"

"Many states have tenure laws, which means that a teacher cannot be fired except by some kind of court procedure. Are you for giving teachers tenure or are you against tenure?"

"Do you know what the metric system is?"

12 "This revolutionary new invention, installed in less than fifteen minutes, is so different that it had to be given a brand new name—The Fire Injector." (Ad for a spark plug substitute that has been around for at least twenty years.)

Application 2. Identify the devices—half-truth, invincible ignorance, faulty comparison, false analogy, questionable cause, neglect of a common cause, causal oversimplication, slippery slope, and post hoc—used in these passages to downplay by omission.

1 On July 2, 1973, a decade after the product first appeared in stores, the Food and Drug Administration removed Pertussin Medicated Vaporizer from the market. The FDA had associated it with eighteen deaths, which evidently had resulted from the victims' inhaling the product's propellants and solvents. The ingredients listed on the can indicated that the product contained only oil of eucalyptus and menthol, two harmless, stock ingredients of such products. What device did the manufacturers employ?

2 Since more suicides occur during the Christmas season than at any other time of the year, something about Christmas must lead people to take their lives.

3 Right after Egyptian President Anwar Sadat started his crackdown on political dissidents, he was assassinated. Proof enough that one of those dissident groups was behind Sadat's murder.

4 STUDENT: How come I failed this course?
   PROFESSOR: You didn't perform.
   STUDENT: Not perform! You said that to pass we had to attend class, take all the tests, and do a term paper.
   PROFESSOR: Correct.
   STUDENT: Well, I did all that and still failed!

5 "Perhaps intimidated by flak from Capitol Hill, the Social Security Advisory Council has backed away from a proposal to increase the maximum pay subject to Soc-Sec taxation from $14,000 to $24,000 to keep the plan on a pay-as-you-go basis. Instead it has recommended shifting the cost of Medicare to the general fund. The proposal, if adopted, would begin the process of transferring SS into an out-and-out welfare program. Once we start in that direction, where do we stop?" ("A Quick About-Face," *New York Daily News*, January 21, 1975, p. 37.)

6 A survey indicates that more than half of all college students with below-average grades smoke pot. In contrast, only 20 percent of nonsmokers have below-average grades. On the basis of this, one person concludes that pot smoking causes students to get lower grades. Another person concludes that getting lower grades causes one to smoke pot. Comment.

7 President Reagan suggesting a way to pacify those who object to the sight of oil rigs off their beaches: "Maybe we ought to take some of those liberty ships out of mothballs and anchor one at each one of the oil platforms between that and onshore, because people never objected to seeing a ship at sea." ("Reagan Supports Watt Stand," *Santa Barbara Evening News Press*, August 5, 1981, p. A4.)

8 JUDY: I've decided to go to U.C.L.A. rather than Swarthmore.
   JIM: Really? Swarthmore's a fine, small liberal arts college, you know—a really good choice for an English major like you.

JUDY: I know. But Swarthmore's in Pennsylvania, and I hate winters. U.C.L.A., on the other hand, is in sunny, southern California, just minutes from the beach!

9 The Federal bail-out of big companies such as Chrysler and Pan American is wrong because the government makes no effort to rescue small businesses that are failing.

10 BILL: I certainly wish we'd start constructing nuclear power plants on a wide-scale basis.

LISA: Me, too.

BILL: They're probably cleaner and more dependable than the alternatives.

LISA: And when you consider the electric bills of ratepayers on projected commercial operation of nuclear power, they're also more economic.

Application 3. Identify the devices—genetic appeal, ad hominem, poisoning the well, humor or ridicule, fear or force, two wrongs, straw man, and red herring—used in these passages to downplay by diversion.

1 "Many of my colleagues in the press are upset about the growing practice of paying newsmakers for news. The auction principle seems to them to strike somehow at the freedom of the press, or at least the freedom of the poor press to compete with the rich press. But I find their objections pious and, in an economy where everything and everybody has its price, absurd." (Shana Alexander, "Loew's Common Denominator," *Newsweek*, April 14, 1975, p. 96.)

2 "If America wins the war on inflation, will your company be a casualty?" (Ad for Westinghouse Credit Corporation)

3 "Repressive environmentalists and population and economic zero-growthers have requested President Reagan to oust James G. Watt as Secretary of the Interior. Those stop-all-progress destructionists have thick-skinned craniums. They lack the intelligence to realize that the United States of America is no longer a subsidiary of the baby-and-people hating and business-repressive do-gooders. President Reagan and Secretary Watt have done what should have been done long ago. Their critics can go to blazes on a one-way ticket." (Letter to the Editor, *Los Angeles Times*, July 24, 1981, part 2, p. 6.)

4 "*Victory* floats by like the Goodyear blimp, familiar, benign, with no particular urgency. It does not feel like the film director John Huston at his most enraged; to tell the truth it feels like a film directed from a nearby parked car with the windows rolled up." (Sheila Benson, "Victory: Boiling War Down to a Soccer Match," *Los Angeles Times*, July 31, 1981, part 6, p. 1.)

5 Comments on the air traffic controllers' strike of 1981, all but the last reported in *Newsweek*, August 17, 1981: President Reagan: "Dammit, the law is the law, and the law says they cannot strike. If they strike, they quit their jobs" (p. 19); Indianapolis businessperson Joseph Horvath: "The controllers are idiots. When any group of people can paralyze the nation, they should all be fired and replaced" (p. 21); Lane Kirkland, AFL-CIO President, explaining why he refused to urge his foundation's member unions to back the controllers' union: "It's all very well to be a midnight-gin militant and call for a general

strike. I am not going to make that appraisal" (p. 22); a controller, Thomas Connelly, explaining the refusal of some controllers to strike: "It's a weakness of character. It's fear." (Paul Bernstein, "Ideals, Self-Interest, Both Work to Keep a Controller on the Job," *Wall Street Journal*, August 13, 1981, p. 1.)

6 "President Reagan is scheduled to sign his economic package into law in a ceremony that will celebrate his January political victory in Congress and give him a new opportunity to promulgate his political mythology. If his past performances are any guide, we will likely hear again how the people last November issued a mighty mandate for fundamental change in relations between citizens and their government, how they have begun triumphantly to have their will transformed into action and how, if they continue to support the administration, all the people will benefit together from the great new beginning that is underway in America. This is part of a large effort by Mr. Reagan and his White House minions to create a legend around him." (Morton M. Kondracke, "Democrats Must Do More to Oppose Reagan," *Wall Street Journal*, August 13, 1981, p. 23.)

7 Justice Lynn Compton of the California State Court of Appeals, explaining her decision to overturn the conviction of a salesman in the rape of a waitress who was hitchiking: "A woman who enters a stranger's car advertises that she has less concern for the consequences than the average female." ("Rape and Culture," *Time*, September 12, 1977, p. 51.)

8 "Precisely what is Nixon accused of doing . . . that his predecessors didn't do many times over? The break-in and wire-tapping at the Watergate? Just how different was that from the bugging of Barry Goldwater's apartment during the 1964 presidential campaign?" (Victor Lasky, "It Didn't Start with Water-gate," *Book Digest*, November 1977, p. 47.)

9 "Didn't evolution have to take place day by day, month by month, and year by year? You never hear anything about what happened on a year-to-year basis. I submit to you this: No evolution per years multiplied by however many millions of years you wish still equals no evolution." (Letter to editor, *Science Digest*, September 1981, p. 10.) Here's an excerpt from Charles Darwin's *Origin of Species:* "It may be said that natural selection is daily and hourly scrutiniz-ing throughout the world every variation, even the slightest; rejecting that which is bad, preserving and adding up all that is good. . . .We see nothing of these slow changes or progress, until the hand of time has marked the long lapses of the ages and then so imperfect is our view into the long past geological ages that we only see that the forms of life are now different from what they formerly were." (From *Great Books of the Western World* [Chicago: *Encyclopaedia Britannica*, vol. 49, 1952], p. 101.)

Application 4. Identify the devices—equivocation, division, composition, accent, inconsistency, and begging the question—used in these passages to downplay by confusion.

1 **BOB:** I think I have a very good chance of not getting mugged for the rest of this year.

BILL: Why?

BOB: Because one out of two people in this city can expect to get mugged each year.

BILL: I don't follow.

BOB: Well, I've already been mugged this year.

2 A labor department official agreed to an interview on the condition that the newspaper would not print his name. The next day the newspaper presented the interview, with an accompanying photograph that carried a most unusual caption: "Labor official who briefed reporters under the condition that his name not be used."

3 "Well, I condemn the [Watergate] cover-up of virtue. I don't mind if they bring up and reject the cover-up of Watergate. Nixon was wrong to try to help his friends and to cover up for them. But we are wrong to cover up our salvation which we owe to Nixon." (Rabbi Baruch Toruff, confidant of former President Nixon, in a speech to the U.S. Citizens Congress in Mission Hills, Kansas, 1976.)

4 "The pawnbroker thrives on the irregularities of youth; the merchant on a scarcity of goods; the architect and contractor on the destruction of buildings; lawyers and judges on disputes and illegalities; the military on war; physicians on sickness, and morticians on death. If then, we have more profligacy, destruction, lawlessness, war, disease, and death, we shall have unparalleled prosperity." (Michel de Montaigne, "The One Man's Profit Is Another's Loss," *The Complete Works of Montaigne*, trans. Donald M. Jrame [Stanford, Calif.: Stanford University Press, 1957], pp. 72–77.)

5 As a presidential candidate Ronald Reagan opposed extending the Voting Rights Act of 1965, including the controversial section that opposed additional sanctions on nine states and parts of thirteen others that have a history of ballot discrimination against minorities. Reagan said it was unfair to require only twenty-two of the country's political jurisdictions to obtain prior approval of changes in their election laws from a federal court or the Justice Department (preclearance). If the requirement is a good one, he claimed, it should be applied everywhere. In June 1981 Reagan repeated his stand, arguing that, if maintained, preclearance requirements should be applied to all states, even though that would probably nullify their enforcement because of the many changes in state election laws every four years. In August Reagan came out in favor of extending the Voting Rights Act for another ten years. He noted that applying it to the fifty states would make it cumbersome and ineffective.

6 CONNIE: It's foolish to claim that God didn't create the world.

VICKI: Oh, I don't know.

CONNIE: Well, think for a minute. Matter has always existed, right?

VICKI: I suppose.

CONNIE: Then the world must have always existed.

VICKI: So it couldn't have a creator.

CONNIE: Exactly.

9

Applying a Format

If you have mastered the material in the preceding chapters, you are well on your way to becoming an effective critical thinker. What you now need is some kind of systematic procedure that integrates argument analysis and evaluation. We now present a seven-step format that achieves this integration.

Format for Analysis and Evaluation

All evaluation of arguments presupposes some analysis, but the amount of analysis preceding the actual evaluation depends on the complexity of the argument. A short, simple argument may require very little detailed analysis. The following seven-step procedure, then, is offered with the qualification that it may not always be necessary to work through each step of the analysis.

1. Clarify meaning.
2. Identify conclusion and main premises.   }   **Analysis**
3. Cast the argument.
4. Fill in the missing premises.

5. Examine the main premises and support for justification.
6. Examine the argument for devices that intensify and downplay.
7. Give an overall evaluation.

You should view this format as a general guide for thinking critically about what you read and hear. Your instructor may use some variation of it, or you may come across another book that takes a slightly different approach. In short, there's nothing sacred about this procedure; others might serve just as well. But following this format *will* enable you to assess arguments effectively.

Before applying this format, let's take a look at each of the steps. Doing so will serve as a review of much of the material covered in the preceding chapters.

Step 1: Clarify Meaning

Before even attempting to clarify meaning, read a passage all the way through. This will give you a feel for the argument as a whole. Even if you happen to disagree with the position advanced, don't allow your disagreement to color your interpretation. If you don't understand some words, consult a dictionary. Unless otherwise indicated, assume that the words used follow common usage. Beware of blocks to critical thinking in the passage itself and in your own reaction. Recall those clichéd patterns of thinking and of viewing things: cultural conditioning, reliance on authority, hasty moral judgment, black-and-white thinking, labels, and limited frame of reference. (See Chapter 1.) Be sensitive to the functions of language: informative, expressive, directive, and performative. (See Chapter 2.) And be alert for (1) vague or ambiguous language, including jargon; (2) shifts in word meaning; (3) bias communicated by highly emotive words, assumption-loaded labels, rhetorical questions, innuendo, extreme quantifiers (such as "all" or "no") or intensifiers (such as "absolute" or "certainly"); and (5) euphemism. (See Chapter 2.) If the passage includes a definition, note what kind it is (denotative, logical, stipulative, or persuasive). Be particularly alert to the use of persuasive definition—redefining a term while at the same time preserving its old emotive impact. Lastly, make sure you can state precisely what the argument is attempting to demonstrate.

Step 2: Identify Conclusion and Premises

Recall that single words such as the following are helpful in identifying premises and conclusions:

Conclusion signals: then, therefore, consequently, it follows that (and so forth)
Area premise signals: since, because, for, insofar as (and so forth)
Specific premise signals: first . . . second . . . third, for one thing . . . for another (and so forth)

When an argument contains no such words, ask yourself, What is being advanced? What is the arguer trying to demonstrate as true? The answer to these questions most probably is the argument's conclusion. Similarly, to locate premises in the absence of signals, ask yourself, Why is this conclusion claim so? What bases does the arguer give for drawing the conclusion? (See Chapter 4.)

Step 3: Cast the Argument

Short, simple arguments don't need to be cast, but longer, more involved ones do. The casting method developed in this book consists of three steps: (1) putting brackets at the beginning and end of each assertion, (2) numbering assertions consecutively, and (3) setting out the relationships among the assertions in a tree diagram to be read down the page. When casting a passage with rhetorical devices

1. Cast each separate assertion.
2. Don't cast repetitions of the same assertion.
3. Don't cast asides.
4. Don't cast background information.
5. Don't cast examples that merely illustrate or clarify a point.
6. Cast examples used to support a point being made; that is, examples that indicate why the point is so.
7. Don't cast as separate assertions information that follows a colon.
8. Cast as separate assertions information separated by a semicolon. (See Chapter 5.)

Step 4: Fill in Missing Premises

In general, fill in missing premises whenever an argument is incomplete and its missing premise is not exactly obvious. An argument is incomplete when (1) the conclusion would not have to be true if the stated premise (or premises) is true (that is, if a counterexample is possible) or (2) if the conclusion contains topics that are uncovered in the stated premise (or premises). In filling in missing premises, follow these guidelines:

1. Apply the topic coverage strategy; that is, determine whether the conclusion covers topics not covered in the premises. The reconstructed premise must, when taken together with the expressed premise, entail the conclusion.
2. Reconstruct a premise that is strong enough to help support the conclusion but no stronger.
3. Reconstruct a premise that illuminates the argument and doesn't just repeat it.

Longer arguments may contain many missing premises that when reconstructed help generate mini-arguments. (See Chapter 6.)

Step 5: Examine the Main Premises and Support for Justification

This is the first step of the evaluative part of the seven-step procedure. Recall that an argument's premises can be considered true only when they are justified; that is, when there is enough reasonable evidence to support them. For some assertions (laws of logic and semantic, systemic, and basic assertions), justification poses no problem. But for hypothetical assertions, whose truth must be confirmed by sense experience outside the self, justification is a problem. Hypothetical statements (such as "There is life outside our planet" or "U.S. productivity and competitiveness has declined in the last ten years") must be backed up by observations that are expressed or implied in the assertion. When evaluating observations keep in mind these five key points: (1) the physical conditions under which the observations were made, (2) the sensory acuity of the observer, (3) necessary background knowledge, (4) the objectivity of the observer, and (5) supporting testimony. When evaluating value assertions (assessments of worth in ethics, art, political philosophy, and so forth), you should (1) clarify the language used; that is, determine whether it can be interpreted as personal preference, social preference, or conformity to law, principle, or standard and (2) determine whether the claim meets minimum adequacy requirements; that is, whether it is consistent with the basic assumptions, standards, criteria, and scholarship in the field and whether it is supported by appeal to principle and/or consequence. (See Chapter 7.)

Step 6: Examine the Argument for Devices that Intensify or Downplay

Even if assertions are justified, they may have no logical bearing on an argument. Possibly they are being used unfairly to intensify by association with what already is approved or disapproved of by the intended audience. Or maybe they're being used to downplay by omission, diversion, or confusion. Look especially for the following common techniques that are used to intensify or downplay:

Intensify by association: testimonial, popularity, tradition, novelty, jumping to a conclusion, guilt by association, positioning, provincialism, and mob appeal

Downplay by omission: half-truth, invincible ignorance, faulty comparison (incomplete or selective), false analogy, questionable cause, neglect of a common cause, causal oversimplication, slippery slope, and post hoc

Downplay by diversion: genetic appeal, ad hominem (abusive and circumstantial), poisoning the well, humor or ridicule, fear or force, two wrongs make a right (also common practice), straw man, and red herring

Downplay by confusion: equivocation, division, composition, accent, and begging the question (see Chapter 8)

Simply because an argument uses these devices doesn't necessarily make it unsound. You must decide whether the argument is relying exclusively or chiefly on them to support its claim. If so, then the argument is indeed incorrect, either because the premises are not justified or because the inference is invalid. But if the evidence is justified regardless of the devices and does entail the conclusion, then the argument is sound. This step is the key to argument evaluation.

Step 7: Give an Overall Evaluation

Having completed the preceding steps, you are now in a position to give the argument an overall assessment. Does it have force? If so, how much? Are you ready to go with the argument on balance, or against it? Has the arguer won you over? To answer questions like these, return to your criticisms, especially to Steps 5 and 6. Are the argument's essential premises so flawed that they provide little or no support for the conclusion? Or are the flaws contained in premises that are not essential to the claim? In a very short argument, it's rarely necessary to ask questions like these, for the judgments made in Step 6 will dictate the overall evaluation. But a complicated argument poses the same problem of overall judgment that the intelligent voter faces when voting. Inevitably there are reasons that argue for a vote and reasons that argue against it. Your job and mine is to decide whether, when all things are considered, we should endorse one candidate rather than another. Similarly, a long, sophisticated argument may offer many reasons for advancing its claim, some fair and legitimate and others unfair and illegitimate. We must decide which reasons are legitimate and whether they are sufficient to endorse the claim.

Rendering an overall evaluation is an important part of the evaluative process, for—if nothing else—it keeps critical thinking from becoming a blood-less, abstract exercise. It allows you to decide whether or not to believe, to endorse, and possibly to act on a claim. It also gives you an opportunity, which you should take, to show how the argument could be improved. Finally, it allows you to clarify your own beliefs as you respond to the argument in a creative and constructive way.

Applying the Seven Steps

It's now time to apply the seven-step format in argument analysis and evaluation. The following examples, which present arguments exhibiting a variety of defects, show how you can use the format to detect these defects and assess the arguments. Although I will proceed through each of the steps, keep in mind that it is not always necessary to do so.

Argument 1

The Argument: Surely life exists elsewhere in the universe. After all, most space scientists today admit the possibility that life has evolved on other planets. Besides, other planets in our solar system are strikingly like earth. They revolve around the sun, they borrow light from the sun, and several are known to revolve on their axes and to be subject to the same laws of gravitation as earth. What's more, aren't those who make light of extraterrestrial life soft-headed fundamentalists clinging to the foolish notion that life is unique to their planet?

Step 1: Clarify meaning.

"Life" is ambiguous: What kind of life is meant—vegetable, animal, human, amino acids? "Surely" is an extreme intensifier. The last sentence is directive and expressive but also informative. It's also a rhetorical question. The arguer is claiming that life exists somewhere other than earth.

Step 2: Identify conclusion and premises.

Conclusion: Life exists elsewhere in the universe.

Premise: Space scientists admit the possibility that life has evolved on other planets.

Premise: Other planets in our solar system are strikingly like earth.

Premise: Those who make light of extraterrestrial life are soft-headed fundamentalists clinging to the foolish notion that life is unique to this planet.

Step 3: Cast argument.

Surely [life exists elsewhere^1 in the universe.] After all, [most space scientists today admit^2 the possibility that life has evolved on other planets.] Besides, [other planets in our solar system^3 are strikingly like earth.] [They revolve around^4 the sun,] [they borrow^5 light from the sun,] and [several are known to revolve^6 on their axes] and [to be subject to the same^7 laws of gravitation as earth.] What's more, [aren't those who make light of extraterrestrial life soft-headed fundamentalists^8 clinging to the foolish notion that life is unique to their planet?]

Step 4: Fill in missing premises.

There are none that I feel aren't obvious, although the arguer may disagree, as we'll see in Step 7.

Step 5: Examine the main premises and support for justification.

Assertion 2 is a true hypothetical statement. Mini-premises 4, 5, 6, and 7 are true hypothetical statements. The justification of assertion 3 depends on whether the arguer has overlooked significant differences between earth and other planets that are relevant to the claim that life exists elsewhere in the universe. Assertion 8 is a false hypothetical statement because not everyone who makes light of extraterrestrial life is a "soft-headed fundamentalist clinging to the foolish notion that life is unique to our planet."

Step 6: Examine argument for intensifying or downplaying devices.

Assertion 2, which supports assertion 1, contains a legitimate appeal to authority or expert opinion: There is general agreement among the experts about the *possibility* of extraterrestrial life. However, assertion 2 is a red herring because it only supports the claim that there *may be* life elsewhere in the universe and *not* the argument's claim, made in assertion 1, that such life "surely exists." So assertion 2 does not entail assertion 1. Assertion 3 draws an analogy between earth and other planets such that, given the similarities stated in assertions 4, 5, 6, and 7, we are to infer that other planets likely share with earth an additional characteristic: the existence of life. But the arguer downplays by omitting at least one significant difference between earth and other planets: Not all planets revolve around the sun at the same distance from it that earth does, and a difference in distance could produce such a difference in temperature that life as we understand it would be impossible. Given this consideration alone, the analogy is false. Besides this, the arguer omits the fact (thereby offering a half-truth) that space probes to some other planets, for example Mars, have provided no substantial evidence to support a claim for extraterrestrial life. It's possible that the arguer will object to my criticism that assertion 2 is a red herring by saying "You've overlooked my assumption, which is 'What most space scientists believe to be the case is actually the case.' Given this unexpressed premise a, my claim that most space scientists believe in the possibility of life elsewhere in the universe is altogether relevant to the conclusion." I would accept this explanation and concede that premise 2, taken together with unexpressed premise a, does entail conclusion 1 and would then quickly point out that the unexpressed premise is a patent falsehood. Similarly, with respect to the inference from 8, the arguer might say "I'm assuming that 'The contradiction of what only fundamentalists believe is actually the case.' This unexpressed premise b, when added to premise 8, does logically entail conclusion 1." Fine, but this assumption also is preposterous. The point is that even if the reasoning process from premises 2 + a to conclusion 1, and from premises 8 + b to conclusion 1 are valid, the assumptions themselves are false. And of course premise 8 itself is false. The reason that I did not include these assumptions under Step 4 (filling in the missing premises) is that they, or something like them, would not redeem the argument. More important, they divert attention from the gross fallacies the arguer commits. Furthermore, the inference to 1 from 3 is invalid because even the best analogy doesn't prove anything conclusively. Good analogies offer a high probability. Thus, if this analogy were a good one, the strongest conclusion it would warrant would be something like "Life *probably* exists somewhere else in the universe."

Step 7: Give an overall evaluation.

There is nothing to weigh in balance concerning this argument. It is clearly a bad one. While there may be good reasons for believing that life exists elsewhere in the universe, this argument doesn't provide any of them. As a matter of fact, given current evidence, there is no basis for arguing that such life *certainly* exists. A good argument for the *probability* of extraterrestrial life would begin by indicating what kind of life is intended and then show through statistics culled from the study of astronomy that the chances of that life form existing elsewhere in the universe are extraordinarily high.

Argument 2

The Argument: In the fury that surrounds the debate about school prayer, it is
sometimes forgotten that prayer is an essential part of religion. To permit
school prayer is virtually the same as endorsing religion. What can be said,
then, for religion? Not much, I'm afraid. Indeed, religion is dangerous. It
has spawned numerous wars throughout history. Today it continues to
sow the seeds of discontent and destruction in Northern Ireland and the
Middle East. It divides people by emphasizing their differences rather
than their similarities. It breeds intolerance of people of opposed views. Is
there any doubt, therefore, that the responsible citizen should oppose
school prayer?

Step 1: Clarify meaning.
"Prayer" and "religion" are ambiguous. I will take "prayer" to mean a
spiritual communion with God or an object of worship and "religion" to
mean an organized system of belief in and worship of that God or object of
worship. "Virtually" is a weasel. Every assertion made about religion in this
argument is an unqualified generalization. "Spawns," "breeds," and "sows
the seeds" are emotive. The last sentence is directive but also informative,
a rhetorical question and a persuasive definition.

Step 2: Identify conclusion and main premises.
Conclusion: The responsible citizen should oppose school prayer.
Premise: To permit school prayer is virtually the same as endorsing
religion.
Premise: Religion is dangerous.

Step 3: Cast the argument.

In the fury that surrounds the debate about school prayer, it is

sometimes forgotten that [prayer is an essential part of religion.]¹ [To

permit school prayer is² virtually the same as endorsing religion.] What

can be said, then, for religion? Not much, I'm afraid. Indeed, [religion

is³ dangerous.] [It has spawned numerous⁴ wars throughout history.]

[Today it continues to sow the seeds of discontent and destruction in

Northern Ireland and the⁵ Middle East.] [It divides people by

emphasizing their differences⁶ rather than their similarities.] [It breeds

intolerance of⁷ people of opposed views.] Is there any doubt, <u>therefore</u>,

that [the responsible citizen should⁸ oppose school prayer?]

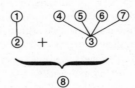

Step 4: Fill in missing premises.
Mini-conclusion 2 follows from mini-premise 1 plus the unexpressed

premise a: "Permitting an essential part of religion to be practiced in school is virtually the same as endorsing religion."
Thus

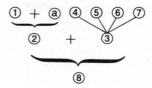

Step 5: Examine main premises and support for justification.

It's difficult to evaluate mini-premise 1 because "prayer" and "religion" are ambiguous. But if these terms are stipulated as in Step 1, then I will accept the assertion as true. Unexpressed premise a is vague and misleading. "Endorsing" literally means "supporting." If the state allows school prayer and if prayer is an essential part of religion, then I suppose it could be argued that the state "supports" religion in the sense that it provides a constitutional basis for the practice of religion in the classroom. I will say considerably more about this unexpressed premise in the next step. Mini-conclusion 3 is a value judgment ("dangerous") that needs considerable support, which presumably is provided by mini-premises 4, 5, 6, and 7. An evaluation of these support assertions is best left to the next step. In sum, I can accept assertion 1; assertions 2 and 3 (together with assertions 4, 5, 6, and 7) warrant closer inspection.

Step 6: Examine argument for devices used to intensify or downplay.

Returning to unexpressed premise a, and by implication mini-conclusion 2, I find "endorsing" loaded with subjective connotations. An example will illustrate. The state permits the publication and sale of pornographic materials. Can it be said, then, that the state "endorses" pornographic enterprises? Yes, but only if "endorses" is taken to mean "support," and "support" in turn is taken to mean providing a judicial basis for the manufacture and sale of pornographic materials. But "endorsing" carries the subjective connotations of "approval" or "actively advancing the interests of." But the state does not endorse pornographic enterprises in either of these senses. In fact, if you read the Supreme Court rulings on pornography, you'll find that the justices who comment without exception express revulsion toward pornography. The court's "permission," then, is based not on approval, and certainly not on active support of the interests of pornographers, but on an interpretation of the constitutional right to freedom of expression. Therefore I'd be inclined to think that, at the very least, to say that the state "endorses" pornography is misleading. Similarly, it seems to me just as misleading to argue that permitting school prayer is tantamount to endorsing religion in the sense of approving of or actively supporting the interests of religion. For this reason I'm calling "endorsing" in unexpressed premise a and mini-conclusion 2 a loaded word.

But even if the arguer insists that "permit" implies "endorse" and "endorse," in turn, implies "approval of" or "actively advancing the interests of," then we must be clear about what it is that's being approved or advanced. It isn't religion but individual freedom, specifically the opportunity for the individual to say (or refrain from saying) a prayer in a public classroom, so long as that practice does not conflict with the constitutional doctrine of church/state separation. Stated another way, if school prayer does not violate church/state separation, then there is no constitutional basis for restricting individual freedom to worship. Consider the pornography example again. If the manufacture and sale of pornographic material is permitted, what is being approved of and actively advanced is the individual right to freedom of expression. To say that what is being underwritten is the pornography industry is a distortion, a straw man. It is as much a straw, in my judgment, to say that permitting school prayer is tantamount to endorsing (that is, approving or actively advancing) religion. And the straw lies in the subjective connotations of "endorsing."

My judgment that unexpressed premise a and mini-conclusion 2 introduce a straw is supported by what follows in the argument, namely, an attack on religion. Having identified prayer with religion, the arguer then attempts to show why religion is dangerous. The diversionary tack here is to discredit school prayer by discrediting religion. Whether or not this strategy proves effective very much depends on the audience's perceptions of religion. But I do think that it's easier to "blow over" religion, and with it school prayer, than it is to repudiate school prayer on legitimate grounds, namely, by attempting to show how school prayer violates the doctrine of church/state separation. In other words, even if mini-premises 4, 5, 6, and 7 are true, so what? All they would do is support the claim that religion is dangerous, mini-conclusion 3. But how does this address the school prayer issue? The arguer undoubtedly will point to mini-argument

$$\underbrace{① + ⓐ}_{②} ,$$

which is intended to identify prayer with religion and school prayer with endorsing religion. At this point I would reintroduce my criticism of that mini-argument on the grounds of ambiguity, loaded language, and straw man.

But if I wanted to be saintly charitable, I could concede the legitimacy of

$$\underbrace{① + ⓐ}_{②}$$

and then closely inspect mini-argument

Mini-premises 4, 5, 6, and 7 are generalizations that need qualification. They are also half-truths, for they omit to mention that religion also has contributed to understanding and human betterment, to the establishment and maintenance of social services (such as schools, orphanages, hospitals, and disaster relief agencies), and the formulation of humanity's highest ideals. Moreover, 4 and 5 are causal oversimplifications. Beyond this, in the context of the main argument, all these mini-premises are diversionary appeals to fear and slippery slope, such that if school prayer is permitted, presumably those dreadful things associated with religion will inevitably follow.

Step 7: Give an overall evaluation.

The argument is unsound: The premises and their support downplay by various appeals of omission, diversion, and confusion, namely half-truth, straw man, fear, causal oversimplication, and loaded and ambiguous language. When the premises and support are stripped of these ploys, they collapse, thus rendering the conclusion unwarranted. It seems that any compelling argument against school prayer must establish that permitting school prayer violates the doctrine of church/state separation and perhaps that this doctrine is worthwhile. The preceding argument doesn't do this, nor does it develop an alternatively compelling argument against school prayer.

Argument 3

The Argument: When you call 911 in an emergency, some police departments have a way of telling your telephone number and address without your saying a word. The chief value of this, say the police, is that if the caller is unable to communicate for any reason, the dispatcher knows where to send help. But don't be duped by such paternalistic explanations. This technology is a despicable invasion of privacy, for callers may be unaware of the insidious device. Even if they are, some persons who wish anonymity may be reluctant to call for emergency help. Remember that the names of complainants and witnesses are recorded in many communities' criminal justice systems. A fairer and more effective system seemingly would include an auxiliary number for callers who wish anonymity.

Step 1: Clarify meaning.

Some highly emotive language is used: "duped," "despicable," "insidious," "calamitous." "Paternalistic" is used accurately, but it does have negative connotations. The sentence beginning "This technology ..." is both informative and expressive; the one beginning "Remember ..." is both informative and directive. The arguer carefully qualifies generalizations by using words such as "some," "may be," "many," and "seemingly." I find the term "emergency help" vague. What kind of emergency is intended: a heart attack, an accident, a fire, a crime? What is clear is that the arguer doesn't want to scrap the emergency phone system by which telephone numbers and addresses of callers are recorded but to supplement it with a system that protects caller anonymity.

Step 2: Identify conclusion and main premises.

Conclusion: A fairer and more effective system seemingly would include an auxiliary number for callers who wish anonymity.

Premise: This technology (i.e., the system that records personal information about callers) is a despicable invasion of privacy.

Premise: If they are aware, some persons who wish anonymity may be reluctant to call for emergency help.

Step 3: Cast the argument.

When you call 911 in an emergency, some police departments have a way of telling your telephone number and address without your saying a word. The chief value of this, say the police, is that if the caller is unable to communicate for any reason, the dispatcher knows where to send help. But don't be duped by such paternalistic explanations. [This technology is a despicable invasion of privacy,]¹ *for* [callers may² be unaware of the insidious device.] [Even if they are, some persons³ who wish anonymity may be reluctant to call for emergency help.] [Remember that the names of complainants⁴ and witnesses are recorded in many communities' criminal justice systems.] [A fairer and more effective system⁵ seemingly would include an auxiliary number for callers who wish anonymity.]

I consider the first three sentences background, and not part of the argument proper. The argument, then, can be cast as follows:

Step 4: Fill in missing premises.

There are a number of missing premises but most are obvious. One might be worth reconstructing, however. Underlying mini-conclusion 1 seems to be the unexpressed premise that collecting information about people without their informed consent is an invasion of privacy. The argument, then, could be recast as follows. Thus the diagram should read:

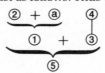

Step 5: Examine main premises and support for justification.

I have no trouble with unexpressed premise a: When data about people are collected without their knowledge and agreement, their privacy is indeed invaded. I'm prepared to accept it on semantic grounds: "Invasion of privacy" includes, among other acts, those taken to collect information about parties without their informed consent. Assertion 2 is a true hypothetical statement. Mini-conclusion 1, then, devoid of the inflammatory terms "despicable" and "insidious," is valid. After all, if 2 and a are justified, it would be contradictory to deny this conclusion. (Of course I assume that the arguer doesn't mean that the technology literally is an invasion of privacy, but that certain acts involving the use of the technology are.) Mini-conclusion 3 is a hypothetical statement. Studies do show that people are most reluctant to get personally involved in reporting crimes. But are people equally reluctant to report things like accidents and fires? That's doubtful. It's even more doubtful that they are reluctant to identify themselves in seeking emergency help for something like a heart attack. Despite these reservations I'll accept 3, giving the arguer the benefit of the doubt since he/she has carefully qualified the generalization with the words "some" and "may be." Mini-premise 4, which supports mini-conclusion 3, is a fact.

Step 6: Examine argument for devices used to intensify or downplay.

The sentence "But don't be duped by such paternalistic explanations" is well poisoning, but is not essential to the argument. Assertions 1 and 2 contain the highly emotive "despicable" and "insidious." "Emergency help" in assertion 3 is ambiguous.

Step 7: Give an overall evaluation.

It is true that assertions 1 and 2 use emotive language and assertion 3 is ambiguous ("emergency help"). But the argument doesn't rely exclusively or even primarily on either of these devices. In other words, stripped of these devices, the premises are justified and do provide legitimate support for the qualified conclusion that a fair and more effective system *seemingly* would include an auxiliary number. (Remember, even though an argument may intensify or downplay, it is not necessarily unsound. The key point is whether the argument relies solely or chiefly on intensifying or downplaying devices. If it does it's fallacious. If it doesn't, then it may be sound. In this case the argument appears to be sound.) In my opinion this argument carves out some middle ground regarding an emergency telephone system. It reminds us that the system needn't be construed in black-and-white terms as one that either (1) records information about callers and thus violates privacy and discourages calls or (2) does not record information, which would respect privacy and encourage the otherwise reluctant to call but would leave in the lurch those unable to communicate. As an alternative the argument proposes a system that preserves privacy and anonymity while safeguarding those unable to communicate. The argument's few intensifying devices do not undercut the support for its conclusion. In brief the argument has convinced me that the auxiliary number approach probably would make a fairer and more effective call system. Barring an overriding counterargument, I'd support such a system.

Summary

The format for argument analysis and evaluation that was developed in this chapter consists of the following seven steps:

1. Clarify meaning.
2. Identify conclusion and main premises.   } Analysis
3. Cast the argument.
4. Fill in missing premises.
5. Examine the main premises and support for justification.
6. Examine argument for devices that intensify or downplay.   } Evaluation
7. Give an overall evaluation.

In applying this format, remember

1. It isn't always necessary to proceed through each step. If an argument is

short or simple, you can usually move directly to the evaluation part (steps 5, 6, and 7).

2. Although an argument may contain intensifying or downplaying devices, it isn't necessarily unsound. These devices result in fallacious arguments only when they are used exclusively or primarily to make a point. If when stripped of a device an assertion can still be evaluated for truth and is relevant to the argument, then the device does not invalidate it. But if the assertion collapses when the device is knocked out from under it, then the assertion is illegitimate.

3. When in doubt about the arguer's meaning or intent, always give the arguer the benefit of the doubt. This especially applies to reconstructing missing premises. Remember, critical thinking doesn't aim to embarrass or humiliate. It does not entail nitpicking. Rather, it aims to make sense of written and oral communication and to raise *substantive* points of criticism about it.

4. In giving an overall evaluation, state whether the argument has force for you and explain why it does or does not. Since critical thinking aims to raise discussions to a more illuminating level and to help you develop your own positions on issues, you should also indicate how the argument could be improved; that is, what points it would need to make to win you over.

Applications

Application 1. Apply the seven-step format to the following arguments.

1 There's no question that everyone should take vitamin E daily. For one thing vitamin E increases the sex drive. Not only have I noticed this myself, but friends who have taken the vitamin regularly for a year report the same thing. Studies confirm that this wondrous elixir also strengthens the heart muscles. Besides, if you don't take vitamin E regularly, then your cells will lose vital oxygen, thereby depriving your body of critical restorative powers. The upshot will be a general deterioration in your health.

2 "*The prayer for others.* Such prayers are potent because, first of all, they are a wonderful way of getting ourselves off our hands. And they are powerful because they *can* change the lives of others.

"An elderly woman once told me how she had been dangerously ill in the hospital and in pain. She had lost her courage and was fighting against tests she needed because it seemed to her that she could bear no more pain. But one day a note came from her church—a place where prayer meetings had long since gone out of fashion—to tell her that her friends had formed a prayer circle and would pray all that night for her. 'About one o'clock' she said, 'I fell asleep and slept as soundly as a child.' The next day she went cheerfully to take her tests and began a slow but steady convalescence." (Ardis Whitman, "Six Special Powers of Prayer," *Reader's Digest*, May 1980, p. 71.)

3 "Although men as well as women struggle with extra pounds, in our culture fat seems to be particularly a woman's problem. I do not know whether there are more fat women than fat men, although women's bodies do contain a higher proportion of fat. But women far outnumber men in organizations like Weight Watchers or Overeaters Anonymous. Almost every issue of most women's magazines announces the 'newest diet,' not so magazines for men. Whether or not women are fatter than men, they worry about it more." (Elsa Dixler, "Fat Liberation," *Psychology Today*, May 1980, p. 110.)

Application 2. Apply the seven-step procedure to the arguments found on the following pages in this text:

1 Page 115, d.
2 Page 172, 4.
3 Page 116, j.
4 Page 147, d.
5 Page 201, 5.
6 Page 146, b.
7 Page 116, d.
8 Page 147, e.
9 Page 173, 7.
10 Page 202, 7.

Application 3. Revise one of the preceding arguments that you found inadequate. Construct a version that you think is sound and has force. (Your instructor may then have class members swap arguments for analysis and evaluation, using the seven-step procedure.)

Application 4. Apply the seven-step format to five arguments that you find in newspapers or news magazines.

The Extended Argument

So far we have considered relatively short arguments, ones consisting of no more than a paragraph or two. But many arguments come in multiparagraph form and are commonly termed "argumentative essays" or (when oral) "speeches of conviction." Open a newspaper to the opinion/commentary page, look at an article in some magazine, or listen to a policy address made by an important public figure, and chances are you'll find an extended argument. Indeed it is the extended argument that you will most have occasion to ponder. Any introduction to critical thinking that aims to make you a more searching reader and thinker therefore would be incomplete without consideration of this widespread argumentative form.

The extended argument contains all the elements of a short argument: signal words, unexpressed premises, premise support, and various intensifying and downplaying devices. In fact, the extended argument can be viewed as a string of shorter arguments, all of which support a main idea. As a result, if you have mastered the seven-step procedure developed in the preceding chapter, you should be able to respond intelligently to longer discourses.

This chapter shows how the seven-step format applies to extended arguments. It also covers an alternative approach to assessing arguments that makes use of the outline. But before turning to these topics, let's familiarize ourselves with the anatomy of the extended argument, specifically its four principal parts:

thesis, organization, main points, and developmental patterns. As a convenience I will use the terms "argumentative essay" or simply "essay" to mean "extended argument." This convention seems warranted since you typically will encounter the extended argument in essay form.

Thesis

The thesis is a statement of the main idea of the essay. It resembles the theme in fiction, in which an underlying idea or moral is expressed through dialogue and action. Since the whole purpose of the essay is to compel the audience to accept a position, the thesis is really what the essay is all about. Without a thesis, or main idea, an essay would be a snarl: a collection of incoherent paragraphs and sentences. The thesis, then, is the essay's counterpart to the conclusion in short arguments.

As you can imagine, if you're seriously interested in evaluating an essay you first must determine its thesis. This is crucial because everything offered in support of the thesis can be assessed only in terms of whether or not it in fact supports it. If you don't know what the thesis is, or if you misrepresent it, you can't intelligently evaluate the essay.

There is no foolproof way of determining the thesis, or main idea, of an extended argument. Sometimes an author states it directly by providing a thesis statement in the essay. But even when the author doesn't expressly state the thesis, but only implies it, you can infer what the thesis must be from a close and intelligent consideration of the argument. *The reason is that an argumentative essay deals with some topic, and its author always has an attitude toward that topic.* When you combine topic and attitude, you come up with the main idea. And when you state the main idea, you have a statement of the thesis.

But how do you determine the topic of an essay? The topic is the subject that the essay deals with. To discover the topic, scrutinize the paragraphs. Paragraph scrutiny is the key to extended argument analysis. Paragraphs always are about somebody or some thing. And that somebody or some thing is the topic of the argument. To find out what the topic of the argument is, discover the common concern of the paragraphs. Once this is apparent find out what the author is interested in telling you about it. That will reveal author attitude or viewpoint. Thus, having isolated topic and attitude, you'll have the main idea, which when stated is the thesis.

What I've said so far can be graphically illustrated by a simple tree diagram, to be read from top to bottom:

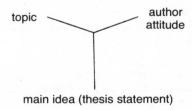

topic   author attitude

main idea (thesis statement)

If we were dealing with actual essays, we might get relationships such as these:

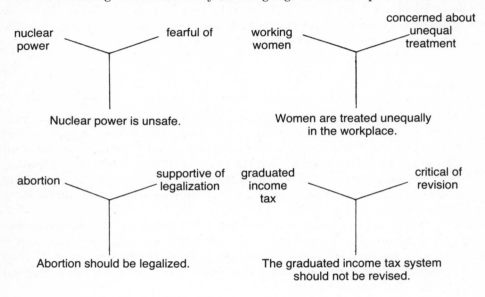

Quick Check on Thesis Identification

These passages are excerpts from essays. For each, identify the topic and the author's attitude, then write an appropriate thesis statement.

1   Capital punishment is meted out to some groups in society more than to others. Minority groups are hit hardest by this imbalance of justice.

In addition, wealthy people seldom receive the death penalty because they can afford better counsel. All the people executed in the United States in 1964 were represented by court-appointed attorneys.

Finally, the death penalty can wrongfully execute an innocent person. There are documented cases of this happening.

2   We have seen "hunting" rifles used to kill a President, Martin Luther King, and numerous others. It is said that these and other guns would not kill if there were not people to shoot them. By the same token, people would rarely kill if they lacked the weapons to do so.

But there is an even more pressing threat to our lives than the sniper or assassin. Blacks, after centuries of exploitation, are openly rebellious. Given the weapons, young blacks could ignite the bloodiest revolution in this country since the Civil War.

On the other side are white racists arming in fear. And don't forget the militant right-wingers storing up arsenals against the Reds whom they see under every bed.

3   "... This weekend, the city of Indianapolis is hosting approximately 500,000 people to create a two-day saturnalia out of the annual celebration of grease, gasoline, and death.

"... the stands inside the Indy Speedway will be filled on Monday with hundreds or thousands of real racing fans. I can't help but think of them as vultures who come to watch the 500-mile race on the highway of death to nowhere, hoping that the monotony of watching cars flick by at speeds in excess of 190 mph will be relieved by mechanical—and human—catastrophe.

"The beltway around Indianapolis is staked with grim white crosses, mute reminders to travelers of the fatal consequence of a too-heavy foot on the accelerator.

"Watching the race from the Indy grandstand is a little like watching hyperactive hamsters tread a cage wheel. The cars fly by like brightly painted berserk vacuum cleaners sucking the ground." (Joan Ryan, "Grease, Gasoline, and Death," *The Washington Post*, May 1979)

4   "Feminists have long complained that playing with dolls is one way of convincing impressionable little girls that they may only be mothers or housewives. ... But dollplaying may have even more serious consequences for little girls than that. Do girls find out about gravity and distance and shapes and sizes playing with dolls? Probably not.

"A curious boy, if his parents are tolerant, will have taken apart a number of household and play objects by the time he is ten, and, if his parents are lucky, he may even have put them back together again. In all this he is learning things that will be useful in physics and math. ...

"Sports is another source of math-related concepts for children which tends to favor boys. Getting to first base on a not very well hit grounder is a lesson in line, speed and distance. Intercepting a football thrown through the air requires some rapid intuitive eye calculations based on the ball's direction, speed and trajectory. ..." (Sheila Tobias, "Who's Afraid of Math, and Why?" *The Atlantic Monthly*, November 1979)

Comments

1.

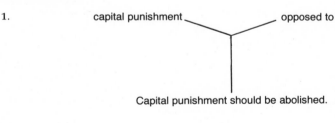

capital punishment — opposed to

Capital punishment should be abolished.

2.

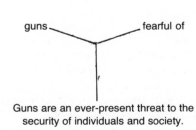

guns — fearful of

Guns are an ever-present threat to the security of individuals and society.

3.

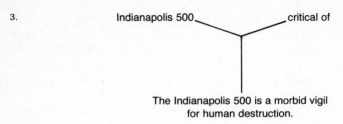

The Indianapolis 500 is a morbid vigil
for human destruction.

4.

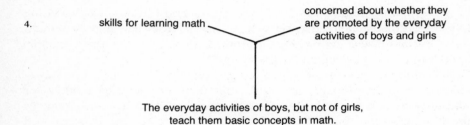

The everyday activities of boys, but not of girls,
teach them basic concepts in math.

Organization

The *organization of an argumentative essay refers to how it is structured.* In the next chapter we will discuss specific ways of organizing essays. Here, however, we are concerned with their overall organization.

In general the argumentative essay can be organized in two ways, both involving the location of the thesis. First, the thesis may be stated or implied early in the essay; that is, in its opening paragraphs, which hereafter we'll take to mean the first two or three paragraphs. These paragraphs are then followed by paragraphs that provide supporting materials. The movement, therefore, is roughly from the general to the specific, much in the form of an inverted pyramid:

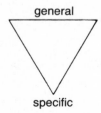

Sometimes, however, writers present their supporting materials first, especially when dealing with controversial topics. It is not until the closing paragraphs—hereafter taken to mean the final two or three paragraphs—that they state or imply their thesis. The movement, then, is roughly from the specific to the general, much in the form of a pyramid:

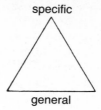

Since a well-constructed argumentative paragraph is really a microcosm of a well-constructed extended argument, we can illustrate these basic organizational patterns with the help of two simple paragraphs, which happen to be adapted from advertisements:

Inverted pyramid (general to specific): Even though our country enjoys one of the highest standards of living and is the largest producer of food products in the world, there are serious gaps in our national diet, most frequently because of poor eating habits. These deficiencies are not limited to low-income groups but cut across all economic and social levels. According to the most recent information, 20 to 50 percent of Americans run some risk of not meeting the U.S. Recommended Daily Allowance for at least one or more of the vitamins C, A, B_1 (thiamine), B_2 (riboflavin), and folic acid. Minerals such as iron and calcium are also likely to be insufficient. If you're dieting or skipping meals, you may be eliminating foods that contain many vitamins, including C, E, and B-complex vitamins.[1]

Pyramid (specific to general): Watch a kangaroo go. At Tidbinbilla they hop to it at better than thirty miles per hour. Buy a boomerang from a man called Mulga Bill and chances are he'll throw in some instruction for free. Add to your rock collection. The local scene produced the Bee Gees, Helen Reddy, Peter Allen, Olivia Newton-John. Go to jail. Stand in the tiny cell where Ned Kelly, the notorious bushranger, was incarcerated. Get out to the Outback—to Ayers Rock, the world's biggest monolith. Around its base secret caves with painted walls telling of the Aboriginal Dreamtime. Stare at stalactites and stalagmites at Jenolan Caves. Meet a jackeroo or a jilleroo. They're young ranch hands learning the business on a sheep station. Outside Canberra you can see a sheep dog "round 'em up." He takes the shortest route from one side to the other: across the backs of the woolies. Come see the wonders Down Under in Australia. They could well turn your world upside down.[2]

Main Points

Main points are the principal support assertions offered to advance the thesis. Elsewhere we've called them main premises. They are crucial to any extended argument, for the argument's thesis stands or falls on the strength of these underpinnings. Furthermore, these main points are the object of the bulk of your analytical work. Usually it's not difficult to isolate the main points of an argument, especially when the essay is tightly organized. But even when it isn't,

[1]A Hoffmann-La Roche ad
[2]A Qantas advertisement

a close reading of the paragraphs and sensitivity to the connections between them should be enough to reveal the main points.

In evaluating the essay you will have to determine whether each of the main points is justified. That in turn requires a close and critical inspection of the paragraphs in which the points are made. For this inspection an awareness of how authors develop their supporting points is helpful.

Developmental Patterns

Developmental patterns are devices used to present the evidence or support for an essay's thesis. In arguing their cases authors use a variety of techniques to develop their main points. Among the most common of these patterns are (1) fact and opinion, (2) illustration, (3) analogy, (4) cause and effect, (5) authority or testimonial, and (6) statistics.

Fact and Opinion

The evidence offered to support a thesis takes the form of fact or opinion or a combination of the two. Providing facts and opinions is the most common way to develop an argumentative essay.

In everyday parlance, facts are what is actually the case. They are objective and verifiable. That water boils at 212 degrees Farenheit, that Sacramento is not the capital of the United States, that the sun rises in the east all are facts. Anyone who wants to can confirm these assertions. Relevant facts support a thesis to a greater or lesser degree.

Always make sure that the facts an author presents are accurate and complete. What is untrue is not a fact; what suppresses significant counterinformation is a half-truth. If the facts are not pertinent to the point they are intended to support, they're irrelevant and probably red herrings as well. If the facts are insufficient, the point they are intended to support is unwarranted and consequently does not support the thesis.

In contrast to facts, opinions are what someone believes to be the case. Opinions are subjective. While we can verify that the author holds a given opinion, we can't verify the opinion itself. If we could, then it would be a fact. Thus, if a ballistics expert testifies that two particular bullets came from the same gun, that's an opinion, not a fact. But don't misunderstand. Opinions can be a potent source of evidence, especially where there is a consensus of expert opinion. If all or most ballistics experts asked agreed that the two bullets came from the same gun, then the testimony would carry the weight of fact. Authority, then, figures prominently in the credibility of opinions. So remember that appeals to authority are legitimate when the authority invoked is indeed an expert in the field and when there is a consensus of expert opinion.

Illustration

Illustrations are authors' attempts to make something clear, to show what they are talking about, or to establish a point. Ordinarily authors telegraph their illustrations with phrases like "for example" and "for instance." But often a single word in a sentence signals an illustration: "A *number* of stories are told about President Lincoln"; *"Many* things are inefficient about the postal system"; "To understand why the Equal Rights Amendment should be passed, Americans should be aware of *several* facts."

Illustrations can take the form of a single example or a series. An example is a specific instance used to make a point clear.

> Throughout history, men have tried various ingenious methods for sorting out truth tellers from liars. A medieval "truth by trial" technique called for thrusting a suspect's hand into a fire; if it was not burned, he was judged innocent. An ancient Chinese test required a suspected wrongdoer to chew rice powder while being questioned. If the powder was dry when he spit it out afterward, the man was condemned—on the theory that the tension of lying had blocked his salivary glands, producing a dry mouth.[3]

Other times illustrations take the form of anecdotes, which are brief clarifying stories. Here's one you've already met:

> Even though they'll rarely admit it, little boys do like little girls and vice versa. A teacher recently observed this courting ritual between second graders during recess break. A little boy, the acknowledged "tough guy" in the class, found a dead snake on the playground. To the accompaniment of cheers and jeers from the other boys, he picked it up and slung it carelessly around his neck. Then he marched purposefully across the playground to where the girls were huddled, shrieking and squealing. Unerringly he sought her out, the loudest squealer of them all, and stopped in front of her. In the silence that followed, the young lover cast his trophy at the feet of his beloved. Secure in the knowledge that he had bestowed a gift of inestimable value, he turned and strode away, while behind him the shrieks and squeals of outraged femininity broke out anew.[4]

This illustration suggests several guidelines for evaluating illustrations intended to demonstrate a point. (Recall that illustrations intended primarily to clarify are not considered a part of an argument, but those intended to advance or support a point are.) First, an illustration must accurately illustrate the generalization or abstraction that it is intended to advance. The anecdote about little boys and girls presumably illustrates that kids do indeed like members of the opposite gender. Does it? I'm inclined to think that at the very best this anecdote illustrates that little *boys* may like little girls but not necessarily that little girls like little boys. If this were the only illustration given, it would be insufficient to warrant the generalization that "little boys do like little girls *and vice versa"* [italics added].

[3]Berkeley Rice, "The Truth Machine," *Psychology Today,* June 1978.
[4]Joan C. Roloff and Virginia Brosseit, *Paragraphs* (Encino Calif.: Glencoe, 1979), pp. 109–110.

Second, the force of the illustration should not depend primarily on the author's subjective interpretation of it. In this anecdote the author wants to illustrate that little boys really do like little girls and so interprets the little boy's behavior as a sort of ritualistic display of affection. But perhaps the boy was being sadistic. After all, he left the girls shrieking and squealing with outrage, didn't he? Why, then, interpret the behavior as a sign of affection? If we accept the anecdote as a report of something that actually occurred, then the writer seemingly serves up a mix of fact and *opinion*, the opinion being the interpretation of the behavior.

An effective use of illustration is provided by this selection from Studs Terkel's "Here Am I, a Worker." Terkel is attempting to advance the thesis that today's workers desire to be thought of as human beings and not just workers.

> Steve Hamilton is a professional baseball player. At 37 he has come to the end of his career as a major-league pitcher. "I've never been a big star. I've done about as good as I can with the equipment I have. I played with Mickey Mantle and with Willie Mays. People always recognize them. But for someone to recognize me, it really made me feel good. I think everybody gets a kick out of feeling special."
>
> Mike Fitzgerald was born the same year as Hamilton. He is a laborer in a steel mill. "I feel like the guys who built the pyramids. Somebody built 'em. Somebody built the Empire State Building, too. There's hard work behind it. I would like to see a building, say The Empire State, with a foot-wide strip from top to bottom and the name of every bricklayer on it, the name of every electrician. So when a guy walked by, he could take his son and say, 'See, that's me over there on the 45th floor. I put that steel beam in.' Picasso can point to a painting. I think I've done harder work than Picasso, and what can I point to? Everybody should have something to point to."
>
> Sharon Atkins is 24 years old. She's been to college and acidly observes, "The first myth that blew up in my face is that a college education will get you a worthwhile job." For the last two years she's been a receptionist at an advertising agency. "I didn't look at myself as 'just a dumb broad' at the front desk, who took phone calls and messages. I thought I was something else. The office taught me differently."
>
> Among her contemporaries there is no such rejection; job and status have no meaning. Blue collar or white, teacher or cabbie, her friends judge her and themselves by their beingness. Nora Watson, a young journalist, recounts a party game, Who Are You? Older people respond with their job titles: "I'm a copy writer," "I'm an accountant." The young say, "I'm me, my name is so-and-so."
>
> Harry Stallings, 27, is a spot welder on the assembly line at an auto plant. "They'll give better care to that machine than they will to you. If it breaks down, there's somebody out there to fix it right away. If I break down, I'm just pushed over to the other side till another man takes my place. The only thing the company has in mind is to keep that line running. A man would be more eager to do a better job if he were given proper respect and the time to do it."[5]

I have presented this selection at length not just to give an example of an illustration that's appropriate to the thesis and does not gain its force from a controversial interpretation but because it points up a third guideline to keep in mind when evaluating illustrations: The illustration should offer a fair represen-

[5]Studs Terkel, "Here Am I, a Worker," in Leonard Silk (ed.), *Capitalism: The Moving Target* (New York: Quadrangle, 1974), pp. 68–69.

tation of the point it's supposed to promote. Otherwise, the illustration will be in effect a biased sample. Notice the variety—in age, sex, and occupation—that Terkel employs in his illustration. Suppose in contrast that he had confined his illustration to males under twenty-five working in automotives. Such a restricted illustration, no matter how many examples were used, would not support his thesis.

So in evaluating illustrations make sure that (1) the illustration accurately illustrates the point it's intended to advance, (2) the force of the illustration does not depend chiefly on a subjective interpretation that may be questionable, and (3) the illustration fairly represents the point. When an illustration fails to meet these criteria, it can end up a red herring, a biased sample, or any other intensifying or downplaying devices being used illegitimately.

Quick Check on Evaluating Illustrations

Evaluate the use of illustration in the following passages according to the three criteria just developed.

1 Barney Clark, a 61-year-old Seattle dentist, suffered from congestive heart failure—an irreversible deterioration of the heart muscles. His condition was so bad that he couldn't walk even a few yards without intense pain. By the night of December 1, 1982, his condition had so degenerated that physicians didn't expect him to live beyond a few hours. So University of Utah surgeons decided to treat Clark with a revolutionary new device. They successfully implanted an artificial heart in Clark, thereby making him the first known person to receive a mechanical heart designed to remain permanently in his chest. This wondrous achievement is a dramatic example of the prudent collaboration of financial and human resources in the service of human health.

2 "When god-like Odysseus returned from the wars in Troy, he hanged, all on one rope, some dozen slave girls whom he suspected of misbehavior during his absence. The hanging involved no question of propriety, much less justice. The disposal of property was then, as now, a matter of expediency, not of right and wrong. Criteria of right and wrong were not lacking from Odysseus's Greece. The ethical structure of that day covered wives, but had not been extended to human chattels." (Aldo Leopold, "The Conservation Ethic," *The Journal of Forestry* 31 [1933])

3 "Sexual morality is a bottomless pit of problems. A competent employee with ten years of experience in one company happened to be a young woman who dated lots of men, including other workers. Her amours were a favorite subject of office gossip. On two occasions a jilted sweetheart stomped into her office and threatened her. Management got so irritated it told her to leave: she was a loose woman and a danger to morale. Rushing to her defense, the union claimed that her private life was her own business and that it was management's job to keep out intruders, not hers. When the case went to arbitration, the union's argument prevailed over management's and the

young woman got her job back." (David W. Ewing, *Freedom Inside the Organization: Bringing Civil Liberties to the Workplace* [New York: Dutton, 1977], p. 221.)

Comments

1. The illustration does not point up the "prudence" of marshalling enormous financial and human resources in behalf of this device. The author imposes this valuation on the example cited. People inside and outside the medical profession have in fact argued that these resources could have been more prudently directed toward cardiac research and therapy with more widespread application. In short, the illustration is irrelevant to the claim that the implantation of a mechanical heart is *prudent* therapy.
2. Acceptable illustration.
3. I'm disinclined to take this one example as enough to justify the generalization that "sexual morality is a bottomless pit of problems." In fact, in most cases workers' sexual morality poses no on-the-job problems, as far as we know. Furthermore, the relevancy of the example is questionable, for it seems more to illustrate that workers' private lives sometimes spill over into their work lives or that management must learn to balance its responsibilities to respect worker privacy on the one hand and to foster a healthful work climate on the other. In fact, given the case's resolution, it seems fair to infer that had management kept out the jilted sweetheart, there wouldn't have been any problem at all, or that at least the problem cited—firing the worker—probably wouldn't have arisen.

Analogy

The analogy is another developmental pattern that authors sometimes employ to establish points. Although when used properly analogies can be extremely effective, remember that many argumentative analogies are deficient because they overlook significant differences in the things being compared. So beware the false analogy in an essay that reasons analogically to make a point. (See Chapter 8.)

Cause and Effect

Like the preceding patterns, cause and effect sometimes figures prominently in the argumentative essay. Whenever an essay's points are developed by cause and effect, be especially alert for the following downplaying by omission devices: questionable cause, causal oversimplification, neglect of a common cause, slippery slope, and post hoc. (See Chapter 8.)

One additional point. Generally causal analysis takes the form of reasoning from cause to effect or from effect to cause. Here's an example of a cause-to-effect development pattern, excerpted from Paul Ehrlich's *The Population Bomb.* Having just established that at present the world's population doubles about every thirty-seven years, Ehrlich writes

Let's examine what might happen on the absurd assumption that the population continued to double every thirty-seven years into the indefinite future. If growth continued at that rate for about 900 years, there would be some

60,000,000,000,000,000 people on the face of the earth. Sixty million billion people. This is about 100 persons for each square yard of the Earth's surface land and sea. A British physicist, J. H. Fremlin, guessed that such a multitude might be housed in a continuous 2,000-story building covering our entire planet. The upper 1,000 stories would contain only the apparatus for running this gigantic warren. Ducts, pipes, wires, elevator shafts, etc., would occupy about half of the space in the bottom 1,000 stories. This would leave three or four yards of floor space for each person. I will leave to your imagination the physical details of existence in this ant heap, except to point out that all would not be black. Probably each person would be limited in his travel. Perhaps he could take elevators through all 1,000 residential stories but could travel only within a circle of few hundred yards' radius on any floor. This would permit, however, each person to choose his friends from among some ten million people! And, as Fremlin points out, entertainment on the worldwide TV should be excellent, for at any time "one could expect ten million Shakespeares and rather more Beatles to be alive."[6]

In contrast, here's an example of an effect to cause development:

The National Commission on Diabetes, a panel appointed by Congress to study the problem, reported in 1975 that diabetes and its complications cause more than 300,000 deaths in the United States each year, making it the third leading cause of death, behind heart disease and cancer. The number of diabetics in the United States is doubling every fifteen years. A newborn child now faces a 1-in-5 chance of developing diabetes. Ironically, this increase is a direct result of improvements in the treatment of the disease. Diabetics who once might have died young or during periods of stress, such as giving birth, are now living relatively normal lives. They are bearing children who are more likely to develop diabetes.[7]

Authority or Testimonials

Frequently argumentative essays rely on testimonials or appeals to authority in developing points. When evaluating such essays keep in mind the criteria for legitimate appeals to authority. And be watchful of false authority, including appeals to popularity, positioning, and appeals to traditional wisdom.

Statistics

Although statistics are a form of appeal to authority, they sometimes play such a central role in essay development that it's useful to isolate them. The Ehrlich selection is a case in point. Recall or review what you learned about statistics in Chapter 8, as well as what was discussed concerning studies, polls, and surveys.

These six developmental patterns occur frequently enough in argumentative essays for you to be familiar with them. Just recognizing the pattern should

---

[6]Paul Ehrlich, *The Population Bomb* (New York: Ballantine, 1969), pp. 14–15.
[7]Thomas H. Maugh II, "The Two Faces of Diabetes," *Science Year, 1978* (Chicago: Field Enterprises Educational Corp., 1979), p. 58.

alert you to the common intensifying and downplaying devices associated with them and thereby ready you to apply a most important step in argument evaluation. An awareness of an essay's patterns, together with knowledge of its thesis, organization, and main points, gives you a kind of map of the essay and prepares you for the challenge of analysis and evaluation.

An Essay Critiqued

With these preliminary remarks behind us, let's now see how the seven-step format can be applied to argumentative essays. The following piece deals with voluntary euthanasia, the practice of allowing the terminally ill to elect to die.

AGAINST LEGALIZING EUTHANASIA

The Karen Ann Quinlan case once again has raised the issue of euthanasia. A number of voices have been heard advocating the legalization of voluntary euthanasia. While the agonizing plight of many of our terminally ill makes this proposal understandable, there are good reasons to resist liberalizing our euthanasia laws.

First of all, no matter how you look at it, euthanasia is killing and thus is wrong. The Bible is clear on that point, and our society always has forbidden it.

Second, it is questionable whether a terminally ill patient can make a voluntary decision to begin with. Those who advocate voluntary euthanasia believe that patients should be allowed to die on request when they've developed a tolerance to narcotics. But exactly when are those patients to decide? When they're drugged? If so, then surely their choice can't be considered voluntary. And if they're to decide after the drugs have been withdrawn, this decision can't be voluntary either. Anyone who's had a simple toothache knows how much pain can distort judgment and leave us almost crazy. Imagine how much more irrational we'd likely be if we were suffering from some dreadful terminal disease and suddenly had our ration of morphine discontinued.

But even if such a decision could be completely voluntary, isn't it really unwise to offer such a choice to the gravely ill? I remember how, before she died of stomach cancer, my mother became obsessed with the idea that she was an emotional and financial burden on her family. She actually kept apologizing to us that she went on living! Had she had the option of euthanasia, she might have taken it—not because she was tired of living but because she felt guilty about living!

I shudder to think of the stress that such a choice would have put on us, her family. Surely we would have been divided. Some of us would have said "Yes, let mother die," while others would have resisted out of a sense of love or devotion or gratitude, or even guilt.

Then there's the whole question of mistaken diagnoses. Doctors aren't infallible. Even the best of them errs. The story is told of the brilliant diagnostician Richard Cabot who, when he was retiring, was given the complete medical histories and results of careful examinations of two patients. The patients had died and only the pathologist who'd seen the descriptions of their postmortems knew their exact diagnoses. The pathologist asked Cabot for his diagnoses. The eminent Dr. Cabot muffed both of them! If a brilliant diagnostician can make a mistake, what about a less accomplished doctor? Let's face it: There's always the possibility of a wrong diagnosis.

But suppose we could be sure of diagnoses. Even so, there's always the chance that some new pain-relieving drug, or even a cure, is just around the corner. Many years ago the President of the American Public Health Association made this point forcefully when he said "No one can say today what will be incurable tomorrow. No one can predict what disease will be fatal or permanently incurable until medicine becomes stationary and sterile."

But what frightens me the most about legalizing voluntary euthanasia is that it will open the door for the legalization of *involuntary* euthanasia. If we allow people to play God and decide when and how they'll die, then it won't be long before society will be deciding when and how defective infants, the old and senile, and the hopelessly insane will die as well.

Step 1: Clarify meaning

The arguer clearly opposes easing euthanasia laws to allow even voluntary euthanasia. While the position is clear, the language used often is fuzzy. "That point" (paragraph 2), "killing" (paragraph 2), "voluntary decision" (paragraph 3), "just around the corner" (paragraph 7) all are ambiguous. The sentence beginning "Imagine how much . . ." (paragraph 3) is both directive and informative. The opening sentence of paragraph 4 is a rhetorical question. "No matter how you look at it" (paragraph 2) and "Let's face it" (paragraph 6) are extreme intensifiers.

Step 2: Identify thesis (conclusion) and main points (premises)

The most efficient way to identify the thesis and main points of argumentative essays is to paraphrase them. Of course, make sure that your paraphrase does not distort or omit important details.

Thesis: Voluntary euthanasia should not be legalized.
Point: Euthanasia is wrong.
Point: It's impossible to ascertain that consent is voluntary.
Point: Allowing a death decision is unwise.
Point: Diagnoses can be mistaken.
Point: Relief or cures can be imminent.
Point: Abuses will follow the legalization.

(You might conceivably consider the third point as support for the second, in which case the essay could be viewed as having five, rather than six, main points.)

Step 3: Cast the argument

AGAINST LEGALIZING EUTHANASIA

The Karen Ann Quinlan case once again has raised the issue of euthanasia.

A number of voices have been heard advocating the legalization of voluntary

euthanasia. While the agonizing plight of many of our terminally ill makes this

proposal understandable, [there are good reasons to resist liberalizing our
euthanasia laws.]

    First of all, no matter how you look at it, [euthanasia is killing] and thus is
[wrong.] [The Bible is clear on that point], and [our society has always
forbidden it.]

    Second, [it is questionable whether a terminally ill patient is capable of
making a voluntary decision to begin with.] Those who advocate voluntary
euthanasia believe that patients should be allowed to die on request when
they've developed a tolerance to narcotics. But exactly when are those patients
to decide? When they are drugged? [If so, then surely their choice can't be
considered voluntary.] And [if they're to decide after the drugs have been
withdrawn, their decision can't be voluntary either.] [Anyone who's had a
simple toothache knows how much pain can distort judgment and leave us
almost crazy.] [Imagine how much more irrational we'd likely be if we were
suffering from some dreadful terminal disease and suddenly had our ration of
morphine discontinued.]

    [But even if such a decision could be completely voluntary,] [isn't it really
unwise to offer such a choice to the gravely ill?] I remember how, before she
died of stomach cancer, my mother became obsessed with the idea that she was
an emotional and financial burden on her family. She actually kept apologizing
to us that she went on living. [Had she had the option of euthanasia, she might
have taken it—not because she was tired of living, but because she felt guilty
about living!]

    [I shudder to think of the stress that such a choice would have put on us,
her family.] Surely [we would have been divided.] [Some of us would have said
"Yes, let mother die,"] while [others would have resisted out of a sense of love or
devotion or gratitude, or even guilt.]

    Then [there's the whole question of mistaken diagnoses.] Doctors aren't
infallible. Even the best of them errs. The story is told of the brilliant
diagnostician Richard Cabot who, when he was retiring, was given the complete
medical histories and results of careful examinations of two patients. The
patients had died and only the pathologist who'd seen the descriptions of their
postmortems knew their exact diagnoses. The pathologist asked Cabot for his
diagnoses. The eminent Dr. Cabot muffed both of them! If a brilliant

diagnostician can make a mistake, what about a less accomplished doctor? Let's face it: There's always the possibility of a wrong diagnosis.

But suppose we could be sure of diagnoses. Even so, [there's always the chance that some [19] new pain-relieving drug, or even a cure, is just around the corner.] Many years ago the President of the American Public Health Association made this point forcefully when he said "No one can say today what will be incurable tomorrow. No one can predict what disease will be fatal or permanently incurable until medicine becomes stationary and sterile."

But what frightens me the most about legalizing voluntary euthanasia is that [it will open the door for [20] the legalizing of *involuntary* euthanasia.] [If we allow people to play God and decide when and how they'll die, then it won't be long [21] before society will be deciding when and how defective infants, the old and senile, and the hopelessly insane will die as well.]

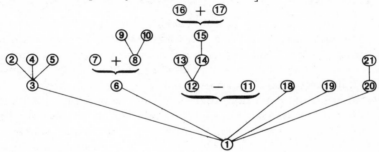

Step 4: Fill in missing premises

In the mini-argument

$$
\begin{array}{c}
② \\
\mid \\
③
\end{array}
$$

the arguer must be assuming that killing is wrong (unexpressed premise a). Thus

$$
\underbrace{② + ⓐ} \\
③
$$

In mini-argument

$$
\underbrace{⑦ + ⑧} \\
⑥
$$

the arguer must be assuming that only one of the two alternatives is possible: that the choice be made either under the influence of powerful drugs, in which case it wouldn't be free because the person's judgment would be clouded; or after the drugs were withdrawn, in which case the choice wouldn't be free because the person would be racked with pain (unexpressed premise b). Thus

In mini-argument

the arguer must be assuming that to choose out of guilt for depleting a family's emotional or financial resources is wrong (unexpressed premise c). Thus

$$\underbrace{⑬ + ©}_{⑫}$$

Step 5: Examine main points (premises) and support for justification

Main point 3 is a value assertion whose justification depends on the meaning of "wrong" and the support provided for that meaning. Mini-premise 2 is a fact, for euthanasia can be considered a form of killing. But unexpressed premise a is in doubt. What about self-defense or capital punishment or soldiers in combat? If the arguer allows that each of these or any other form of killing is justifiable, then he/she can't hold that killing *always* is wrong. If killing is not always wrong, then euthanasia may not be wrong. Should the arguer admit that killing is not always wrong but that euthanasia is an unacceptable form of killing, then he/she must demonstrate why. In any event the arguer leaves this crucial value judgment unsupported. Well, not entirely. The arguer does mention the Bible in mini-premise 4. But is the Bible "clear on that point"? If "that point" refers to killing, then it's not at all certain that the Bible prohibits all forms of killing. In fact, most interpretations of the Bible find exceptions to the commandment "Thou shalt not kill." If on the other hand "that point" refers to euthanasia, it is not true that the Bible clearly takes a stand against euthanasia. As for mini-premise 5 offered in support of main point 3, the reference to "it" in "our society has always forbidden it," must refer to euthanasia, since our society has not always forbidden every form of killing. Although some might question the literal truth of this assertion, I'll grant it and reserve further comment until the next step. In short, I can accept mini-premises 2 and 5 with qualifications; I can't accept unexpressed premise a or mini-premise 4.

Whether or not main point 6 is true depends largely on mini-premises 7 and 8 and unexpressed premise b. The mini-premises probably are true hypothetical statements, and the arguer has made fair use of an analogy in assertion 9 in making point 8. But is the unexpressed premise true? Must consent be obtained only when patients are drugged or when they're crazed with pain after drugs have been withdrawn? If these are the only two choices, the arguer probably is correct in asserting that the death decision may not be voluntary (main point 6). But there is another possibility: Offer patients a choice when they are faced with imminent death but not yet lapsed into excruciating pain or have been heavily sedated. The arguer could reply that consent in such situations is an uninformed and anticipatory consent and that patients can't or shouldn't commit themselves to be killed in the future. Still, there may be cases where patients not in pain indicate a desire for ultimate euthanasia and reaffirm that request when under pain. In any event, the question of what constitutes consent is a tricky one that cannot be dismissed by the black-and-white thinking evident in this unexpressed premise. This doesn't mean that the arguer is necessarily incorrect in making main point 6 but that he/she hasn't presented those cases in which consent seems at least possible. Nor has the arguer attempted to define precisely what is meant by "consent" and "voluntary decisions." Therefore I don't regard the support offered as justifying main point 6.

Main point 12 is a value assertion ("unwise") whose justification depends on the support offered by mini-premises 13 + c and 14, which follows from assertion 15, together with assertions 16 + 17. Given the qualifying "might have" in mini-premise 13, I can accept the assertion as a possibility only. There's no way of knowing for sure that the arguer's mother would have chosen euthanasia, or if she had, that she would have done so for the reasons given. Unexpressed premise c, which is a value assertion, needs considerable support before it can be taken as justified. Mini-premise 14 can be considered justified on the basis of a confirmation found within the arguer and supported by the similarly justified assertions 15, 16, and 17. Whether these assertions and mini-premise 13 give enough support to main point 12 are questions best taken up in the next step.

Main point 18 is not in doubt: Diagnoses can be mistaken. (Incidentally, I didn't cast the example because it seems intended to reinforce the point, not to demonstrate it.)

The truth of main point 19 cannot be determined because "around the corner" is so vague. The example cited merely repeats the point.

There is no evidence to support main point 20. Mini-premise 21, which is offered in support of it, is purely speculative, an observation that I'll return to presently.

Step 6: Examine the argumentative essay (i.e., the argument) for devices used to intensify or downplay

Regarding mini-arguments

mini-premise 4, besides being ambiguous and doubtful, is a questionable testimonial. Mini-premise 5 is an appeal to tradition: Even if society has always forbidden euthanasia (itself a questionable assertion), that fact doesn't demonstrate that society has been justified in doing so or that the tradition is worth following. Stripped of these intensifying devices, mini-premises 4 and 5 provide no support for main point 3. This, together with unexpressed premise a's problems, noted earlier, leaves main point 3 a controversial value assertion that the arguer has not established. Until the arguer does, I can't regard main point 3 as entailing the argument's thesis, 1. In other words thesis 1 cannot be inferred from main point 3.

I already have indicated the black-and-white thinking evident in unexpressed premise b of mini-argument

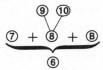

This mini-argument also can be viewed in terms of downplaying by means of a half-truth. The arguer overlooks cases falling between the two extremes that have been set up. But I do admit that even if there are other alternatives, the question whether anyone under a death sentence can make a "voluntary decision" may remain. So the black-and-white assumption may not gut this mini-argument. Nevertheless main point 6 is at best only tenuously related to the thesis. Even if we can question whether a terminally ill patient is capable of making a voluntary decision, that only suggests that we should determine the conditions under which we reasonably can assume that a person is making a voluntary decision. It doesn't support the claim that euthanasia should not be permitted. Maybe society should not allow death decisions made under the influence of powerful drugs or when people are mad with pain. But it doesn't follow that society shouldn't allow death decisions at all. So even if main point 6 is true, I'd consider it a red herring and thus irrelevant to thesis 1.

The support offered for main point 12 consists of intensifying through provincialism. The personal illustration is insufficient to support the implied unqualified generalization in main point 12. Furthermore, the arguer downplays by half-truth when, in writing about the stress these decisions place on families (mini-premise 14), he/she conceals or ignores the fact that under current law families experience stress that sometimes strains the limits of human financial, emotional, and spiritual endurance. (Curiously the arguer implies as much by arguing earlier that patients will choose euthanasia out of concern for their suffering families.)

Another thing. Mini-argument

$$\underbrace{⑯ \; + \; ⑰}_{⑮}$$

is a straw man. The real issue is whether the dying should be allowed to choose death; the straw is whether family should be allowed to choose death for a dying loved one. Although legislation concerning voluntary euthanasia could be so written as to allow a proxy death decision, it needn't be. Up to this point in the essay, the arguer clearly is discussing voluntary euthanasia in the context of terminal patients making their own decisions. This mini-argument raises the possibility of others making the decision for them. It would have been perfectly legitimate to raise this matter if earlier the arguer had defined voluntary euthanasia to include cases of proxy decisions. But in the absence of such stipulation and in the context of the rest of the essay, I feel justified in interpreting "voluntary euthanasia" more narrowly to include only decisions made by individuals themselves. I think this interpretation is correct because even in cases of proxy decisions, individuals have expressly indicated (for example, through a so-called Living Will) that under carefully circumscribed conditions, they prefer death to artificially sustained life and have designated someone to implement their wishes if they themselves can't. So to raise the specter of a family battle over whether to allow mother a quick and painless death is unfair. It's a straw man and an appeal to fear. By this account mini-premise 14 provides no support for the value assertion made in main point 12. Since the premises 13 + c don't either, the value assertion is left unsupported and consequently fails to support the thesis.

Although main point 18 is true, it smacks of fear. It also can be considered a half-truth because the vast majority of diagnoses are correct ones. But the arguer's reason for using this point to support the thesis obviously is that even the slightest possibility of miscalculation should discourage the relaxation of prohibitions against euthanasia. Fair enough. But what are we to say about the many medical procedures and operations that are performed daily? These always carry a risk of wrong diagnosis, in which case patients can be harmed, sometimes irreparably. Indeed any operation carries a risk to life, and often the risk is grave. The medical profession itself admits that too many operations and other medical procedures are unnecessary. What are we to say of all this? That medical procedures shouldn't be allowed? It is true that euthanasia is unique in that its object is not to save or prolong life but to end it. But euthanasia also aims to end pain, and the saving of pain is widely considered to be a legitimate aim of medical practice. The arguer could object that we don't know for sure that euthanasia in fact effects a net saving of pain. True enough, but how are we to find out? Apparently by trying voluntary euthanasia. To dismiss summarily the possibility that voluntary euthanasia may result in a net saving of pain would be to downplay by invincible ignorance. Finally it's possible to question the relevance of the arguer's whole point about mistaken diagnoses, that is, to see it as a red herring. After all, the issue of mistaken diagnoses is a medical not legal one. Even if mistaken diagnoses of terminal diseases were highly likely, is that relevant to the question of whether or not individuals should have the legal right to euthanasia? So although main point 18 obviously is true, the arguer has failed to demonstrate why the possibility of mistaken diagnoses argues against permitting voluntary euthanasia. Thus the thesis cannot be inferred from this point.

In main point 19 the phrase "just around the corner" downplays by confusion. Will a day, week, month, year, or several years pass before relief or a cure is found? Not only is "just around the corner" ambiguous, it's a half-truth concealing the fact that when medical discoveries are made usually several years pass before the new drug or therapy is available for widespread use. It's not as if one day we can't perform liver transplants, for example, but the next day we can. In the interim between discovery and general availability of a drug or therapy, the euthanasia option could be halted for those affected, or at least those affected could be informed of the possible new treatment. Moreover, the arguer conceals the fact that relief or cure would apply only to those in the group to whom the discovery applies. Are we to leave the remainder to suffer to preclude risk to these patients? The arguer leaves this point underdeveloped, citing instead a testimonial that, while legitimate, repeats main point 19 instead of illuminating it. In short, the arguer relies totally on ambiguity and half-truth in asserting this point. Therefore I can't accept 19 as entailing 1.

The last mini-argument

is a "wedge" defense. The arguer claims that should voluntary euthanasia be permitted, various forms of involuntary euthanasia are bound to follow. But there's nothing inevitable about this anticipated chain of events. This mini-argument, then, consists of downplaying by slippery slope. The thesis cannot be inferred from it.

Step 7: Give an overall evaluation

Although there may be good reasons for not permitting voluntary euthanasia, this essay has not marshalled them. It has relied heavily on ambiguity, straw man, half-truth, and red herring in an attempt to demonstrate its thesis. Perhaps a more fruitful approach would be to present an alternative care system for the dying that would greatly reduce, if not dissolve, the desire and need for death decisions. The hospice approach is an alternative that has gained widespread attention in England and the United States. Hospices are special settings devoted exclusively to the care of the terminally ill. The hospice approach to the care of the dying differs from conventional care in a number of ways. Most important, hospices stress comfort and care, which includes pain and symptom control and assistance at all levels to patients and their families during and after death. Specifically, hospice practitioners contend that pain, especially chronic pain, is a complex phenomenon that involves the emotional, social, and spiritual dimensions of the patient as well as the physical. Drawing on this view, they take a preventive rather than reactive approach to pain and symptom control. Thus every attempt is made to keep patients pain-free. Is this possible? Medical experts claim that most of the painful symptoms connected with terminal disease can be treated effectively but are not because health care professionals have not received proper training in symptom control. (See J. M. Hinton, "The Physical and Mental Distress of Dying," *Quarterly Journal of Medicine* 5 (1963): 1–21; W. D. Rees, "The Distress of Dying," *Nursing Times* 68 (1972): 1479–1490; and M. A. Simpson, "Planning for Terminal Care," *Lancet* 1

(1976): 192−193.) If in fact the pain connected with terminal disease can be reduced to a tolerable level, then the major reason for allowing death decisions loses much of its force. Of course, The hospice approach is not applicable in cases of extremely debilitating chronic disease. For such patients mercy death is still a viable alternative.

Notice that what I've done in this overall evaluation is present points that the arguer could have presented in discussing voluntary euthanasia. I've also taken the opportunity to clarify my own beliefs on the issue. By so doing, I have attempted to move discussion of this important social issue to what appears a more constructive level of discourse.

An Alternative Casting Method: The Outline

The casting method we've been using throughout our study is just one way an essay's structure can be portrayed. Another is the outline, with which you're probably familiar from your writing and speech courses. An outline presents the thesis of an essay and then lists in their order of appearance the main points (represented by roman numerals) and support materials (represented by capital letters).

If you prefer the outline to the tree-diagram method, use it in Step 3 of the seven-step format. Indeed, if you have properly identified thesis and main points in Step 2, you have the basis for an outline, which you must complete with any support material given in the argument. In implementing Step 4 you will then insert in the outline any missing premises that are not obvious.

Here is an outline of the essay under discussion. Notice that the missing premises, when inserted, have been indicated with a wedge (⟨ ⟩).

Thesis: Voluntary euthanasia should not be legalized.

 I. **Euthanasia is wrong.**
  A. Euthanasia is killing. + ⟨Killing is always wrong.⟩
  B. The Bible says so.
  C. Society forbids it.

 II. **It's impossible to ascertain that consent is voluntary.**
  A. If patients are drugged the consent cannot be voluntary.
  B. If the drugs are withdrawn the consent cannot + ⟨These are be voluntary because the patients will be mad the only two with pain. options.⟩
   1. A common toothache illustrates how much pain interferes with judgment.
   2. The excruciating pain associated with a terminal illness would blur judgment even more.

III. Allowing a death decision is unwise.

    A. Had she the choice, my mother might have chosen euthanasia out of guilt. ⟨Choosing out of guilt is wrong.⟩

    B. Families will be strained.

        1. My family's experience is a case in point.

IV. Diagnoses can be mistaken.

V. Relief or cures may be imminent.

VI. Abuses will follow the legalization.

    A. Permitting voluntary euthanasia will lead to death decisions imposed on defective infants, the old and senile, and the hopelessly insane.

Once you have outlined the essay and inserted the missing premises, you can then proceed with Steps 5, 6, and 7—the evaluation. In fact, if your outline is complete, you may not have to refer to the essay at all. You may be able to rely exclusively on the outline to determine whether the premises and support are justified and what intensifying and downplaying devices are used. Used properly, then, the outline is an economic way of portraying the structure of argumentative essays and evaluating them.

Summary

Many arguments come in multiparagraph form and are commonly termed "argumentative essays" or (when oral) "speeches of conviction." The argumentative essay consists of four principal parts: thesis, organization, main points, and developmental patterns.

In identifying the thesis, determine the essay's topic and the author's attitude toward it.

The typical argumentative essay may be organized in two ways: The thesis may be stated in the opening paragraphs, followed by support material, or (2) the support material may come first, followed in the closing paragraphs by the thesis.

An essay's main points usually can be identified by a close reading of the paragraphs, which includes a sensitivity to the connections between them.

Developmental patterns fall into the following categories: (1) fact and opinion, (2) illustration, (3) analogy, (4) cause and effect, (5) authority or testimonial, and (6) statistics.

Being aware of the anatomy of an essay provides a departure point for analysis and evaluation. The seven-step format can be applied as profitably to the extended argument as it can to the shorter one. If you prefer you may cast the essay (Step 3) in the form of an outline rather than a tree diagram, making sure to add to the outline the missing premises (Step 4).

Applications

Apply the seven-step format to the following argumentative essays.

LET'S STOP GIVING RICH KIDS A FREE RIDE THROUGH COLLEGE[8]

When Gov. George Deukmejian took office last month, he inherited a budget crisis of the first magnitude. The imminent deficit of the state of California was measured in billions rather than hundreds of millions. Clearly this looming disaster was not the new governor's fault. After all, he had just been inaugurated.

It would have been easy for Deukmejian to get in front of the television cameras and say, "Now, look at this mess. I inherited it, but it's not my fault. It's Jerry Brown's fault. So, I'm going to ask for a large income-tax increase and I will send to the Legislature a bill which I call the 'Jerry Brown Tax Rescue Act of 1983.'"

That would have been easy, but it would have been wrong, and that's for sure.

I think that before long, the governor will have to ask for a tax increase. But in the meantime, he is making a heroic effort to cut the budget without worrying about whether what he does is politically appealing. One aspect of that struggle shows what a fine mind and independent spirit George Deukmejian has in a day of conformers and me-tooers.

Deukmejian has suggested to the Legislature that a modest fee be attached to attending state universities and colleges. This idea is the beginning of an avalanche of good sense that has been due for some time. Students attending state institutions of higher education should absolutely pay tuition and fees unless they come from poor families. This is a matter of the most elementary justice and fairness to the working people of California.

Ten years ago, I was a teacher at the University of California at Santa Cruz. There was no tuition to speak of. There was only a trivial charge for room and board. The students lived in the most fabulous, incredibly beautiful dormitories on Earth, overlooking magnificent Monterey Bay, framed by towering redwoods, gardens and pathways tended ceaselessly by armies of landscapers.

All of this was paid for by the taxpayers of the state of California. In my classroom were mostly children of doctors and lawyers, IBM computer executives, proprietors of large and small businesses. For their Christmas vacations, the students took planes to Hawaii, Puerto Vallarta, Mazatlan, New York City. In the summer, the kids went to Europe, to South America, to artists' retreats.

In other words, these were well-to-do kids. It nearly drove me mad to think that the ordinary dime-store clerk, agricultural laborer, retired policeman, school janitor, assembly-line worker at Lockheed, typist at the Bank of America

---

[8]Ben Stein, "Let's Stop Giving Rich Kids a Free Ride Through College," *Los Angeles Herald Examiner*, February 7, 1983, p. A9.

or oilfield roustabout in Bakersfield were paying for these upper-class school-children to loll about in the redwoods, blowing pot and talking about revolution.

Now, I admit that my case was extreme. But, as a fact of life, the mean income of families of students at all the UC campuses exceeds the mean income of all California taxpayers. That means the poor of California are subsidizing the rich kids' education. This is a fundamental attack on fairness and equity in a free society. To soak the poor for the benefit of rich children insults the whole idea of a society in which persons are helped or assessed according to their means.

(For the students to say that they do not want to be dependent on their parents is just a rich kids' whine echoing a rich parents' whine. The kids are legally dependent in any event, and the "I want to be independent" nonsense would legitimize giving food stamps to the wife of a Rockefeller.)

I heard reports of a rally at UCLA at which state Sen. Alan Robbins said we should give a "free" education because we get a more highly skilled and productive labor force from a free state university system. Alas, that, too, is nonsense. If students are made more productive by their educations at UC or Cal State, the primary beneficiaries are the students themselves. Their incomes are raised, not the income of the taxi driver or the factory worker, except by the most remote form of trickle-down theory.

Since the college education of young Californians benefits them and is an investment in their future, they should pay for it themselves. I have to pay for a new typewriter that raises my productivity. The *Herald* has to pay for new delivery trucks that raise its productivity. Why shouldn't well-to-do California kids pay for investments that will increase their productivity? The child of the doctor or small-business owner or lawyer is madly ripping off the ordinary taxpayer of California if he or she does not pay for his or her own education, and if the parents do not chip in a lot of that money.

Of course, there will be some students too poor to pay for their education. For those with genuine need, both social compassion and the welfare of the state dictate public assistance. But for the poor to pay the bills of the rich at the university level is simply not fair. Gov. Deukmejian has made a start toward correcting this basic inequity. More power to him.

WOMBS FOR RENT: NEW ERA ON THE REPRODUCTION LINE[9]

Admittedly, the economy is in bad shape, but somehow I never expected to see a new breed of entrepreneurs arrive on the scene hanging out shingles that offer Wombs for Rent.

Remember when the real-estate moguls of the 1970s dealt in houses? It appears that their 1980s counterparts are dealing with uteri. While they aren't doing a land-office business quite yet, surrogate motherhood is an expanding market.

---

[9]Ellen Goodman, "Wombs for Rent: New Era on the Reproduction Line." © 1983, the Boston Globe Newspaper Company/Washington Post Writers Group; reprinted with permission.

At the moment, the star of the surrogates is Judy Stiver of Lansing, Mich., who was set up by a lawyer in her own cottage industry. According to Judy's testimony, surrogate motherhood, pregnancy and delivery were a little bit like taking in a boarder. She was promised $10,000 to give womb and board to a fetus for nine months and then deliver the baby to its reputed biological father, Alexander Malahoff of Queens, N.Y.

When asked why she decided to take this moonlighting job, Judy explained that she and her husband wanted some money to take a vacation and maybe fix up the house a bit—that sort of thing.

Would I buy an egg from a lady like that? Frankly, I wouldn't even buy a pair of genes from her.

But that was just the beginning, or the conception, of this tale. The baby was born last month with microcephaly, a head smaller than normal, which usually means that he will be retarded. Suddenly, this most wanted child was a pariah. Baby Doe was put in a foster home. The Stivers claimed that he wasn't theirs. Malahoff claimed that he wasn't his.

Pretty soon there were blood tests and lawsuits all around and a climactic scene on a Phil Donohue Show that looked like a parody of a Phil Donohue Show. Live and in color from Chicago—Whose baby is Baby Doe? Will the real father stand up, please?—we learned the results of the blood test. Hang onto your seats: Malahoff was not the father; Judy's husband, Ray Stiver, was.

By any standards, this was a thriller with more identity crisis than *H.M.S. Pinafore.* The fate of the baby was resolved right there on camera as the Stivers promised to bring him up just as if he were one of their own. So much for their vacation.

But, for all its freakishness, I don't want to dismiss the story as just another human sideshow. This one was a long time in the making.

I don't know a soul who can't sympathize with the feelings and desires of an infertile couple. Over the past several years, we have grown used to reading about dramatic help for infertile couples. By now, artificial insemination seems routine, and in vitro fertilizations have been eased off the front page. We applaud their births as happy endings.

We have been, I think, numbed into regarding motherhood-for-hire as just another option. There are now at least eight and perhaps as many as 20 surrogate-parenting services in the country. Anywhere from 40 to 100 children have been born by surrogate mothers paid $5,000 to $15,000 in states where such payment is legal. At least one entrepreneur aims to become "the Coca-Cola of the surrogate-parenting industry."

The tale out of Michigan was a jarring reminder that surrogate mothering is something qualitatively different, with hazards that we are just beginning to imagine.

Being a surrogate mother is not, as has been suggested, the "flip side" of artificial insemination. The infertile couple have contracted for more from a woman than an infusion of sperm. The pregnant woman has a stronger relationship with a fetus than a man has with a vial. The law governing this business, governing this web of parenting, is far murkier.

If the Stiver story has a bizarre twist, there are other and equally mind-boggling risks. What if the biological mother decides, as at least two have done, to keep the baby? Would a court hold that the contract was more sacred than the mother's rights?

What effect is there on a couple when the man seeks another woman to bear his child? The Malahoffs, it should be noted, separated when the child he believed was his was conceived.

What do you tell a child when he or she asks, "Where did I come from?" And what if the baby isn't perfect? Who holds the final responsibility for a child conceived through a contract?

In the Stivers' home, the boarder is now a son. They've learned something about chance.

We've learned something about a business and an idea that encourages people to regard parents as customers rather than as caretakers. We've learned something about people who look on motherhood as biological work on a reproduction line. We've learned to be wary of people who regard babies as just another product for an eager and vulnerable market.

WHY NOT SEND KIDS TO SCHOOL AT AGE 4, CUT GRADES TO 11?[10]

New York state's commissioner of education proposed recently that kindergarten begin at age 4 and first grade at age 5, and that the public-school curriculum be completed at the end of the 11th grade. These are the first really new ideas in public education since former California Supt. of Public Instruction Wilson Riles made it economically feasible a decade ago for schools to provide pre-kindergarten programs.

Both ideas are sound, and should be implemented. Experience and research tell us that an earlier start makes sense, saves dollars and is long overdue. There is no magic, or special developmental, reason for formal schooling to begin at age 6. That age was selected for political, not educational, reasons.

Nineteenth-Century factory owners found that most 5-year-olds could not reliably work a 12-hour day, and so the people trying to end child labor selected 6 as the age for beginning compulsory education. It is true that a 5-year-old is unlikely to stand up to 12 hours a day of repetitive labor, but, unless we want to run classrooms like factories for 12-hour days, that fact is irrelevant. Limiting schooling to age 6 and above makes no more sense, educationally, than does the nine-month school year—few of our children are needed for chores on the family farm anymore.

Experimental studies of pre-school education have demonstrated clearly—and with disadvantaged children—that an early start can reduce the need for later special education or for repeating grades, and that children who have been in good pre-schools are more likely to graduate from high school and, subsequently, to find and hold jobs and go on to post-secondary education.

[10] Irving Lazar, "Why Not Send Kids to School at Age 4, Cut Grades to 11?" *Los Angeles Times,* February 7, 1983, part 2, p. 5. Reprinted with permission.

The differences in later performances of pre-school graduates and those who did not attend pre-school are so great that the savings resulting from pre-school exceed its costs.

An earlier start in school offers additional advantages: It capitalizes on the eagerness to learn that 4-year-olds usually display; it establishes a greater commitment to learning and valuing of education, which is essential to school success, and it provides an opportunity for earlier identification of both the talented and the handicapped, permitting more effective schooling for each. Then, too, parents of younger pupils are far more likely to get involved in their education. The cost of re-tooling lower grades will be more than made up by the savings in remedial education and by the elimination of the 12th grade.

The proposal to contract the length of schooling by 8%—from 12 grades to 11—is another sensible idea. About half our youngsters drop out of school by the 12th grade, making it the most costly and least productive year in school. Of those who remain, about half go to college. The normal age for college entrance in the United States used to be 16, and it still is in most of the world. On the other hand, 12th grade has become a bore for able students and simply a "holding tank" for the rest.

Compressing the curriculum by 8% would make high school more challenging, and would result in a higher percentage of students graduating. Reducing the number of years in school wouldn't mean that we would have to teach less. A more efficient curriculum could more than compensate for the difference, and the addition of one class period a day would make up the time. Japanese children are in school eight hours a day and 11 months a year, with results that we feel in our pocketbooks.

Both these ideas offer real benefits to our society—and our economy:

—Our school resources would better match the age distribution in our country.

—The need for, and costs of, special and remedial education would probably be reduced.

—We would have a better-educated labor pool 12 years from now.

—An earlier start would free more mothers for work. The shortage of decent day care is so acute that the day-care industry would not suffer at all if the number of 4- and 5-year-old users were gradually reduced. The resulting increase in family income would have a beneficial effect on tax receipts and commerce.

Taking into account current dropout rates and college enrollments, the New York commissioner's plan would increase the number of teen-agers in the labor market by about 20% a dozen years from now. In today's economy, that would be awful. But if our economy is still in the doldrums a dozen years from now, it wouldn't make any difference anyway.

This plan would not solve all our educational problems. We would still need real curriculum reform, more sensible parental involvement and other changes, such as a more constructive use of summer months.

But an earlier start and earlier graduation are ideas that merit serious consideration.

THESE TESTS ARE MEANT TO SCARE PEOPLE[11]

Sen. Sam J. Ervin Jr. was right when he called polygraph interrogations "20th century witchcraft." But despite the frequency with which these examinations fail to detect deception and wrongly accuse people of lying, they do "work."

They work for the same reason that torture works—because the subject decides that resistance is futile.

Polygraphy is little more than a form of psychological one-upmanship enabling an interrogator to intimidate a person into revealing highly private information most of us would regard as nobody else's business. Afraid that his emotions will cause the needles to jump and thus "incriminate" him, the subject will pour out embarrassing admissions to questions that have nothing to do with his job, in hope of producing a smooth graph.

President Nixon, during an effort to stem leaks, said to his staff, "I don't know anything about polygraphs and I don't know how accurate they are, but I know that they'll scare hell out of people."

Like Nixon, the people who inflict polygraph interrogations on employees and applicants know the procedure is unreliable and produces false accusations. They don't care, so long as the test scares people.

Polygraph interrogations are unfair. They deny due process not only by being unreliable but by violating the privacy of beliefs and associations, the freedom from unreasonable searches, the privilege against self-accusation, and the presumption of innocence.

Polygraphers claim that their subjects voluntarily waive their rights, but there's nothing voluntary about waiving basic human rights to keep or get a job. Moreover, no waiver can be voluntary if it's made without full knowledge of the risks, and few polygraph subjects know what they're getting into.

Polygraphers should be required to give subjects this warning: "Before you waive your rights, you should know that many decent people have come out of these interviews feeling demeaned.

"You should also know that your superior or personnel manager will receive my report, and, if he is typical, will rarely risk his career by employing a person who has damaging information of any kind in his record. If you reveal embarrassing information, it may remain in somebody's file for years and you can never be sure who will see it or use it against you. And you should know that polygraphers have been known to wrongly accuse more than 10 percent of those they question.

"That said, are you sure you want to go through with this?"

LIE DETECTORS ARE ACCURATE AND USEFUL[12]

When used responsibly, the lie detector can be an effective, reliable tool for businesses and law enforcement agencies to screen prospective employees.

[11]Christopher H. Pyle, "These Tests Are Meant to Scare People," *U.S.A. Today*, February 17, 1983, p. A10. Reprinted with permission of *U.S.A. Today*.

[12]Lynn Marcy, "Lie Detectors Are Accurate and Useful," *U.S.A. Today*, February 17, 1983, p. A10. Reprinted with permission of *U.S.A. Today*.

Since the 1960s, the nation's population has become tremendously mobile. An applicant is less likely to come from the community where he or she seeks a job, or to have lived there long enough to establish an easily verifiable record.

The polygraph is particularly useful for small businesses that cannot afford to employ large security, personnel or audit departments. It may cost a business or law enforcement agency up to $1,500 to check an applicant's background; by using a polygraph, the employer can get the answers he needs for $50 to $100.

It's a simple, cost-effective way to verify the information a prospective employee has put on an application form. It's also useful in our litigious society, when many counsels advise their corporations not to respond at all to reference requests, for fear the subject of an inquiry will later sue.

Businesses which require their employees to handle cash or valuables find polygraphs useful. Convenience stores, jewelry retailers, drug chains and trucking firms have all begun using polygraph tests.

When administered correctly by qualified operators, the tests are accurate more than 90 percent of the time. Responsible operators bend over backwards to avoid asking questions which embarrass, demean or upset the subject. And 40 states have passed laws regulating polygraph use, to ensure responsible operation.

And the great majority of employers are responsible—they use the tests as one indicator among many indicators in the employee selection process. Few job applicants are denied jobs on the single criterion of failing a polygraph test.

Legislation we support will be reintroduced in this Congress to set minimum standards for polygraph operators and prevent abuses. It sets guidelines: No inquiries can be made concerning sexual or religious preference or union relationships, or about activities that occurred more than seven years before the interview. And I would support rules that, as a part of informed consent, would let subjects approve question areas in advance.

There are an estimated 200,000 to 400,000 polygraph tests a year in this country. They save employers money and help them make informed decisions about whom to hire; for the applicants, the test speeds up the process—within a couple of hours, they know whether they'll get the job.

PART FOUR

Generation

Writing the Argumentative Essay

So far this book has taught you how to analyze and evaluate ordinary arguments, long or short. You should now be able to respond critically to what you read and hear. You should not, however, confine your critical thinking skills to the information you receive. You should also apply them to the arguments that you yourself generate.

As you make your way through college, you will have many occasions to express yourself. Quite often the occasion is a written assignment that requires you to argue some point. Indeed, how well you do in school is determined in large part by your ability to write argumentative essays.

This final chapter to our study of critical thinking is intended to help you write good argumentative essays. It not only shows you what an argumentative essay consists of but also gives you strategies for writing one that are based on the critical thinking skills you have acquired.

Argument and Persuasion

As you know, there are many kinds of writing: fiction, biography, poetry, textbooks, news reports, letters, and so forth. Classical rhetoricians, however, distinguished only four forms of discourse, or expression of ideas, under which all kinds of writing could be classified. The first form of discourse is narrative or story telling, either fictional or factual. The second is description, which tells how something looks, sounds, feels, tastes, or smells. Description is used mostly in narration to provide a setting and help establish characterization. The third is exposition, which is an informative usage designed to express or clarify facts and ideas. The fourth form of discourse is persuasion, which is intended to induce readers to accept the opinion of the writer. Sometimes this form is referred to as persuasion *and* argument, because it is difficult to distinguish them in practice. In fact, most arguments carry persuasive elements, and most persuasion is grounded in the same rational approach that characterizes argument. But there are theoretical differences between argument and persuasion that are useful to pinpoint.

In theory argument and persuasion are differentiated by both purpose and technique. The purpose of an argument is to establish the truth of a contention wholly on the basis of a supporting body of logically related assertions that are true. Ordinarily, then, *the purpose of the argumentative essay is to win assent; that is, acceptance of a contention.* For example, in the argumentative essay we analyzed in the preceding chapter, the author tried to convince us that voluntary euthanasia should not be permitted by assembling a number of reasons that, taken together, supposedly constituted a rational appeal to our understanding.

In contrast, persuasion tries to make an audience think or act in accordance with the writer's will. Thus *the purpose of a persuasive essay is to move an audience to action—to win* consent *as well as assent.* For example, the author might have tried to persuade us to write our legislators expressing opposition to any legislation permitting nonrestrictive euthanasia. The author might have relied mostly on emotional techniques to win our consent, as persuasive writing usually does.

Actually, many argumentative essays, including the best, carry a persuasive function: They are directed at the audience's will as well as its intelligence. Thus argumentative essays are not merely bloodless exercises in preparing tidy little arguments. Although they are based on rational procedures and are developed logically, they also make wise use of emotional techniques. Just as part of the job of intelligent reading is to sort out the legitimate emotional appeals from the illegitimate, part of the job of effective argumentative writing is to know how to use emotional appeals legitimately.

So although there are theoretical differences between persuasion and argumentation, these distinctions are blurred in argumentative essays. Indeed, the argumentative essay typically enlists several forms of discourse. (The author who opposed the legalization of euthanasia used narrative in recalling his/her mother's dilemma and exposition in reporting that mistaken terminal diagnoses do occur.) The point is that it is impossible to draw a sharp line between argument and persuasion in an essay. For this reason I will use the term "argumentative essay" to include persuasion as well.

To write an argumentative essay you must be familiar with some of its principal features: thesis, main points, and organization. But before discussing these from the writer's point of view, let's examine an important consideration in writing argumentative essays—indeed, in any form of communication—the audience.

Audience

Have you ever wondered what makes a comic like George Carlin or Richard Pryor so funny? Certainly mannerisms, temperament, delivery, timing, and a sense of the tragic and absurd all contribute. But ultimately what makes any comic funny is the audience: Without audience response—laughter—a comic "dies."

This is why comics spend much time studying their audiences, learning their age, social and educational backgrounds, sexual and racial makeup, biases, inhibitions, fears, and basic outlook on life. Indeed, audience characteristics influence the comic's choice of words, dialect, and points of reference. Such considerations help the comic draw and then walk that thin line between being funny and being offensive, between good humor and bad taste. When comics overstep the line, chances are it's because they have ignored or misjudged their audience.

There is a lesson in this for you, the would-be argumentative writer. While you are not trying to entertain or amuse your readers, you *are* trying to win them over. For the comic, winning over the audience means getting them to laugh often. For the writer it means getting the audience to agree with you. Whether or not either succeeds depends largely on how well each has shaped the material to suit the audience.

Shaping an argument to suit your audience requires the same kind of audience study that the comic makes. Keep in mind the values, prejudices, and basic assumptions of the people you want to influence. Also be aware of their educational, economic, and social backgrounds; their ages; their occupations; and their feelings about current issues. Here is an inventory of key areas to think about when analyzing your audience before putting pen to paper:

1. **Age:** How old are the members of my audience? What effect, if any, will their ages have on what I'm trying to say?

2. **Values:** What is important to my audience—family, job, school, neighborhood, religion, country? What are their fundamental ideals—being successful, getting married, realizing their potential, ensuring law and order, guaranteeing civil liberties, establishing international harmony?

3. **Economics:** Is my audience wealthy, middle-class, poor? Are they currently employed, unemployed, training for employment?

4. **Social status:** From which social group does my audience come? What's important to this group? What references will they identify with?

5. **Intellectual background:** What does my audience know about my subject? What can I take for granted that they will know? Which words can I expect them to understand; which ones should I make sure to explain?

6. **Expectations:** What will my audience be expecting of my essay? Why will they be reading it? What will they be looking for?

7. **Attitude:** What can I assume will be my audience's attitude toward my topic? Will they likely be sympathetic, hostile, or indifferent?

   Taking an audience inventory makes your writing job simpler than it otherwise would be. To see why, let's suppose that you're interested in lining up George Carlin for a show that your college club is sponsoring. You approach Mr. Carlin and find him receptive. In short order you work out arrangements and set a performance date. Now, you would certainly think it odd if Mr. Carlin didn't ask you at some point "Who's the audience? Tell me something about them." Indeed, if Mr. Carlin didn't ask, you'd undoubtedly volunteer the information to ensure that his material will be appropriate. Once Mr. Carlin knows who his audience will be, then he can start shaping his material accordingly; he can start creating material that a group of college students will likely find amusing.

   The same applies to writing an argument. If you don't know your audience, you lack any sound basis for selecting material, choosing vocabulary, employing persuasive devices, and, most important, knowing how to strike the pose that will win your audience's respect, sympathy, and approval. Audience consideration thus assists you in deciding what to include, how to express it, and what role to play when preparing an argument. We will return to the concept of role shortly, but first let's examine another example that will further show how crucial audience awareness is.

   Suppose that you are a member of a student group that has been selected to meet with a board of professors and administrators to consider giving students academic credit for work experience. You have been chosen to argue the case in favor of such a policy.

   In preparing your case you should first identify the characteristics of the members of your audience. First, they will be mostly middle-aged, from thirty-five to fifty-five. Second, they probably never received any such credit when in school and just as likely have never been associated with any institution that gave such credit. Third, they will be intelligent, educated people who see themselves as open-minded, reasonable, and flexible. Fourth, they will be concerned about the institution's academic integrity. Fifth, they will be troubled about the "nuts and bolts" of implementing the policy. (Will *any* kind of work experience count for credit? If not, what conditions should be met to warrant credit?) Sixth, they will be sensitive to the opinions of alumni, the board of trustees, and parents, all of whose financial and moral support the school needs. Armed with this kind of commonsense information about your audience, you can give your argument form and character.

   Now to the point about image. I indicated that taking an audience inventory can help you decide which role to project as writer. In fact, deciding the role that you will play for your audience follows directly from audience analysis and is related to it.

Persona[1]

Rhetoricians use the term "persona" to refer to the role or identity assumed by a writer or speaker. The persona that you select depends largely on audience considerations. For example, in arguing your case before the group of professors and administrators, you will want to appear thoughtful, intelligent, serious, and mature. But suppose you were addressing a student audience. While your argumentative purpose remains the same—to win assent for the granting of academic credit for work experience—you would probably be more effective if you struck the pose of an angry young person who sees elements of elitism and a fundamental injustice in the traditional policy of giving academic credit only for course work. You might heighten this image by projecting yourself as a youthful progressive locked in combat with academic traditionalists out of step with the times.

Before writing a single word, then, you must learn about your audience. Although the purpose of the argumentative essay always is to win assent (and, when the essay tries to persuade, to win consent), how and whether it will do so depends largely on audience considerations. These same considerations greatly influence the choice of persona. With these important observations behind us, we may now turn to three essential ingredients of the argumentative essay: thesis, main points, and organization.

Quick Check on Audience and Persona

1   Pretend that you are writing a letter to the editor of your local paper protesting the city council's decision to impose a 10 P.M.-to-7 A.M. curfew in all city parks. What particularly rankles is that the curfew will prevent you from jogging between 6 A.M. and 7 A.M. in a neighborhood park, as is your custom. Identify your audience and persona; that is, list the specific characteristics of the audience and the important characteristics of the role you must play for it.

2   You are asked to write an argumentative essay for some course you are currently taking. Presumably the paper will be read only by your instructor. What specific characteristics of this person must you keep in mind? What important characteristics must you convey to this person? Suppose that the paper was intended more for a student audience. In what ways would the audience and persona characteristics be different?

3   Using the preceding exercises as models, create two situations that call for you to argue some case. Then identify audience and persona characteristics.

[1]*Persona* comes from the Latin word for the masks worn by actors in ancient classical drama to immediately delineate their roles for the audience. Accordingly, a smiling mask signaled a comic character, a sorrowful mask a tragic character.

In preparing your audience, follow this scheme:

Situation: _____

Specific characteristics of the audience I must keep in mind:

1. _____

2. _____

3. _____

4. _____

Others: _____

Important characteristics to convey to the audience:

1. _____

2. _____

3. _____

4. _____

Thesis

As you learned in Chapter 10, every argument has a contention, which in. an argumentative essay usually is termed the "thesis."

The thesis is the argument's main idea; that is, the main point being advanced. Thus the thesis gives the writer a purpose; the essay will be little more than a collection of sentences and paragraphs without it. Argumentative writers often have trouble formulating a thesis because (1) they fail to construct arguable assertions, (2) they don't know how to go about writing a thesis, or (3) they can't select a subject to write a thesis about.

Arguable Assertions

Not every contention is so arguable that it can or should be developed in an essay. Some contentions are easily verified. "Millions of Americans smoke cigarettes," "Nearly half the households in the United States are supported primarily by working women," and "A spirochete causes syphilis" are assertions that can be easily confirmed or disconfirmed. The ease with which these assertions can be evaluated precludes the need—and certainly the wisdom—of constructing essays to demonstrate their truth.

Other contentions defy objective verification altogether; they cannot be confirmed outside the self in the real world. The preceding assertions are at least objectively verifiable, although they need not be argued in essays. In other words we can go outside ourselves into the world, collect data and evidence about these contentions, and thereby confirm or disconfirm them. But what about statements such as "I am nervous," "I feel that something dreadful is about to happen," or "Drinks with sugar taste better than the sugar-free kind"? Confirmation of these statements lies within the persons expressing them. Personal experience, if honestly reported, is enough to verify such statements. Since what is needed to confirm these basic statements is available only to the persons making them, there is no point in constructing arguments to prove them. Yes, I might explain why I feel something dreadful is about to happen, but I probably wouldn't attempt to demonstrate to you in an argumentative essay that I feel this way.

In contrast are contentions so disputable, controversial, or opinionated that they lend themselves to elaboration. "Life exists outside our solar system," "Coffee is bad for one's health," "Many of today's films subtly attempt to justify violence directed against women," and "Television network news departments practice racism in hiring on-camera personnel" are examples. These assertions need to be supported by appropriate documentation and so could serve as arguable assertions to be developed in essays.

Thus only assertions demanding elaboration should serve as theses of argumentative essays and not assertions that can be easily verified or that defy objective verification. Of course, such assertions can and do appear as support material. For example, in attempting to demonstrate that female workers deserve the same pay as their male counterparts, I might point out that half the households in the United States are supported primarily by working women. Or to demonstrate how effective a suspense film is, you might report that throughout the film you were filled with presentiment. In such cases these facts would serve to support the arguable contentions that were being advanced.

So much for assertions that are not appropriate for development. What about assertions that are? These typically fall into five categories: assertions about meaning, value, consequences, policy, and fact.

1. **Assertions about meaning.**   Assertions about meaning are generalizations that focus on how we define or interpret something. For example, what we mean by such concepts and terms as pornography, equal opportunity, the just state, person, death, and mental incompetence often are the concern of lengthy essays, even books.

2. **Assertions about value.**   Assertions about value are generalizations that express an assessment of worth. Some examples are "Abortion is never right," "*Godfather II* is a better film than *Godfather I*," and "The two-party system is the most effective way of structuring our political system." Although value assertions rarely can be argued conclusively and always present unique problems in argument, they do constitute a large part of what people argue about, as we have seen.

3. **Assertions about consequences.**   Assertions about consequences are generalizations about the causal patterns of certain ideas or actions. Such arguments usually constitute responses to hypothetical "what if" questions. Accordingly they often take the form of "If X, then Y": "If the Equal Rights Amendment were passed, then women would be subject to the draft"; "If voluntary euthanasia were permitted, then involuntary euthanasia would follow"; "If government cuts back support to the arts, then many local cultural activities will dry up."

4. **Assertions about policy.**   Assertions about policy are generalizations that usually deal with approaches to social or institutional issues. Such conten-

tions typically are expressed as proposals using the words "ought" or "should" (which, incidentally, often signal value assertions as well). Examples are "Capital punishment should be reinstated," "College professors ought to take attendance in their classes," "Prisoners should be allowed to exercise cohabitation rights," and "Terminally ill patients ought to be informed of their condition."

5. **Assertions about facts.** Assertions about facts are generalizations dealing with alleged descriptions of actual states of affairs. "The universe will continue to expand," "China is preparing for a war with Russia," "People can communicate with one another over great distances without using any of the conventional means of communication," "An earthquake registering at least 7 on the Richter scale will probably rock California within the year," and "Shakespeare wrote all the plays and poems attributed to him" are statements that purport to describe things as they actually are, were, or likely will be.

In formulating a thesis writers generally focus on one of these five types of assertion, but in developing the essay they often call on several types. Thus you might draw up an argument whose thesis is "Gun control should be mandatory in every state" (a policy assertion). In supporting your position you might stipulate what you mean by "gun" and "gun control" (meaning), point out that certain states with gun control have lower rates of crime involving handguns than states without gun control (fact), discuss the social merits of gun control (consequences), and conclude that failure to enact such legislation is immoral (value).

Writing the Thesis

As indicated earlier, writing the thesis is vital because it helps the writer limit, focus, and organize the topic. Although there is no one way to write a thesis, the following steps do provide a logical and useful approach. You may have encountered a similar sequential strategy elsewhere, but reconsidering these steps will reinforce your learning and skill.

Step 1: Decide on a subject   The subject is the area of concern or interest. "Education in the United States," "the electoral process," "drugs," "feminism," "the penal system," "religion," and "conflict between the generations" all represent subjects or areas that are ripe for argumentative exploration. The first job of the argumentative writer, then, is to decide on a subject. Often instructors do this for students. "Write a 500-word essay on advertising," your English professor might tell you. Faced with such an assignment, you could be confused. "What *about* advertising?" you wonder. Your instincts rightly tell you that advertising is far too broad and unwieldy a subject to be handled in a mere 500 words. Therefore before proceeding with your essay you must identify some aspect of advertising that can be managed within the prescribed length.

Step 2: Identify possible topics   Your asking "what about" when faced with the assignment can be viewed as a groping for a topic. The topic is some aspect of the subject. Obviously subjects can spawn countless topics. For example

Subject	*Possible Topics*
Football	Salaries of players
	The strike of 1982
	A uniquely American pastime
Education in the United States	The high costs of college education
	Shortcomings in public secondary education
	Misplaced priorities
Religion	The Moral Majority
	The decline of institutional religion
	The increasing interest in Eastern religion
Advertising	Relationship to the law
	Deceptive practices
	Impact on the economy

In this step of argumentative writing, the writer must list the topics that could be developed in the essay. Accordingly this stage can be viewed as a brainstorming session in which you identify as many possible aspects of a subject as you can. From this list will come the topic you will write about.

Step 3: Select and limit the topic   Having composed a list of possible topics, you should then select one you want to write about and limit it. Note that this step consists of two operations: selection and limitation. The second operation is very important, for failing to limit your topic may mean that you later find it unmanageable. The proper limits of the topic usually are determined by the length of the proposed essay. The possible topics we've listed could be, and have been, the subjects of books. So to tackle any of them in a 500-word essay would prove unwise. They must be narrowed to allow development within 500 words. Here are some possibilities for the subject "Advertising":

Possible Topics	*Limited Topic*
Relationship to the law	The impact on consumers of three landmark decisions in consumer law
Deceptive practices	The use of ambiguity to sell aspirin, toothpaste, and mouthwash
Impact on the economy	Effects on the retail prices of alcoholic and nonalcoholic beverages

It is worth noting that the limited topics suggested here exhibit a common and effective method of controlling an essay—*dividing it into parts*. Thus the first limited topic refers to *three* landmark decisions; the second to *aspirin, toothpaste*, and *mouthwash*; the third to *alcoholic* and *nonalcoholic* beverages. From the writer's viewpoint these divisions reveal precisely what the essay must discuss and even the order to be followed (for example, aspirin, then toothpaste, then mouthwash). From the reader's viewpoint these divisions focus the topic and suggest the order of consideration: The reader knows what you will discuss and roughly when. Using division is enormously helpful because it maximizes the chances of effective communication.

Step 4: Determine your attitude toward the topic   A thesis not only consists of a topic but of the author's attitude toward it. Determining your attitude will help you decide what it is you're trying to demonstrate. For example, you may be *fearful* of the impact of the three landmark decisions; *critical* of the use of ambiguity to sell aspirin, toothpaste, and mouthwash; or *convinced* of the significant effects of advertising costs on the retail prices of alcoholic and nonalcoholic beverages. In identifying your attitude, remember the types of assertion that arguments ordinarily make; this will simplify your task of composing the thesis statement. Thus your fear about the three legal decisions springs from a concern about *consequences*, your criticism of ambiguity in advertising probably concerns *value* or *policy*, and your conviction about the impact of advertising costs reflects some ultimate assertion of *fact* and perhaps of *value* ("significant" implies a value assertion).

Step 5: Write the thesis statement   The next step consists of wedding the topic and your attitude toward it in a single assertion, which typically is a generalization. In writing the thesis statement you should be certain of the type of contention you want to make; this will ensure a sharp focus. As for the topics under discussion here, you might write a thesis statement such as the ones in the following diagrams:

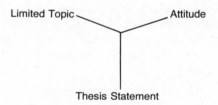

Limited Topic — Attitude

Thesis Statement

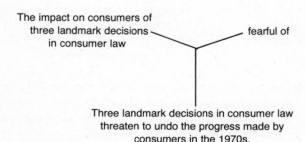

The impact on consumers of three landmark decisions in consumer law — fearful of

Three landmark decisions in consumer law threaten to undo the progress made by consumers in the 1970s.

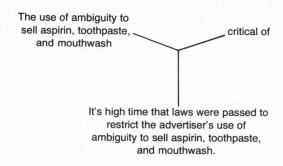

The use of ambiguity to
sell aspirin, toothpaste,
and mouthwash

critical of

It's high time that laws were passed to
restrict the advertiser's use of
ambiguity to sell aspirin, toothpaste,
and mouthwash.

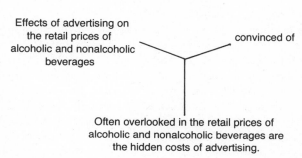

Effects of advertising on
the retail prices of
alcoholic and nonalcoholic
beverages

convinced of

Often overlooked in the retail prices of
alcoholic and nonalcoholic beverages are
the hidden costs of advertising.

Step 6: Test the thesis statement   After writing the thesis statement it's a
good idea to check it for focus. After all, you want to make sure that your topic
and viewpoint are crystal-clear. A good way to check your statement is to have
somebody else read and react to it. Ask the person "What do you think I'm trying
to demonstrate in my essay?" If the reply corresponds with your purpose, you
have a well-focused thesis statement. If it doesn't, then back to the drawing
board!

Quick Check on Thesis Formulation

By using the six steps just discussed, write a thesis statement for each of the
following subjects:

1 Job opportunities for women
2 Freedom of the press
3 The judicial system
   in the United States
4 Drug usage among minors
5 The state of marriage twenty
   years from now
6 Restoring cities
7 Gun control

8 Premarital sex
9 College curricula
10 Defense spending
11 The plight of the handicapped
12 Extracurricular activities in college
13 Junk foods
14 Changing sex roles
15 Contemporary music

Selecting Subjects

Clearly every thesis derives from a subject. When instructors assign you a subject, or even a topic, your job of formulating a thesis is simplified. But often they leave the choice up to you; they assign what is termed a "free-choice subject," which means that you can write on whatever you choose. Faced with no subject limitations, students sometimes falter; they can't formulate a thesis because they can't even select a subject, let alone some aspect of it they may wish to write about. The problem here is a failure of imagination. And it helps you precious little to sit patiently waiting for the muse to arrive. You must instead take measures to quicken that sluggish imagination. Here are four things you can do when stymied by a free-choice assignment.

First, you can select something that you are familiar with and about which you would like to learn more. Perhaps you've had a health course and learned something about vitamin therapy in the treatment of disease. If you want to learn more, why not make vitamin therapy your subject? Or maybe you recently read a newspaper article entitled "The American Indian: The Forgotten Minority." You remember being moved by the piece and wishing that you had the time to explore the plight of American Indians further. Here again is a possible subject. Or perhaps one of your outstanding gripes with colleges is the weight that admissions officers sometimes place on standardized tests. If you want to learn more about the pros and cons of such testing, make it the subject of your paper.

Second, you can choose a subject that you know nothing about but would like to investigate. A good place to begin is with terms you encountered once and glossed over, such as "supply-side economics," "circles of work," "big bang," "astral plains," or "cybernetics." Such terms are potential subjects for essays.

Subjects you'd like to learn something about can originate in conversations. A few years ago a student did an essay on what some experts on organizational psychology and management term "Theory Z," which is a way of approaching and structuring work that is new to the United States but has been common throughout Japan for decades. When asked how he had decided on such an unusual subject, the student explained that some time before he had struck up a conversation with a passenger on a flight from San Francisco to Los Angeles. As it happened, the exchange turned to the subject of work and young people's attitudes toward it. The passenger thought that the Japanese approach to work organization might be more appealing to young American workers and help improve U.S. productivity. The flight ended before the passenger could explain very much about this approach. The student didn't think much more about the encounter until, a few months later, he was asked to write a free-choice essay. Recalling the conversation, he discovered his subject.

Third, you can skim newspapers, magazines, and other periodicals for possible subjects. A good newspaper (and sometimes even a poor one) is a treasure trove of subjects. Daily columns, commentaries, and editorials abound with information about current events, science, medicine, the arts, sports, religion, and education. In fact, brief news reports often inspire a subject.

Another enterprising student once chanced upon an item explaining that the Food and Drug Administration had banned for sale in the United States an intrauterine device called the Dalkon Shield. A few weeks later the student came across another item concerning the export of the Dalkon Shield for sale abroad. She found this odd and began to wonder how many other products that were banned in the United States were being shipped overseas for sale. "Why not write an essay on this subject?" she thought. She did, and was it an eyepopper!

Fourth, you can consult the library for a subject of interest. Because the card catalogs contain information on every subject, merely perusing them should yield a clutch of ideas.

Of course, after you have chosen a subject, you must identify possible topics, then select one and narrow it, as indicated.

Quick Check on Subject Selection

1 Suppose that you have been assigned a free-choice subject in a course you are taking. Identify four different subjects: (1) select something you are familiar with and about which you would like to learn more; (2) select something you know nothing about but would like to investigate; (3) select something from a newspaper, magazine, or other periodical; and (4) select something you have discovered in the library.
2 Identify possible topics for each of the free-choice subjects and limit those topics.

Anticipation of Objections

When you argue a position, you imply that another position exists. After all, if an issue were one-sided, arguing it would be as pointless as trying to prove a widely known fact.

Whether or not you argue effectively depends largely on whether or not you anticipate the other side or sides. But, you might wonder, how do I know for sure that my audience holds the opposite position? You don't. But you must assume that, like yourself, they are critical thinkers. As such, they probably will raise questions just as you would. Good argumentative writers, then, recognize that the audience might raise objections even though raising objections doesn't necessarily imply adherence to an opposing position. Writers who know their craft also realize that leaving too many important questions unanswered may turn their audience into opponents.

For example, suppose you were writing a paper in support of mandatory retirement. You must not ignore the studies that indicate that forced retirement is a threat to workers' physical and mental health. Nor can you overlook the fact that taxpayers incur costs for maintaining people in retirement. Simply acknowledging these objections and proceeding with your argument probably won't settle these matters for your audience. You must try to blunt these potential objections to your thesis. One way to do this would be to find legitimate grounds for challenging the validity of the studies. Another would be to demonstrate that, for example, while society pays for maintaining retirees, it also pays to support younger workers who cannot find employment because the job ranks are glutted with older workers.

In anticipating counterarguments keep your audience in mind. Their background will largely determine the kind of objections they will raise. For example, in an essay supporting the teaching of creationism in high school biology classes, a general audience likely will raise different objections from those raised by a group of scientists. Anticipating your audience's objections helps you decide which points to emphasize to win them over.

Main Points

Every argumentative essay contains main points; that is, principal support assertions offered to advance the thesis. Recall the essay opposing voluntary euthanasia that we considered in the preceding chapter. In attempting to show why voluntary euthanasia should not be permitted (thesis), the author developed six main points:

1. Euthanasia is wrong.
2. It's impossible to ascertain that the consent is voluntary.
3. Allowing a death decision is unwise.
4. Mistaken diagnoses are possible.
5. Relief or cures can be imminent.
6. Abuses will follow the legislation.

Since any argumentative essay must demonstrate its thesis, writers must look for statements that answer *why* or *how* the thesis is justified. These statements are reasons. Thus, *why* should voluntary euthanasia not be legalized? *Why* are stricter regulations needed to restrict the widespread use of ambiguity to sell aspirin, toothpaste, and mouthwash? *How* does even a cursory look at the pricing structure of alcoholic and nonalcoholic beverages reveal the enormous effect of advertising costs? The writer's job is to marshal reasons that answer the *why* or *how* questions.

If the writer assembles enough of the right kinds of reasons, then the persuasion will be logical. If the reasons satisfy the audience, then they are persuasive. In writing essays, then, you must (1) select reasons that prove your thesis and (2) limit the essay to the reasons that are likely to be most persuasive; that is, the reasons that likely will have the greatest impact on your audience. Having discovered and selected your reasons—your main points—you must then support them with evidence.

In collecting reasons and support for them, you can call on several sources. One is *observation*. Observation is awareness of what occurs outside the writer. Usually observations are first-hand studies of scenes, people, objects, and events. Recall that in the euthanasia essay, the author called on observation to make judgments about the effect of drugs and pain on free, rational choice and to indicate the possibility of mistaken diagnoses.

Personal experience is a second source of reasons. As distinguished from observation, personal experience refers to what goes on *inside* the writer. It is one's consciousness of thoughts, ideas, and involvement with incidents, persons, places, and things. Used together with other sources, personal experience can be a rich source of support material. But be careful: Over-reliance on personal experience to make points results in provincialism. This, I think, occurred in the euthanasia essay when the author recounted his/her family's ordeal in attempting to establish main point three. The author erred not in invoking this touching personal experience but in relying on it exclusively to make the point and ignoring counterevidence.

Informed opinion is a third and most important source for developing reasons and support material. Informed opinion is the views of others who have studied the same subject. The euthanasia essay could have been greatly improved had the author made proper use of informed opinion.

Finally, *organized research* is a fourth source of material. Organized research is the systematic sifting of evidence from records, reports, and other printed sources. The author of the euthanasia essay didn't call on this source, but could have; for, as indicated in the overall evaluation, some material is available on alternative approaches to the treatment of the dying.

You can and should use these sources when assembling your main points and support material. Indeed, brainstorm in terms of these sources. Make a list of observations, personal experiences, informed opinion, and organized research relevant to your thesis. From this list select the most effective points; then shore them up with support material by again using these sources.

Quick Check on Formulating Main Points

Assume that you have become interested in three of the theses you wrote for the Quick Check on Thesis Formulation. Based on your own experience and observations, write down everything you can think of that is relevant to each one. Then select three points from each that you think are the most important for supporting that thesis.

Organization

Organization is the framework that ties together the reasons you assemble to support your thesis. An essay generally is structured to move from the general to the specific (inverted pyramid) or from the specific to the general (pyramid). But more narrowly defined patterns can be used to write a logically compelling paper. The most common of these are exhibited in (1) the inductive essay, (2) the pro-and-con essay, (3) the cause-and-effect essay, and (4) the analysis-of-alternatives essay. The choice of organizational plan depends largely on considerations of your purpose and audience.

Inductive Essay

Without getting into all the nuances of induction, I will simply describe an inductive essay as one that typically moves from the specific to the general, from bits and pieces of evidence to a probable conclusion. In an inductive essay examples, illustrations, facts, opinions, and other forms of evidence are used to draw a general, probable conclusion that is in effect the thesis.

Induction is especially useful when your purpose is to convince the audience of a rather controversial assertion—for example, "The use of saccharin should be prohibited," "The United States should have a national health insurance program that guarantees all citizens health care and services despite their ability to pay," or "Public schools are not giving young people what they need to survive in a highly technological society." Audiences often greet such controversial assertions of value, policy, or fact with prejudice and distrust. The inductive approach helps you turn audience attention to the evidence, which is allowed to speak for itself. Thus the support material usually is presented first; then in the final paragraph or two the assertion is made. Ideally, having seen the evidence, members of the audience will change their minds or will at least be receptive to your controversial conclusion.

For example, suppose your purpose is to convince a skeptical audience that Americans are not as well fed as they think they are. Using the inductive approach you might structure your essay as follows:

Fact 1: According to the most recent information, 20 percent to 50 percent of Americans run some risk of not meeting the U.S. recommended daily allowance for at least one or more of the vitamins C, A, B$_1$ (thiamine), B$_2$ (riboflavin), and folic acid.

Fact 2: Although the diets of most Americans may be richer in minerals than they were fifty years ago, our intake of such minerals as iron and calcium still is likely to be insufficient.

Fact 3. Many people today, young and old, are dieting and skipping meals. As a result they may be eliminating foods that contain many vitamins, including C, E, and B-complex vitamins.

Conclusion: These facts point to an unmistakable conclusion: There are serious gaps in our national diet, most frequently because of poor eating habits.

Pro-and-Con Essay

Notice that in the preceding example you tried to present a "closed case" for your contention. But you might not have been so one-sided in your presentation. Instead you might have presented a more balanced approach.

The pro-and-con essay attempts to reach a balanced conclusion by treating an issue as an open question worth thinking about. In it the arguer usually begins by discussing the pros and cons of an issue. The discussion serves as a basis for a balanced conclusion. This format, then, consists of (1) the confirmation of an idea, (2) the objection to the idea, and (3) a balanced conclusion. This approach has special audience appeal because it flatters their intelligence and sense of fair play. It also makes the writer appear thoughtful and impartial. Here's an example:

Confirmation: Undoubtedly the United States enjoys one of the highest standards of living and is the largest producer of food products in the world. Our agricultural and industrial resources understandably make many Americans and non-Americans alike consider us the best-fed people on earth.

Objection: Current evidence suggests that we are far from realizing the nutritional promise of our bountiful resources. For one thing 20 percent to 50 percent of us run some risk of not meeting the U.S. recommended daily allowance.

Conclusion: Calling ourselves the best-fed people on earth is misleading. Rather, we appear to be potentially the best-fed people on earth. Whether we realize our potential depends largely on whether we can close the gaps in our national diet by improving our eating habits.

Cause-and-Effect Essay

The cause-and-effect essay, which is especially appropriate for advocating consequential assertions, attempts to ascertain the conditions that have produced some phenomenon. One way to do this is to present the major causes in chronological order, as in treating some historical event. Another is to arrange the causes in order of importance. Often writers of a cause-and-effect essay have in mind some remedy, which they present after they have discussed the causal conditions underlying a problem. In that event the writer's purpose is twofold: (1) to make the audience aware of the causes and (2) to make it accept the proposed solution. The cause-and-effect essay, then, often follows this structure: statement of problem, various causes, proposed solution. Here's an example:

Statement of Problem: It is commonly thought that Americans are the best-fed people on earth. Yet current evidence indicates that there are serious gaps in our national diet.

First Major Cause: The deficiencies in our national diet are attributable to several factors. Perhaps the most important is poor diet.

Second Major Cause: Lack of education is another reason for the deficiencies in our national diet. Although public school curricula inevitably include a "health" component, very little of it is devoted to the study of proper nutrition.

Third Major Cause: Still another factor that explains our nutritional deficiencies is the medical profession's traditional ignorance of or lack of interest in proper nutrition. Historically doctors have spent little time impressing on patients the link between poor diet and ill health.

Conclusion Proposal: Undoubtedly we Americans have the potential for being the best-fed people on earth. But until we change our eating habits, schools start instructing students in proper nutrition and health professionals begin reinforcing this instruction, we stand little chance of realizing our potential.

Analysis-of-Alternatives Essay

Often the purpose of an essay is to make the audience accept one of several alternatives. This is accomplished by structuring the presentation according to options. Thus the essay that analyzes alternatives tries to make the audience accept one option as preferable by examining and eliminating other less desirable options. This strategy is especially useful in making the audience accept the "lesser of the evils" or an untried approach. For example

Thesis: The eating habits of elementary school children can be improved in many ways.

First Alternative: One way is for the U.S. Department of Health and Welfare to exercise tighter control over the school lunch program. Undoubtedly this approach will invite a full-scale social debate about the proper role of government in relation to business and consumers.

Second Alternative: Another approach is for schools to prohibit the sale of junk food on campus. Where this has been tried, it has met widespread opposition from children, parents, and, of course, the junk-food industry.

Third Alternative: A third alternative is to make nutrition a basic and continuing part of a child's education. This approach has the advantage of being far less controversial than either of the other two. More important, it respects the autonomy of individuals by equipping them to make informed food choices but not restricting their choices. Perhaps most important, this approach stands the best chance of getting students to eat properly outside school and to develop sound eating habits for life.

Quick Check on Organization

1 Which organizational format is used in the essay opposing the legalization of voluntary euthanasia (Chapter 10)? How would you describe the author's audience? The author's persona?

2 Which organizational patterns would you use for the three theses you selected in an earlier Quick Check?

3 Identify the organizational patterns evident in the following essay excerpts.

    a   The United States certainly has both the human and material resources to reduce its crime rate. We have enough money and know-how to devise and underwrite innovative ways of dealing with crime and criminals. Indeed, some communities have done just that. Yet a presidential commission recently reported that as a whole the United States is losing its fight against crime.

What we lack, of course, is the will. We Americans value our creature comforts too much to allow our personal incomes to be taxed for ambitious crime-prevention expenditures.

So to say that as a nation we have a serious crime problem really is to admit that we are unwilling to devote more than a minor fraction of our great wealth and human resources to the enterprise of crime prevention.

b   "There are many different methods of achieving limitation of births.

"Abortion is undoubtedly preferable to infanticide, though we know too little about the physiological and psychological damage which it may cause to recommend it without serious qualms.

"Contraception certainly seems preferable to abortion, and indeed the moral objection to contraception in principle seems to be confined to a single major branch of the Christian church. Even there, the difference in practice between this church and the rest of society is much smaller than the difference in precept. Contraception, however, also has its problems, and it is by no means an automatic solution to the problem of population control.

"The fact that we must recognize is that it is social institutions which are dominant in determining the ability of society to control its population, not the mere physiology of reproduction." (Kenneth E. Boulding, *The Meaning of the Twentieth Century* [New York: Harper & Row, 1979], p. 79.)

c   "Political pressures in this presidential year have given a militant minority of women powerful leverage for enactment [of the Equal Rights Amendment]. However, the respective state of the Union may come to regret ratification, if the two-thirds majority approves.

". . . legal scholars from the University of Chicago, Yale, and Harvard [have argued] that while the amendment would have no effect upon discrimination, it would 'nullify every existing federal and state law making any distinction whatever between men and women, no matter how reasonable the distinction may be, and rob Congress and the 50 states of the legislative power to enact any future laws making any distinction between men and women, no matter how reasonable the distinction may be.'

"Like the civil rights movement, Women's Lib is seeking, by using the power of the state, to forbid individual discrimination as opposed to discrimination legally enforced.

"But like some elements of the civil rights movement, militant feminists are not really interested in reform, but rather in revolution and destruction of the existing social fabric of the society." (Jeffrey St. John, "Women's Lib Amendment Not Simple Legal Formula," *Columbus Dispatch*, May 9, 1972, p. 23.)

d   "America's young people have found a potent, sometimes addictive, and legal drug. It's called alcohol.

"Why are youngsters rediscovering booze? One reason is pressure from other kids to be one of the gang. Another is the ever-present urge to act grown up. For some, it eases the burden of problems at home or at school.

And it's cheaper. You can buy a couple of six-packs of beer for the price of three joints of pot.

"Perhaps the main reason is that parents don't seem to mind. They tolerate drinking—sometimes almost seem to encourage it.

"The Medical Council of Alcoholism warns: The potential teen-age drinking problem should give far more cause for alarm than drug addiction. Many schools have reacted to teenage drinking. They've started alcohol-education programs. But a lot of experts feel that teen-agers are not going to stop drinking until parents do." (Carl T. Rown, "Teenagers and Booze" in *Just Between Us Blacks* [New York: Random House, 1974], pp. 95–96.)

Comments: Number 3

a. pro-and-con
b. analyzing alternatives

c. inductive
d. cause-and-effect

Testing the Logic of the Essay

An argument demands a systematic building of a case, and you will want to ensure that your argument hangs together by supporting your thesis convincingly and legitimately. To do so you will want to control your material with an outline. The outline is an excellent device for testing the web of logical relationships in your essay.

Most student writers (and non-student writers, for that matter) don't fully exploit the outline, which is the primary tool for structuring an essay. Typically, when they do use an outline, they formulate some main and subordinate headings and immediately launch into the writing. Rarely do they pay enough attention to the logic of the relationships connecting their ideas, to their missing premises, or to the intensifying and downplaying devices that are implicit in their outline and that may come back to haunt them in the essay. To get the most out of your outline, follow these four steps:

Step 1: *Construct the outline*, using Roman numerals to indicate main points and letters and Arabic numerals to indicate support material. (I am assuming that you have learned how to do this elsewhere.)

Step 2: *Indicate on the outline the relationships between the main points and the thesis and between the support material and the main points, with reference to these developmental patterns: fact and opinion, illustration, authority or testimonials, cause and effect, analogy, or statistics (including polls, surveys, and studies).* The reason for identifying these patterns is that they will alert you to potential pitfalls. For example, if you're using an illustration, you must ensure that it's appropriate, that it doesn't depend for its force on a subjective or controversial interpretation of it, and that it is a fair representation of the point it's supposed to make.

Step 3: *Fill in the missing premises that aren't obvious.* Doing this is as crucial in writing essays as in evaluating them. If you don't fill in your missing premises, you can't be sure of that your assertions and inferences have a logical basis.

Step 4: *Examine the outline for intensifying and downplaying devices.* If you expect the audience to agree with you, you must make sure that the force of what you say doesn't rely chiefly on one of the many ways that we bias communication.

Let's now see how to apply these steps to test the logic of a hypothetical essay that argues for restricting the access of consenting adults to pornographic materials. For illustrative purposes I will repeat the outline in applying each step, although you needn't do this when actually outlining an essay.

Step 1: Construct an outline.

Thesis: The state should restrict consenting adults' access to obscene and pornographic materials.

  I. Pornography leads to crime.

    A. Newspapers recently reported the story of an unstable young man who raped a woman after he'd been aroused by lurid scenes in an obscene comic book.

    B. The 1965 Gebhard study confirmed the reports of police officers that sex offenders often have pornographic materials in their possession or admit to having seen them.

  II. Pornography threatens society's moral well-being.

    A. It makes people preoccupied with sexual gratification.

    B. It leads to impersonal expressions of sexuality.

    C. The state has the right and duty to control what threatens society's physical well-being.

  III. People need standards of decency and direction in sexual matters.

    A. Religious leaders have always said so

    B. Polls indicate people desire this.

Step 2: Indicate relationships between main points and thesis and between support material and main points.

Thesis: The state should restrict consenting adults' access to obscene and pornographic materials.

Cause and effect	**I. Pornography leads to crime.**
Illustration	**A.** Newspapers recently reported . . .
Study	**B.** The 1965 Gebhard study . . .
Opinion	**II. Pornography threatens society's moral well-being.**
Opinion	**A.** It makes people preoccupied . .
Opinion	**B.** It leads . . .
Analogy	**C.** The state has the right . . .
Opinion	**III. People need standards of decency and direction** . . .
Authority	**A.** Religious leaders have always said so.
Poll	**B.** Polls indicate people desire this.

Step 3: Fill in missing premises.

Thesis: The state should restrict consenting adults' access to obscene and pornographic materials.

Cause and effect	**I. Pornography leads to crime.**	+ ⟨The state ought to restrict people's access to anything that leads to a crime.⟩
Illustration	**A.** Newspapers recently . . .	+ ⟨Viewing the lurid scenes caused the man to commit the rape.⟩
Study	**B.** The Gebhard study . . .	
Opinion	**II. Pornography threatens . . .**	+ ⟨The state ought to restrict people's access to anything that threatens society's moral well-being.⟩
Opinion	**A.** It preoccupies people . . .	
Opinion	**B.** It leads . . .	+ ⟨Preoccupation with sexual gratification and impersonal expressions of sexuality threaten society's moral well-being.⟩
Analogy	**C.** The state has the right . . .	
Opinion	**III. People need standards . . .**	+ ⟨If people need standards of decency and direction, the state should provide them.⟩
Authority	**A.** Religious leaders . . .	
Poll	**B.** Polls indicate . . .	+ ⟨If people want standards, the state should provide them.⟩

Step 4: Examine for intensifying and downplaying devices. (The outline completed.)

Thesis: The state should restrict consenting adults' access to obscene and pornographic materials.

Cause and effect	**I. Pornography leads to crime.** (probably a causal oversimplification)	+ ⟨The state ought to restrict ...⟩ (unsupported value judgment)

Illustration	**A.** Newspapers recently . . . (Is this typical? If an isolated case, it's a biased sample.)	$+ \langle$Viewing the lurid scene caused . . .$\rangle$ (post hoc)
Study	**B.** The 1965 Gebhard study . . . (Where are specifics of study? Did it prove a *causal* relation?)	
Opinion	**II. Pornography threatens** . . . **("moral well-being" is ambiguous; unsupported value judgment)**	$+ \langle$The state ought to restrict . . .$\rangle$ $\langle$unsupported value judgment; ambiguity$\rangle$
Opinion	**A.** It makes people preoccupied . . .	
Opinion	**B.** It leads . . .	$+ \langle$Preoccupation with sexual gratification and impersonal expressions of sexuality threaten society's moral well-being.$\rangle$
	(unsupported opinions; questionable causation)	(unsupported value judgment; ambiguity)
Analogy	**C.** The state has the right . . . (false analogy: one major difference is that we can pretty much agree on what threatens our physical well-being but not on what threatens our moral well-being)	
Opinion	**III. People need standards** . . . **(irrelevant reason: this only shows that** *somebody* **should provide them)**	$+ \langle$If people need standards . . .$\rangle$ (unsupported opinion)
Authority	**A.** Religious leaders . . . (false authority)	

Poll   **B.** Polls indicate . . .   + ⟨If people want standards,
                      (Where are specifics?)   the state should provide
                                                                them.⟩
                                                          (unsupported opinion)

This outline indicates serious problems in the logic of the relationships between thesis and main points and between main points and support material. If the writer wishes to write a compelling argumentative essay advancing this thesis, he/she must drastically revise the plan.

Here is one additional observation that further points up the value of outlining. Sometimes an outline will suggest a different approach altogether, perhaps even a scrapping of the original thesis. Don't resist this possibility, for it offers you a chance to elevate an issue to a more enlightening level. In any event, it's better to alter a course at the planning stage than midway through the writing of the essay.

Quick Check on Outlining

Using the four steps just developed, work up an outline for each of the theses you selected in an earlier Quick Check.

Writing the Essay

Once you are satisfied with your outline, you then must write the essay. Essays of any length consist of a beginning, a development, and an ending.

Beginning

Here are six strategies you can use in beginning your argumentative essay.

1. **Clarify your topic.**   Illustration from a paper linking the media with widespread anxiety: "It is little wonder that many people today show intense anxiety and worry. An uncertain economy makes them wonder whether they will be able to maintain themselves and their families. The deplorable state of the environment makes them question whether the struggle for survival is even worth it. The worsening of international relations leaves them fearful that the world is headed for a nuclear holocaust. In all this, the media play a crucial role in producing anxiety."

2. **Indicate your feelings about the topic.**   Illustration from a paper opposing pornography: "Rarely do we consider it politically interesting whether men and women find pleasure in performing their duties as citizens, parents, and spouses; or, on the other hand, whether they derive pleasure from watching their laws and customs ridiculed on stages, in films, or in books. Nor do we consider it politically relevant whether the relations between men and women are depicted in terms of an eroticism separated from love and calculated to

undercut the family. Nevertheless, much of the obscenity from which so many of us derive pleasure today is expressly political."

3. **Relate your topic to something current or well known.** Illustration from a paper dealing with the evolution of the term "competition": "In the winter of 1982, two monumental antitrust cases came to an end. In the first, AT&T (American Telephone and Telegraph) agreed to divest itself of a score of subsidiaries; in the second, the Justice Department dropped its suit against IBM (International Business Machines). Some heralded these events as a great victory for the free-enterprise system. Others deplored them as a defeat for free enterprise at the hands of big business. Whether one sees these cases as good or bad for free enterprise depends very much on one's definition of *competition*, a concept whose current meaning does not always parallel its eighteenth-century classical formulation."

4. **Challenge a generally held assumption about your topic.** Illustration from a paper on the virtues of not voting: "In the last presidential election, at least half of those eligible did not vote. These nonvoters faced the combined scorn of political parties, school teachers, chambers of commerce, Leagues of Women Voters, and sundry high-minded civic groups and individuals. In upcoming elections we can expect to see these same forces again heroically trying to 'get out the vote.' Yet the notion that 'getting out the vote' makes for better election results is not nonpartisan, patriotic, or logical."

5. **Show something paradoxical about your topic.** Illustration from a paper on the deficiencies in textbooks: "Textbooks certainly are one of the most influential factors in an individual's intellectual, cultural, and social development. Yet, though they are called 'educational,' textbooks often teach little. Although they are thought 'liberalizing,' they sometimes inculcate narrowmindedness and intolerance. Though they are viewed as disseminating American values, they sometimes work to undermine them. Yes, textbooks are influential, but not always in a positive way."

6. **State some striking facts or statistics related to your topic.** Illustration from a paper dealing with the overconsumption of medical drugs in the United States: "The volume of drug business in the U.S. has grown by a factor of one hundred during the twentieth century. Twenty thousand tons of aspirin are consumed per year, about 225 tablets per person. Central-nervous-system agents are the fastest-growing sector of the pharmaceutical market, now making up 31 percent of total sales. Dependence on prescribed tranquilizers has risen about 290 percent since 1962. Medicalized addiction has outpaced all self-chosen forms of creating well-being, such as marijuana or alcohol."

Developing

In developing your essay you will be arguing your thesis, using the material you have gathered to make your points. Your outline contains your whole developmental strategy. Take care, then, that your outline contains a sensible order of ideas. There basically are two ways to ensure this.

1. **Let the thesis dictate the order.**   If your thesis contains divisions, you should take up the points in the order indicated in your thesis. For example, reconsider two of the thesis statements we developed earlier:

> It's high time that laws were passed to restrict the advertiser's use of ambiguity to sell aspirin, toothpaste, and mouthwash.

and

> Often overlooked in the retail prices of alcoholic and nonalcoholic beverages are the hidden costs of advertising.

In ordering an essay based on the first thesis, you should take up ambiguity in selling aspirin, then in toothpaste, then in mouthwash. Likewise, in the second, take up the hidden costs of advertising in the price structure of alcoholic and then in nonalcoholic beverages.

2. **Let the organizational structure determine the order.**   In inductive essays the reasons are usually presented in order of importance. In a pro-and-con essay the confirmation of an idea is followed by an objection to that idea, which then is followed by a balanced view. In a cause-and-effect essay causes and effects are arranged either in chronological order or in order of importance. And in an analysis-of-alternatives essay alternatives typically are presented in order of the most common, most popular, or best-known first.

Besides an ordering of ideas, developing your paper also calls for an inspection of the kinds of assertions you are making and of the logical relationships among them. So be conscious of the need to support your assertions with facts, illustrations, and examples. Since your paper will include a mix of fact and opinion, you must be careful to distinguish between them and to avoid associated fallacies—false authority or testimonial, popularity, and tradition—and the misuse of statistics, surveys, and polls. If you invoke comparison or analogy, beware of faulty comparison and false analogies as well as the fallacies of hasty conclusion and half-truth. Should you employ cause-and-effect reasoning, be careful to avoid questionable causes, causal oversimplification, neglect of a common cause, post hoc, and slippery slope.

Always define key terms, or terms that are ambiguous. When you do, avoid downplaying by confusion.

Finally, since you want to guide the reader through an orderly arrangement of ideas, be sure that your paper is coherent. Helpful here is the use of signal words (such as "nevertheless," "however," "therefore," and "as a result"). These terms will show readers the logical connections among your ideas and help direct them to the conclusions that you have drawn. Again, the best way to ensure logical relationships is by using an outline as indicated.

Ending

The conclusion of your paper should reinforce your thesis, tie your paper together, and emphatically end it. Here are three strategies for ending the argumentative essay.

1. **Make some statement about your thesis rather than merely repeating it.** Illustration: "In their editorial decisions, communication methods, and marketing devices, the media contribute dramatically to our individual and collective anxiety. For those in print and electronic journalism to ignore or minimize this psychological impact or glibly subordinate it to some lofty mission guaranteed by the Constitution seems irresponsible. To be sure, we need an unfettered press. But we also need a citizenry that is self-confident, optimistic, and panic-free."

2. **Show how you have proved, disproved, or enlarged on your thesis.** Illustration: "'Getting out the vote,' then, does not necessarily make for better election results. On the contrary it is always partisan, for a calm and dignified effort benefits the party in power and a frenetic one benefits the party out of power. It is no more patriotic than the time-honored American attitude of 'a plague on both your houses.' Nor is it logical. Since a successful 'getting out the vote' campaign generates votes from the poorly informed, uninformed, misinformed, and the downright indifferent and ignorant, it undercuts the votes of the intelligent electorate. No, let's not get out the vote; let's get out the *informed* vote."

3. **Tie your paper to something known or a future possibility.** Illustration: "When classical capitalists such as Adam Smith talked about competition, they did so in a social and economic atmosphere quite different from today's. Whereas the economy of the industrial revolution was characterized by a comparatively free and open market system, the economy of the twentieth century is made up of relatively few enormous holding companies that can secretly fix prices, eliminate smaller companies, and monopolize an industry. Ironically, through intense competition such corporate giants have reached a point at which they can now make a mockery of the classical doctrine of competition. The challenge that lies ahead for society and government is to redefine competition in such a way that the classical notion is integrated into present-day realities. As the AT&T and IBM cases well illustrate, this is no mean undertaking."

Quick Check on Writing the Paper

1 Using the strategies provided, try to write an opening for each of the three theses you have selected in an earlier Quick Check.
2 Using the strategies provided, try to write a conclusion for each of the three theses.

Summary

Argument and persuasion can be theoretically differentiated by purpose and technique. The purpose of an argumentative essay is to win assent through rational appeal; the purpose of a persuasive essay is to win consent through emotional appeal. In practice, however, the two cannot easily be separated: Argumentative essays often try to win consent and to use emotional techniques legitimately. For our purposes the term "argumentative essay" includes persuasive essays.

To write effective argumentative essays, you must know your audience. This calls for an audience inventory that isolates key audience characteristics. Armed with this information, you can then give an argument shape and character. Just as important, you must decide on the appropriate persona or role you will play; that is, the characteristics that must be conveyed to the audience to gain their respect and win their approval.

The thesis, which typically is a generalization, is the essay's main idea. In formulating a thesis, you must make sure that it is arguable—that it is an assertion disputable, controversial, or opinionated enough to allow development in an essay format (such assertions might include "Life exists outside our solar system" or "Coffee is bad for one's health"). Assertions worthy of development generally fall into five categories: assertions about meaning, values, consequences, policy, and fact.

In arguing your case it's crucial to anticipate objections. Taking stock of your audience's background usually will alert you to the kinds of objections they're likely to raise.

In writing a thesis follow these six steps: (1) decide on a subject, (2) identify possible topics, (3) select and limit the topic, (4) determine your attitude toward the topic, (5) write the thesis statement, and (6) test the thesis statement.

Main points are principal support assertions. In developing your main points and support material, use observations, personal experience, informed opinion, and organized research.

You can organize your argumentative essay according to an inductive, pro-and-con, cause-and-effect, or analysis-of-alternatives format.

Essential to a good argumentative essay are logical relationships between main points and thesis and between support material and main points. A good test of your essay's logic is an outline. In using an outline follow these four steps: (1) construct the outline; (2) indicate the relationships by reference to developmental patterns: fact and opinion, illustration, authority or testimonial, cause and effect, analogy, or statistics; (3) fill in the missing premises; and (4) examine the outline for intensifying and downplaying devices.

Applications

1   Write a 500-to-1000-word essay on one of the theses you have worked with in this chapter. Remember to keep in mind your audience and persona.

2   A chairman of the Federal Communications Commission once described television as "a vast wasteland." What he meant was that most network (CBS, NBC, ABC) programming offered nothing of value to adult viewers. Would you agree? Use detailed evidence from shows that you have watched to write an essay (500 to 1000 words) arguing your case. Present your material *inductively.*

3   Write a *pro-and-con* paper in answer to one of the following questions:

Should the draft be reinstated?
Should college students be required to take English composition?
Should the United States limit future immigration?
Should the sale of marijuana be legalized?
Should federal employees, such as postal workers and air traffic control-lers, be permitted to strike?

4   Write an essay in which you analyze the *major causes* of one of the follow-ing: marital problems and divorce, cheating on exams, illiteracy among high school graduates, the epidemic proportions of venereal disease among people under twenty-five, or incomplete and biased news coverage.

5   Write a paper in which you analyze *major alternatives* for achieving one of the following goals: a reduction in violent crimes, a more integrated public school system, equal job opportunities for women, avoidance of nuclear war, a more favorable U.S. image abroad, a fair allocation of the costs of environmental cleanup, energy independence, or a more equitable dis-tribution of the world's wealth and resources.

Index